THE SHADOW WAR

THE SHADOW WAR

IRAN'S QUEST FOR SUPREMACY

BRANDON J. WEICHERT

REPUBLIC

BOOK PUBLISHERS

To Ashley, for riding the storm with me.

CONTENTS

FOREWORD

ROBERT G. KAUFMAN

Brandon Weichert has emerged as one of our most well informed, original defense intellectuals in the tradition of the great Herman Kahn: telling us what we do not want to hear but need to know about the gathering dangers imperiling our freedom and prosperity. His first book, *Winning Space*, ranks high among the most important national security studies of the past two decades. Weichert makes an unassailable and chilling case for why the mounting military challenge of China and Russia in the vital strategic domain of outer space could negate the information dominance essential for sustaining American military primacy. Any Administration should embrace—as President Trump prudently did by creating the Space Force as the sixth independent branch of our armed services—Weichert's diagnosis and prescriptions for winning the Space Race.

Weichert's new book brings the same rigor, originality, and persuasiveness to analyzing the gathering danger of Iran across a spectrum of domains. His well-researched, powerfully argued, and historically well-informed analysis of the origins and trajectory of Iran's Revolutionary regime demolish the fallacious assumption of the Carter, Obama, and Biden Administrations that the mullahs running Iran since 1979 are reasonable statesmen with whom the United States can safely do business. Weichert demonstrates, on the contrary, that revolutionary Iran's implacable quest for regional hegemony is inimical to America's vital interest, the vital interest of our regional allies, and the very existence of decent, democratic Israel—a nation that has consistently stood alongside the United States in its darkest hours.

Mincing no words, Weichert assails the logic and consequences of the Carter, Obama, and Biden Administration's policies for enabling Iranian ambitions—especially Obama's nuclear deal that President Biden today hopes to revive. The Iran nuclear agreement is a deal that facilitates Iran crossing the nuclear threshold and developing a ballistic missile capacity menacing to America's regional allies and eventually directly threatening to the United States itself. Weichert well sets the Iranian nuclear threat in the broader context of the revolutionary Iranian regime using regional surrogates, such as Hezbollah and Hamas, in their existential struggle to eradicate Israel.

By Weichert's sound reckoning, Iran envisages nuclear weapons, among other things, as a mechanism for eroding America's military deterrent without ever having to face US military personnel in direct conflict. Thus, Tehran's leaders seek to invert Clausewitz's dictum by using negotiations to wage war by other means upon their Western enemies.

Weichert's book on Iran also displays an exquisite sense of strategic proportion, taking due measure of the Middle East's significance relative to America's other greater geopolitical priorities. His analysis and policy prescriptions for dealing with Iran rest on the sound premise that the Middle East has long dominated America's foreign policy agenda to the detriment of addressing the nation's most significant long-term challenges. Weichert applauds the former Trump Administration's National Security Strategy that began prudently to recalibrate America's overall grand strategy, thereby rearranging America's ranking of interests and threats to reflect geopolitical realities of the 21st century—namely that America must maintain a strong, though defensive, position in the Middle East while focusing its greater energies on deterring a rising China and a resurgent Russia.

Even at the apogee of the Middle East's significance during the Cold War, preventing hostile powers from dominating either Europe or Asia loomed as the paramount challenge to the United States. Still, the United States rightly deemed it vital to prevent either the Soviet Union or any other hostile power from directly or indirectly dominating the Middle East's oil reserves on which the United States, its allies, and much of the world depended. Now that the United States has become an energy superpower, the significance of the Middle East will continue to diminish, especially relative to the Indo-Pacific, by far the world's most important power center for the 21st century and to Europe, now ranked second.

The Trump Administration—like Weichert in his own words—rightly defined "the central challenge to U.S. prosperity and security" as "the emergence of a long term, strategic competition" by what the 2018 Summary of the National Security Strategy classifies as a "revisionist Russia and China" striving for "a world consistent with their authoritarian model—gaining veto power over other nations' economic, military, and political decision."

Correspondingly, the Trump Administration—in accordance with Weichert's inclinations—scaled back American strategic ambitions in the Middle East to pursuing more traditional and limited ends, while remaining engaged in the region:

1. Preventing a single hostile hegemon from dominating the region.

2. Deterring rogue regimes from crossing the nuclear threshold and/ or sponsoring terror.

3. Broadening and deepening cooperation with a decent, democratic Israel and Sunni allies in the region sharing our strategic objectives of containing, deterring, defanging, and if necessary, defeating Iran's revolutionary rogue regime.

If these objectives are not met by the Americans and their allies, then Iran will achieve regional dominance by crossing the nuclear threshold, sponsoring terror, and/or annihilating Israel. All these things will happen in short order if the Biden Administration's Iran agenda is followed. And, as Weichert warns, this could spark a world war wherein Iran draws in its great state allies, like Russia and China, and attempts to overrun the region as the Americans struggle to hold these rivals back.

Weichert's superb book, a worthy companion to his excellent first book, exemplified prudence in a Thomistic sense—right reason about right things to be done. His policy prescriptions strike a felicitous balance between taking the Iranian threat seriously and addressing it vigilantly, on one hand, without detracting from our greater geopolitical priorities, on the other. Above all, America's greatest geopolitical challenges today are the hegemonic ambitions of a revisionist, aggressive, increasingly repressive Chinese regime striving to eclipse the United States as the world's dominant power, with an authoritarian, revisionist Russia looming as a distant but significant second.

May the next American President read and heed both of Weichert's books in tandem. Pray in the meantime that Winston Churchill is right: that the United States will eventually do the right thing after trying everything else with Iran. For the Biden Administration is on the autobahn to doing the same thing as Carter and Obama, with predictable dismal results.

—ROBERT G. KAUFMAN

INTRODUCTION

THE MULLAHS JUST AREN'T

INTO US

WHILE CAMPAIGNING FOR THE IRANIAN PRESIDENCY, Hassan Rouhani, a man the Obama administration had hailed as a "moderate," stood before a frenzied crowd and exhorted that, "The beautiful cry of 'Death to America!' unites our nation!"[1] The crowd assembled before him was a cross-section of Iranian society. For many of the Iranians gathered, Rouhani's comments were nothing more than an affirmation of the same propaganda that had flooded their land since the rise of the

---

1 Embassy of Israel, "The Beautiful Cry of 'Death to America' Unites Our Nation," November 21, 2014. 11:36. https://twitter.com/IsraelinUSA/status/535834105150451712

1

bloody-minded Islamist revolution in 1979. This revolution, as you'll see in this work, has torn Iran apart from within; murdered countless innocents, and made Iran an international pariah.

During religious ceremonies, birthdays, and funerals—basically any social occasion, large or small—"Death to America!" can invariably be heard resonating from the crowds. It's almost an automatic reply—especially when cameras are present. Yet after the cameras are turned off and the security services momentarily turn their backs, many of those same Iranians—notably the younger ones—dream of living a different, freer life somewhere else in the West. Anywhere but in Iran.

The Islamists who rule Iran have made a prison of one of the most ancient countries in existence. Thought crimes, or apostasy, are punishable by death. People have no civil rights. Iran is democratic the way that East Berlin was democratic—in name only. Iran's political system holds sham elections at times, but the powers that be, Islamists in this case, determine the results. They hold all the power and control the future. Anyone can be elected, so long as they support the theocracy and further the objectives of the religious leaders, the mullahs, who truly control Iran.

In fact, in the 2021 presidential "elections," the purported moderate, Hassan Rouhani, was thrown out of office and replaced by a rabid Islamic jurist named Ebrahim Raisi.[2] The former chief justice of Iran, Raisi, is a close friend of the Ayatollah Ali Khamenei, the spiritual leader of Iran's theocracy. Raisi was chosen specifically because of his virulent antipathy toward the United States, his rabid religious opposition to the Sunni Arab states that surround Iran, and his hardline anti-Semitism. The first thing that Raisi did when he became Iran's president was to announce that Iran's ballistic missile program was "nonnegotiable".[3] He refused to meet with President Joe Biden and stated that Iran under his

2 "Iran's Ebrahim Raisi: The Hardline Cleric Set to Become President," BBC, 21 June 2021. https://www.bbc.com/news/world-middle-east-57421235

3 "Iran Nuclear Deal: President-Elect Raisi Issues Warning Over Talks," BBC, 21 June 2021. https://www.bbc.com/news/world-middle-east-57552639

leadership would not engage in negotiations over its nuclear weapons program "for the sake of negotiations."[4]

Home to the largest group of Shiite Muslims, a minority in the Middle East, Iran (ancient Persia) has long been an outcast. Yet Iran has a long and rich history of greatness. Since 1979, however, the growth of its greatness has been stunted by the radicals who now rule the country. The Islamists have made it their mission to wage war upon the West, whether it be the United States, Britain, or European countries. What's more, Iran, as a minority in the Islamic community, does not believe it will be welcomed as an equal, either by the Sunni Arab states or the Jewish state of Israel. So Iran has embraced a supremacist strategy for itself in the wider Middle East.

Ending America's role in the region, erasing the Jewish state of Israel, and subordinating the Sunnis to enact a long-term plan of vengeance upon them for killing the man that most Shiites believe was the true heir of the Prophet Muhammad at the Battle of Karbala in 680 CE— these are the Iranian strategic ambitions. Because Iran is outnumbered in the region, the Islamist leaders of Iran believe they need nuclear weapons. Iran's military has embraced radical unconventional warfare methods, such as cyberwar, electromagnetic pulse (EMP) weapons, the targeting of oil flows, and transnational terrorism as acceptable tactics for achieving their strategic ambitions.

Since the rise of the Islamist revolution in 1979, American policy-makers have completely missed the mark on what Iran is and the threat it poses to the wider world. From former President Jimmy Carter to Barack Obama and now Joe Biden, a succession of Democratic presidents assumed that Iran could be reasoned with. Considering Iran an unruly child, Carter, Obama, and Biden all believed they could simply be nicer and treat the Islamist regime of Iran as if it were any other regime, and

---

4 Najmeh Bozorgmehr and Andrew England, "Iran's President-Elect Ebrahim Raisi Signals Tough Line on Nuclear Deal," *Financial Times,* 21 June 2021. https://www.ft.com/content/1e257cb9-da14-4ebf-9bea-869f64918273

Iran would suddenly abandon their ambitions for regional hegemony. At every turn, the Iranian regime has used and abused the largesse that Democratic presidents gave them. Although Republican presidents have tried to contain and strangle Iran with sanctions, Democratic presidents have long sought an elusive deal with the Islamic Republic. Each time the Democrats have attempted to make a deal with Iran's leadership, they weaken the sanctions that Republican presidents imposed earlier upon Iran—and Iran's leaders have used that lull in pressure to become more aggressive and reach in the Greater Middle East.

Many Democratic leaders have not fully understood the adage that Iran's mullahs just aren't that into us. The Republicans, for their part, aren't that much better. Republican administrations have vacillated between ignoring Iran and threatening the Islamic Republic with total war. Neither of these solutions are helpful. They either do not commit enough resources to containing the Iranian threat, or they risk overcommitting the United States to fighting Iran at a time when the United States military is stretched to its breaking point.

The greatest gifts to Iran were given when Ronald Reagan pulled American forces out of Beirut after Hezbollah, Iran's terrorist arm in Lebanon, blew up the Marine barracks. That year, 1983, saw Americans flee the region en masse. In response, the Reagan administration quietly encouraged Iraq's Saddam Hussein to make war upon what he thought was his weaker neighbor, revolutionary Iran. A decade later, the Iraqis had been defeated by the fanaticism of the Iranians. Iraq became weak. Iran got stronger.

To regain his strength, Saddam Hussein of Iraq annexed neighboring Kuwait, precipitating Desert Storm in 1991. After the US-led coalition kicked Saddam's forces out of Kuwait, the United States and its allies maintained a strict no-fly zone over northern and southern Iraq and imposed onerous sanctions upon the Baathist regime. Iraq became a pariah and remained weak in a region where weakness invited attack. Saddam pretended to have nuclear weapons to keep the Iranians from attacking his ailing regime in the 1990s and early 2000s.

Saddam's subterfuge was so good, however, that it deceived the West into believing he really did possess nuclear weapons—something that no American leader could allow after 9/11.

By 2003, President George W. Bush, a Republican, believed he needed to oust Saddam. While successful in ending Saddam's rule, Bush's "war of choice" simply handed Iraq over to Iran (Iraq has a massive Shiite population). The moment the statue of Saddam Hussein was torn down by a ferocious mob (with the help of US Marines), the stage was set for Iran to break out from its containment.

Between Democratic Party presidents playing footsie with the mad mullahs and Republican administrations inadvertently empowering Iran by making Iran's regional rivals weaker, the United States has been ill served. Because of these feckless actions, Iran is poised to become capable of building nuclear weapons—which will only harm the United States. Time is not on our side.

The United States has been forced to pay far more attention to the Middle East than it would like to since 9/11. The whole region has been consumed with Islamist fervor. And while Iran did not attack the United States on 9/11, it does have a history of consistently undermining and attacking the United States, infamously murdering over 200 Marines in Beirut in 1983. Beyond that, Iran has a clear track record of targeting sensitive American infrastructure, of stoking the flames of war with Israel, and threatening the Sunni Arab states that the United States has historically aligned with.

At no point would the Islamists in Iran find common ground with the United States. At some rare times the Americans have cooperated with the Iranians, such as when US forces helped to target Iranian dissidents who had taken cover in neighboring Iraq, in the run-up to the US-led invasion of Iraq in 2003. American forces ostensibly cooperated with Iranian-backed militias fighting ISIS in 2014 too. Each time, the Iranians were always gaming the Americans, and Iran usually got the better of the Americans.

Tehran did not consider America an ally. Iran's leaders used

American airpower to fundamentally alter the strategic balance on the ground in their favor—and to harm American interests in the long run. Iran treated America like their patsy. And most American leaders, Democrats and Republicans alike, were happy to play that role.

While al Qaeda and ISIS threaten the United States daily with terrorism, Iran's mullahs dream of doing something bigger. Iran is a nation-state with a rich history of independence. The threat the mullahs pose to the United States goes beyond terrorism (though they certainly love to support terrorism in Tehran). Iran's threat is geostrategic.

Call it "Death to America, Plus." Iran definitely wants to visit death upon the United States, just as al Qaeda and ISIS do. Yet Iran also wants to weaken and blunt America *on the strategic level.*

Iran's leaders want to push the Americans out of the Middle East entirely, destroy Israel, and dominate the Sunni Arabs. Iran's ambition, however, will not be sated with regional dominance. The regime, after all, believes it has a mission from their god to visit death and destruction upon those who have wronged Iran in the past and upon those who do not conform to their particular brand of Islam. Their exclusionary fundamentalism views compromise as a weakness and believes fate is always working in their favor—so long as they stay true to their interpretation of Shia Islam.

It is the question of Iran's role in the region that has defined all aspects of American policy in the Middle East. The failure to understand this has led to major mistakes that continue to haunt the United States. It's as though US policymakers have attempted to put together a jigsaw puzzle with half the pieces missing.

Since the formation of Islam in the seventh century, the great dividing question in the region has always been Iran's place there. As Shiite Muslims and ethnic Persians, Iranians see themselves as a minority group among a majority of Sunni Muslims and ethnic Arabs. There's no circumventing this fact—and the pathway to war between these two opposing sides is unlikely to be averted, so long as the current Islamist regime rules in Tehran.

In fact, the Iranian leadership views the world in either/or terms: there are those who believe in their brand of Shia Islam, as the Iranian leadership does, and those who do not believe as they do (a large and growing camp). To defeat such a large group, Iran's mullahs believe they need nuclear weapons. And Iran will inevitably try to deploy these weapons against the Americans, whom they view as the "Great Satan."

Ignoring these trends and denying what Iran's leaders have said since the rise of their regime is a recipe for disaster. This has been the pattern since Jimmy Carter was in office. In fact, Jimmy Carter and Barack Obama were completely oblivious to the dangers that cooperation with the Islamists of Iran posed. Today, Joe Biden is repeating the mistakes of his Democratic presidential predecessors.

The path forward requires containing Iran and standing strong with America's traditional allies in the region, the Israelis and Sunni Arab states—possibly even Turkey. Right now, the region is teetering on the brink of a major war, one that could easily turn into a world war and involve the use of nuclear weapons. America *cannot* go to war again in the Middle East without severely weakening itself. It needs allies. There are natural allies waiting to be called upon, if only the Americans would set aside ridiculous Western standards of human rights and democracy and dance with the ones who brought us: Saudi Arabia and Israel, for example.

Iran is not a rational actor and will not behave just like any other state, as former President Obama believed when he crafted the Joint Comprehensive Plan of Action (JCPOA), otherwise known as the Iran nuclear deal, in 2015. Giving in to Iranian ambitions, as this work will show, will not stabilize the Middle East. Instead, it will destabilize the region further and ensure that the United States gets sucked into a deadly war precisely when Americans want to step back and focus on bigger threats, like China or Russia.

The Shadow War: Iran's Quest for Supremacy, will describe how dangerous Iran's current Islamist regime is. This book will show why Iran cannot be trusted with nuclear weapons under any circumstance. And this work will describe what might happen if the Biden administration continues its perilous detente with Iran.

The world is approaching a critical moment when one misstep in its dealings with Iran could produce a nuclear third world war. Iran's leaders are keenly aware of the dangers. Tehran has proven they are comfortable with the risks; indeed, the fears surrounding an Iranian bomb have actually compelled Iran's reckless leadership to push harder for nuclear weapons.

In essence, the Iranian regime is courting nuclear world war. At some point, the Iranians just might get what they wish for. And the Americans, divided against one another and distracted with an assortment of other problems, will be taken by complete surprise.

When the First World War broke out, America was at peace and still experiencing rapid industrial growth. The question of Germany's place in Europe and the wider world was the reason why that war erupted when and how it did. When the First World War started in 1914, Americans were far more concerned about Mexican bandits along the southwestern border than the Kaiser Wilhelm II's aggressive plans.

President Woodrow Wilson, a Democrat, ran for reelection in 1916. He had campaigned on a promise of keeping the United States out of any European conflict, while his Republican challenger, former Supreme Court Justice Charles Evans Hughes, criticized Wilson for not having taken the "necessary preparations" to face war in Europe.[5] Shortly after his reelection, Wilson became the biggest cheerleader for American intervention in World War I.

The results were devastating.

While America had helped to turn the tide of that war, American politics, as well as the internal dynamics of Europe, had proven to be a hindrance in creating a lasting peace. By the end of that war, 20 million people had died, parts of Europe had turned into a devastated

---

5 "1916 Election," The President Woodrow Wilson House, Accessed on 23 February 2021. http://www.woodrowwilsonhouse.org/1916-election

moonscape, and chemical weapons of mass destruction had been used wantonly. Further, the stage was set for the far more devastating Second World War. The same horrible pattern awaits the United States in the Middle East if it persists in playing footsie with Iran's mullahs and feeding their nuclear ambitions.

The issue of Iran's place in the wider Middle East is akin to the question of Germany's place in Europe before the First World War. The regime in Iran is at once convinced of its moral and spiritual superiority while simultaneously obsessed with its physical insecurity, a fact exacerbated by the regime's own malign actions over the course of decades. Courting the present regime of Iran will court only disaster.

The solution is *not* to replicate the failed regime change policy that the George W. Bush administration attempted in Iraq in 2003. Instead, Washington must revitalize its once close support of Sunni Arab autocrats, like Saudi Arabia, now led by the Crown Prince Mohammed bin Salman (MBS), and the current government of Israel. Allowing these alliances to fray, as the Obama administration did and the new Biden administration threatens to do, will ensure that mere anarchy is loosed upon the region—and the world. Preventing that means stopping Iran from building a nuclear weapons arsenal; America must back the efforts of both Israel and the Sunni Arab states to contain Iran, and it requires resolve and steadfast vigilance against desperate Iranian attempts to break that containment and split America from its traditional regional allies.

As the Biden administration takes shape, it appears that containing Iran and preventing the country from getting nuclear weapons is not their priority. Instead, Biden's team, like Obama's and Carter's, wants to work Iran into the wider regional framework. The only problem is that neither the Sunni Arabs nor Israelis will accept that. Even if they did, Iran would be emboldened to expand their attempts to achieve regional supremacy at the expense of the Israelis and Sunni Arab states.

Before the First World War, both Britain and Germany were interconnected through trade and culture. The decade before war erupted and eviscerated the European world order, Sir Norman Angell wrote an infamous book, *The Great Illusion,* in which he argued that conflict between the two industrial juggernauts, Britain and Germany, was impossible because the two great powers were relative equals. Any conflict would destroy the great money-making opportunities that trade offered. And it would eradicate the great cultural achievements their two countries had made in the decades leading up to 1914.

Norman Angell was wrong. Shortly after his work was published, the Europeans entered into the suicide pact known as the First World War, and the United States eventually got sucked into that morass. Europe was never the same, and some have argued that the United States was forever changed as well. Men and women purporting to represent the forces of peace and reason, such as those on the foreign policy teams of Jimmy Carter and Barack Obama, as well as the new Biden administration, all believe about Iran what Norman Angell believed of Germany. The Democratic Party's greatest foreign policy thinkers all assume that Iran is a rational actor, that Tehran only wants to be treated as an equal country alongside the other nations of the Middle East. In their opinion, if Iran is given what they want, then peace will break out and the United States can finally extricate itself from the quicksand of Mideast politics.

These assumptions are as wrong—dangerous—as the assumptions that undergirded the works of men like Norman Angell in the previous century. Should the United States follow the Carter, Obama, and now Biden policies into making peace with Iran and letting that rogue state acquire nuclear weapons, it will rip apart the already tenuous stability in the region. It will spark a nuclear arms race. And it might very ignite a nuclear world war.

The Shadow War: Iran's Quest for Supremacy is a warning that describes what America's future might be if it follows the destructive path to superficial "peace." If the United States does not see the dangers posed by the Islamist regime of Iran before it is too late, these nightmarish scenarios will unfold. This book is meant to both warn us and show a path forward *before* the shooting begins.

—**BRANDON J. WEICHERT,** JUNE 20, 2022, NAPLES, FL

1

GROUND ZERO FOR

WORLD WAR III

AN IMAGE WENT VIRAL on the internet at the beginning of 2020. The image showed a severed left hand, bloodied and covered in dirt, that was lying on a patch of grass, with a distinctive oversized red ring on the wedding ring finger. The graphic image originated in Baghdad. Even though the ancient Middle Eastern city has become synonymous with bloodshed over the past few decades, there was nothing common about this image.

The severed hand belonged to General Qassem Soleimani, a man who had led the Quds Force, the covert overseas arm of the Iranian Revolutionary Guard Corps (IRGC), the terrorist wing of Iran's military, since 1997. While many in Iran mourned the image, still others around the world celebrated, for it symbolized the death of one of the world's most prolific mass murderers.[1]

Soleimani had traveled to Baghdad with a small cadre of IRGC guards—including his son-in-law—to meet with Mohammed Ridha, a senior figure in Iraq's Shiite paramilitary force that the pro-Iran government of Iraq had merged into their military, known as Hashed Al-Shaabi.[2] Soleimani and his cadre had landed at the Baghdad airport on the evening of January 3, 2020. Western intelligence believed Soleimani's flight to Baghdad had originated either from Syria or Lebanon, two areas where Iran's Quds Force has been increasingly deployed to over the last few years, as Iran's malign influence expanded in the Greater Middle East.[3]

As the Iranians were surreptitiously whisked away from the Baghdad airport in two black SUVs, four Hellfire missiles streaked from an American drone that was stealthily tracking the group from above and blasted the vehicles to smithereens. Later, Iranian state television would report that ten people were killed in the explosions; five of them were IRGC personnel, including Soleimani and his son-in-law. Soleimani was so badly mangled by the blast that he could only be identified by the fat red ring on his severed left hand.[4]

Shortly after the devastating attack, President Donald J. Trump

1 "Iran's Qassem Soleimani: Global Mass Killer," Al Arabiya, 4 January 2020. https://english.alarabiya.net/en/features/2020/01/04/Iran-s-Qassem-Soleimani-Global-mass-killer

2 "Hashd al-Shaabi/Hashd Shaabi/Popular Mobilisation Units/People's Mobilization Forces," Global Security, Accessed on 1 November 2020. https://www.globalsecurity.org/military/world/para/hashd-al-shaabi.htm

3 Nader Uskowi, "The Evolving Iranian Strategy in Syria: A Looming Conflict with Israel," Atlantic Council, September 2018. https://www.atlanticcouncil.org/wp-content/uploads/2019/09/The_Evolving_Iranian_Strategy_in_Syria.pdf

4 "Four Hellfire Missiles and a Severed Hand: The Killing of Qassem Soleimani," *The Times of Israel*, 3 January 2020. https://www.timesofisrael.com/four-hellfire-missiles-and-a-severed-hand-the-killing-of-qassem-soleimani/

took to the airwaves to claim responsibility for the killing of Soleimani and his traveling companions on the service road of the Baghdad airport.[5] Trump had rightly accused Soleimani of being responsible for the deaths of "thousands" of people throughout the region during his time in command of Iran's Quds Force. Since 2007, US intelligence had suspected that Soleimani's Quds Force had killed countless American troops fighting in neighboring Iraq during the ill-fated Iraq War (2003–2010). US intelligence was so concerned about Soleimani that they had created an elite unit specifically tasked with tracking the Iranian general's movements. It had followed him throughout the region for more than a decade by the time President Trump had ordered Soleimani's assassination.[6]

Despite having known for some time how dangerous Soleimani was, a succession of US presidents, beginning with George W. Bush, refused to kill Soleimani, despite his growing body count.[7] Soleimani's paramilitary activities had become brazen throughout the region. As Iran's involvement in the Syrian Civil War and in the fight against the Sunni Islamist terror organization, the Islamic State of Iraq and Syria (ISIS), became more pronounced, Soleimani became an increasingly visible figure in those conflicts (which often blended together).

Iranian-backed fighters would often post "images on social media of him on the battlefield, his beard and hair always impeccably trimmed."[8]

---

5 Donald J. Trump, "Remarks by President Trump on the Killing of Qasem Soleimani," The White House, 3 January 2020. https://www.whitehouse.gov/briefings-statements/remarks-president-trump-killing-qasem-soleimani/

6 Tom Vanden Brook, "Qasem Soleimani: The Pentagon Had Tracked Iranian General for Years Before He Was Killed," *USA Today*, 3 January 2020. https://www.usatoday.com/story/news/politics/2020/01/03/us-military-tracked-iran-general-soleimani-years-killed-thursday/2806630001/

7 Grace Panetta, "Why Neither Bush nor Obama Killed Iranian Commander Qassem Soleimani, Who the US Took Out in an Airstrike," *Business Insider*, 4 January 2020. https://www.businessinsider.com/why-neither-bush-or-obama-killed-iranian-general-qassem-soleimani-2020-1

8 Babak Dehghanpisheh, "Soleimani was Iran's Celebrity Soldier, Spearhead in Middle East," Reuters, 3 January 2020. https://www.reuters.com/article/us-iran-security-soleimani-newsmaker/soleimani-was-irans-celebrity-soldier-spearhead-in-middle-east-idUSKBN1Z20C4

Although the Quds Force was supposed to be a covert unit of Iran's military, its commander, Soleimani, came to embrace his newfound celebrity. He became a symbol of Iran's growing power in the region. Soleimani was the embodiment of Iran's "holy" opposition to the extremism of their Sunni co-religionists as well as to the infidel crusaders—as represented by the Americans—and their Jewish enemies, as represented by Israel.

General Soleimani had acquired more power and stature in Iran's system over the years; indeed, it was believed he had more influence over Iran's foreign policy than the country's foreign minister. His power in Iran's foreign policy was matched only by the supreme leader, Ayatollah Khamenei. Yet Soleimani had essentially painted a big red target on his back for US intelligence, believing that the Americans would never risk assassinating him. As Bob Woodward reported in *Rage*, his 2020 exposé of the Trump administration, during a golf game at Trump International Golf Club in West Palm Beach, Florida, on December 30, 2019, President Trump informed Senator Lindsey Graham (R-SC) that he was contemplating assassinating Soleimani. Graham cautioned Trump against the move.[9]

The Americans under Trump were finally tired of Soleimani's antics, though. As the Iranian general's media stature had grown in the region, he had also become more brazenly hostile toward the United States. Not satisfied with the murder of US troops who had been waging the war in Iraq from 2003–2011, Soleimani had targeted American personnel in Iraq who had been tasked with helping the Iraqi government defeat ISIS. In the run-up to his assassination, the regional cat-and-mouse game between Iran and Israel (as well as Israel's allies, notably the United States) had reached a critical point.

The week before Trump had ordered the assassination of Soleimani, Kataeb Hezbollah, a Shiite terrorist group operating in Iraq and backed by Soleimani's Quds Force, murdered an American contractor on a base

9 Bob Woodward, *Rage* (New York: Simon & Schuster, 2020), pp. 195–97.

in Kirkuk, Iraq. The United States fired missiles at Kataeb Hezbollah's bases in both Iraq and Syria, killing twenty-five of their fighters. After the US missile strike against Kataeb Hezbollah, pro-Iran militiamen broke into the massive US embassy in Baghdad. After this violation of the sovereignty of the US embassy in Iraq, President Trump tweeted that Iran would pay a "BIG PRICE" for their aggression against the United States.[10] Shortly after that tweet, Soleimani and his cadre were incinerated in the American drone attack.

After the killing of Soleimani, the Iranian regime vowed to take its vengeance upon the Americans. Tensions between the United States and Iran reached levels not seen since the early days of the Islamic Republic of Iran's rise to power. Curt Mills, an editor of *The American Conservative,* went on the Fox News Channel's highly rated primetime program, *Tucker Carlson Tonight,* to warn viewers that the slaying of Soleimani might become a "Franz Ferdinand moment," in which "a great power [the United States] gets involved with a smaller power [Iran], and gets the world into a world war."[11] The Iranian response to the assassination was, fortunately, something less than that which followed the assassination of the Austro-Hungarian Empire's Archduke Franz Ferdinand and his wife by a Serbian nationalist while they toured the Austro-Hungarian military's barracks in Serbia in 1914.

Far from beginning another world war, the Iranian response was haphazard and made Tehran look weak. On the evening of January 8, 2020, a dozen missiles were launched from Iran, arced deep into the early morning sky, and slammed into several US bases in neighboring Iraq. It was a caustic experience for the US military personnel stationed on those bases. One hundred US servicemen would be treated

---

10 Donald J. Trump, 31 December 2019, 4:19 pm, https://twitter.com/realDonaldTrump/status/12121210260725923384

11 YouTube. The American Conservative, "The American Conservative's Curt Mills Talks Iran and General Soleimani on Tucker Carlson Tonight," 3 January 2020, 4:42, https://www.youtube.com/watch?v=bvI-5rI2RX8.

for traumatic brain injuries associated with the missile fusillade.[12] Thankfully, no American deaths were reported.

Sadly, however, the shambolic Iranian missile attack did claim the lives of 176 innocent people who were traveling on an outbound international flight from Tehran International Airport to Kiev, Ukraine. An IRGC missile operator had misinterpreted a radar signal, identified the Ukrainian airliner as an incoming American cruise missile, and launched a missile that knocked the planeload of innocent men, women, and children out of the sky.[13] Nothing about Iran's counterattack was militarily effective, nor did it help win international sympathy for the assassination of Soleimani. After the embarrassing Iranian missile attack on January 8, Iranian President Hassan Rouhani told the international press that, "We have responded to that terrorist act, and *will respond to it* [emphasis added]."[14]

What happened at the start of 2020 was not an isolated incident. It was another round of many rounds of escalating hostilities between the United States and Iran, going back decades. As I have written in *The American Spectator,* the "Little Cold War" occurring between the United States and its regional partners against Iran is increasingly turning hot.[15] Or, in the formulation of irregular warfare expert, Sean McFate, a "shadow war" exists between the United States and Iran.[16] And this

---

12 Shawn Snow, "American Troops Had Only Hours to React to Iranian Ballistic Missile Attack. Here's What They Did." *Military Times,* 21 April 2020. https://www.militarytimes.com/flashpoints/2020/04/21/american-troops-had-only-hours-to-react-to-iranian-ballistic-missile-attack-heres-what-they-did/

13 Michael Safi, "Iran Admits It Fired Two Missiles at Ukrainian Passenger Jet," *The Guardian,* 21 January 2020. https://www.theguardian.com/world/2020/jan/21/iran-admits-it-fired-two-missiles-at-ukrainian-passenger-jet

14 "Iran President Says Iran Responded, Will Respond to Assassination of Soleimani," *Reuters,* 18 March 2020. https://fr.reuters.com/article/uk-iran-us-soleimani-idAFKBN215124

15 Brandon J. Weichert, "Trump Is Winning the Little Cold War with Iran," *The American Spectator,* 23 June 2019. https://spectator.org/trump-is-winning-the-little-cold-war-with-iran/

16 Janine di Giovanni, "Why America Isn't Equipped for the New Rules of War," *MIT Technology Review,* 24 October 2019. https://www.technologyreview.com/2019/10/24/132194/america-isnt-equipped-for-shadow-war-disinformation-sean-mcfate/

shadow conflict is becoming increasingly hard to keep in the shadows.

At the time of Soleimani's killing, some in the Western political establishment insinuated that it had happened because President Trump was an irresponsible leader simply trying to distract the American public away from a contentious impeachment hearing against him.[17] As you've seen, however, Soleimani's killing *was* a response to an escalating series of Iranian attacks against the West. While the Soleimani hit was a direct response to the Iranian assassination of an American contractor in Kirkuk and the subsequent Iranian attack on the US embassy in Baghdad, the series of hostilities that resulted in the assassination of Qassem Soleimani goes back much farther in time.

In fact, the Islamic Republic of Iran has been at war with the United States and Israel since its rise to power in 1979. One of the first actions the Islamic Republic of Iran took was to storm the US embassy in Tehran. After they captured the embassy and its staff, the subsequent hostage crisis lasted for over 400 days. "Death to America!" is a chant synonymous with the Iranian regime since its inception forty-two years ago. As the introduction of this work notes, through its Hezbollah proxy in Lebanon, Iran blew up the US Marine barracks in Beirut in 1983, murdering 241 US military personnel. Almost from the beginning of the regime, Iranian forces have worked to spread its violent Islamist revolution to the rest of the Middle East.

Further, Iran has consistently called for the destruction of the Jewish state of Israel while seeking to subjugate its Sunni Muslim neighbors. These are not new aims. The current Islamist regime of Iran is merely returning to the historical foreign policy objectives pursued by former great Shiite regimes of Iran (formerly Persia).

In pursuit of its expansionistic agenda, Iran has made common cause with other American rivals, such as North Korea, Venezuela, Cuba,

---

17 "Warren Implies Trump Had Soleimani Killed to Distract from Impeachment," *The Times of Israel*, 6 January 2020, https://www.timesofisrael.com/warren-implies-trump-had-soleimani-killed-to-distract-from-impeachment/

and Syria. Iran has sought—and received—protection from China and Russia, America's great rivals. Meanwhile, the Iranians have worked assiduously to undermine the American war effort in both Afghanistan as well as Iraq.

More importantly, though, Iran has remained committed to creating a nuclear weapons arsenal that it can use to keep American military power at bay. By keeping American power over-the-horizon, Tehran believes it will be able to intimidate its Sunni Arab neighbors while potentially obliterating its rival Israel. Given its penchant for terrorism and its obsession with nuclear weapons, Iran could possibly hand off its nuclear material to its terrorist proxy, Hezbollah, who could use that nuclear material in a terrorist attack directed against either Europe or the United States.

Iran has also attempted to use its status as the world's fourth largest oil producer to hold the oil-dependent world hostage to its ideological whims.[18] And since Iran straddles the Strait of Hormuz, a vital maritime trade route, Tehran can and has threatened the safe passage of oil tankers and other ships through that waterway. Iran believes these moves will produce an irreparable spike in the international price of oil, which they hope will harm the US economy. The Iranians tried to do this most recently in 2018.[19] Thankfully, Iranian actions have thus far failed to harm the US economy.

As you can see, though, Iran is a long-term threat that has plagued US foreign policy for years with little sign of abatement. Curt Mills's concern that the killing of General Soleimani could be a trigger for a third world war did not pan out. Yet if a third world war were to start, it would likely begin in the Middle East—and be triggered by Iran, given its incessantly destabilizing behaviors: its support for terror, its

---

18 Brandon J. Weichert, "Iran Keeps Asking for It," *The American Spectator,* 15 September 2019. https://spectator.org/iran-keeps-asking-for-it/

19 Brandon J. Weichert, "Iran Will Strike Again," *The American Spectator,* 22 September 2019. https://spectator.org/iran-will-strike-again/

aggression against its neighbors, or its pursuit of nuclear weapons. This is especially true when we consider the intractable historical animosities between Iran and its neighbors and the fact that so many rival great powers have taken competing stands on Iran.

2

A WEAK IRAN IS JUST AS

DANGEROUS AS A STRONG ONE

IF 2020 STARTED WITH A BANG when Trump assassinated Solei-mani, things only got worse. The outbreak of the novel coronavirus that originated in Wuhan, China, eviscerated the Iranian regime. Beginning in 2019, Iranians began protesting against their regime. The Trump administration's sanctions were adding to the woes of ordinary Iranian people, and the regime was viewed in a negative light.[1]

According to David P. Goldman of *The Asia Times*, "there is a

---

[1] "Iran Protests: All You Need to Know in 600 Words," Al Jazeera, 20 November 2019. https://www.aljazeera.com/news/2019/11/20/irans-protests-all-you-need-to-know-in-600-words

good deal of evidence of extreme dissatisfaction with the regime due to economic stress." Goldman concluded:

> Few countries have endured this level of deprivation outside of full war mobilization, and few have seen such a drastic decline in births. The only modern comparison is Venezuela. Governments with a monopoly of economic resources and the willingness to kill significant numbers of their own citizens can stay in power for quite some time, but there seems no question that Iran's regime is fragile and prone to destabilization.[2]

This assessment was written *before* the outbreak of COVID-19 in Iran. The negative trends that David Goldman highlighted have only been exacerbated by the pandemic. The outbreak of COVID-19 was the ultimate stress test for every system in the world, from computer networks, to healthcare systems, to the system of nation-states that has defined the international order since the Treaty of Westphalia of 1648 CE. After the outbreak of the novel coronavirus from Wuhan, China, the *Guardian* reported that Iran was "struggling to cope as trust in government diminishes, sanctions weaken the economy and hospitals report overcrowded intensive care units."[3]

Far from being the powerhouse about to annex the region away from the Americans, however, the Iranian regime is a wounded animal today. However, a wounded animal is most dangerous. What's more, should Western pressure on Iran weaken, the Islamist regime could restore its strength. Today, Iran faces a significant internal political crisis. An increasing level of domestic dissatisfaction risks undercutting the mullahs' carefully laid plans for regional dominance.

---

2 David P. Goldman, "How Fragile is Iran's Regime?" *The Asia Times,* 13 January 2020. https://asiatimes.com/2020/01/how-fragile-is-irans-regime-2/

3 Patrick Wintour, "Iran at Breaking Point as It Fights Third Wave of Coronavirus," *The Guardian,* 14 October 2020. https://www.theguardian.com/world/2020/oct/14/iran-at-breaking-point-as-it-fights-third-wave-of-coronavirus

American observers of Iran, at times, are encouraged because Iran is buckling under the pressure. They believe that Iran's internal contradictions will cause the regime to collapse as bloodlessly as the old Soviet Union did. We can only hope so. Yet, for every peaceful regime collapse like that of the Soviet Union in 1991, there are several more examples of the collapse of a great power causing a cascade of chaos.

The First World War saw three great empires in their twilight—the Austro-Hungarian, Russian, and Ottoman Empires. Their actions threw Europe, and then the world, into one of the bloodiest conflicts imaginable. These three European empires were all enduring decline before the First World War erupted in Europe. By the war's end, these great empires had collapsed—and taken millions of lives with them.

The weaknesses of these regimes made the Great War more (not less) possible and helped to exacerbate the conflict. We are still dealing with the fallout from the collapse of these great empires more than a century later.[4] Iran is a very likely candidate to precipitate a great power conflict because of its current internal weakness.[5]

The likelihood of Iran causing a third world war has been made all the greater because of its alliances with both Russia and China.[6] Recently, the desperate Iranian regime made a bizarre, twenty-five-year trade deal with China. Observers like Dr. Majid Rafizadeh have described this deal as a betrayal of the Iranian people to rapacious foreign powers. According to Rafizadeh (and others), the deal appears "colonial"

---

4 Geoffrey Mock, "How the Trauma and Struggles of World War I Helped Shape the Modern World," Duke Today, 8 November 2018. https://today.duke.edu/2018/11/how-trauma-and-struggles-world-war-i-helped-shape-modern-world

5 Brandon J. Weichert, "Trump Strikes the Right Balance with Iran," American Greatness, 3 January 2020. https://amgreatness.com/2020/01/03/trump-strikes-the-right-balance-with-iran/

6 Tom O'Connor, "Iran Seeks Deals with Russia and China to Build Coalition to Resist U.S.," Newsweek, 22 July 2020. https://www.newsweek.com/iran-russia-deal-china-agreement-coalition-1519467

in nature, wherein Tehran has granted "a foreign country significant rights over Iran's resources."[7]

Over the first five years of the Sino-Iranian agreement, China will invest $400 billion in Iran's oil, gas, and petrochemical industries. On top of that, China will be given first rights to any contract that is connected to the oil, gas, and petrochemical industries in Iran. They will receive these benefits, all while being given a 12 percent discount and a two-year delayed repayment option on any of those favorable contracts.

Think about it this way: while the Iranian people are suffering and Iran's economy is collapsing, the desperate Iranian regime has opted to give away to a foreign power Iran's only real hope of economic revitalization—their energy resources—at a discount rate. This deal will not benefit the ordinary Iranian citizen. Instead, this one-sided deal will merely prop up the unpopular regime in Iran that helped to foster the abysmal conditions that most Iranians are now living under.

China's deal with the mullahs allow for up to 5,000 Chinese "security personnel" to be deployed to Iran. This prompted the Iranian newspaper *Arman-e Melli* to ask, "Will Iran Become a Chinese Colony?" By definition, it is now a Chinese colony, much as Kenya is today.[8] The Iranians, as the Kenyans are learning, may soon become foreigners in their own land.[9]

The Chinese have shown their preferred pattern of making deals with developing countries: the rapacious Chinese move their workers in to a country, like Kenya, and displace the people there. The jobs

---

7 Dr. Majid Rafizadeh, "Iranian Regime Betrays Its Principles with China Deal," Arab News, 12 July 2020. https://www.arabnews.com/node/1703671

8 Su-Lin Tan and Jevans Nyabiage, "Kenya Keen to Renegotiate Debt, Fees with China as Coronavirus Hits Unprofitable Mombasa-Naivasha Rail Line," 3 October 2020. https://www.scmp.com/economy/china-economy/article/3103710/kenya-keen-renegotiate-debt-fees-china-coronavirus-hits

9 Akol Nyok Akol Dok and Bradly A. Thayer, "Takeover Trap: Why Imperialist China Is Invading Africa," *The National Interest,* 10 July 2019. https://nationalinterest.org/feature/takeover-trap-why-imperialist-china-invading-africa-66421

that are created usually do not go to the locals. Instead, they go to the Chinese expatriates living there.[10]

In a decade's time, the Chinese who move to Iran, attracted by the vast energy resources and opportunities to exploit the country, will essentially make Iranians second-class citizens in their own country. This will repeat a pattern that China has followed in every developing region where it does business. The relationship will be extractive: the Chinese will take, and the Iranians will be made to give, just so the unpopular Islamist regime of Iran can survive.

Meanwhile, Iran has made itself a conduit for the projection of Russian power into the Middle East.[11] Beginning with Russia's attacks in Syria several years ago, Iran allowed Russian bombers to deploy from its territory.[12] Further, Iranian troops, along with those of the Syrian Arab Army loyal to Syria's strongman, Bashar al-Assad, have waged a ceaseless ground war against jihadist groups in Syria while the Russian air force bombed the jihadists from above.[13] In essence, the Iranians and Syrian Arab Army do the dying while the Russians do the flying in the Syrian Civil War.

Iran's ruling mullahs believe that bolstering Assad in Syria while propping up the pro-Iranian regime in Iraq will allow for the Iranians to build a land bridge connecting their country to the Levant, where

---

10 Lily Kuo, "The Worst Thing About Kenya's New Power Plant Isn't That Chinese Workers Are Being Brought In to Build It," Quartz, 28 July 2016. https://qz.com/africa/743461/the-worst-thing-about-kenyas-new-power-plant-isnt-that-chinese-workers-are-being-brought-in-to-build-it/

11 Jeffrey Mankoff and Andrew Bowen, "Russia Doesn't Care if Assad Wins. It's about Russian Power Projection," Foreign Policy, 22 September 2015. https://foreignpolicy.com/2015/09/22/putin-russia-syria-assad-iran-islamic-state/

12 Andrew Osborn, "Russia Uses Iran as Base to Bomb Syrian Militants for the First Time," Reuters, 16 August 2016. https://www.reuters.com/article/us-mideast-crisis-russia-iran/russia-uses-iran-as-base-to-bomb-syrian-militants-for-first-time-idUSKCN10R0PA

13 Laila Bassam and Andrew Osborn, "Iran Troops to Join Syria War, Russia Bombs Group Trained by CIA," Reuters, 1 October 2015. https://www.reuters.com/article/us-mideast-crisis-russia-syria/iran-troops-to-join-syria-war-russia-bombs-group-trained-by-cia-idUSKCN0RV41O20151002

the Iranians can then empower Hezbollah in Lebanon to threaten Israel. Instead, the Iranians have suffered high numbers of casualties after almost a decade of fighting in Syria, while only the Russians have gained any meaningful benefits from their alliance with Iran.[14]

The Islamists of Iran want to marry their power to Chinese and Russian power to offset the unwanted influence of the United States and its allies in the region. Not only have China and Iran entered into a large development deal, but Iran has also connected its trade with that of Russia. Since 2018, total bilateral trade between Russia and Iran has increased to around $2 billion, "driven by exports of machinery, steel, and agricultural goods from Russia, and fruits, vegetables, and dairy products from Iran," according to *The Middle East Institute*.[15] What's more, Iran and Russia have currently been driven closer by the sanctions that the United States has imposed upon both Russia and Iran.

Due to these sanctions, the Russo-Iranian relationship has seen a marked increase in economic integration and a deepening of energy ties. The *Tehran Times* reported in August of 2020 that Moscow was planning to build a $1.6 billion port in Lagan on the coast of the Caspian Sea to further expand its trade relations with Iran. Toward that end, a new shipping route between Russia and Iran via the Caspian Sea went active in September 2020.[16]

Despite this progress, however, as Alex Vatanka of the Middle East Institute noted, the Russo-Iranian trade relationship has fallen short of what it could be. This is partly because of logistical limitations—which is why Russia and Iran created the new shipping route along the Caspian

---

14 Ardavan Khoshnood, "Iran-Russia Ties: Never Better but Maybe Not Forever?" The Middle East Institute, 12 February 2020. https://www.mei.edu/publications/iran-russia-ties-never-better-maybe-not-forever

15 Alex Vatanka, "Russia, Iran, and Economic Integration on the Caspian," The Middle East Institute, 17 August 2020. https://www.mei.edu/publications/russia-iran-and-economic-integration-caspian

16 "Iran, Russia to Launch Cargo Shipping Line in September," *Tehran Times,* 12 August 2020. https://www.tehrantimes.com/news/451144/Iran-Russia-to-launch-cargo-shipping-line-in-September

Sea—but also because of the complex history between the two powers that still resonates with the Iranian people today.

Since America imposed sanctions on Russia, Moscow has moved aggressively to sell its oil and natural gas products to consumers that usually bought from the US-sanctioned Iranian energy sector. These recent Russian moves have complicated Iran's trade and economic policies at a time when the country is already feeling the squeeze from American sanctions. In turn, the Russian moves have made it difficult for Iran's ruling elite to increase the trade relations they desire with Russia.

Still, the Iranian regime continues behaving like a colonized nation to both China and Russia. The regime has made these deals because the Islamists of Iran believe they need the aid of larger states, like Russia and China, to counteract the Americans and their regional partners of Israel and the Sunni Arab states, notably the Kingdom of Saudi Arabia. Given the rising tensions between the United States, Russia, and China, it is likely that these alliances will make Iran and the Middle East ground-zero for the next great power war. Again, Iran's weakness has made it a grave threat to regional stability and American national security.

3

ANOTHER INTIFADA WITH ISRAEL?

IRANIAN FANTASIES OF EXPANDING beyond their present borders, exterminating the Jewish state of Israel, permanently pushing the Americans out of the region, and subjugating their Sunni Arab neighbors continue—in spite of how brittle Iran's regime may be at home. In fact, the weakness of the mullahocracy likely forces it into a "use-it-or-lose-it" mentality when it comes to achieving their dreams of regional hegemony. Iran's leaders assume that if they can report success in subjugating the region, then they will have bought their regime a new lease on life.

Iran's ongoing support of Hezbollah, which operates out of southern Lebanon and routinely terrorizes nearby Israel, has intensified now that Iranian forces have a physical connection from Iran through Iraq and Syria. Because Iranian power is connected in these three countries, Iranian reach can theoretically touch Israel.[1] The more closely that Iran is connected to its terrorist proxies in the Eastern Mediterranean, the more it can foster another round of communal fighting involving its proxy Hezbollah and the Sunni Hamas terrorist organization in the Gaza Strip against Israel. In fact, there is some evidence that Iran has been helping Hezbollah and Hamas plan yet another intifada.[2]

THE FIRST TWO INTIFADAS

The first two intifadas—meaning "resurgence" in Arabic—were waged by the Palestinian Liberation Organization (PLO) against Israel. The PLO would ultimately become the political party known as Fatah, which today is the governing party of the Palestinian quasi-state. The first intifada began in 1987, after an Israeli Defense Force (IDF) jeep killed four Palestinian youths engaged in a protest against Israel.

At the time, Israel had expanded from a small settlement in 1947 to a major regional power after Israel's Arab neighbors lost a series of wars meant to roll back Israeli gains since the United Nations recognized Israel as an independent country in 1948. Hamas, a Sunni Muslim extremist organization that today rules the Gaza Strip, can trace its lineage to the First Intifada, which ended in 1992. In fact, the PLO's longtime dominance of the Palestinian territories was challenged by Hamas during this conflict. That internal conflict for mastery of the Palestinian territories between Hamas and the PLO, now Fatah, continues to this day.[3] The First Intifada, while bloody, was also a failure

---

1 Ralph Peters, "The Stakes in Syria Now Include US-Russia War," *New York Post*, 19 June 2017. https://nypost.com/2017/06/19/the-stakes-in-syria-now-include-us-russia-war/

2 Ahmad Majidyar, "Iranian Cleric Calls for Arming Palestinians for 'Third Intifada,'" The Middle East Institute, 15 December 2017. https://www.mei.edu/publications/iranian-cleric-calls-arming-palestinians-third-intifada

3 Mitchell Bard, "Israel's Wars & Operations: First Intifada (1987–1993)," Jewish Virtual Library, Accessed on: 2 November 2020. https://www.jewishvirtuallibrary.org/first-intifada

for the Palestinians and their Arab allies.[4]

The Second Intifada differed markedly from the first. It started in September 2000, when Ariel Sharon, then prime minister of Israel, visited the Temple Mount in the contested city of Jerusalem. The heads of the Israeli security forces, as well as the commander of the Palestinian Preventative Security Organization, advised Sharon that, so long as he and his colleagues did not enter the mosques near the Temple Mount, there would only be limited protests. They were catastrophically wrong.

What soon followed was the explosion of the Second Intifada. The First Intifada had been a distant affair for most Israelis, generally affecting only to those men and women who were serving in the IDF. The Second Intifada, however, was the conflict in which bus bombings and rocket attacks directed against Israeli civilians became the norm.

Whereas the First Intifada began as violent protests against Israeli rule of the Gaza Strip and West Bank, "the Second Intifada was far bloodier, taking on the aspects of armed conflict, guerilla warfare, and terrorist attacks," in the words of Israeli analyst Ziv Hellman. "The stone-armed Palestinian child of [the First Intifada] was replaced by the armed adult fighter of [the Second Intifada]."[5] It should be noted that the Israelis do not share the Palestinian view of how the Second Intifada began. According to most Israeli intelligence experts at the time, they began detecting troubling patterns of increasing hostility coming from the Palestinian side that prompted the Israelis to enact certain contingencies when it became clear that some conflict would erupt between the two sides.[6]

---

4 Sonja Karkar, "The First Intifada—Historical Overview," American Muslims for Palestine, 10 December 2007. https://www.ampalestine.org/palestine-101/history/intifadas/first-intifada-historical-overview

5 Ramzy Baroud, "'Children of the Stones': The Day Palestine was Reborn," Al Jazeera, 8 December 2017. https://www.aljazeera.com/opinions/2017/12/8/children-of-the-stones-the-day-palestine-was-reborn

6 Ziv Hellman, "The Second Intifada Begins," My Jewish Learning, Accessed on 2 November 2020. https://www.myjewishlearning.com/article/the-second-intifada-begins/

Regardless of the origins of the crisis, the nature of conflict between the Israelis and the Palestinians has clearly changed since the First Intifada. Modern guerilla warfare and terrorist tactics would come to define the increasing discord between the Palestinians and Israelis. While Iran had little input in the two intifadas, afterwards Iranian influence over both Hezbollah and Sunni terrorist groups, such as Hamas, has steadily increased over the years. Therefore, the already changing nature of the Palestinian terrorist threat to Israel has become increasingly more complex and better funded, thanks to Iran's greater level of involvement.

As Iranian power has grown in the region, Tehran has been able to take a more proactive stand with these likeminded anti-Israeli terrorist organizations in pushing hard against Israeli power in the Levant. The Iranian regime, which views the United States as its greatest threat, believes that in the Middle East, there is no difference between US national interests and Israeli interests. Just as Iran views Hezbollah as a proxy for its own power, Tehran believes that Israel is little more than a proxy for American power in the region.[7]

IRAN JOINS THE FIGHT: THE HEZBOLLAH-ISRAEL WAR OF 2006

In 2006, a full-blown war erupted between Israel and Hezbollah. On July 12, 2006, Hezbollah fighters secretly crossed the Israel-Lebanon border and ambushed an IDF patrol. Five IDF soldiers were in the vehicle. Three were killed and two were taken prisoner by Hezbollah's fighters. The Israelis attempted to rescue the two captured soldiers, only to lose five more of their soldiers in the ensuing battle.

For their part, Hezbollah demanded that Israel release Lebanese political prisoners in exchange for the two captured IDF soldiers. Israel, with its long-standing policy of not negotiating with terrorists, launched

---

7 Dalia Dassa Kaye, Alireza Nader, Parisa Roshan, *Israel and Iran: A Dangerous Rivalry* (Santa Monica: RAND Corporation, 2011), pp. 57–60. https://www.rand.org/content/dam/rand/pubs/monographs/2011/RAND_MG1143.pdf

a full-scale invasion of Lebanon. The objective at that point was for Israeli forces to disarm and disband the Lebanese Shiite Muslim terrorist group Hezbollah. After thirty-four days of intense fighting, though, the Israelis failed to achieve their strategic objective. In fact, Israel ultimately withdrew its forces entirely from southern Lebanon and left their two captured soldiers to their fates.[8]

Even though Hezbollah received a brutal pounding from the IDF, its leader, Hassan Nasrallah, claimed that his organization had enjoyed a victory.[9] After all, it is likely that neither Nasrallah nor anyone else in Hezbollah anticipated the robust Israeli military response to Hezbollah's simple kidnapping of two IDF soldiers. Once committed fully to war, however, Israel had a long history of achieving its strategic objectives— no matter how badly the odds were stacked against it. In the case of the 2006 war, though, Israel failed to achieve the victory it was looking for.

Not only did Hezbollah survive the direct assault on their forces, but they prospered thereafter. In Israel, the military leadership correctly understood that the 2006 war was a failure. Following that consensus, Israeli strategists spent the next several years pioneering research and development of "gray zone" operations, or the war between the war.[10] Meanwhile, Hezbollah has only grown wealthier and stronger as Iranian power and influence has extended beyond its own borders and into Iraq, Syria, and Lebanon.

Hezbollah is a foreign entity based in Lebanon. Unlike other Islamist terror groups, such as al Qaeda or ISIS, Hezbollah does not belong the Sunni sect of Islam. Instead, Hezbollah is the proudly militant arm of

---

8 Rebecca Stead, "Remembering Israel's 2006 War on Lebanon," *Middle East Monitor,* 12 July 2018. https://www.middleeastmonitor.com/20180712-remembering-israels-2006-war-on-lebanon/

9 Michael Slackman and John O'Neill, "Hezbollah Chief Leads Huge Rally," *New York Times,* 22 September 2006. https://www.nytimes.com/2006/09/22/world/middleeast/23lebanoncnd.html

10 Matt M. Matthews, "We Were Caught Unprepared: The 2006 Hezbollah-Israeli War," U.S. Army Combined Arms Center Combat Studies Institute Press, The Long War Series Occasional Paper No. 26 (2006): 61–65. https://www.armyupress.army.mil/Portals/7/combat-studies-institute/csi-books/we-were-caught-unprepared.pdf

Shiite Islam (or, at least that's what their members tell everyone). The terrorist organization receives support from the even more distant Iran. Despite it being a foreign terror group, Hezbollah—and therefore its Iranian backers—has come to play a vital role in the ongoing war against Israel. What's more, Hezbollah is but one of many foreign groups participating in the ongoing Israel-Palestine conflict. As you will see in the next chapter, the Sunni-Shia split in Islam defines the Islamic world and drives politics in the Middle East. Despite their differences with each other, Iran has in recent years striven to empower not only its Hezbollah proxy in Lebanon but also Hamas and Fatah to further weaken Israel and, in its eyes, the United States.

Recently, Iran, its proxy Hezbollah, Hamas, and Fatah have been showing signs of a reconciliation. In February of 2020, both Hamas and Iran were sending signals of their growing cooperation, and Israeli intelligence feared that Hamas, with Iranian assistance, was stockpiling arms for a new round of religious warfare against Israel. As far back as December of 2017, leaders of Fatah met with the leaders of Hezbollah. At that fateful 2017 meeting in Beirut, "Fatah agreed to collaborate with [Hezbollah]" and to "activate a third intifada [against Israel]."[11] For two years, Iran continued its expansionistic behavior throughout the region as their conflict with Israel simmered—all while supporting the three greatest threats to Israel: Hezbollah, Hamas, and Fatah.

Sensing the danger, Israel quietly stepped up its activities in the "gray zone." Israeli forces have "conducted more than 200 airstrikes" in Syria since 2011 "and 1,000 targets linked to Iran and its Islamic Revolutionary Guards Corps Quds Force (IRGCQF), and against IRGC-QF backed groups such as the Lebanese Hezbollah." According to the Center for New American Security, "this campaign has slowed Iran's military buildup in Syria while avoiding a broader regional

---

11 "Palestinians Meet with Hezbollah Terror Leader to Spark Third Intifada," *Jewish News Syndicate,* 8 January 2018. https://www.jns.org/palestinians-meet-with-hezbollah-terror-leader-to-spark-third-intifada/

conflagration that would have been damaging to Israel's interests."[12]

While Israel increased its operational tempo against Iranian proxies in Lebanon and Syria, Israeli forces also engaged in a series of offensives in the Hamas-controlled Gaza Strip. The Israeli writer Caroline Glick likened the Israeli actions in Gaza to "mowing the lawn."[13] Such moves are part of a larger Israeli strategy that American football fans might refer to as a "prevent defense."[14]

Thanks to Iran's support, Hezbollah and Hamas are now proving increasingly effective against Israel—though Hezbollah continues to pose the more serious challenge.[15] Israel's enemies have learned the key lesson all successful guerilla movements have learned: it is better to be decentralized and dispersed instead of centralized. In order to prevent these diffuse threats from coalescing into an effective fighting force that could potentially push Israelis out of their hard-won territory, Israel is attempting to slow their momentum with pinpoint strikes. At some point, though, Israel's "mowing the grass" strategy will be insufficient to the threat level these increasingly coordinated elements pose to Jerusalem.[16]

Iran remains undaunted in its antagonism toward Israel, despite

---

12 Ilan Goldenberg, Nicholas Heras, Kaleigh Thomas, and Jennie Matuschak, "Countering Iran in the Gray Zone," Center for New American Security, 14 April 2020. https://www.cnas.org/publications/reports/countering-iran-gray-zone

13 Caroline B. Glick, "Column One: Mowing the Lawn in Gaza," *The Jerusalem Post,* 18 October 2018. https://www.jpost.com/opinion/column-one-mowing-the-lawn-in-gaza-569775

14 For those who may be unfamiliar with the concept, prevent defense is a tactic that teams use to stymie a rival team's offense from moving too rapidly down the field or from successfully scoring with a long pass. It is a defensive strategy meant to run out the all-important play clock during a football game. Former NFL coach John Madden, as well as this author, have argued that "The only thing that prevent defense does is prevent you from winning."

15 Chuck Freilich, "Hamas Is a Distraction for Israel Compared to Hezbollah and Iran," *Haaretz,* 19 November 2018. https://www.haaretz.com/israel-news/.premium-conflict-with-hamas-is-hardly-the-main-threat-facing-israel-1.6432549

16 Maren Koss, "Flexible Resistance: How Hezbollah and Hamas Are Mending Ties," Carnegie Middle East Center, 11 July 2018. https://carnegie-mec.org/2018/07/11/flexible-resistance-how-hezbollah-and-hamas-are-mending-ties-pub-76782 .

Israel's brilliant mastery of the gray arts since its 2006 war with Hezbollah. On June 21, 2020, Hezbollah's squat, white-bearded leader—clad in black, as all villains prefer—introduced a stylishly edited video at one of Hezbollah's lavish conventions (yes, apparently, there really is such a thing as a terrorist convention). In that video, Nasrallah could be heard chortling that "today, we can hit the city of Tel Aviv but also, if God wants and with his help, can hit very precise targets within Tel Aviv," as the images shifted from Nasrallah speaking to the hauntingly specific coordinates of Israel—thereby intimating that Hezbollah possessed weapons capable of striking deep and hard into Israeli territory with consistent accuracy. It would have been easy to write this off as mere posturing on the part of Nasrallah.

However, my Israeli colleagues have learned not to underestimate the Iranian-backed terrorist supervillain. The last time Israel's leadership underestimated Hezbollah, it ended up losing the 2006 war against Hezbollah in Lebanon. During this thirty-four-day conflict, Hezbollah is estimated to have fired around 4,000 short-range rockets into northern Israel and murdered fifty Israelis.

The week of July 28, 2020, saw the Israeli government claim that it had stopped a Hezbollah attack that was about to commence against Israel. In the skirmish between the IDF and Hezbollah, a Hezbollah fighter was killed. This must have felt like *déjà vu* for the Israeli leaders who had lived through the opening phases of the 2006 war with Hezbollah when, as you've read above, Hezbollah fighters breached Israel's borders and attacked an unsuspecting IDF patrol.

Elsewhere, Hezbollah and Israeli border security personnel engaged in a protracted firefight. In response to the shootout, Nasrallah cryptically told the international press that the firefight was "unrelated" to the initial killing of the Hezbollah fighter by the IDF on July 28. Just as Iranian President Rouhani had left open the possibility of still more attacks against the United States for the assassination of Qassem Soleimani, Hezbollah's leader, Nasrallah, insisted that his organization's retaliation against Israel was "still coming."[17] Observers should have taken Nasrallah and Rouhani at their word: it is likely that Iran and its proxy Hezbollah were planning a major military action against Israel as a retaliation for the sustained assault that the Israelis, Americans, and Saudis had subjected Iranian forces to across the region for the last few years.

The makings of a Third Intifada, I believe, were in the offing during the summer of 2020. Yet the Western alliance of Israel, the United States, and the Sunni Arab states appeared to have Iran's number. A great war has raged between the Western alliance and Iran in the shadows for years. The tempo of this shadow war, however, intensified over the last few years, ever since President Donald J. Trump in 2018 abandoned the nuclear agreement created by his predecessor, Barack Obama, three years earlier.

The pieces for another intifada or certainly another round of warfare with Hezbollah (or both) are in place today. This time, however, the wars between Israel and its enemies—especially Hezbollah—will be far deadlier than any earlier conflict that Israel has endured. Now the various groups in the Middle East are jockeying for better positioning when the shooting actually starts. These rival groups are basically preparing the battlefield for the inevitable conflagration to come.

17 "Lebanon Accuses Israel of Provoking Border Escalation," AP, 28 July 2020. https://www.baynews9.com/fl/tampa/ap-online/2020/07/28/lebanon-accuses-israel-of-provoking--border-escalation

4

THE BEIRUT BLAST:

BUNGLED OR BRILLIANT MOVE?

IN AUGUST OF 2020, the world awoke to an incredible explosion in the port of Beirut. The blast was felt all of the way to the island nation of Cyprus. The unpopular Lebanese government's official claim was that poorly stored fireworks at an abandoned warehouse near the Beirut harbor exploded after years of malign neglect from the regime.[1] The blast killed 203 people and injured nearly 4,000.[2]

---

1 "Lebanon's Army Finds Firework Cache at Devastated Beirut Port," Reuters, 19 September 2020. https://www.reuters.com/article/uk-lebanon-crisis-port/lebanons-army-finds-firework-cache-at-devastated-beirut-port-idUSKCN26A0H8

2 "Lebanon Explosion: Deadly Fuel Tank Blast Rocks Beirut," BBC, 9 October 2020. https://www.bbc.com/news/world-middle-east-54486402

Given that 2,750 tons of ammonium nitrate were present at the explosion site, the narrative quickly shifted to the possibility of improperly stored fertilizer being the cause of the explosion.[3] Another mundane, though nonetheless disturbing, explanation from Lebanon's embattled government was that the regime had known about the ammonium nitrate; the massive quantity of explosives had been stored in Hangar 12 at the port after the explosives were confiscated from a Russian freighter, *MV Rhosus,* that was abandoned at the port in 2013. The Lebanese government went on to claim that due to incompetence on their part, the regime did not know what to do with the explosive fertilizer—while ignoring warning signs that the dangerous fertilizer was unstable and could explode at any moment.[4]

Yet some observers, such as this author, could not help but to suspect that if ammonium nitrate was present, it was possible that a Hezbollah weapons cache exploded in Beirut. It is well known that the Lebanese Christian government of President Michel Aoun is essentially an arm of Hezbollah. For decades, Hezbollah has been based in Lebanon, and an alliance of convenience has existed between the Shiite Muslims of Hezbollah and the Christians of Lebanon.[5] We know also that ammonium nitrate is a critical element in the creation of bombs.[6] Because ammonium nitrate is readily available on the civilian market, it is one

3 Bassem Mroue, Zeina Karam, Sarah El Deeb, "Negligence Probed in Deadly Beirut Blast Amid Public Anger," AP News, 5 August 2020. https://apnews.com/article/global-trade-ap-top-news-international-news-middle-east-lebanon-4475998de078a93bbe91b7ac9d43ada2

4 Timour Azhari, "Beirut Blast: Tracing the Explosives That Tore the Capital Apart," Al Jazeera, 5 August 2020. https://www.aljazeera.com/news/2020/8/5/beirut-blast-tracing-the-explosives-that-tore-the-capital-apart

5 Helim Shebaya, "Where Do Lebanon's Christians Stand on Hezbollah?" Al Jazeera, 30 November 2017. https://www.aljazeera.com/opinions/2017/11/30/where-do-lebanons-christians-stand-on-hezbollah/?gb=true

6 Brandon J. Weichert, "Official Narrative About Beirut Explosion Not Adding Up," The Weichert Report, 8 August 2020. https://theweichertreport.wordpress.com/2020/08/08/official-narrative-about-beirut-explosion-not-adding-up/

of Hezbollah's favorite chemicals to use in its perfidious bombs.[7]

In fact, the Israelis themselves postulated that the warehouse in question was a Hezbollah weapons depot.[8] Given this belief, Israeli officials argued that the August 2020 explosion in Beirut was likely the result of improperly stored ammonium nitrate that Hezbollah had housed there for use against Israeli targets in the future. Western intelligence services have since accused Hezbollah of purchasing and storing large quantities of ammonium nitrate in covert depots from Germany to Belgium to England—to be used in a future campaign of unmitigated terror against Israel.[9] The German newspaper *Die Welt* reported that "Iran's Revolutionary Guards made three deals with Hezbollah at the price of nearly 400,000 Euros between July 2013 and April 2014—and delivered the goods via land, air, and sea." By the way, according to *Die Welt,* the deal was "overseen by Quds Force commander Qassem Soleimani."[10]

There is reason to suspect that the official narrative is inaccurate. For example, "the detonation of ammonium nitrate would result in a *gray* mushroom cloud *not* the reddish-brown one we witnessed." Given this discrepancy, an alternative explanation is needed. There is a chemical that creates a reddish-brown plume when it explodes—Octogen (HMX), which has ammonium nitrate as a precursor element.[11]

---

7 "Hezbollah Procured Hundreds of Tons of Ammonium Nitrate from Iran, Report Says," *Haaretz,* 2 August 2020. https://www.haaretz.com/middle-east-news/.premium-hezbollah-procured-hundreds-of-tons-of-ammonium-nitrate-from-iran-report-says-1.9087357

8 "Israel's Netanyahu Says Hezbollah Has 'Arms Depot' in Beirut," Arab News, 30 September 2020. https://www.arabnews.com/node/1741846/middle-east

9 Lahav Harkov, "Hezbollah Stockpiled Chemical behind Beirut Blast in London and Germany," *The Jerusalem Post,* 5 August 2020. https://www.jpost.com/middle-east/hezbollah-stockpiled-chemical-behind-beirut-blast-in-london-637578

10 Daniel Dylan-Böhmer, "Die explosive Spur führt zur Hisbollah," *Die Welt,* 19 August 2020. https://amp.welt.de/politik/ausland/article213884822/Libanon-Die-explosive-Spur-fuehrt-zur-Hisbollah.html?__twitter_impression=true

11 Brandon J. Weichert, "HMX Explosives Present at Beirut Port," The Weichert Report, 5 August 2020. https://theweichertreport.wordpress.com/2020/08/05/hmx-explosives-present-at-beirut-port/

According to *Defense World,* "Octogen (HMX) is used exclusively for military purposes to implode fissionable, as a component of rocket propellant, and as a high explosive buster charge." In 2016, *Defense World* reported, "Iran's Defense Ministry announced … plans to produce [Octogen] to boost the penetration and destructive power of missile payloads."[12] Stephen Bryen, an American defense expert, tweeted that, "The explosion in Beirut looks like red fuming nitric acid used in rockets and scuds [sic]. Seems like a work accident by Hezbollah."[13]

Shortly after the explosion took place, many speculated that the blast was, in fact, the result of a nuclear explosion. Indeed, as Professor Andrew Tyas of Sheffield University in England assessed, the Beirut blast "[had] the equivalent yield to something that's on the scale of the smallest tactical nuclear weapon." Tyas added, "Had the warehouse storing the [explosives] been 400 metres closer to the city, however, fatalities would have measured in the 'thousands, if not tens of thousands.'"

Certainly a compelling case could be made immediately after the explosion, based only upon the startling visual evidence, notably the massive crater and the mushroom cloud, that a nuke had detonated in Beirut. Despite these conjectures, even those experts who did not accept the Lebanese government's ridiculous, "Aw, shucks!" explanation of the explosion disagreed that it was nuclear. Ed Lyman of the Union of Concerned Scientists argued that the lack of increased radiation levels or radiation-related injuries to people who were near the blast site disproves the nuclear weapon theory.[14]

Still, given both Hezbollah and Iran's objective of acquiring nuclear

---

12 "Iran to Produce Octogen Explosive Materials to Power Weapons Systems," *Defense World,* 8 April 2016. https://www.defenseworld.net/news/15772/Iran_To_Produce_Octogen_Explosive_Materials_To_Power_Weapon_Systems#.X6BhDi9h3xt

13 Twitter. Stephen Bryen, 4 August 2020, 1:22 pm. https://twitter.com/stevebryen/status/1290699671174819840

14 Jeff Schogol, "No, That Mushroom Cloud in Beirut Doesn't Indicate a Nuclear Bomb Went Off," *Task & Purpose,* 4 August 2020. https://taskandpurpose.com/analysis/beirut-explosion-nuclear-blast-debunked

weapons and the increasing threat that Iran and Hezbollah pose to Israel, the case for a nuclear explosion in Beirut was not entirely unfounded. What's more, if HMX was indeed present at the warehouse in Beirut, that could point to a new Hezbollah capability. *The Wisconsin Project on Nuclear Arms Control* lists HMX—Octogen—as one of three catalysts needed to detonate the shape charge of a rudimentary "implosion type" nuclear weapon.[15] A low-yield implosion-type nuke might just be the kind of weapon a violent terrorist organization, like Hezbollah, would like to deploy against soft targets in Israel.

We've seen that Israel's enemies underwent a rapid evolution in warfare during the two previous intifadas against Israel and the Israel-Hezbollah War of 2006. After going from merely throwing rocks at IDF troops to full-blown guerilla warfare tactics, all of the way to sustained rocket sieges, Israel's enemies just might be ready for a deadlier form of warfare to employ against their ethnic and religious foes in Israel. The skeptics are probably correct that nukes were not responsible for the Beirut blast—*this time*. Given the intentions of Iran and its proxies, though, it is only a matter of time before that changes.

Think about it: in 2018, Israeli Prime Minister Benjamin Netanyahu revealed to the world that Israeli intelligence had gained access to "half a ton" of Iranian nuclear weapons research materials.[16] In that tranche of documents, Israeli intelligence found numerous references to Iranian research and development of HMX. Writing for the BESA Center in 2019, retired IDF Lieutenant Colonel Dr. Raphael Ofek, a munitions expert, reported:

> Another important facility that was unknown until the Iranian archive
> revelation was Sanjarian, adjacent to Tehran. Initial information on
> the facility which has not yet been verified, was reported in 2009 by

---

15 "Nuclear Weapons Primer," Wisconsin Project on Nuclear Arms Control, Accessed on 2 November 2020. https://www.wisconsinproject.org/nuclear-weapons/

16 YouTube. CBS News, "Netanyahu Claims Proof of Secret Iranian Nuclear Activities," 30 April 2018, 18:06. https://www.youtube.com/watch?v=Bmpgaig54-k&feature=emb_logo

the National Council of Resistance of Iran (NCRI), an opposition organization to the Tehran regime based in Paris. The purpose of the Sanjarian facility was to produce the explosive system that surrounds the uranium core of a nuclear weapon, the function of which is to compress the core through the explosion in order to bring it to super-criticality. This process is called implosion. The explosive system is called MPI (Multi-Point Initiation system) or "Shock Wave Generator." The main explosive in the MPI envelope is Octol, a mixture of HMX and TNT. The channels inside the shell contain special exploding bridgewire (EBW) detonators that are suitable for simultaneous ignition and are ignited only when high voltage is applied.[17]

Don't be fooled. Sometime soon the world may yet wake up to the prospect of a dirty bomb being detonated in one of the West's great cities, either in Israel, Europe, or the United States. Iran is building the capability even now, and its alliance with Hezbollah would allow Iran to move such a weapon surreptitiously to a target city. Let Beirut be a warning of where things are heading in the Middle East in the Iranian/Hezbollah war against Israel. It will get uglier, not prettier, over time.

Former CIA agent and Mideast expert Robert Baer stated that the orange ball of fire, makes it clear that what detonated in Beirut was "a military explosive." Baer also explained that "white powder seen in the videos of the incident before the major blast are likely an indicator that ammonium nitrate was present and burning," but Baer insisted that "[ammonium nitrate was not] responsible for the massive explosion that ensued." More puzzling to Baer and myself, though, was the fact that a "a lot of munitions [were] going off ahead of the larger explosion."[18]

---

17 Lt. Col. (ret) Dr. Raphael Ofek, "What the Smuggled Archive Tells Us About Iran's Nuclear Weapons Project," The Begin-Sadat Center for Strategic Studies, 22 July 2019. https://besacenter.org/perspectives-papers/smuggled-iran-nuclear-archive/

18 Tara John, Melissa Mecaya, Mike Hayes, et al., "Beirut Explosion Rocks Lebanon's Capital City," CNN, 5 August 2020. https://edition.cnn.com/middleeast/live-news/lebanon-beirut-explosion-live-updates-dle-intl/h_0f646d1827f2f246b9c48701b5c8eac5?fbclid=IwAR2VyQVipSk_jsZwxJguZaTASML5KXcGIA4AL4jugiB-IWXY4r2aVepSkeo

The Beirut blast in August 2020 was not a single explosion. It was actually six tiny explosions followed on by one large explosion, and the main explosion did the most damage and garnered media attention. According to Israel Defense, a private defense contracting firm with close ties to Israel's military and intelligence establishment, "such a sequence could be consistent with 'weapons systems that are activated in a chain,' and which might have been stored in the port and set off accidentally or deliberately."

Another Israeli munition expert, Boaz Hayoun, asserted that "the Beirut incident involved underground explosions. The 43-metre (140-foot) deep crater at the port could not have been left by the explosion of the amount of ammonium nitrate reported by Lebanese authorities." Hayoun told Reuters that, "[The crater] would have been shallower, maximum 25 or 30 metres."[19]

We know that Hezbollah has utilized extensive tunnels both to transfer their fighters covertly from one location to the next as well as to store weapons in its irregular warfare against Israel. Oddly enough, following the devastating explosion in Beirut, both *Sky News* of Britain and the Russian state-owned *Sputnik News* reported the existence of subterranean tunnels. As with every aspect of this story, the corrupt Lebanese government issued stringent denials.[20] Yet, more shockingly, *Sky News* actually aired live footage of the suspected tunnels![21]

Given that a hard news network like *Sky News* took the provocative step of airing such footage, it will be hard for detractors to argue that this is merely "fake news." If military grade explosives such as HMX

---

19 Dan Williams, "Seismic Data Suggests String of Blasts Preceded Beirut Explosion: Israeli Analyst," Reuters, 13 August 2020. https://www.reuters.com/article/us-lebanon-security-blast-seismology/seismic-data-suggests-string-of-blasts-preceded-beirut-explosion-israeli-analyst-idUSKCN2591S2

20 Seth J. Frantzman, "Were Suspicious Tunnels Near Beirut Port Discovered After the Blast?" *The Jerusalem Post*, 11 August 2020. https://www.jpost.com/middle-east/were-suspicious-tunnels-discovered-near-beirut-port-after-explosion-638131

21 "Underground Shelters Found at Beirut Port Spark Hopes of Unlikely Survivor Stories," NBC, 7 August 2020. https://news.yahoo.com/underground-shelters-found-beirut-port-162926443.html

were indeed buried in the secret Hezbollah weapons caches that Boaz Hayoun thinks were present at the explosion site, it would explain why the crater from the blast was so much deeper than it should have been.

This brings us back to HMX. After all, HMX is used not only as a catalyst in an implosion-type nuclear weapon but also as a solid rocket propellant. I've shown you how Iran has committed itself to expanding its HMX production capabilities as far back as 2016. Given that HMX burns a reddish-orange hue, as the stark images from the Beirut blast showed, and that ammonium nitrate *is* a precursor element in the creation of HMX, it is quite possible that what detonated in Beirut was some kind of a production or storage facility for HMX. The HMX in question could have eventually been used as a solid rocket propellant in Hezbollah's vast and growing missile arsenal, which would have ultimately threatened Israel in a future war.

Perhaps it was not HMX but, as Stephen Bryen mused on Twitter, the orange, brown, and gray plume of the explosion in Beirut may have come from inhibited red-fuming nitric acid (IRFNA), a propellant for Scud missiles. Meanwhile, the BESA Center's Mordecai Kedar said, "What probably happened on August 4 was an explosion of volatile material and flammable materials that were incorrectly stored by Hezbollah for at least a day in a metal, non-air conditioned warehouse."[22] So whether or not it was HMX or IRFNA—"volatile material," as Mordecai Kedar so eloquently put it—that caused the massive explosion in Beirut, the possibility exists that Hezbollah was either building or storing components needed for their long-range missiles, which indicates a significant escalation on their part against Israel and its allies, including the United States.

More to the point, a June 2020 report by The Washington Institute for Near East Policy assessed that, through what the Iranians refer to

---

22 Seth J. Frantzman, "Beirut Explosion Wrapped in Conspiracies, Fueling Online Sleuths," *The Jerusalem Post,* 11 August 2020. https://www.jpost.com/middle-east/beirut-explosion-wrapped-in-conspiracies-fuelling-online-sleuths-638125

as the "Precision Project," Iran has enhanced the accuracy and range of Hezbollah's missiles—and continues doing so to this day. The Iranian Precision Project with Hezbollah has led to the construction of several missile production facilities throughout Lebanon and Syria. According to The Washington Institute for Near East Policy report, Iran directed Hezbollah to build many of the missile production facilities in crowded Lebanon to deter Israel from striking those missile plants out of fear of collateral damage to the Lebanese civilians nearby.[23]

On June 27, 2020, Paul Iddon wrote an article in *Forbes* that made the case that Israeli leaders will have to "contend with increasingly lethal Hezbollah missiles" when another conflict erupts between Hezbollah and Israel. Iddon further assessed that "the Lebanese Hezbollah militia has amassed an enormous arsenal of surface-to-surface missiles and rockets. With Iran's help [through the Precision Project], the group is continually improving the accuracy and range of this arsenal so it can threaten Israel in any future war."[24]

The precision-guided missiles would give Hezbollah the capability to target critical Israeli civilian infrastructure and bring the civilian life of Israel to a halt. That, in turn, would ratchet up fear among the population, create political instability, harm Israel's otherwise strong economy, and likely push Israel back, changing the power dynamic in the conflict between Israel, Hezbollah, and Iran. It would also be a natural evolution on the part of Hezbollah from their limited missile attacks in the 2006 war with Israel and would allow Hezbollah to visit total warfare upon its enemies in Israel.

---

23 Katherine Bauer, Hanin Ghaddar, and Assaf Orion, "Iran's Precision Missile Project Moves to Lebanon," The Washington Institute for Near East Policy, December 2018. https://www.washingtoninstitute.org/policy-analysis/view/irans-precision-missile-project-moves-to-lebanon

24 Paul Iddon, "In a Third Lebanon War, Israel Will Have to Contend with Increasingly Lethal Hezbollah Missiles," *Forbes*, 27 June 2020. https://www.forbes.com/sites/pauliddon/2020/06/27/in-a-third-lebanon-war-israel-will-have-to-contend-with-increasingly-lethal-hezbollah-missiles/?sh=705682a84b5e

Hezbollah's missile development program, thanks to Iranian technical assistance, has seen extraordinary changes in its distribution of missile production. Rather than maintaining their stockpiles in an easily identified and destroyed central location, Hezbollah has spread its capabilities across Syria and Lebanon. If one production facility is destroyed, many more will continue on. Therefore, Hezbollah's precision-guided missile threat to Israel had redundant capabilities that would allow Hezbollah to strike back against Israel even if the Israelis did destroy some of the missile production facilities. In all, Iddon concluded that "in the event of another Lebanon war, neutralizing Hezbollah's rocket capabilities could become the most significant challenge faced by the Israeli military in over a generation."[25]

It is likely that the Beirut explosion was the result of weapons-grade explosives, either HMX or some other chemical related to Hezbollah's expansive precision-guided missile program being present. The question of what triggered the blast is another matter entirely. The conventional wisdom, if you don't buy the Lebanese government's explanation, involves incompetent terrorists improperly storing highly dangerous explosives.

Another variation of this tale has Hezbollah operatives prepositioning detonators inside explosives. These then produced a series of accidental detonations that precipitated the larger explosion in the warehouse. Danilo Coppe, an Italian explosives expert, doesn't believe the official narrative. As Coppe told the media shortly after the Beirut blast, "it seems like an explosion of an armament house."[26]

A lesser-known theory says someone detonated the storehouse purposely. This belief was generated by President Trump himself when, upon first hearing of the Beirut explosion, he stated in a press

---

25 Iddon, "Third Lebanon War."

26 Francesco Giambertone, "Beirut, l'esperto di esplosivi: «La nuvola arancione e gli scoppi: ecco perché credo ci fossero anche armi», *Corriere Della Sera,* 5 August 2020. https://www.corriere.it/esteri/20_agosto_05/beirut-esperto-esplosivi-la-nuvola-arancione-scoppi-ecco-perche-credo-ci-fossero-anche-armi-6da4a01e-d71b-11ea-93a6-dcb5dd8eef08.shtml

conference that "it looks like a terrible attack." Trump's comments were made a mere six hours after the explosion occurred. Per the *Asia Times,* "the bombshell assessment came against the backdrop of a spate of confrontations between Israel and Hezbollah, and a string of fires and explosions at sensitive military sites in Iran, sending Trump's cabinet and the concerned parties into damage control mode."

The Trump administration went into "damage control mode" because, if true, "the alternative … would be the logical attribution to Israel, forcing Hezbollah into an equivalent response, which would trigger a war of catastrophic proportions." According to a source close to Hezbollah, "if it was an Israeli attack, then this will not be revealed because it implicates both sides in a war they don't want."[27]

Yet it should be noted that Hezbollah most definitely *does* want a conflict—though at a time and place of *its* choosing. The Israeli "gray zone" operations, along with those of the Americans (such as the assassination of Qassem Soleimani) and the continued pressure that Saudi Arabia is subjecting the Iranians to in places like Yemen and elsewhere, has forced Iran to reassess its plans and change its preferred timetables. All of that, however, could change now that the domestic political leadership in the United States has changed. It may also change if the domestic leadership in Israel changes.[28]

In the summer of 2021, Israel's leadership *did* change. However, the removal of long-time hawkish Prime Minister Benjamin Netanyahu did not lead to the rise of a more pacifist government in Israel. On the contrary, the new prime minister, a younger man named Naftali Bennett, was to the right of Netanyahu. Still, Bennett ousted Netanyahu by aligning his tiny ultra-nationalist right-wing Yamina Party with more

---

27 Alison Tahmizian Meuse, "Trump May Be Right about Beirut 'Attack,'" *Asia Times,* 8 August 2020. https://asiatimes.com/2020/08/trump-may-be-right-about-beirut-attack/

28 Shira Rubin, "Israel's Netanyahu Walks Out of His Own Corruption Trial," *Washington Post,* 8 February 2021. https://www.washingtonpost.com/world/middle_east/netanyahu-corruption-israel-trial/2021/02/08/108453dc-69ee-11eb-a66e-e27046e9e898_story.html

THE BEIRUT BLAST: BUNGLED OR BRILLIANT MOVE?

moderate and left-leaning parties. Some have speculated that Bennett's coalition partners will be instrumental in restraining his more militant impulses on the matter of Iran and the controversial Israeli settlements. A year after Bennett took over as prime minister of Israel, he was ousted and replaced by his government's centrist foreign minister, Yair Lipid, who immediately called for the normalization of ties between Israel, Saudi Arabia, and the rest of the Sunni Arab world.[29]

On November 7, 2020, the Democratic Party's presidential nominee, former Vice-President Joseph R. Biden, was declared to be the winner of the US presidential election, making him the 46th President of the United States.[30] The Biden campaign immediately announced the president-elect's intention to renew the Obama administration's much-criticized nuclear arms agreement with the Islamic Republic of Iran.[31] Biden's team also indicated that it wanted to distance itself from the Trump administration's major Middle East initiative, the Abraham Accords, which was designed to unite Israel and Saudi Arabia in an anti-Iran alliance.[32]

The Biden administration's moves would inevitably produce a fundamental reorientation of US foreign policy in the Middle East; they would undoubtedly weaken the anti-Iran alliance that the Trump administration built and strengthen the Iranian push to redraw the

---

29 Joseph Krauss, "Explainer: Who is Naftali Bennett, Israel's New Leader?" AP News, 14 June 2021. https://apnews.com/article/naftali-bennett-israel-middle-east-religion-technology-20678c93611da0fe e71fbccac80759d5

30 "Joe Biden Elected 46th President of the United States," *Tampa Bay Times*, 7 November 2020. https://www.tampabay.com/news/florida-politics/elections/2020/11/07/joe-biden-elected-46th-president-of-the-united-states-ap-says/

31 "Biden Will Seek to Re-Enter Iran Nuclear Deal within Months, Former Aide Says," *The Times of Israel*, 8 November 2020. https://www.timesofisrael.com/biden-will-seek-to-reenter-iran-nuclear-deal-within-months-aide-says/

32 Prof. Abraham Ben-Zvi, "Biden's Conduct Endangers the Abraham Accords," *Israel Hayom*, 7 February 2021. https://www.israelhayom.com/opinions/bidens-conduct-endangers-the-abraham-accords/

geopolitical map of the region in their favor.[33] In fact, this move would likely precipitate a war between Israel, Hezbollah, and Iran rather than deter one.[34] Since the US presidential election in 2020, the Iranians have proven themselves to be steadfastly committed to their destructive course against Israel, the Sunni Arabs, and the United States.

It must be noted, though, that US intelligence does not believe that Israeli actions caused the Beirut explosion in August 2020. What's more, Trump's comments about the Beirut blast may have been nothing more than a Trumpism. After all, America's 45th president was notorious for his off-the-cuff style of speaking. It very well could have been that he did not actually mean an attack had occurred; he may have just been vamping. For their part, the Israelis explicitly deny any involvement whatsoever.[35] What's more, the Lebanese maintain that it was a terrible accident. Regardless of what actually happened, political stability in the Middle East is clearly collapsing. And the next few years could prove decisive in determining how the region's political situation changes and whether such changes would help or harm American interests there.

Although neither Iran nor Hezbollah want a war now, they are preparing the battlefield for the inevitable campaign. And this conflict will be, at least for Israel, its most serious struggle since the Yom Kippur War in 1973. Hezbollah, Hamas, Fatah, and Iran—these groups are aligning. They may not share identical political objectives, and they may dislike

---

33 Brandon J. Weichert, "Joe Biden's 'Values-Based' Foreign Policy is a Loser," *The Washington Times*, 5 November 2020. https://www.washingtontimes.com/news/2020/nov/5/joe-bidens-values-based-foreign-policy-is-a-loser/?fbclid=IwAR0-zL4UXrEyU2jiyDGVpN1K3y2NXonJuJ5O0ah7cctodlIgva MUIAVKOFE

34 Lahav Harkov, "Israeli Minister Warns of War If Biden Returns to Iran Deal," *The Jerusalem Post*, 5 November 2020. https://www.jpost.com/us-elections/israeli-minister-warns-of-war-if-biden-returns-to-iran-deal-648097?fbclid=IwAR1Ho7lbjhCdsU3Ssjbrgtn8ocw1o4VwkOsxWOh3eTVV4rPAsdLK Kbg2aeg

35 "U.S. Officials Rebut Claim by Trump That Deadly Beirut Explosion Resulted from a 'Terrible Attack,'" *Market Watch*, 5 August 2020. https://www.marketwatch.com/story/us-officials-refute-trump-claim-that-beirut-deadly-explosion-resulted-from-a-terrible-attack-2020-08-05

each other at a religious level, but clearly all these groups are coalescing to defeat their common foes. Those foes, as they have repeated publicly over the decades, are the Israelis and then the Americans.

Was a nuke the cause of the Beirut blast? Was it rocket fuel? Was it an accident? This particular whodunit in the Mideast will never get old because the answers are unlikely to ever be found. Several sources, on condition of anonymity, have expressed the belief that the Beirut blast was the result of "sabotage" rather than incompetence. However, none would dare venture to predict who caused it. If the Beirut blast was part of the ongoing shadow war between the West and Iran, then readers should ask themselves, *"Cui bono?"* ("Who benefits?"). Israel is the obvious answer. But Israel isn't the only state that would benefit from a reduction in Hezbollah's capabilities. So, too, would Israel's allies in the Sunni Arab world (again, notably Saudi Arabia) and the United States.

Yet for political reasons, few in official positions are willing to speak about this possibility, even more than a year after the event. Still, such questions about the Beirut blast should be entertained if only for the fact that I believe we are reaching a period when the shadow war will explode into total war. When that happens, such a war might precipitate a global conflict just as a regional war in the Balkans rapidly transformed into the devastating First World War.

We are unlikely to ever get a definitive official answer from anyone involved in the incident. While it is interesting to speculate, readers should realize that, whatever its cause, the Beirut blast was a serious wake-up call for Western policymakers. It is a cautionary tale for Western leaders to stand ready and not to abandon their campaign of "maximum pressure" on Iran and its proxies, regardless of whether a Democrat or Republican sits in the Oval Office. Should the maximum pressure campaign be reduced, as President Biden appears to be doing, the ramifications will be the loss of a regional order that is friendly to the United States.

Consider this: Nasrallah warned Israel in 2016 that Hezbollah's missiles were capable of hitting an ammonia storage facility in Haifa, a major Israeli port, which would create the same blast effect as a small nuclear weapon—almost identical to the blast created by whatever happened in Beirut in August of 2020. Hezbollah appears to be targeting strategic ports that house explosive chemicals; these products, when detonated under the right conditions by Hezbollah's Iranian-built long-range precision-guided missiles, could yield the same impact as other, more predictable and direct terrorist attacks do. Keeping attribution murky would benefit Hezbollah and its allies, as they would inevitably have more maneuvering room to keep their Israeli and American foes off balance—allowing Hezbollah to press its attacks more directly against Israel.

Assassinations, nukes, terrorism, shadow wars, religious and ethnic blood feuds that go back centuries—all with the United States stuck in the middle—define the Middle East today. This is not the plot of the next David Baldacci novel, nor is this the position that America should desire for itself. This is a sad reality that the United States faces in the Middle East today. Since the rise of the Islamist regime of Iran in 1979, Washington has bungled every major policy in the Middle East. Today, the world stands at a precipice of nuclear war because decades of bad American decisions have empowered Islamists and weakened American allies, such as Israel and the Sunni Arab states. Now is not the time for the Biden administration to be making nice with Iran.

It is the time for the Americans to restore the integrity and strength of its long-time allies in the Sunni Arab states and Israel. A senior Saudi official described Iran as a "paper tiger with steel claws." Those steel claws are its unconventional military forces that have spread far beyond its borders since the destruction of Saddam Hussein's regime in neighboring Iraq; these steel claws have slashed hard and wide across the arc of the Shiite population centers that dot areas outside of Iranian territory. They have proven to be a conduit for Iranian power; a place from which to reach out and strike hard against Iran's enemies in the Sunni Arab world, Israel, and against the Americans in the region. Putting Iran back into its box is the surest way to restore a modicum of peace to the region *without* compromising American interests.

5

ELEVEN DAYS IN MAY

IN MAY 2021, the jockeying between Iran, its proxies, and the West caused an unexpected eruption of renewed hostilities between Hamas, Palestinian Islamic Jihad based in Syria, and Israel. After the Israeli Supreme Court ruled that a group of Palestinian families could be evicted from contested territory that Jewish settlers wanted to move to, the Palestinian Territories erupted in mass protests.

Using this incident as an excuse to demonstrate its resolute support of the Palestinian cause and to catch the Israelis by surprise, Hamas launched a brutal rocket attack upon the unsuspecting Israelis. The conflict between Israel and Hamas lasted just eleven days. But in that time great damage was done, many lives were lost on both sides, and the geopolitical situation in the region was altered—and not necessarily for the better.

Hamas's al-Qassam Brigade, the terrorist organization's armed faction, as well as the Palestinian Islamic Jihad, launched a total of 4,300 rockets in the short conflict. Most estimates place Hamas's total rocket arsenal at 14,000. According to Sebastien Roblin of *Forbes,* "Hamas maintained barrages of 300 to 450 rockets daily despite the IDF's counter-bombardment—50% to 100% higher than the volume of fire in the preceding 2014 war." More disconcerting was the fact that, according to Roblin's excellent reporting, "nearly twice as many rockets were lobbed at more distant cities like Tel Aviv and Jerusalem (roughly one out of six), implying Hamas increased the proportion of long-range rockets."[1]

In fact, Hamas did enhance the size and range of its missiles. And Iran can be given most of the credit for this highly unsettling development. From the very founding of Hamas, Iran has provided training and support for the Sunni Palestinian terror group, whose early charter explained that its goal was to fight and defeat the "warmongering Jews." One estimate indicated that Iranian financial support for Hamas was around $50 million annually from 1992, the year that Iranian-backed Hezbollah taught Hamas's fighters how to create and use suicide bombs against civilian targets, until a brief breakdown in relations between Iran and Hamas occurred in 2011. That cooling of relations between Hamas and Iran occurred during the Syrian Civil War (when Hamas then supported the Sunni Islamists fighting against Syria's dictator, Bashar al-Assad, who was supported by Iran).

Despite the cooling of relations between the two sides, Hamas continued to enhance the capabilities it had received over the decades from Iran. As early as 2014, relations between the two began to increase, and by 2017, both Hamas and Iran were giddily embracing each

---

1 Sebastien Roblin, "How Hamas' Arsenal Shaped the Gaza War of May 2021," *Forbes,* 25 May 2021. https://www.forbes.com/sites/sebastienroblin/2021/05/25/how-hamass-arsenal-shaped-the-gaza-war-of-may-2021/?sh=453c92c479df

ELEVEN DAYS IN MAY

other as comrades in terror. According to a 2014 report by an Iranian Revolutionary Guards Corps (IRGC) commander, Ahmed Hosseini, scores of Hamas operatives had not only been "armed and trained" by Hezbollah, but many eventually came to Iran! In fact, IRGC General Hassan Tehrani Moghaddam, the now-deceased father of Iran's missile program, "armed and guided" Hamas trainees who came to Iran.[2]

Iran taught Hamas engineers how to create an indigenous rocket production capability using everyday household items. This came in handy by the 2010s, as Israel imposed a now fourteen-year blockade on Hamas-controlled Gaza. Before the blockade, however, in the aftermath of the 2008 Gaza conflict, Israeli intelligence discovered multiple Iranian-made weapons in the hands of its Hamas enemies. Just four years later, in 2012, Hamas surprised the Israelis again when the terrorist organization began launching Iranian-style long-range Fajr-5 missiles at Tel Aviv and Jerusalem.

After Israel's blockade of Gaza was imposed, Iran worked assiduously to use its growing influence in the Greater Middle East to create reliable smuggling routes between itself and Hamas-controlled Gaza. Iran did everything from hiring Bedouins in the Egyptian-controlled Sinai Peninsula to paying the thuggish regime of Omar el-Bashir, ruler of Sudan, to facilitate the movement of Iranian arms and military equipment into the Gaza Strip. Analysts have rightly noted that there has been a parallel development between the Iranian-controlled Lebanese Shiite terrorist group, Hezbollah, and the Sunni terrorist organization of Hamas. That's because Iran is now coordinating its larger strategy for breaking Israel with these two bloodthirsty terror groups. Thus, we see an increase in the Iranian-built long-range precision missiles that both Hezbollah and Hamas are building and deploying against an increasingly besieged Israel.

Don't take my word for it. In January 2021, Amir Ali Hajizadeh, the IRGC aerospace commander, boasted to the press that "all the missiles

---

2 Ido Levy, "How Iran Fuels Hamas Terrorism," The Washington Institute for Near East Policy, 1 June 2021. https://www.washingtoninstitute.org/policy-analysis/how-iran-fuels-hamas-terrorism

you might see in Gaza and Lebanon were created with Iran's support."
Further, Western intelligence services came to the sobering conclusion
that Iran was facilitating the illicit transfer of its weapons through Libya,
with the possible assistance of Turkey, a NATO member, and Qatar,
the Sunni Arab rival of Saudi Arabia.

And it isn't only long-range precision missiles that Hamas is
receiving from Iran. It is also acquiring a long-range drone capability. In
a later chapter, I will detail the extent of Iran's drone threat. Just to give
you a preview of the increasing danger that Iranian drone capabilities
pose to the region, during the eleven-day Gaza conflict between Israel
and Hamas in 2021, Hamas deployed up to six *Shahab*-type drones,
which are modeled on Iran's *Adabil* drone, to conduct kamikaze-style
attacks on Israeli targets.

Meanwhile, to show how much sway Iran holds over the various anti-
Israeli terrorist factions in the region, a multiplicity of actors either voiced
or actively engaged in support of Hamas in the May 2021 conflict. The
leader of the Iraqi-based Shiite militia, Kataeb Hezbollah (whose leader
was also targeted in the Trump administration's successful drone strike
on IRGC General Qassem Soleimani in 2020), claimed that many of his
fighters joined the fight in Gaza alongside Hamas. The villainous black-
robed leader of Hezbollah, Hassan Nasrallah, gushed that Hamas's actions
in May 2021 against Israel represented a "historic step in the conflict with
the enemy." The IRGC said, "The *Intifada* has gone from using stones
to powerful, precise missiles … and in the future Zionists [Israelis] can
expect to endure deadly blows from within the occupied territories."[3]

All of this came just four months shy of the one-year anniversary
of the Beirut blast, which everyone—except the multitude of explosives experts I cited in the previous chapter as well as former President
Trump—insist was totally an accident. I think that the IRGC leadership

3 "Iran Leader Urges Muslim States to Back Palestinians Militarily, Financially," Reuters, 21 May
2021. https://www.reuters.com/world/middle-east/iran-hails-palestinian-victory-warns-deadly-blows-
against-israel-2021-05-21/

betrayed their real intent with the effusive praise they heaped upon Hamas for its actions against Israel in May 2021. Iran has been providing a far closer degree of coordination and support, going back decades, for Hamas and Hezbollah than most Western analysts care to admit. The Iranian military has overseen the evolution of the capabilities that both Hezbollah and Hamas now possess.

Who can say that whatever exploded in Beirut was not meant to be Iran's coup de grace against Israel? What if whatever detonated in Beirut was meant to be unleashed upon Israel by Hezbollah? And what if the Iranians manage to eventually accomplish whatever they may have been trying to accomplish with whatever exploded in Beirut in 2020?

Israel heralded their Iron Dome missile defense system as having deflected most of Hamas's rockets. This great technology has saved countless innocent Israeli lives. Yet Israel's enemies Hezbollah and Hamas, thanks to Iran, are already adapting to the new defenses that Israel has created recently to counter the missile threat these terror organizations pose. Despite the success of Iron Dome, sadly, some Hamas rockets got through. What's more, if Israeli intelligence estimates are correct, then about 8,000 rockets remain under the control of Hamas— and given Hamas's indigenous rocket production capabilities, it will likely replenish the 4,500 rockets used in the eleven-day war with Israel.

Hezbollah's missile stockpile is larger and far more diffuse than that of Hamas. Iran is coordinating its strategy of multiple attacks on Israel perfectly. Whatever blow Iran took from the Beirut blast, its proxies in Hamas kept the pressure on Israel from Gaza; Hamas's rocket fusillade over eleven days in May was not a minor outburst. Hamas wasn't lashing out or simply defending itself from whatever type of aggression its leadership accused Israel of. Instead, the Hamas conflict in May 2021 was merely a proof of concept. It was an example of how Iran and its asymmetrical forces spread throughout the region can punch their Israeli, Sunni Arab, and American foes.

Given the kind of assistance and advances Iran's military has provided both Hamas and, to a much larger extent, Hezbollah, it is only a matter of time before Iran breaks through Israel's mighty defenses and accomplishes its goal of eradicating the Jewish democracy in the heart of the Middle East. This would be not only a human tragedy but a geopolitical disaster for the United States, which has spent decades and billions of dollars supporting Israel. Plus, should Iran manage to weaken Israel or remove it entirely from the region, American power projection will be stunted—and Iran's will be greatly enhanced (and also the power projection of their Chinese and Russian allies).

At such a precarious time for Israel and, by extension, the United States, one would think that Washington would be moving closer to its regional allies, like Israel and the Sunni Arab states. Unfortunately, the Biden administration appears uninterested in doing this. Instead, as you'll read in later chapters, Mr. Biden and his policy advisers are intent on downgrading the traditional American alliances with both Israel and the Sunni Arab states and empowering the Russian and Chinese-backed Islamic Republic of Iran.

The eleven-day fight in May 2021 between Israel and Iran-backed Hamas was the start of a much longer, more dangerous movement against Israel and its allies. Far from being cowed by the outward appearance of technologically superior Western forces, Iran is devising extremely innovative ways to overcome the technological advantages of the West, and to force the outcome that Tehran desires: regional hegemony. With Biden in office, Iran just might get what it wants.

6

IRAN'S LATIN AMERICAN

EXCURSION—WITH MISSILES!

JUST WHEN WASHINGTON THOUGHT it could rest easy when it came to Iran, June 2021 proved to be a very dangerous time in the Middle East for the newly installed Biden administration. Not only was Iran pressing hard against the Saudis, the Israelis, and the Americans in Iraq, but two Iranian Navy warships entered the Atlantic Ocean and headed toward Latin America. The destination for the Iranian ships was likely Venezuela.[1] To make matters more frightening, Western intelligence

---

1 Isabel Debre and Jon Gambrell, "Iran Sends Warships to Atlantic amid Venezuela Concerns," AP News, 10 June 2021. https://apnews.com/article/middle-east-iran-10b8da94fa9040ec6348a7b7006d 879b

services suspected that the Iranian ships carried long-range precision-guided missiles of the sort that now plague both Saudi Arabia and Israel.[2]

Most media sources downplayed the actual threat of the arms deal. They focused on the danger of allowing Iran's regional navy to complete the journey because that would give the Iranians critical experience in longer-range naval operations. The Biden administration warned both Venezuela and Cuba not to allow for the Iranian ships to dock.

To deflect any political pressure from the press, the Biden team also stressed that the arms deal between Iran and Venezuela was completed in the Trump administration's final year. Of course, what the Biden people never acknowledged was that former President Trump explicitly threatened Venezuela's leader, the socialist Nicolas Maduro, with severe ramifications if he allowed Iranian weapons to flow into Venezuela.

What most media sources missed was the severe danger the weapons themselves posed to the United States. If the Western intelligence community's suspicions were correct about the weapons the Iranians were ferrying over to Maduro, then Tehran was engaged in a serious escalation. The Islamic Republic is now taking their model of decentralized regional resistance to the West and expanding it beyond the Greater Middle East into Latin America. Iran has given Hezbollah and Hamas the capability to threaten Israel with increasingly precise long-range missiles and Iran has supported the Houthi Rebels in Yemen who are today threatening Saudi Arabia. In much the same way, Iran is using an ally to directly threaten their great enemy, in this case the United States.

In October of 1962, the world was brought to the brink of nuclear war when the United States discovered that the Soviet Union had placed intermediate range ballistic (IRBM) missiles in Cuba. With these systems in Cuba, the USSR could threaten the mainland United States with direct nuclear attack in much the same way Soviets believed the

---

2 Lara Seligman, Andrew Desiderio, Betsy Woodruff Swan, and Nahal Toosi, "U.S. Warns Venezuela, Cuba to Turn Away Iranian Ships Believed to be Carrying Arms," Politico, 9 June 2021. https://www.politico.com/news/2021/06/09/venezuela-cuba-iran-ships-492602

Western alliance threatened them with nuclear weapons in places close to the Soviet Union like Turkey. After nearly two weeks of intense diplomacy and a war of words between Moscow and Washington, nuclear war was *barely* averted. Nuclear conflict was averted as much despite those running the two governments as it was because of their actions.

When the Cuban Missile Crisis occurred in 1962, there existed an international balance of power between the Soviet Union and the United States. The two superpowers were basically equals on the world stage, and they formed the two poles around which many of the world's nations orbited. So long as balance was maintained, war could likely be averted. Today, no such balance exists between the United States and the Islamic Republic of Iran.

While that imbalance appears to favor the Americans, appearances are often deceiving. Therefore, the Iranians have pioneered the development of asymmetrical, or unconventional, warfare as a method of overcoming America's overwhelming conventional military superiority. Judging from Iran's increasingly hostile stance toward the West, American military power does not appear to be having the deterrent effect that it had previously. Iran is expanding its presence and capabilities far beyond its own borders. With its steel claws, as the Saudis have described these unconventional Iranian capabilities, Tehran can reach out and threaten Saudi Arabia, Israel, and now the United States.

It is naïve to think that Iran will be deterred by American threats against their activities in Latin America. There have been few restraints on Iran's nefarious doings in Latin America. Going back to the 1990s, when Hezbollah blew up a Jewish cultural center in Buenos Aires, Iran has always had an active hand in Latin America.[3] And their presence and capabilities in the region have expanded since that time. Thanks initially to their relationship with Cuba, by 2002 Iran had become a key partner for the socialist dictatorship of Hugo Chavez in Venezuela. This

---

3 "Argentina Designates Hezbollah as Terrorist Organisation," BBC, 18 July 2019. https://www.bbc.com/news/world-latin-america-49030561

relationship continues today under Chavez's successor, Nicolas Maduro.

So the Western media missed the lede in the Iranian journey to Venezuela in June 2021. It wasn't just about enhancing Iran's long-range maritime capabilities. It was about moving long-range missiles and other weapons into Latin America to threaten the United States more directly. One thing that most Western sources did note was that the Iranian ships were carrying a shipment of smaller fast-attack boats. Iranian forces regularly use such boats to harass US Navy and Coast Guard warships patrolling the narrow Strait of Hormuz near Iran's shores. The fast-attack boats utilize swarming tactics in order to overwhelm larger ships and to disrupt shipping in the key waterway of the Strait of Hormuz.

Farzin Nadimi of the Washington Institute for Near East Policy is worried that Iran could be sending the fast-attack boats to Venezuela to disrupt critical shipping transiting through the Panama Canal. He also cautions readers, "If Iran decides to expand its kinetic footprint in the Caribbean, it could proliferate even longer-range missiles." Again, think about the evolution of the missile capabilities of both Hezbollah and Hamas thanks to Iran's copious support over the decades. Now imagine Iran moving those same capabilities to Venezuela and other Latin American nations who share Iran's antipathy for the United States.

Nadimi also warns that, even if a long-range missile capable of hitting the Panama Canal or threatening the United States directly were not onboard the Iranian warship, Iran's military might be offloading "smart sea mines, waterborne improvised explosive devices (suicide boats), or high-performance armed and reconnaissance drones." Nadimi correctly worries that introducing these Iranian military systems into Latin America would "alter the balance of power in the Caribbean and cause significant challenges for SOUTHCOM on par with those already posed against CENTCOM."[4]

---

4 Farzin Nadimi, "Iran's Atlantic Voyage: Implications of Naval Deployments to Venezuela or Syria," The Washington Institute for Near East Policy, 15 June 2021. https://www.washingtoninstitute.org/policy-analysis/irans-atlantic-voyage-implications-naval-deployments-venezuela-or-syria

Unlike CENTCOM or USINDOPACCOM, the military command charged with managing the US military's activities in the Pacific, SOUTHCOM, is poorly resourced.[5] American policymakers have long assumed that Latin America poses no significant threats (aside from narco-terrorism and rogue states like Venezuela or Cuba). Yet, a sudden surge of Iranian military capabilities to Venezuela or Cuba would fundamentally undermine the regional dominance in Latin America that Washington clearly takes for granted. It would leave the United States vulnerable in its hemisphere in ways not experienced in decades—and it would force Washington to divert critical, limited resources to USSOUTHCOM to deter the newfound Iranian-provided capabilities to Venezuela or Cuba at an inopportune time.

Iran's relationship with Venezuela is not merely recent and superficial. As noted above, Tehran and Caracas have cooperated for decades. Hezbollah and the IRGC have operated from Venezuela for years. They've trained alongside the Venezuelan military too. Iran is interested in Latin America not just to expand its military footprint outside the Middle East (though that's a key component of it). As with so much of what Iran does, Iran desires access to South America's scientific community and uranium deposits to use in the construction of its indigenous nuclear weapons program.

As Argentine prosecutor, Alberto Nisman, was close to releasing the conclusions of an exhaustive investigation into the 1994 Buenos Aires bombing, he died under mysterious circumstances. A spate of exposes in the Brazilian newspaper *Veja,* in 2012–13, proved that Hezbollah has been operating in the tri-border area (the place where the borders of Argentina, Brazil, and Paraguay meet). Hezbollah routinely engages in criminal activities in the tri-border area (TBA) to fund their operations throughout Latin America and beyond.

---

5 Corey Dickstein, "Four-Stars Tell Senators More Resources Are Needed to Compete with China, Russia, in Latin America, Arctic," *Stars and Stripes,* 17 March 2021. https://www.stripes.com/theaters/us/four-stars-tell-senators-more-resources-are-needed-to-compete-with-china-russia-in-latin-america-arctic-1.666025

Part of the investigation into Hezbollah operations in South America revealed that in 2007 Mahmoud Ahmadinejad, Iran's president at the time, had formulated a special diplomatic airline that traveled between Caracas and Tehran, with one stop in Damascus, Syria. Ahmadinejad and Hugo Chavez nicknamed the biweekly diplomatic flights, which ran from 2007 to 2010, "Aeroterror." The report revealed that few Venezuelan or Iranian diplomats flew on the plane, which operated under the guise of a diplomatic flight. Instead, the plane was used to transport illicit weapons and narcotics—as well as military personnel—between Iran and Venezuela. Because of Hezbollah's nefarious activities throughout South America over the course of decades, Brazil, Argentina, and other Latin American countries labeled Hezbollah a "terrorist organization."[6]

Speaking of Argentina, Iran has been courting Argentina for nuclear knowhow for years. Argentina has many technical capabilities that could assist Iran's nuclear weapons program.[7] The US sanctions imposed upon Iran have been onerous enough to slow down Iran's progress toward a reliable indigenous nuclear weapons capacity. Yet Iran is always searching for a way to overcome those sanctions. Tehran's rulers have looked to South America as way for circumventing those sanctions on their nuclear weapons program, whether it be Argentina, Bolivia, or Venezuela. Inevitably, Iran will find what it's looking for.

Meanwhile, Hezbollah in Latin America is not just a potential threat. It's very real. In 2019, the Trump administration shifted US policy in Venezuela from "incrementalism" to "maximum pressure" (which mirrored President Trump's moves against Iran as well).

In May 2020, the Department of Justice issued high-level indictments of senior Venezuelan leaders, including the president, Nicolas

---

6 Linette Lopez, "AEROTERROR: A Regular Flight from Caracas to Tehran Carried More Drugs and Money Than People," *Business Insider,* 25 March 2015. https://www.businessinsider.com/aeroterror-venezuela-iran-and-latin-america-2015-3

7 Jonathan Tirone, "Iran Offered Nuclear Lessons by Argentina," *Al Jazeera,* 9 August 2019. https://www.aljazeera.com/economy/2019/8/9/iran-offered-nuclear-lessons-by-argentina

Maduro, for international narcotics violations. Two months later, the DOJ indicted Adel El Zebayar, a person with dual Syrian-Venezuelan citizenship and a former member of Venezuela's National Assembly, for "allegedly working with Maduro … on a narcoterrorism conspiracy that involved dissidents of the Revolutionary Armed Forces of Colombia (FARC), drug cartels in Mexico, the Islamic Republic of Iran, Syria, and the Lebanese terrorist group, Hezbollah."[8]

There are plenty of other connections between Iran and Venezuela that should worry you. For example, in 2009 it was reported that the now-deceased dictator of Venezuela, Hugo Chavez, was supplying uranium mined in South America to Iran.[9] In fact, some reports from that time indicate that Iran was helping Venezuela and Bolivia identify uranium deposits that could be mined. This was a ham-fisted attempt by Tehran to circumvent sanctions imposed by the United States because of Iran's continued insistence on developing nuclear weapons.[10]

Long-range precision-guided missiles that could threaten the United States. Fast-attack boats that could be used to harass critical shipping in Latin America. Support for narco-terrorism throughout the Western Hemisphere. Potential uranium mining operations to help Iran achieve its long-sought nuclear weapons capability. American policymakers ignore Iran's growing presence in Latin America, through Venezuela, at America's own risk.

It is true that the Iranian ships carrying the potential long-range missiles and fast-attack boats ultimately turned away from Venezuela

---

8 Joseph M. Humire, "The Maduro-Hezbollah Nexus: How Iran-Backed Networks Prop Up the Venezuelan Regime," Atlantic Council, 7 October 2020. https://www.atlanticcouncil.org/in-depth-research-reports/issue-brief/the-maduro-hezbollah-nexus-how-iran-backed-networks-prop-up-the-venezuelan-regime/

9 The Associated Press, "Secret Document: Venezuela, Bolivia Supplying Iran with Uranium," *Haaretz*, 25 May 2009. https://www.haaretz.com/1.5056591

10 Teresa Cespedes, "Chavez Says Iran Helping Venezuela Find Uranium," Reuters, 17 October 2009. https://www.reuters.com/article/us-venezuela-iran-uranium-sb/chavez-says-iran-helping-venezuela-find-uranium-idUSTRE59G1Y820091017

and meandered around the Atlantic Ocean. The Biden administration should be given credit for using the presidential bully pulpit to cajole Iran into backing down. However, empty threats from an administration that is clearly committed to making a deal with—rather than standing up to—an increasingly aggressive Iran will not go unchallenged forever.

The Iranians deployed their warships to travel to Venezuelan waters just weeks before their presidential "elections" were to be held. What's more likely is that the Iranians were simply probing the Americans; trying to keep the new Biden administration off balance while Tehran selected a new hardline leader, Ebrahim Raisi. The next time Iran decides to send weapons and military equipment to Venezuela, it might not be deterred so easily. Given the way that Iran has helped the Houthi Rebels, Hezbollah, Hamas, and a variety of other malign actors in the Greater Middle East, Washington should not wait to see if Tehran does the same for Venezuela.

What Washington should do is to invest more money into US Southern Command's counterterrorism capabilities, so that SOUTHCOM can go after Iranian terror groups operating throughout the region (as well as their allies in Latin America, like FARC). As Joseph Humire wrote, "curtailing the Maduro-Iran-Hezbollah cooperation is a critical step in stemming illicit networks that are helping to sustain the Maduro regime and prolonging the Western Hemisphere's worst humanitarian crisis."[11]

The next time that Iran deploys naval ships to Venezuela, the Americans should sink them too. Iran cannot be allowed to fundamentally undermine the precarious balance of power in America's backyard. And Washington must be tougher on Maduro and ensure that he understands any attempt to possess advanced Iranian military systems will threaten his regime's existence. According to some reports, Iran veered away from sending the long-range missiles and fast-attack boats

---

11 Humire, "The Maduro-Hezbollah Nexus: How Iran-Backed Networks Prop Up the Venezuelan Regime."

to Venezuela a year ago because the Trump administration threatened to bomb any sites in Venezuela where Iranian missiles would be found.

However, these measures will only work for so long. The Maduro regime wants to make a deal with Washington, but since any deal between the socialist government of Venezuela and the United States has been fleeting, Washington will have to do a better job of protecting its interests in Latin America from outside powers, like Iran. That includes taking sterner measures against the Maduro regime and the communist regime in Cuba. As the situation in Venezuela deteriorates, the regime will only move closer to Iran, Russia, and China. Iran's threat to the United States through Venezuela will only intensify unless real actions are taken to divorce Venezuela from Iran and to prevent any greater expansion of Iranian power in the Western Hemisphere.

7

WHY PEACE WITH IRAN

WON'T WORK

THE BIDEN ADMINISTRATION, like the earlier Obama administration, assumes that it can extricate the United States from the messy Middle East by abandoning its flawed (though committed) regional allies and making a nuclear weapons deal with Iran (and normalizing relations with it). The argument is that Iran has been treated as a perennial pariah in the region. Biden's Mideast team believes that Iran behaves as it does because the rest of the world treats it like a rogue state. If President Biden can just restore the Obama-era nuclear deal with Tehran, distance the United States from its traditional regional allies (the Sunni Arabs and Israel), and work Iran into the international trading and economic system, peace will eventually break out in the region.

This all sounds wonderful on paper. Yet the facts of history do not indicate that this policy is realistic or desirable. In fact, Iran's current regime does not want to be incorporated into the wider regional order, much less the US-led international system. Instead, Tehran wants to see an alternative system created. In that system, Iran is the dominant power of the Greater Middle East and a preferred partner for the alternatives to the US-led world, China, and Russia. Ceding any ground to the Islamic Republic will not serve American interests.

WAR IN THE HOUSE OF PEACE

Islam was birthed in war. Founded by Muhammad, a man Muslims believe to be their holy prophet, Islam was imposed by the sword upon the various tribes, Jewish groups, and Christians who populated the Arabian Peninsula. In thirty years, Muhammad took his religion from a band of brigands and vagabonds to being a potent empire that was pushing out from the conquered Arabian Peninsula into all directions. By 661 CE, however, the Prophet Muhammad was dead. He left no heirs.

Muhammad had conquered and converted the tribes of Arabia. While Islam was now their faith, the old tribal politics still played out beneath the new religion. Without a suitable heir, Muhammad's death created a power vacuum in the Islamic caliphate. Two opposing factions formed after Muhammad's death. One group, the minority group known as the Shiites, believed that only a blood relative of the prophet could succeed him. The Sunnis did not believe that a blood relative was necessary for succession.

For many years after Muhammad's death, these tensions simmered just below the apparently peaceful surface of Islam. It was not until the year 680 CE that the simmering tensions between the larger number of Sunnis and the minority Shiites boiled over into open warfare. Al-Husayn ibn 'Ali was the fourth grandson of Muhammad. He challenged Yazid I of the Umayyad Caliphate, based out of Damascus. When all other Muslims were swearing fealty to Yazid I, Husayn refused to bend his knee. Instead, he opted to make haste with seventy-two of his traveling companions toward the Shiite city of Kufa, in present-day Iraq, which was in open rebellion against the Sunni-led Umayyad Caliphate.

Fearing that the grandson of the prophet himself would link his cause with those of the rebellious Shiites in Kufa, Yazid sent a large force from Damascus to intercept Husayn and his companions on the road to Kufa. What followed was an historic event that changed the development of the Islamic world forever and solidified the very divisions that drive the Greater Middle East today. Here the much larger force of Sunnis engaged in an epic battle against the poorly defended—and surrounded—Shiites who marched with Husayn. Among them were Husayn's family members, including his infant son, the great-grandson of the Prophet Muhammad.

The Shiites were massacred that day, and Husayn's severed head was delivered to Yazid I in Damascus. From October 10, 680 CE, the day that the Shiites lost the Battle of Karbala, until the present, the fault lines in the Middle East were drawn. Although Shiite communities are spread throughout the Greater Middle East today, the largest concentration is found in Iran. The Shiites lived under constant repression by and fear of their Sunni caliphs.

THE TWELFTH IMAM WILL RETURN

In 1501 CE, the Shiites living under the Sunni-dominated Baghdad-based Abbasid dynasty were unruly. Although the Shiites and Sunnis shared the same deity and followed the same prophet, Muhammad, the murder of Husayn and all of those who rode with him in the Battle of Karbala in 680 ensured that Shiites would chafe under the rule of Sunnis. The Abbasid rulers were fearful of Shiite rebellion against their rule, so they imprisoned the tenth imam of the Shiite faith, a man whose standing was similar to that of the pope of the Catholic Church. While in captivity, the tenth imam had a son, Hasan al-Askari.

The young al-Askari was described as a prodigy. When he was twenty-two, al-Askari's father died. Most Shiites believed that al-Askari would naturally bring the twelfth imam into the world. Once the twelfth imam arrived, he would restore the Shiites to their rightful place and bring justice to those who had wronged the Shiites. Thus, the twelfth imam would be a Shiite messiah figure. Or, as the Shiites referred to him, the *Mahdī*.

The Abbasids did not believe that al-Askari's future son would be a messianic figure. But they feared their Shiite subjects would view al-Askari's progeny as a messiah—and that the twelfth imam could become a source of resistance to Abbasid rule. Rather than contend with that possibility, the Abbasids assassinated al-Askari, who was still in their custody. Yet the Shiites did not believe that al-Askari was murdered before he could produce an heir. Many Shiites—especially those who rule Iran today—firmly believe that the twelfth imam was merely occluded, or hidden away, by loyalists. According to the Shiite narrative, the twelfth imam remains "occluded" today and will reveal himself to the world during "a time of chaos and crisis" and will "reestablish the righteous rule of God on Earth."[1]

The messianic convictions about of the *Mahdī* are still important. The group better known as the "Twelver" (after the twelfth imam) sect of Shia Islam defines the politics of present-day Iran. In fact, the Iranian Revolution of 1979 was birthed by the Twelvers. Their political and religious preferences dominate Iran to this day. The Twelver branch of Shiism is the largest sect of the Shia faith, is spread out across the largest amount of territory in the Middle East today, and is the most powerful Shiite group.

According to Oxford University's Islamic Studies department:

> The twentieth century interpretation of Ayatollah Ruhollah Khomeini holds that [until the twelfth imam returns from his occlusion] the position of ruler of state should be filled by the most learned *faqih* (jurist) as the imam's representative, a position Khomeini held until his death.[2]

---

1 Michael Axworthy, *Empire of the Mind: A History of Iran* (New York: Basic Books, 2008), p. 129.

2 "Hidden Imam," Oxford University Islamic Studies Online, Accessed on 19 November 2020. http://www.oxfordislamicstudies.com/article/opr/t125/e838

The Twelver sect of Shia Islam has been the unifying force in Iranian politics. The Twelver interpretation of Shia Islam is the driver of Iranian regional ambitions as well. It is essential that Western policymakers comprehend this fact. Thus far, the Shiite experience at Karbala and the indignity of having been subjected to Sunni supremacy have defined Shia Islam. Iran's pre-Islamic history also remains a powerful force in Iranian culture and politics today.

In the words of the much-maligned Iranian foreign minister, Javad Zarif, "you must remember [Iranians] have a PhD in sanctions."[3] When he spoke those words in a 2019 speech to the Asia Society in New York City, Zarif was stating that since the Battle of Karbala, when the Umayyads deprived Husayn and his fellow Shiites of water for days before the fateful battle began, Iranians believe they've been punished for their faith.

While it is not true that the United States is sanctioning Iran today because of its Shiite Islamic beliefs, modern Iranian leaders have deftly manipulated the religious component to blunt the anger of their own people toward their regime. Remember, this regime refuses either to abandon its commitment to building a nuclear weapons program or to end its pervasive support for international terrorism directed against the United States, Israel, and its allies.

The deep disagreement between Sunni and Shia is the key for American policymakers to understanding the region's internal dynamics. It is an intractable divide. It has played out for centuries and will continue to, so long as Islam remains the dominant force in the region—which, of course, it will. American policymakers interacting with the region need to subordinate their own grand ambitions for the region to the idea that religion and, as you will see, ethnicity define all politics here.

Of course, as has been apparent since the 9/11 attacks, American

---

3 Dan De Luce, "Trump Pressure Will Fail Because Iran Has a 'Ph.D. in Sanctions Busting,' Says Iran's Zarif," NBC, 25 April 2019. https://www.nbcnews.com/news/world/trump-pressure-will-fail-because-iran-has-ph-d-sanctions-n998711

elites, both Democratic and Republican alike, are utterly incapable of understanding, let alone acknowledging, religion as a force in the world. Mideast scholars like Dr. Ussama Makdisi disagree with this assertion. Makdisi belongs to a new school of thought in the Mideast policy community that finds the entire idea of analyzing the Middle East through the lens of sectarianism, either religious or ethnic, to be offensive; he argues that focusing on the religious sectarianism of the region is "misleading" and "puts the cart before the horse," as it "conflates a religious identification with a political one."[4]

Makdisi and those in the West, who agree with his criticism of the sectarian model for analyzing Mideast politics, are correct to worry that such analysis could, in fact, obscure truth in certain instances. However, it is prima facie absurd to claim that religion and politics in the Mideast are not fused. They are—notably in Iran, which is run by a group of mullahs of the Shiite faith, who rose to power in a bloody revolution and who named their regime the "Islamic Republic of Iran." Ignoring that fact is wrong and will blind American policymakers to the realities they face in the region.

The story of Husayn and the plight of his seventy-two companions at Karbala in 680 provides far greater insight than anything that modern practitioners of statecraft in the West can concoct. In addition to the Battle of Karbala, there are several instances when the Shiite population of the region resisted Sunni rule. With each iteration of Sunni-Shia conflict, the Shiite worldview was only reinforced and perpetuated down the generations. Little has changed. In fact, extremism has increased in succeeding generations of Shiite and Sunni alike, the more negative interactions they've shared with each other.

Today, the world is witnessing the return of the Sunni-Shia conflict in a new form. Iran seeks to acquire nuclear weapons not only to push

4 Ussama Makdisi, "The Mythology of the Sectarian Middle East," James A. Baker III Institute for Public Policy, 2017, p. 2. https://www.bakerinstitute.org/media/files/files/5a20626a/CME-pub-Sectarianism-021317.pdf

the Americans out and to crush the Israelis, but to also keep their Sunni Arab neighbors down. From there, the Iranians will let the Chinese and Russians in—a net loss for the United States. As this traditional religious blood feud returns to the forefront of modern Middle East politics, American leaders must understand the primary role of Islam in the political and cultural affairs of all Middle Eastern states and calibrate their expectations accordingly.

ISLAMIC GUNPOWDER EMPIRE IN IRAN

By 1501 CE, the Safavid Dynasty—Iran's "Gunpowder Empire"—came into being. The Safavids are important for Iranian history because they made Shia Islam the official religion of the land. Douglas E. Streusand argues that "the Safavid rulers, and their Zand, Qajar, and Pahlavi successors, considered themselves legitimate rulers in the absence of [the twelfth imam]," which explains how ethnically foreign invaders, such as [Ismail] and his Safavid clique, were able to galvanize the people of Persia under his reign.[5] Safavid rulers also took on the title of "Shāh."

From that point, the legacy of the Shāhs and Shia Islam were fused in Iranian history. Inevitably, Iran would struggle in its interactions with Russia and the European powers throughout the nineteenth and early twentieth centuries. It was a monarchy of Shiites in a region dominated by Sunnis. And Iran (known as Persia back then) was being pushed around by the more powerful and technologically sophisticated European and Russian empires. They also had to contend with the more powerful Sunni Ottoman Empire, based in Turkey.

DEMOCRACY COMES TO IRAN

It was not until 1906, when momentous changes, because of Iran's repeated interaction with foreign European powers, occurred. In response to massive disruptions caused to Iran's local economy by the influx of cheap foreign goods the year before, pro-democracy protests

---

5 Streusand, *Islamic Gunpowder Empires*, p. 138.

erupted throughout Iran. The autocratic Shāh at the time, Mazofar o-Din Shāh, created the first democratic assembly, the *Majles*. This assembly drafted Iran's first democratic constitution. The interesting thing about Iran's democratic revolution in 1906 was that the aspiring middle classes, the merchant guild, and the conservative clerical community led the movement. Contrary to popular notions about democratic reform or revolutionary movements, the most conservative and traditional groups in Iranian society championed the change.

These democratic trends would only continue roiling Persian politics from that point until the present—which is to say that modern Iran, while it is technically ruled by a religious order, does have democratic trappings. Thus, we in the United States must be careful when advocates call for democracy in the Middle East. Democracy is a relative term; it means something different to everyone. Western democracy advocates might get what they wish for when it comes to democracy in the Middle East—yet it might just be the wrong thing for both the region and the United States.

In the new national constitution, the democratic reformers specifically decreed that the legitimacy of the Shāhs' rule derived not from their deity but instead from *the people*. A natural balance against this newfound strain of secularism was forged in the constitution when those who had crafted the document also named Shiism the official state religion and embraced shariah law, which is the legal code based on Islamic precepts, as the law of the land. Further balance was instituted within the new constitution in the form of minority rights. This proves how influential non-Shiites were in the formation of the constitution—notably members of the otherwise oppressed Jewish, Armenian, and Bahi'a communities.

During this revolutionary time, there was a proliferation of newspapers and a widening scope of interest in the political realm among many Iranians. Soon ordinary Iranians were gathering in what could be described as local salons to discuss the news of the day and to demonstrate their newfound political freedoms. The idea of a constitutional republic was clearly imported from the Europeans. And that idea was flowering among many Persians who ordinarily would be kept in both poverty and political repression. Soon, Europeanized Iranian nationalists and liberals were joining the ranks of the more conservative merchants and clerics in the burgeoning constitutional regime.

The more that Europeanized intellectuals took charge of the revolution, the more marginalized the original conservative elements became. Whereas the conservatives just wanted to make the system more responsive to their needs without destroying the Persian and Islamic roots of that system, the liberals and nationalists wanted to reimagine Iranian society from the ground up, using democracy as the vehicle to do it.

Thus the conflict between tradition and modernization that has played out for centuries in Persia ruptured the hard-won consensus that had arisen in 1906 in Persia. This would not be the first time that secular modernization in Iran met stiff resistance from the clerical class. Nor would it be the last time that these two forces, once divided, would allow the corrupt and incompetent political class they had revolted against to reassert their control over the land.

While all of these changes had been underway, as rivalries among the pro-democracy elements in Iran became intractable, a new Shāh rose to power. Mohammad Ali Shāh replaced his father and was far less inclined to accept the democratic yearnings of his people. By June 1908, as the revolution divided against itself, the new Shāh believed his time to act against the revolution was at its apex. With the assistance of a brigade of Russian Cossack soldiers, the Shāh's forces shelled the building the *Majles* had gathered in. After the shelling, Persia's nascent parliament disbanded.

The political turmoil in Persia created an opportunity for the Russian and British Empires to impose a treaty upon the doomed Middle Eastern power. The treaty, enacted in 1911, divided Persia into three zones: a British-controlled area, a Russian zone, and a neutral zone. Democratic ideals, however, did not die in Persia. They continued to appeal to many who were both incensed at the presence of foreigners in their lands and wanted reform to occur. The *Majles* would continue as well, even after the country officially ended its flirtation with democracy. In fact, by 1924 the *Majles* would force the end of the ruling Qājār dynasty. Reza Khan would be made the new Shāh and would create the Pahlāvi dynasty, the last dynasty of Iran, which would be overthrown by the Grand Ayatollah and his fellow Islamists in 1979.

Reza Khan would prove to be an enemy of the democratic movement. He would become an opponent of a young rising democrat, Mohammed Mossadegh. Khan had further engendered animosity from the clerics because he was interested in making secular reforms to Persia just as Atatürk had in Turkey in the 1920s. Under the flag of modernization, Reza Khan ordered changes to the way that Persians dressed, gave women more rights, and attempted to replace Islam with the ancient Persian religion of Zoroastrianism. Reza Khan also officially changed Persia's name to "Iran," which it is still known as today.

The young Mossadegh aligned with the Iranian cleric Hassan Modarres in an attempt to stunt Reza Khan's autocratic changes to Iran. Because of this opposition to the autocratic Reza Khan as Shāh, Mossadegh was exiled. Modarres met a darker fate: he was arrested and murdered by the Shāh's loyalists. Like Ali at Karbala in 680 CE and the twelfth imam who is believed by Shiites to have been occluded shortly after his birth to prevent the Abbasids from murdering him, Modarres was viewed as one of the great Shiite imams who was martyred for Islam and the peasant masses. Parliament Day in modern Iran takes place on the anniversary of Modarres's assassination in 1937. By these actions Reza Khan saved his regime. But the damage was done. He'd not remain in power for very long.

Reza Khan's rule was ensured by Britain, which required the free flow of oil from Iran. Yet as the Second World War erupted, Reza Khan went looking for new allies. He found one in Hitler's Germany. Reza Khan was not a Nazi, but he wanted to use Nazi Germany as a counterweight against the British Empire to extract better trade deals from Britain. Reza Khan was also a fierce anticommunist and viewed

Nazi Germany as a check against Soviet expansionism. Inevitably, the British and Soviet Union ended Khan's reign, with the British replacing the aging Iranian ruler with his son, Mohamed Reza Pahlāvi.

Despite the influence of foreign powers over Iran, the fact remains that Iranian politics were driven primarily by Iranian leaders, culture, and history. Yes, new influences from the West, such as the advent of the printing press and ideas related to democracy, nationalism, human rights, and secularism were imported into Iran during its long interaction with Western powers. But the pattern of historical facts suggests that Iran has long been subject to ostracism and hardship because of its existence as a Shiite power in a majority Sunni region.

That difference has created an extraordinary willingness among Iranians to endure hardship—as well as a stubborn commitment to their cause (becoming the regional power at the expense of their rivals). There is no escaping this. And for all the propaganda coming from the Islamists about Western perfidy in Iranian history, the truth is more complex. For example, the 1953 coup in Iran, which was supported by the British and implemented by the Americans, is viewed by many in the West as the reason for Iran's current hatred of the West. As the following chapter indicates, however, the coup in 1953 was the result of internal Iranian politics, and the Americans and British were only supporting the lawful government of Iran at the time—the Shāh.

8

THE TRUTH ABOUT

THE 1953 COUP IN IRAN

IN THE POSTWAR ERA, nationalism and anticolonialism were pro-
pulsive forces that defined much of what we now call the developing
world. In many cases, these two forces often traveled arm-and-arm with
communism, which during the Cold War was a major point of contention between the two superpowers. Iran's representative assembly, the
Majles, voted to make Mohammad Mossadegh their next prime minister.

As was noted earlier, Mossadegh had already run afoul of the
Shāh's father, Reza Khan, when Mossadegh opposed Khan's decision
to depose the last Qājār ruler and make himself the next Shāh. After
he had spent many years in political retirement, Mossadegh's political

fortunes changed with the Anglo-Soviet invasion of Persia. When the British and Soviets deposed Reza Khan and replaced him with his son, the man who would be Iran's last Shāh, Mossadegh returned to politics. Mossadegh ran for parliament in 1944 and was successfully elected to the *Majles*. From there, he came to lead the National Front, a coalition party aimed at stunting foreign influence in Iranian politics.

Mossadegh was not just opposed to the monarchy though. Initially, Mossadegh had the tenuous support of the clerical elite. However, Mossadegh soon made powerful enemies within the clerical class in Iran. They soon realized that Mossadegh intended to displace the Shāh and then diminish the importance of Shiism in Iranian life, replacing it with a more secular, progressive lifestyle that most Iranian monarchists and clerics—even many in the business community—found offensive.

When Mossadegh was made prime minister in 1951, he immediately nationalized the Anglo-Iranian Oil Company, fulfilling the wishes of all involved with the National Front. Iran's oil supply was the lifeblood of Britain's economy. London moved rapidly to impose harsh sanctions upon Iran at a time when its domestic stability was yet again in question.

For Britain, the issue of Iran was simply a matter of the survival of their empire that was already under severe threat everywhere. After Iran attempted to nationalize it, the Anglo-Iranian Oil Company removed their technicians from Abadan, complicating Iranian attempts to drill the oil on their own. The British Royal Navy then blockaded the vital port. Britain also cut off exports to Iran—effectively starving the country and further contributing to domestic instability in Iran at that time.

Britain then took their case against Iran's nationalization of property belonging to the Anglo-Iranian Oil Company to the United Nations, as well as the World Court. At every turn, however, the British were rebuffed by the international entities they appealed to. Both the UN and World Court effectively refused to rule on the matter, prompting Britain to seek a resolution to the crisis through less honorable means, such as a coup directed against Mossadegh.

Because the British Empire was so weakened, however, London

could not stop the Iranian government from nationalizing the oil. So London appealed to their stronger American friends. Washington ultimately intervened because it feared that Mossadegh was not strong enough to keep the communist elements in Iran at bay. Should Iran have become a communist state, America's entire containment strategy against the Soviet Union would have collapsed.

Many in the West feared that Mossadegh was a Soviet sympathizer aligned with the Tudeh Party, Iran's communist party.[1] While the Tudeh Party had, at times, agreed with Mossadegh's stance on key issues—notably his plans to nationalize Iran's oil industry—most historians believe that Mossadegh was *not* a communist sympathizer.

Although, it must be noted that Gregory Copley, who today serves as the president of the International Strategic Studies Association, who has decades of experience in Iran as well as deep ties to British and Australian defense communities insists that Mossadegh was indeed a communist. And there is some evidence in recently declassified State Department cables from the 1953 coup in Iran that indicate there was more than a sneaking suspicion on the part of American and British policymakers that Mossadegh was, in fact, working with the communist elements in Iran.

Further, it was well-known that the pro-Soviet Tudeh Party in Iran did try to prevent the 1953 coup against Mossadegh in Iran. Unfortunately for the Reds, though, the Tudeh Party was far too internally divided and could not muster the resources to stop the coup. It should be noted here that, according to the noted historian of the communist movement in Iran, Maziar Behrooz of San Francisco State University, that the Tudeh Party relied heavily on the Soviet Union (particularly after the overthrow of Mossadegh) for organizational and ideological support.[2]

---

1 Rajeesh Kumar, "What New Declassifications Reveal about the 1953 Coup in Iran," E-International Relations, 7 September 2017. https://www.e-ir.info/2017/09/07/what-new-declassifications-reveal-about-the-1953-coup-in-iran/

2 Arash Azizi, "Communists Tried to Stop the 1953 Coup—But It Was 'Too Little, Too Late,'" *Iran Wire*, 24 August 2017. https://iranwire.com/en/features/4789

Consequently, few in either the Western intelligence services or in the Shāh's government in Iran believed that Mossadegh was not a sympathizer to the Tudeh Party and, therefore, a Soviet agent. This explains why the prominent Iranian political leader and long-time friend of the Iranian monarchy, General Fazlollah Zahedi (a long-time colleague of the aforementioned Gregory Copley as well) assembled a team of top Iranian military and political leaders to help him craft a plot to overthrow Mossadegh. Zahedi, according to Copley, was the real mastermind of the 1953 coup in Iran, not the British or American intelligence services, which merely tagged along for the ride. So, Copley and several analysts have made the claim that far from being the plot of rapacious foreigners from America and Britain, the 1953 coup plot was entirely an Iranian ordeal with some minor assistance from the West.

Lastly, as Copley and others who supported General Zahedi's counter-coup argue, Mossadegh had exceeded his mandate as prime minister. Because of this, the legitimate head of state, the Shāh, ordered him removed from power. Yet, rather than give up power, Mossadegh began trying to rewrite the Iranian government to ensure he would remain in power—going so far as to threaten the existence of the monarchy itself. It was because Mossadegh had overstepped his authority, as Copley has claimed, that Zahedi and the pro-Shāh military stepped in to preserve the constitutional order of the monarchy and prevent an unwanted communist takeover of Iran.

Thus, rather than being a foreign plot to overthrow the legitimate government of Iran, Zahedi's counter-coup becomes a necessary, last-ditch effort to save the actual government of Iran—its constitutional monarchy—from a power-mad, communist sympathizer. It is important to bear this in mind whenever listening to popular narratives in the West about the 1953 coup (most of which are meant to make the United States and Britain look as guilty as possible for why Iran is in its present decrepit state).

Yet the West needed a strong and stable Iran to keep the oil flowing and, for America's sake, to prevent Iran from becoming a Soviet client state.

THE COLD WAR CONNECTION

Since the start of the Cold War, the Americans had embraced a strategy of containment against the Soviet Union. This inherently defensive strategy was predicated on mutual assured destruction through nuclear warfare (in 1949, the Soviets successfully tested their own nuclear weapon and became the existential threat we all remember). The containment strategy was designed to prevent the Soviets from making any further territorial gains in addition to what they already had at the end of the Second World War.

If Iran had become a Soviet ally, though, the entire containment strategy would have been called into question. Remember also that the Soviet Union, as the inheritor of the Russian Empire, also had the age-old Russian desire for access to warm-water ports. Not only could the Soviets acquire a lucrative partnership with a communist-friendly, oil-rich Iran, but Moscow could also conceivably gain access to those warm-water ports, as the tsars of old had long dreamed of doing.[3]

The threat to America's strategy of containment if Iran became a Soviet satellite, therefore, drew the Americans in. American firms were ultimately given a 40 percent stake in the British Petroleum-led National Iran Oil Consortium (NIOC) that was created with the Shāh's blessing after Mossadegh was overthrown in 1953. But, while beneficial to the United States, access to Iran's oil was *not* the cause of America's involvement in the coup.

---

3 As Stephen Kotkin describes in his epic biography of Josef Stalin, *Stalin, Volume I: Paradoxes of Power, 1878–1928* (New York: Penguin Press, 2014), "Stalin [shattered] any attempt to contain him within binaries. He was by inclination a despot who, when he wanted to be, was utterly charming. He was an ideologue who was flexibly pragmatic. He fastened obsessively on slights yet he was a precocious geostrategic thinker ... who was, however, prone to egregious strategic blunders. Stalin was as a ruler both astute and blinkered, diligent and self-defeating, cynical and true believing. The cold calculation and the flights of absurd delusion were products of a single mind." Stalin moved away from Lenin's attempt to shatter the nation-state and instead embraced a concept of "socialism in one country." Stalin's grand strategy was entirely Russocentric—so much so that Stalin earned the nickname of the "Red Tsar," by many who lived under him. Like the tsars who preceded the communist reign of terror in Russia, Stalin ultimately shared many of their long-term strategic goals (such as expanding his borders to more defensible positions in Europe, the Middle East, Central Asia, and along the Pacific coast as well as acquiring warm water ports).

There was another aspect to the story of Mossadegh's overthrow that few scholars have yet to fully understand. Writing in the *Texas National Security Review,* Gregory Brew has asserted that the United States feared a collapse of the government in Iran even more than they feared the possibility of Mossadegh being a communist agent there. According to Brew, "the collapse narrative incorporated concerns over oil with the well-articulated fears of Iran 'falling behind the Iron Curtain.'"[4]

In response to the British embargo of Iran, Mossadegh attempted to create an economy in Iran that did not depend as heavily on oil as it had before the British embargo. The idea of an oil-less economy in Iran was one that the Americans could not comprehend. Washington policymakers believed that the Iranian regime would collapse due to economic failure.

There was an old notion that communism marched on empty stomachs. American leaders assumed that an economically depressed Iran with a weak leader, Mossadegh, who was already nominally aligned with the communists in Iran, would inevitably lead Iran into the waiting arms of Uncle Joe Stalin and the Soviet bloc. So the concern of an imminent communist takeover under Mossadegh was likely not the primary impetus for America's involvement in the 1953 ouster of Mohammad Mossadegh. Instead, it was more likely that the United States feared that if Mossadegh or his allies remained in power, over the longer term Iran would simply drift into the Soviet Union's orbit.

The collapse narrative that Brew wrote about in 2019 makes sense. Several months before the Americans took part in the overthrow of Mossadegh, the Truman administration had told the British that any attempt to overthrow Mossadegh was reckless. That all changed, though, by August of 1953. By then the old wartime partners, Britain's Winston Churchill and America's Dwight D. Eisenhower, had found themselves yet again partners in power. Churchill, as the British prime minister,

---

4 Gregory Brew, "The Collapse Narrative: The United States, Mohammed Mossadegh, and the Coup Decision of 1953," *Texas National Security Review,* vol. 2, issue 4, (November 2019), pp. 38–59. https://tnsr.org/2019/11/the-collapse-narrative-the-united-states-mohammed-mossadegh-and-the-coup-decision-of-1953/

despised the wave of nationalists who were splitting apart the British Empire in the decade following the Second World War.

Eisenhower was also weary of the result of these movements, but not because they would liberate peoples who had been colonized by the British. Instead, these movements would leave their countries weakened and, therefore, ripe for Soviet annexation. When Eisenhower took power from Truman and Churchill was returned to Downing Street, the conditions were set for a move against Mossadegh in Iran.

One reason for the shift might have been events in Iran in 1952. At that time, the National Front—the alliance of nationalists, clerics, liberal reformers, and even communists in Iran that Mossadegh led—was breaking down due to its own internal contradictions. The greater the breakdown of Mossadegh's National Front, the more that CIA analysts feared Mossadegh would depend on the pro-Soviet Tudeh Party to augment his own power. Thus American policymakers believed that a coup to oust Mossadegh and his supporters from power in Iran was key.[5]

Western fears about Mossadegh and his associations with the communists in Iran came to the fore in August 1953. Mossadegh had been a fiery anti-monarchist. The Shāh had instructed the military to arrest Mossadegh. However, the Shāh underestimated Mossadegh, who was better informed than the Shāh realized. The night before his arrest was to take place, Mossadegh had learned of the Shāh's plot to arrest him, so Mossadegh outmaneuvered the Shāh.

Fearing for his safety, the Shāh packed up and fled the country, basically abdicating. Before Mossadegh could act decisively and name himself president of Iran, Washington and London moved quickly to restore the Shāh to the throne and rebuff any potential communist advances in the oil-rich country of Iran.

---

5 Mark J. Gasiorowski, "U.S. Perceptions of the Communist Threat in Iran during the Mossadegh Era," *Journal of Cold War Studies,* vol. 21, no. 3, (Summer 2019), pp. 185-221. https://www.mitpressjournals.org/doi/pdf/10.1162/jcws_a_00898

MOSSADEGH GETS PUSHED OUT

Operation AJAX, a joint British and American CIA operation, overthrew Prime Minister Mohammad Mossadegh and replaced him with
the autocratic Shāh. The Iranian constitution written in 1906 would
become a meaningless scrap of paper after the coup.[6] After the ouster
of Mohammad Mossadegh as the duly elected prime minister of Iran,
the Shāh shut down the *Majles,* Iran's parliamentary body. He allowed
another assembly of the consultative parliamentary body to form, but
yet again shuttered it in 1961. Essentially, from the 1953 coup until
his own ouster by the clerics in the 1979 Islamic Revolution, the Shāh
enjoyed absolute rule over Iran.[7]

The removal of Mossadegh from power has been cited by nearly
every observer of modern Iran as the catalyst for the Iranian revolution in 1979. Most academics believe the Anglo-American removal of
Mossadegh is the reason why Iran despises the United States and its role
in the Middle East. The Americans and their British allies took extreme
steps to keep rulers friendly to their interests in power in Iran. Although,
the fact remains that the current situation in Iran is hardly the fault of
the United States or the West—especially if the claim of Gregory Copley
and Iranians like Fazlollah Zahedi, the man who ultimately replaced
Mossadegh as Iranian prime minister following Mossadegh's ouster in
the 1953, are completely accurate.

Even before the Anglo-American coup attempt, the political scene
in Iran was chaotic. While Mossadegh enjoyed popular support in the
beginning of his short-lived tenure as prime minister, the various factions he purported to lead were divided against each other. Their unity
was always tenuous and had started to fragment almost from the start
of his tenure as prime minister.

---

6 Dariush Borbor, "A Comparative Overview of the Iranian Constitutions of 1906–07 and 1979,"
Iran & the Caucasus, vol. 10, no. 2 (2006), pp. 263–86. https://www.jstor.org/stable/4030928?seq=1

7 Joseph Kraft, "Letter from Iran," *The New Yorker,* 18 December 1978. https://www.newyorker.com/
magazine/1978/12/18/letter-from-iran

Mossadegh was a weak prime minister. Had he remained in power, it is likely that the Iranian government would have either collapsed or become coopted by stronger powers—most probably the USSR, which, like their tsarist Russian predecessors, always lurked just over Iran's horizon. This fact is often overlooked by Western scholars. Iran's current predicament, as described in the first chapter of this book, is almost entirely the result of internal and regional factors that had little to do with the United States (not that the Anglo-American coup helped the situation).

Besides, Mossadegh's National Front did not ultimately include the most powerful political group in Iran: the clerics. At first, Mossadegh did play nice with the clerics—especially as his spat with the Shāh and, more importantly the Shāh's foreign backers, became more pronounced. Mossadegh had aligned himself with a longtime critic of British influence in Iran, the highly regarded Shiite *mojtahed* Abol-Ghasem Kashani. Kashani had been a noted anti-capitalist for most of his life and had used his position as a Shiite religious leader to attack both capitalism and British influence over Iran. When Mossadegh rose to power in 1951, Kashani had only just returned from exile (he had been banished from Iran when the Anglo-Soviet invasion occurred during the Second World War).

Kashani shared Mossadegh's antipathy toward the British and also viewed the AIOC oil development deal in Iran as one-sided. He was outraged that the AIOC paid the British more than the Iranians for an Iranian product. Kashani ultimately served as speaker of the *Majles* when Mossadegh was the prime minister. So long as Mossadegh had Kashani in his corner, the controversial prime minister would have the backing of the Iranian people as well. But, as you've seen, Mossadegh was not just a committed anti-monarchist and anti-colonialist, but anti-clerical also. These contradictions between Mossadegh and Kashani could not be papered over for very long—especially after Mossadegh's successful first act, nationalizing Iran's oil supply, had been completed. The two men, despite their shared enemies, drifted apart.

Mossadegh eventually repeated the same mistakes of other noted reformers in Iran. He pushed too far, too quickly—and did so *without* the religious establishment on his side. Iran was always a place of religious passion. Whether referring to the Zoroastrianism that had dominated ancient Persia or the fiery Shiism that charges through Iranian society today, the attempt to divorce Iran from both its monarchy as well as its religion—to say nothing of the foreign influences—at the same time was an absurdity.

Without the clerics (or the monarchists) behind him, Mossadegh was always waging a losing battle at home, while also losing to the foreign powers on the international stage. Eventually, domestic forces inimical to his leadership would have removed Mossadegh, even if the British and American intelligence services had not overthrown him in 1953. He had simply made too many enemies and lost too many followers.

9

ISLAMISM ASCENDANT

IN MODERN IRAN

AROUND THE TIME that Mossadegh successfully headed the National Front, with Kashani and many of the other Shiite clerics backing that movement, a young firebrand in the Shiite community, Navvab Safavi, was cutting a swathe through Iran's sociopolitical scene. Born to a prestigious family, Safavi, who had worked for the AIOC as a young man, began an explosive journey to Shiite Islam.

Known for his dashing good looks and stunning oratory, the young man became a cult figure in Iranian religious circles. Many even compared him to Hassan-i Sabbah, the man who in the nineteenth century had founded the controversial Assassins (one of the many strands of Shiism that evolved over time and is not widely covered in this work). For the record, the Assassins were a sect of Shiites who, as their name suggests, believed it was their duty to assassinate those leaders who were polluting the land. While they had never been as popular as Twelver Shiism, the Assassins have always fascinated both Iranians and foreigners alike.[1]

Safavi was not his original surname, though. Many believe that he adopted the "Safavi" surname for political purposes, as that was the title of those who served the Safavid dynasty that had made Shiite Islam the official religion of Iran. That name came in handy when Safavi initiated his meteoric—though bloody—rise in Iranian society and politics.

Navvab Safavi is an important figure in the foundation of the Islamic Revolution of 1979. For starters, Safavi was a close friend and colleague of the young Ruhollah Khomeini; he, like Safavi, was a rising young star in the Shiite clerical community. Safavi had founded the potent Islamist organization in Iran known as the Fada'iyn-e Islam in 1945. The group, like its founder, was heavily influenced by the larger Islamist movement known as the Muslim Brotherhood, which had been born in opposition to British colonialism in Egypt in the 1920s.

The Muslim Brotherhood remains the most important element of Islamist radicalism. Under the umbrella of the Muslim Brotherhood, all other modern Islamist parties—Sunni and Shiite alike—found ideological affirmation and purpose. Safavi took the teachings of the Muslim Brotherhood to heart, even meeting its infamous founder, Sayyed Qutb, in 1953, and he adapted the Muslim Brotherhood's ideology to a Shiite political context. Safavi's Muslim Brotherhood–inspired Islamism was disseminated to Ruhollah Khomeini, as the two men would spend hours together discussing politics, history, and faith.

Safavi's organization then set about assassinating any Iranian government minister they believed to be responsible for leading their country astray from the true teachings of Islam. Safavi, like Kashani, initially

---

1 For the best explanation of this movement, see: Bernard Lewis, *The Assassins: A Radical Sect in Islam* (New York: Basic Books, 1967).

believed that Mossadegh would not just reduce the unwanted influence of foreigners over Iran. In addition, the dynamic prime minister would also purify Iran. Over time, however, Safavi and Kashani both concluded that Mossadegh was as opposed to Shiism's role in Iran as he was opposed to the British and the Shāh's place in Iranian society.

Remember that the revolution in 1905, which led to the creation of Iran's first constitution in 1906, was brought about by the conservative cleric and business communities. In Iran, as you've seen going back to the eleventh imam, the Shiite religious leaders enjoy an exalted status in their society. The clerics always believed that Mossadegh was too secular and too liberal (and, in their view, Mossadegh was possibly an irredeemable communist). Men like Kashani and Safavi, though, took a chance on Mossadegh, believing him preferable to the Shāh and British influence in Iran. Mossadegh's break with Kashani sealed both Mossadegh's and Safavi's fate.

ISLAMIST OPPOSITION TO MOSSADEGH

When the coup took place in 1953, many elements of the Shiite religious community in Iran—the same elements who would lead the Islamic revolution against the Shāh in 1979—cheered on the American coup. There are reports that some members of the clerical community even assisted the British and American intelligence services in restoring the Shāh to the Peacock Throne.[2] Notably, Safavi's Islamist group attacked Mossadegh's supporters in the run-up to the coup. Inevitably, Safavi would be arrested after the coup and executed in 1956. But his influence, as noted above, would resonate through the later generations due to his close friendship with Ruhollah Khomeini, the future grand ayatollah of the Shiite faith in Iran.[3]

---

2 Brandon J. Weichert, "Blame Iran for Iran's Problems," Real Clear World, 16 January 2020. https://www.realclearworld.com/articles/2020/01/16/blame_iran_for_irans_problems_255091.html

3 Amir Taheri, *The Spirit of Allah: Khomeini & the Islamic Revolution* (Bethesda, MD: Adler & Adler, 1986), pp. 98–102.

Ayatollah Seyyed Hossein Borujerdi, a mentor of Ruhollah Khomeini and a contemporary of Kashani, was supportive of the Shāh. It was known that Borujerdi openly declared that "the country needs the king" to his masses of followers. As a respected leader of the Shiite faith, Ayatollah Borujerdi and his Shiite supporters played a large role in ensuring the success of the 1953 coup against Mohammad Mossadegh, simply by throwing cold water on the other Shiite clerics who were openly opposed to the Shāh.

However, Borujerdi's support of the Shāh was part of his wider belief in Shiite "quietism," a theory that the role of an austere religious leader was to have as little impact on politics as possible. Not only did Borujerdi refuse to oppose the Shāh, but he also refused to condemn what many Muslims saw as the unjust treatment of Palestinian Arabs by Israel. Ambivalence about politics—especially radical politics—was an essential aspect of quietism.

Because Khomeini was a protégé of Borujerdi, he felt compelled to honor his mentor's request to avoid involvement in radical politics. Khomeini played no role in the 1953 coup and likely supported it, for he viewed Mossadegh as negatively as Kashani had. Once Ayatollah Borujerdi died in 1962, so too would the principle of Shiite quietism in Iranian politics. Khomeini would immediately step forward as a leader and become the focus of opposition to the Shāh at that point. Khomeini was smart to have honored the wishes of his wise mentor, Borujerdi. After all, Safavi was ultimately executed in 1956 for his radical position. He had at first supported Mossadegh, then turned against him. Once Safavi believed that the Shāh would not purify Iranian society by forcefully imposing shariah law, he soon turned on Mossadegh's successors, who were all handpicked by the Shāh.

All these trends, despite their links to both the oil industry and Britain's development of Iran's petroleum resources, have far deeper resonance with events that occurred in Iran and the wider region long before European colonialism entered the fray of Mideast politics. The divide between Ayatollah Borujerdi's quietism and the views of Kashani harken back to the divisions that formed within the Shiite faith during the eleventh century, documented earlier in this book. Even without Britain's interest in oil or America's fears that the Soviets would bring Iran behind its menacing Iron Curtain, the Iranian political scene was a disaster. Of the three groups in Iran who were driving politics—the monarchists, the Islamists, and the nationalists—the traditional religious and monarchist institutions had far greater staying power than the nationalists or liberal reformers.

What's more, the rise of Islamism in Iran is deeply connected to the earlier rise of Islamism in Egypt and the wider region, as represented by the Muslim Brotherhood. These movements, while outwardly directed against European—specifically British—colonialism, were fixated on purifying Islamic polities internally. And such purification movements have historically only been nominally linked to foreign interference in Islam.

While many reactionary autocrats who ruled Muslim lands enjoyed the support of outside powers, whether Western states or the Soviet Union, there is no guarantee that these leaders, or others like them, would not have risen regardless of the presence or absence of foreigners in the region. Even within the history of the caliphate, there were notoriously unpopular rulers, such as Yazid I of the Umayyad dynasty or the Abbasid rulers who ultimately helped create the notion of the *Mahdi* in Shiism through their brutal mistreatment of the Shiites under their rule.

The internal politics of Iran made it a powder keg waiting to explode, with or without foreign meddling. Events in Iran were shaped first and foremost by the Shiite-Sunni split, the long history of great dynasties that ruled the territory—both before and after the rise of Islam—and the interaction between Iran and other regional powers. The real power brokers in Iranian politics have always been the clerics. Their preferences have usually won out over all others. It was true during the Safavid dynasty. It was true in 1905, when the constitutional revolution occurred. It was true during the overthrow of Mohammad Mossadegh as prime minister. And as you will soon read, it was true in 1979. It is true today, as the Iranian people yearn for greater democratic freedom and yet their calls are muted by the Mullah council and the Ayatollah Khamenei in favor of increasingly hardline presidents, such as the recently "elected" Ebrahim Raisi. The internal sociopolitical and economic dynamics of Iran, while periodically influenced by foreigners, were controlled by Iranians. Iranians, therefore, did far more to shape Iran than anything the Western imperial powers ever did.

WAS THE 1953 COUP THAT IMPACTFUL?

Nearly sixty-eight years have passed since the Anglo-American coup against Mossadegh. It has been more than forty years since the Islamic Revolution overthrew the Shāh. Since that time, two generations have gone through the Islamic Republic of Iran's education system. And as Ervand Abrahamian established in 2009, high school history textbooks in Iran all but ignore the 1953 coup when teaching their pupils about Iranian history.[4]

How could the Anglo-American coup, then, have so profound an impact on modern-day Iran if most Iranians today are taught little about it? Given the role during the 1953 coup played by the clerics, the men who would go on to lead the Islamic Revolution in 1979 against the Shāh, how can anyone seriously believe that the coup was this decisive moment in Iran's modern history? The coup was important because it enhanced foreign influences over Iran. It was not, however, the defining moment many Western analysts assume it to be.

---

4 Ervand Abrahamian, "History Used and Abused," PBS, 19 August 2009. https://www.pbs.org/wgbh/pages/frontline/tehranbureau/2009/08/history-used-and-abused.html

10

THE MIXED BAG OF

MODERNIZATION

BY 1954, Mossadegh was gone, and the Shāh was firmly ensconced as the monarch yet again. Once the Shāh was restored to power, all concerns about the nationalization of the oil industry were gone. Instead, the Shāh allowed the British to expand their oil operations in Iran. British Petroleum was allowed to create a new consortium that would dominate Iran's oil industry from the overthrow of Mossadegh until the Islamic Revolution in 1979. This was the National Iranian Oil Company (NIOC), in which American firms were given a 40 percent stake. The money generated from increased oil development was used to fund the Shāh's dream of modernizing Iran, as his father, Reza Khan, had desired to do. To accomplish these ambitious goals, the Shāh believed he needed the West on his side.

The year 1962 proved to be a momentous one for the Shāh. He and his coterie of advisers took a plane to the United States. President John F. Kennedy had invited the Shāh to come and visit the United States. Kennedy took his guests to visit the NASA launch center in Cape Canaveral, Florida. The Iranian monarch went to top-of-the-line American military installations so his partners could show the Iranian delegations what an alliance with the United States could do for them. Meanwhile, the Shāh sojourned to the National Press Club in Washington, DC and talked about his hopes to make Iran a great power in the modern age.

During that trip, President Kennedy pressed the Shāh. The Kennedy administration rightly recognized that Iran was a key strategic partner for the West. Should it be lost as a partner, America's defense against the Soviet Union would have been greatly damaged. Yet JFK assessed that Iran was in dire need of rapid modernization.

However, Kennedy also knew that modernization by itself was insufficient to meet the needs of Iran's people as well as the demand for legitimacy both at home and abroad. He believed that democratization was key to ensure Iran's long-term stability and prosperity. JFK's purpose was to imbue the Shāh with the sense that his regime's long-term survival was contingent upon the liberalization and ultimate democratization of his state. It was not merely enough to impose radical modernization upon the populace; the Shāh had to grant them liberty.

For his part, the Shāh had come to the United States looking to reaffirm that his alliance with the United States was essential and to be seen near the advanced NASA launch sites and the bristling military bases of the United States. This was a signal to the Shāh's enemies back home—and the skulking Soviets—that the Shāh would not be intimidated and could not be removed. The Shāh even addressed Congress and spoke in flowery language about his love for America and his dream to make Iran more like the United States.[1]

This was mere window dressing, sadly. The Shāh needed weapons, diplomatic cover, and technical insights so he could spur modernization in his homeland. Not a single component of the Shāh's ambitious modernization program, however, had anything to do with democracy.[2] In the mind of the Shāh, that experiment had been tried and had failed. No, the fate of Iran was inextricably bound up with the Shāh's. Modernization would strengthen the Shāh's vice-like grip on power while also empowering Iran on the world stage. At least that's what the Shāh believed.

In reality, the Shāh came to view the United States much as the rest of the world viewed American largesse during the postwar era: America was a cash cow they should take advantage of whenever it suited them. The Shāh intended to take foreign aid and support from the Americans, but there was no way he would democratize. Had it not been for the assassination of JFK, it is likely that the Shāh would have been made to conform to Kennedy's wishes. Then again, if the Shāh had done as Kennedy wished, it is probable his reign would have ended as badly in the 1960s as it did in 1979. And that is the rub: modernization does not always march hand-in-hand with democracy. When one tries to force democracy alongside modernization, particularly in the context of the Middle East, you end up accomplishing neither modernization nor democratization. Instead, you either perpetuate the strongman rule or, more dangerously, empower religious totalitarians who will take power and keep their population locked under their extreme, dogmatic interpretation of their faith. What's more, as the examples of South Korea or Colombia show, very often a US-backed autocracy intent on modernization can evolve into an actual democracy. This is a concept

---

1 "John F. Kennedy and the Shah," Radio Farda, 2 June 2017. https://en.radiofarda.com/a/kennedy-sha-visit-iran-alliance/28524785.html

2 April R. Summit, "For a White Revolution: John F. Kennedy and the Shah of Iran," *Middle East Journal*, 58, no. 4 (2004), pp. 560–75. https://www.jstor.org/stable/4330063?seq=1

that modern Liberal Internationalists seem incapable of understanding.

The dark side of modernization became visible when the Shāh created his domestic security arm, codenamed SAVAK. This group of highly skilled spies would hunt down and disrupt any domestic threats to the Shāh's continued reign. They became a feared intelligence body in Iran that routinely policed and brutalized the population in the name of the Shāh. SAVAK eventually grew into a powerful asset for the West, augmenting Western forces in the struggle against the Soviet menace. In 1961, the Shāh cemented his absolute rule by yet again shuttering the *Majles*. Closing down Iran's parliamentary body allowed the Shāh to move forward with modernization in land reform laws—or the "White Revolution."

The first thing that the Shāh had to do was create programs meant to elevate the vast majority of Iranians from systemic poverty. Modernization was the way. Yet the Shāh, like other modernizers throughout history, believed that the religious establishment in his country hindered true modernization. Shiism in Iran has always rested on the worship of martyrs—Ali, who was killed by the Umayyads at Karbala, and the twelfth imam, who is thought to have been occluded by fellow believers when the Sunni Abbasids came to assassinate him.

Shiism has always enchanted the masses of dispossessed and poor in Iran. This explains why the mullahs have always been so popular, with a revered place in Iranian society: they have significant influence over the masses. What's more, as you've seen, Shiism in Iran has been locked in a long-term struggle with the forces of modernization for control of Iran's destiny.

With Mossadegh out of the way and any democratic forces in Iran now fully under monarchical control, the Shāh next focused his ire on the religious leadership. Taking his cues from Atatürk's example in Turkey, the Shāh believed it necessary to disentangle religion from the country's politics. Not only did the Shāh advocate using Iran's money from the oil industry to support education reforms for the masses or to reinvest in national industries, but he also believed the Iranian people needed land to create their own wealth and chart their own course.

Although the Shāh ruled as an absolute monarch from 1953 until 1979, he spoke openly about freedom in Iran under his rule. While people were not free to criticize the Shāh or question his policies, the Shāh believed that his firm hand would guide the country from medievalism to modernity. For the Shāh, then, material prosperity was synonymous with freedom.

The Shāh also oversaw an expansive industrialization of his country along Western lines. All of this was done to build the capacity of Iran, as his father, Reza Khan, had desired to do. In building up Iran's capacity, the Shāh believed that he could make Iran competitive with the West. By making Iran competitive with the West, the Shāh hoped Iran could deal with the Western powers on a more even footing—while still rebuffing the ravenous Soviets.

Of course, the Shāh's push for modernization was not only about empowering ordinary Iranians but also about elevating his place in his country and the world. The year 1971 saw the Shāh crown himself as emperor of Iran in a scene reminiscent of Napoleon. In a glittering gold room, while he was surrounded by his closest supporters and wearing royal robes, his head was adorned with a glittering crown, a symbol of his supreme power. Here stood not just the king of kings in Iran, but a man who had tapped into a deeper, richer vein of Iran's *pre-Islamic* history in a direct shot at the religious clerics who purported to guide Iranian society.[3]

During this period, the Shāh celebrated the 2,500th anniversary of the pre-Islamic Persian monarchy. A lavish party was thrown at the ancient pre-Islamic capital of Persepolis that was attended by the world's most prominent royal figures—including Prince Philip, the Duke of Edinburgh. This decadent event, held in an expensive tent city specially constructed outside the ruins of Darius the Great's capital city, was meant to be the Shāh's "coming out" party.

More importantly, though, the Shāh and his ministers envisioned

---

[3] "Decadence and Downfall: The Shah of Iran's Ultimate Party," The Royal Watcher, 27 February 2017. https://royalwatcherblog.com/2017/02/27/persepolis-1971/

the great event as the official announcement that Iran had finally arrived on the world stage. After centuries of being abused, Iran had become a modern state with a rich people and hopeful future. Iran would be as important and potent as any of the other developed countries of the West. By inviting the world's royalty, as well as countless well-connected elites from around the world—including emissaries from the Soviet Union—the Shāh was indicating that this new, grand, modern Iran would chart its own course too.[4]

Yet the lavish events in Persepolis would not serve as the beginning of Iran's ultimate victory over the forces of backwardness, foreign oppression, and exploitation. Instead, the party at Persepolis highlighted all the flaws of the monarchy (at least in the eyes of those who should have mattered most, the Iranian people). The event cost the Iranian people $100 million at the time. The exclusive ceremony required massive security; new infrastructure was rapidly built in Persepolis to support the scores of notables who would be there during the festivities as well. The world's media photographed the Shāh and his coterie being treated to immense pampering, all in an effort to show to the world how powerful Iran had become.

But the party could not have come at a more inopportune time. At this point, the Shāh's modernization, on top of unevenly distributing the wealth generated from these reforms, had hit a proverbial brick wall. Inflation had rocked the Iranian economy, stalling the economic momentum that the White Revolution had created. Average Iranian citizens were squeezed the hardest by the downturn.

Iranians already were uneasy with many social reforms the Shāh was imposing, as well as how the Shāh's fearsome SAVAK terrorized anyone who dared to question the Shāh. Thus conditions were set for mass protests and, ultimately, revolution. For the people of Iran, the images of the decadent event in Persepolis were not a source of national

---

4 Hassan Amini, *Decadence and Downfall: The Shah of Iran's Ultimate Party* (2016: BBC Studios, London, 2016), YouTube. https://www.youtube.com/watch?v=fDhGPYWfKFU&feature=emb_logo

pride. They were viewed as yet another sign of just how far the Shāh had strayed from both the will of the Iranian people and Allah, their god. And in the eyes of most people—notably the clerics—it was a caustic example of how their society had been misled by foreigners seeking to merely exploit Iran and her people.

The events at Persepolis in 1971, far from being viewed as Iran's victorious "coming out" party as a modern, industrial state, served as the equivalent of Marie Antoinette's apocryphal statement to the impoverished masses of pre-revolutionary France: "let them eat cake!" It was a continual reminder of how decadent the life of the foreign-supported Shāh was compared to the lives of the dispossessed, impoverished masses of Iran. It would become a galvanizing event—permanently saved on video reels—and the Shāh's enemies among the Shiite clerics would constantly use it to harangue and harry the Shāh's dubious standing among the Iranian people.

A few years thereafter, in 1976, the Shāh abandoned the Islamic calendar in favor of the ancient pre-Islamic calendar. This was yet another sign of the Shāh's opposition to the role of the Shiite clerics in Iranian society. Modernization, the economic downturn, imperial decadence, and unwanted foreign influence were leading to the downfall of the well-meaning—if, at times, misguided—Shāh. A snowball effect of revolution was happening, and all that was needed was a leader to pick up that snowball and throw it at the unwitting Shāh. Such a man was in the offing, an old enemy and a highly regarded religious figure whom the Shāh had exiled a decade before: Ruhollah Khomeini.

The White Revolution was the most serious modernization program in Iran. At first, it was also hugely successful economically. Tehran became a modern city, and as Iranian capacity increased, so too did Iran's importance to the West. Not only was Iran a major oil-producing state for the West, but it was also the strategic lynchpin for containing Soviet expansion into the Middle East. It had formed the anchor for what was known as the "Baghdad Pact," or the Central Treaty Organization (CENTO), a sort of NATO alliance for the Middle East that consisted of Turkey, Iran, Iraq,

Pakistan, and Great Britain.[5] Outwardly, Iran had made true progress toward becoming a major player on the world stage as it had never done before. Sadly, although that progress was outwardly strong, it had been built upon a foundation of sand.

The problems of the White Revolution were twofold: the economic benefits of the modernization program had been unevenly distributed. The rapid industrialization of the country led to the massive dislocation of entire communities that had, over the course of many generations, become dependent on preindustrial methods for earning a living. This exacerbated the socioeconomic divide.

The second problem of the White Revolution would ultimately lead to the Shāh's undoing in 1979: the land reform program redistributed privately owned land from the wealthy to the impoverished. Specifically, it redistributed land that clerics had owned for generations to less fortunate Iranians. This redistribution, coupled with the Shāh's drive for modernization, led Iran's Shiite leaders to believe that the Shāh had effectively declared war on them. In many ways, the Shāh had done just that. Like his father, though, he was picking a fight with an entrenched institution that had a far greater relevance to ordinary Iranians than the monarchy did.

Then there was the Shāh's promotion of women's rights in Iran. This served as a final nail in the political coffin of the aging Iranian monarch.[6] Like the actions of the Shāh's father, Reza Khan, the empowerment of women in Iran was a bridge too far for many Iranians. Each time women have been granted a modicum of civil rights beyond what the *Qur'an* specifically outlines (as the clerics interpret it), political instability has erupted.

The uneven distribution of wealth, the displacement of traditional jobs and lifestyles brought about by the Shāh's massive modernization push, the opposition from the religious establishment to the Shāh's

5 "The Baghdad Pact and the Central Treaty Organization," U.S. Department of State, Accessed on 5 December 2020. https://2001-2009.state.gov/r/pa/ho/time/lw/98683.htm

6 "Iranian Women—Before and After the Islamic Revolution," BBC, 8 February 2019. https://www.bbc.com/news/world-middle-east-47032829

policies, and the granting of women's rights formed the perfect admixture for the political cocktail that led to the Shāh's downfall. Within no time, all of these factors congealed—with the religious establishment stoking the rage of common Iranians—into extreme antipathy toward foreigners, specifically the British and American influences in Iran.

IRAN, OPEC, AND THE BEGINNING OF THE END

For the modernization program to have succeeded, the Shāh had to maintain unbroken economic growth. He may have been able to accomplish that if he had not become embroiled in the politics of OPEC. Founded in 1960, the Organization of Petroleum Exporting Countries was designed to better regulate the price of oil *to ensure that its members got a fair market value for their product.*

OPEC is considered a cartel that favors the sellers of oil rather than the consumers of the product. In most cases, cartels are illegal. In the oil industry, there's no getting around the collective power of OPEC.

OPEC had five founding members: Iran, Iraq, Saudi Arabia, Kuwait, and Venezuela. The cartel held its first meeting in Baghdad, Iraq, in 1960. The cartel was designed to do three major things for its members. First, OPEC was meant to keep oil prices stable. The average acceptable price of oil for OPEC member states has been anywhere between $70 and $80 per barrel of oil. Analysts believe that at those prices, the collective stock of oil held by the OPEC member states would last about 113 years. When prices decline, OPEC members agree to cut production of oil to artificially inflate the price—thereby keeping the global price of oil generally in that $70 to $80 range.[7]

Further, the cartel was intended to preserve oil as a precious commodity, the lifeblood of the economies of the OPEC member states, for as long as possible. Without the collusion of OPEC member states, each oil producer would act individually; they would all compete with each

[7] Kimberly Amadeo, "OPEC and Its Goals, Members, and History," *The Balance,* 10 July 2019. https://www.thebalance.com/what-is-opec-its-members-and-history-3305872

other to produce more oil and sell it at a lower cost. When the global price of oil plummeted, demand for a more affordable product would spike, further draining the supply of oil, a nonrenewable resource, in these countries. Once their oil reserves were drained, the OPEC leaders feared that their countries would yet again be in the proverbial backwater of global politics, for the world's energy consumers would move to other regions that had more bountiful oil supplies or use innovation to move entirely away from the use of oil.

A cursory examination of the news would inevitably lead viewers to see that the price of oil varies. It is a highly volatile product. This volatility is based on the realities of oil production. For the oil market to be stable, oil producers must drill for oil all day, seven days a week. Whenever oil production goes offline for any period of time, the price fluctuates. When the global price of oil gets off balance, a tweak to production often lets the price return to the level oil producers prefer.

Stability is key because the oil-producing countries want to ensure that the world's energy consumers of the world do not feel a pinch in their wallets when they refill their cars. Should consumers feel squeezed by high prices, they may begin looking for alternative energy sources, whether renewable resources (think wind, solar, nuclear, or hydropower) or domestic fossil fuel sources (natural gas or oil shale). Price stability keeps everyone happy.

The third mission of OPEC was to manage the world's oil supply. Whenever there is a disruption, the cartel steps in and helps to overcome the effects the disruption. Saddam Hussein took millions of barrels of oil offline, and other OPEC countries stepped in to produce more oil to make up for Iraq's loss of production. Without the capabilities that the cartel provides its members, the oil industry would likely die.

Before the 1970s, the United States was a major oil producer. It could supply its own needs and was entirely self-sufficient. In the year 1970, however, the United States reached "peak oil."[8] In essence, ana-

8 Marc Lallanilla, "Peak Oil: Theory or Myth?" Live Science, 12 February 2015. https://www.livescience.com/38869-peak-oil.html

lysts then believed that most of the easily accessible oil in the United States had already been tapped. Anything else that could be gotten would be too expensive to tap into.

At this time demand for oil in the United States had reached record levels. As a result, President Richard M. Nixon opted to eradicate the import quotas that were meant to keep the United States from becoming overly dependent on any single foreign supply of oil. His goal was to rapidly meet the growing demand for oil *without* disrupting the economy at home. The result of these decisions was that the energy supply of the United States became increasingly insecure.

In the words of Andrew Scott Cooper, "America's thirst for cheap oil quickly soaked up any excess capacity, tightening the market to the point where prices began spiraling upward for consuming nations everywhere."[9] Inevitably, America's newfound dependence on Mideast oil was exploited for the vulnerability that it was. The Arab members of OPEC voted to stop selling to the United States and its Western allies because they had supported Israel, a blood enemy of the Arab states, in the Yom Kippur War. The Shāh of Iran kept producing and selling oil to the Americans, in defiance of OPEC.

When asked by the *New York Times* in 1973, the Shāh explained his deep concerns about any nation relying exclusively on oil. "Oil should be used for derivatives like petrochemicals," he said. "It seems a sin to use it for heating houses and lighting electrical bulbs. Why not develop coal, atomic energy, solar energy?" the Shāh inquired. But he did not stop there. The Shāh admonished Western governments by saying, "They closed [their] coal pits. They didn't bother to find other sources of energy. They fixed low prices. Now they will have to pay the price." During the incredible interview, done just six years before his regime was overthrown and his grand plans for Iran were dashed, the Shāh defended his decision to continue trading with the Americans

---

9 Andrew Scott Cooper, "A Tale of Two Oil Shocks, Part I: 1973–1976," PBS, 15 June 2012. https://www.pbs.org/wgbh/pages/frontline/tehranbureau/2012/06/a-tale-of-two-oil-shocks-part-1-1973-76.html

even though other Muslim powers in the Arab world (though they were Sunnis) had embargoed the West. He argued that, "I will not accept anyone's pressures, friend or foe … they say we are not Moslems, but we are Aryans. Iraq—a very good Moslem neighbor—did not take part in the embargo. Neither did Nigeria nor Indonesia, which is 90 percent Moslem … I am here to defend the interests of my own country."[10]

However, the Shāh took advantage of his American ally's weakness at that moment and used his position as an OPEC leader to force a drastic increase in the global price of oil. According to Cooper, "the price of oil increased 470 percent in the span of *a single year.*"[11]

Because of the 1973 decision to continue pumping oil and selling it to the West, though, the Iranian economy eventually was wrecked by inflation. As I explained above, the oil market has traditionally been volatile. The major reason for OPEC's creation, at least in part, was to mitigate the volatility of the oil industry. That's the nature of the beast. As the oil revenue into the country increased, it prompted more spending for the Shāh's pet modernization programs. Yet the country could not absorb the massive revenue quickly enough and was ultimately slammed when inflation eventually hit.

One critic described the Shāh's modernization programs for Iran as full of "outrageous simplemindedness."[12] In fact, the Shāh moved too far, too quickly. As he was alienating the clerics at home and terrorizing his people with the SAVAK, his domestic security service, the monarch's reforms weren't yielding the results he had promised. To compound the direness of his situation, the Shāh had twisted the proverbial knife

---

10 Bernard Weintraub, "Their Oil Embargo," *New York Times,* 22 December 1973. https://www.nytimes.com/1973/12/22/archives/shah-of-iran-urges-arabs-to-end-theiroil-embargo-shah-of-iran-urges.html

11 Cooper, "Tale of Two Oil Shocks."

12 Scheherazade Daneshkhu, "The Political Economy of Industrialisation in Iran, 1973–1978," London School of Economics, p. 6, Accessed on 8 December 2020. https://etheses.lse.ac.uk/2794/1/U615743.pdf

in the back of his American allies by more than doubling the price of oil. When inflation inevitably hit, not even the Shāh's regime could spend the massive amounts of money it had accrued from the hike in prices quickly enough to save the economic or political situation in Iran.

Another costly oil crisis would plague Iran in 1979, around the time that the Islamist revolution in the country was reaching a peak. The Iranian revolution began in earnest in 1978. At that time, Iranian oil production was slashed. In response to this sudden decrease in production, countries began hoarding their oil, and global price spikes ensued. Surging demand, according to one report, was caused by the booming global economy at that time as well as the precautionary hoarding that began when Iranian production was cut. This increased the oil prices further.[13] All of this would play into the hands of the Shāh's domestic enemies, notably the clerics who were leading the revolution against his reign.

The Shāh's course to oblivion was irrevocably set. His rendezvous with destiny was at hand. Unbeknownst to the Western powers that had come to rely on Iranian oil supplies and the relative—but superficial—stability of the Shāh's absolute rule, the days of predictability from both Iran and the wider Middle East were over. What would come next would resonate from 1979 until the present. Not only would Iranian oil be removed from Western supply, but the Pandora's box of Islamist extremism would be opened—with no way of putting the horrors back inside that ideological box.

More dangerously, the slow but steady push for Iran to gain nuclear weapons began in the final years of the Shāh's tenuous reign.[14] And this move would fundamentally alter the direction of the Middle East and US foreign policy, and it could possibly lay the groundwork for the next world war, which I fear the world today is rapidly racing toward.

---

13 Laurel Graefe, "Oil Shock of 1978–79," Federal Reserve Bank of Atlanta, 22 November 2013. https://www.federalreservehistory.org/essays/oil-shock-of-1978-79

14 Brandon J. Weichert, *Winning Space: How America Remains a Superpower* (Alexandria, VA: Republic Book Publishers, 2020), p. 153.

11

KHOMEINI PLAYS WESTERN

ELITES LIKE FOOLS

IN 1962 THE Shiite holy leader, Ruhollah Khomeini, began his mission to overthrow the Shāh's autocratic rule in earnest. He challenged the Shāh's rampant modernization program. Specifically, Khomeini and his coreligionists reviled the women's rights that the Shāh had demanded his countrymen embrace.[1]

Khomeini declared the Shāh an apostate who was making war on

---

1 "Women Protest in Iran, Shout 'Down with Khomeini,'" *Washington Post,* 9 March 1979. https://www.washingtonpost.com/archive/politics/1979/03/09/women-protest-in-iran-shout-down-with-khomeini/84d3a780-738a-4dfd-a2a5-c7d4f546323c/

Islam and its holiest leaders. Khomeini was a revered figure in the Shiite community. A year later, he agitated against the Shāh so vociferously that massive riots broke out in the country. Khomeini was arrested by the SAVAK, the internal security services of Iran.

As Khomeini languished in prison, he likely believed that he would soon suffer the same fate as his old friend Navvab Safavi. That Shiite firebrand had once supported the Shāh against Mossadegh, but then turned on the monarch when the Shāh refused to impose shariah law in Iran. Fearing for his life, Khomeini's fellow religious clerics named him an ayatollah, a subject "worthy of emulation" in the Shiite faith. Under Iranian law, ayatollahs were exempt from the death penalty. Therefore, executing him—the likely end of Khomeini's imprisonment—would have led to unforeseen events far more unpleasant than any political upheaval the Shāh had endured until that point.

Yet it was a precarious time for the Shāh. The year 1962 was the same year that the Shāh traveled to the United States and met with JFK to reaffirm America's commitment to his regime. As it would happen, 1962 was also the year when the White Revolution went into effect, which slowly galvanized the clerical elite against the Shāh. Given how highly Khomeini was esteemed by the Shiites of Iran, the Shāh did not believe he could do to Khomeini what he had managed to do to Navvab Safavi a few years before.

By allowing Khomeini's promotion to an ayatollah, the Shāh believed that he was appeasing the Shiites in Iran who were skeptical of his modernization program. As an added measure, the Shāh then exiled Khomeini in 1964. Believing that Khomeini was now far removed from the political scene, the Shāh went about executing his modernization plan while squelching opponents who remained in Iran.

Even though the gains of the modernization program were unevenly distributed, it was still viewed favorably by most Iranians. That would all change when the 1970s began. As you've read, the oil shocks, rapid inflation, and granting of women's rights, to name just a few things, empowered the Islamists in Iran as never before. Marxist groups in

Iran, the Fedayeen-e Khalq (FEK) and Mujahadeen-e Khalq (MEK), had been so successful in inciting massive protests against the regime, based on economic grounds, that the Soviet Union, for which these two groups were unapologetic proxies, was unprepared for.[2]

The Soviets wanted their Marxist proxies to overthrow the pro-American Shāh and replace him with a pro-Soviet revolutionary regime. Marxist guerillas stirred the pot among the Iranian people, taking advantage of the economic downturn in the late 1970s to promote their cause. Alongside them, however, arose another group of guerillas—Islamic reactionaries—led by the clerical establishment.

Khomeini, who had spent his time living in exile in Turkey, Iraq, and eventually France, knew the time was at hand for his grand return.

Ayatollah Ruhollah Khomeini had lived among the Shiite communities of southern Iraq and in Turkey. However, his greatest achievement came when the French government allowed him and his compatriots to reside at a posh retreat in Neauphle-le-Château, just outside Paris. There Khomeini would enhance his links to the Western elite while living beyond the reach of the Shāh's security services. The ayatollah honed his skills at manipulating the West during this period.

At the end of the Second World War, the European continent was left in ruins, becoming nothing more than a geopolitical hot potato for the two superpowers, the United States and Soviet Union, to fight over. Many assumed that national rivalries between the European states were dead. But old patterns die hard in an ancient place like Europe. Long before the rise of the superpowers and the immolation of European power in the cauldron of two world wars, states like the British Empire and France had tussled for global wealth, power, and prestige. Although dormant, these impulses had never been totally eradicated by the world wars or the Soviet threat in the Cold War.

---

2 "Fedā'iān-e Ḵalq," *Encyclopædia Iranica*, 7 December 2015. https://www.iranicaonline.org/articles/fadaian-e-khalq

Iran was a land of great wealth and opportunity. In the eyes of the world, the British and their American allies had exploited Iran deftly for a long time. The British dominated the growing arms trade in Iran, and the Americans had come to take the lion's share of the oil trade there. The French fumed over having been mostly left out of the payday in Iran.

Yet the Shāh's government was very interested in what we would now refer to as alternative energy. Specifically, the Shāh wanted to make Iran a nuclear energy power. And to acquire the knowledge and industrial base needed to create an indigenous nuclear energy capability, the Shāh turned to the French—who were much more advanced in this field. The French were more than willing to create positive trade relations in a niche industry that neither the Americans nor British had yet monopolized.

When the French government permitted Khomeini and his followers to set up shop just outside of Paris, it was hardly altruistic. There were several machinations at play. It has long been rumored that Paris offered to assassinate Khomeini and his followers for the Shāh so they could curry favor with the Iranian ruler and make him more amenable to French overtures. Another aspect explains French permissiveness toward Khomeini; as the British and Americans would eventually conclude, the French felt the Shāh's days were numbered. The religious element in Iran was preferable to the communists. If the Shāh did fall, then the French logic was that it was better for the most likely next Iranian leader—Ayatollah Khomeini—to owe the French government for safe harbor in his hour of extreme need.

In a sense, Khomeini had always been a foreigner in a foreign land. According to various reports, in particular those of Gregory Copley, a former adviser to the Shāh and president of the International Strategic Studies Association, the Ayatollah Khomeini was not Persian. His mother was Kashmiri, and his father was British. In 2016, Melik Kaylan reported in *Forbes* that he possessed documents that corroborated these explosive claims. If these claims are true, it makes sense that Khomeini would have little problem adapting to life in Turkey, Iraq, or even

France after he was exiled from Iran.

For his part, Melik Kaylan has described the evidence about Khomeini's true parentage as "raw."[3] However, Gregory Copley, insists that it is true. Others have asserted this as well, though corroboration is difficult because most people who had direct knowledge of Khomeini's parentage are dead and much of the documentary evidence in Iran has been either destroyed or altered by the regime over the years.

Nevertheless, much about these claims is obviously true because we know that Khomeini himself as well as the regime worked assiduously to keep a lid on biographical aspects of Ruhollah Khomeini. The Islamist regime in Iran clearly believed that honesty about Khomeini's parentage would have undermined his image as the father of a pure Islamist revolution in Iran. The leaders of the Islamic Republic also feared that knowledge of this truth would ruin the regime's overall legitimacy. Think about it this way: If the regime was born from the mind of a half-British non-Iranian, how could it possibly be legitimate, given the Islamic Republic's propaganda that it was the true representation of both Islam and Iranian national identity?

Kaylan reported that Khomeini's father was a British adventurer named William Richard Williamson, who ultimately found a home in Iran and soon converted to Shiism. Although Williamson is a relatively obscure figure today, in his time he was quite the notorious rapscallion. He was a true Victorian (born in 1872), or at least that was the image that author Stanton Hope created of Williamson in his 1951 biography *Arabian Adventurer: The Story of Haji Williamson,* Williamson had chafed under the strictures of English society and fled his homeland aboard a British merchant ship, setting out for Britain's vast empire.

Unhappy with life aboard the merchant ships he had come to call "home," Williamson headed to the United States, where he had a variety of jobs, ranging from actor to cowboy. Still, Williamson could not find happiness or peace—that is, until he landed in the Middle East.

---

3 Melik Kaylan, "Was Khomeini's Father a Brit?" *Forbes,* 8 October 2009. https://www.forbes.com/2009/10/08/ayatollah-khomeini-british-ahmadinejad-iran-opinions-columnists-melik-kaylan.html?sh=309a15d21a53

Soon, William Richard Williamson became Haji Abdullah al-Zobair. He donned the traditional garb of Shiite holy men, taking two Islamic wives—one of them believed to be Khomeini's mother—and eventually raising his many children in the traditional Shiite way. Inevitably, Haji was exiled by Reza Khan during the period between the world wars, because Reza Khan believed Haji was a British agent. (Who could blame Reza Khan for these concerns?)

Haji's first two children were perfect students who went on to become ayatollahs themselves. His third son, the future Ruhollah Khomeini, was an unruly child who initially did poorly in his studies. Failing to make a name for himself in the holy city of Najaf, the future grand ayatollah migrated to Iran's holiest city, Qom.

While there, the future ayatollah soon chose to make the name of the city of Qom (or Khom) the basis of his name—Khomeini. As you've also read, it was while studying in Qom that he became a protégé of the Ayatollah Borujerdi and eventually befriended Navvab Safavi, a member of the Muslim Brotherhood.

When he was 11, Khomeini's mother moved he and his brothers to Northern India for a period of time. According to Khomeini's brother, Ayatollah Pasandideh, the reason for why neither Khomeini nor his siblings were as well-versed in the native Persian language was due to the fact that they had spent so much time living in Northern India. Of course, officially the reason that Khomeini and his family moved to India was because his father, Seyed Moustafa Hindi, was murdered when Khomeini was a young boy. Yet, if the rumors about Khomeini's true father being a British expatriate are true, it would make sense that he'd be moved outside of Iran—especially if his mother was from the subcontinent.

While living in France, though, Khomeini carefully cultivated a media profile very different from the one he had established in the Middle East. Most Iranians knew Khomeini from his picture: a tall, stern, elderly man, clad in the traditional black and white robes of a Shiite holy leader, with his long white beard that indicated his prestigious spot in the Islamic faith. They also knew his voice: a vitriolic warble that constantly castigated the regime in Iran for its impiety, called on the holy to resist the lure of Western decadence, and urged the faithful to impose shariah law at all costs.

But in the West, the same images—a tall bearded elderly man who wore the robes that Shiite leaders have worn since the seventh century—led most elites to view Khomeini as a friendly old shamanic figure. Khomeini seemed simple to the postmodern Western elites. He was a throwback to a bygone era in the most amusing sense. But Khomeini was neither friendly nor simple. In fact, Khomeini was savvy enough to play the role of mystical New Age healer. Iranians at home understood what Khomeini was and what he intended for their country. Westerners, however, were blissfully clueless. And Khomeini, whose heritage was possibly a cross between West and East, could navigate these two different cultural waters expertly.

Culture matters. The ability to navigate foreign cultures is important for anyone traveling or living abroad. Khomeini was not in France seeking political asylum; he was there to live as an ordinary person would—or that was the French government's explanation for allowing such a controversial figure to live in France. However, his ambitions were purely political. And Khomeini never intended to stay in France for long. Thus, Khomeini excelled at exploiting the biases of the elites of France. Khomeini and his inner circle were especially skilled at this. The longer they stayed in France, the wider their circle of support became in the West too.

Remember, the West in the 1960s and 70s was dominated by the hippie counterculture and the New Left.[4] In fact, France was one of the first places where this postwar leftist reaction to Western tradition had occurred.[5] By the time that Khomeini and his coterie of advisers found

4 "Spirit of 68: French Countercultural Art—In Pictures," *The Guardian*, 23 February 2017. https://www.theguardian.com/artanddesign/gallery/2017/feb/23/spirit-of-68-french-countercultural-art-in-pictures

5 Eleanor Beardsley, "In France, the Protests of May 1968 Reverberate Today—And Still Divide the French," NPR, 29 May 2018. https://www.npr.org/sections/parallels/2018/05/29/613671633/in-france-the-protests-of-may-1968-reverberate-today-and-still-divide-the-french

themselves in exile in France, the country had been going through its painful "hangover" from the turbulent 1960s.[6]

At this time in the West, the New Age guru was all the rage.[7] The West had lost its faith in its own institutions and religious traditions.[8] Something else was needed. The raw materialism and greed of the 1980s had yet to rear its ugly head. In the 1970s, Eastern medicine and alternative lifestyles inspired by the East had all become huge fads—especially among the Western elite. The well-connected in France and the wider West, if they knew anything about Khomeini at all, believed him to be nothing more than the next Maharishi Mahesh Yogi, the storied Indian guru who rode with the Beatles.

Khomeini played on the condescension and ignorance of his hosts and managed to gain advocates for his return to Iran at the highest levels. He very often downplayed his exhortations to kill the unbelievers who supported the Shāh in Iran. Even as he let loose wails of "Death to America!" and "Death to Israel!" in his infamous recordings that were played from the rooftops in Iran during the dark days of the Islamist revolution, the Western elites dismissed these statements as mere posturing (if they were aware of them at all).

Then again, the ability of Western elites to remain giddily ignorant of totalitarians in their midst, even when those totalitarians (such as Lenin, Stalin, and Hitler) explicitly tell you—repeatedly—what they intend on doing, has always been part of a tragic pattern that repeats itself every generation. It is likely that this same wishful thinking was at play when dealing with the bearded grand ayatollah. It was far easier to believe he was a New Age mystic and healer, just as it was easier for Europeans

---

6 Damon Linker, "Why I Miss the Gritty Greatness of the 1970s," *The Week*, 28 March 2014. https://theweek.com/articles/448596/why-miss-gritty-greatness-1970s

7 "The Rush of Gurus," The Pluralism Project, Accessed on 8 December 2020. https://pluralism.org/the-rush-of-gurus

8 Mary Eberstadt, "How the West Really Lost God: A New Theory of Secularization," The Heritage Foundation, 30 May 2013, YouTube. https://www.youtube.com/watch?v=DcVyz5C3LPY

to believe that Lenin was a democrat, that Stalin was a utopian central planner of the first order, or even that Hitler "could make the trains run on time" rather than accept that Khomeini was a new representation of an old archetype in Islamic history: a rigid enforcer of shariah law, a seventh-century death-dealer in a postmodern twentieth-century world.

Strangely, France and almost every other Western nation had embassies in Tehran. The Farsi speakers assigned to those embassies undoubtedly heard Khomeini's disembodied voice urging on the bloodlust of the benighted Iranian people, exhorting them to take power from the Shāh. They likely also heard Khomeini's sermons, spoken in his gutter Farsi (he spoke Arabic far better than he ever spoke the Persian language), commanding his followers to make ready to burn Israel off the Mideast map and to make war upon the Americans—all of whom the old paranoiac Khomeini believed were secretly in their midst, conspiring to sap the purity and strength of true Islam.

What's more, Khomeini's exile, which had initially placed him at the periphery of Iranian politics and allowed other potential revolutionary stars to rise in Iran, ended up benefiting Khomeini. The ayatollah could avoid sullying his hands directly in the bloodletting that led to the Shāh's downfall. In fact, when the ayatollah was staying in Iraq, Saddam Hussein offered to "disappear" the ayatollah and his coterie on behalf of the Shāh. The Shāh declined Saddam's offer—much to both men's enduring regret. Thus, Khomeini could appear to be above the fray—all while manipulating his Western hosts and the desperate Iranian people into doing his bidding (which, of course, they all blindly did).

Khomeini also played on the Western concerns about the spread of Soviet Communism. Most people in the West who were monitoring the events in Iran understood that Marxists constituted the most visible elements raging in the streets. While the religious element was present, Western eyes—even the Shāh's eyes—were fixed firmly on the Marxist elements in the streets. Few dared to think that there could have been a rival revolutionary (technically, counterrevolutionary as many clerics saw it) force in Iran to the Marxists. There was. And Khomeini and his followers formed the nucleus of that movement.

Yet, knowing that the Western intelligence agencies were more concerned about the Marxists, Khomeini perfected his message to Western elites in Paris, London, and even Washington: support me and my movement because we are better for your interests than either the ailing Shāh or, obviously, the Marxist radicals are. Khomeini assured his Western audience that the Islamists of Iran, if they gained power, would respect the interests of the West while preventing the spread of Soviet influence into the region. Khomeini was an expert on playing up Western fears of the Marxists and the spread of the Soviet Union while downplaying the threat the Islamists posed to Western interests. As you'll see, Khomeini's manipulation of the West would prove to be the West's undoing in Iran.

12

AN ISLAND OF INSTABILITY

IN A TURBULENT SEA

IN 1975, the Shāh took the extraordinary step of disbanding all political parties in Iran—including those that supported his reign. As you've read in previous sections, since the 1905 constitutional revolution, the proliferation of political parties had often increased the threats to the rule of the Shāh. Rather than face this prospect out of apathy or fear of the ramifications, the Shāh opted to force everyone into a new party, known as the Resurrection Party.

The name "resurrection" was critical to understanding what the Shāh was doing. Between his White Revolution and his disbanding of political parties in favor of the united (which was anything but)

"Resurrection" party, the Shāh was engaged in state building on an epic, though ham-fisted, scale. He was struggling to reconnect Iranians with their ancient, pre-Islamic past in order to make a quantum leap into the future—or at least, that was his reasoning.

The move caused a stir among the Shāh's Western allies. The Western nations grew despondent at the ways the Shāh was squelching any hope of democracy in Iran. A crisis in US-Iranian relations was coming to the forefront. Not only were Iranians becoming increasingly restive under the old order of the Shāh, but Americans were chafing under the perceived corruption and failures of their own leadership at home—and were weary of exporting those failures abroad.

America's elite institutions and its news media quickly picked up the mantle of cleaning America's conscience by holding its autocratic allies accountable. Mike Wallace of CBS News travelled to Iran to interview the autocrat in 1976. Glowering at his American interlocutor, the Shāh flippantly asked, "What is democracy anyway?"

Undeterred, Wallace pressed his truculent subject, clearly trying to get the Iranian monarch to concede that he had violated some unspoken norm by not allowing democracy to flower in Iran. Remember that Iran was an ancient nation with very little experience of Western democracy. "How do you define 'democracy'?" Wallace inquired, preening still further by asking, "Don't we have democracy in the United States?"

The Shāh blithely retorted, "Well, not according to what the Greeks used to say in the public places."[1]

---

1 The first case of Greek democracy arose in the famous city-state of Athens around 500 BCE. It was fundamentally different from the representative democracy that the United States technically is today, as well as from the social democracies of Western Europe, Canada, Japan, and South Korea today. Athens existed under a regime of direct democracy wherein all adult citizens were required to take up an active role in Athenian politics. If Athenian adult citizens did not participate in politics, they could be fined, or some would have red paint splashed on their robes as a mark of shame for not fulfilling their duty to Athenian democracy. The definition of citizen in ancient Athens was different from what it is in the West today. Citizenship was extended only to male Athenians who were not slaves. Citizenship was not conferred upon women or children either. Thus, people in those groups were excluded from voting. In ancient Athens, each year, 500 citizens were chosen to actively serve in the government for one year. These 500 were charged with running the government and making laws. Whenever new laws were proposed, all citizens of Athens had to attend assembly and vote on the measure the day the vote took place. That is nothing like American democracy—or democracy as it is practiced anywhere in the West today.

Wallace, not understanding the reference to ancient Greek politics, pushed on, "[Americans] elect [their] leaders. *You* are *not* elected."

In Washington, you see, democracy is superficially correlated with elections. Decades later, this idiotic postulation would prove to be America's undoing in the Sunni Arab world, when George W. Bush took the country to war in Iraq and Afghanistan to "spread democracy." Or in 2006, when the Bush administration, believing elections equated to democracy and, therefore, legitimacy, supported the takeover of the Gaza Strip by Hamas. This same foolish assumption on the part of Western elites would also form the basis of the Obama administration's bizarre alliance with Islamists in Libya, Egypt, and Syria during the so-called Arab Spring. These ignorant assumptions can all be traced back to the 1970s, when America was unknowingly first coming into contact with the scourge of Islamism in Iran.

Wallace's comment evoked a stinging rebuke from the Shāh, "Yes, but how do you elect your leaders? According to Watergate, it's a special kind."

Mike Wallace still did not comprehend where his subject was coming from. "You will acknowledge that the United States is much more democratic than in Iran?" Despite his seemingly polite New England accent, Wallace's question seemed more like an accusation than honest inquiry.

Indignant, the Shāh again demanded to know what Wallace's definition of democracy was. Wallace, a typical byproduct of elite society in the post–Vietnam War and post-Watergate America, began rattling off perceived freedoms that were present in the United States but not available under the Shāh's rule in Iran. "I mean freedom of thought. I mean freedom of expression. I mean freedom of the press ..."

Arching his eyebrows and puckering his lips, the Shāh spoke over Wallace's bullet points and demanded, *To what extent? To what extent?*

Wallace trilled on, reciting his list of star-spangled awesomeness, "I mean electing leaders. I mean opposition ..."

Undaunted, the Shāh insisted again, "To what extent?"

Wallace burbled some more platitudes about freedom but apparently got lost in a verbal maze of his own misconceptions, born out of the privilege endemic to all American elites: the belief that everyone and everything in the world must be just like them. After much hemming and hawing from Wallace, he eventually realized his subject was unmoved by the superficial bromides that he was offering to the autocrat. Confused and alone in the conversation, Wallace finally gave up and exasperatedly asked the Shāh, "Well, to what extent?"

The Shāh's eyes flashed with anger; his face was stern, and his tone remained hushed albeit harsh. Yet the next words the Iranian monarch spoke were less an answer to Wallace's inquisition than it was a general complaint, possibly even an accusation, directed against his erstwhile American allies. The Shāh's response would perfectly sum up his reign and betray his true—negative—view of the United States.

"Yes, to what extent?" The Shāh mused, clearly sensing his victory in his rhetorical tête-à-tête with the haughty American reporter. The Shāh pressed the apparent advantage he enjoyed over his interlocutor and argued further that, "If it is a self-destructive, masochist kind of [democracy] that would permit you all kinds of fraud and corruption, [America has] it."

The Shāh fired one last parting shot at Wallace when he sneered, *"The permissive democracy!"* at the mere mention of the United States.[2]

The Shāh's assessment of America's political failings wasn't necessarily wrong. Fair was fair, after all. Had not Wallace and America's leaders goaded the Shāh to embrace political standards and processes that were not at all a natural component of either Persian or Islamic society?

Had not the United States, especially after Watergate, appeared to be a democracy adrift? A power in the throes of terminal decline? Who were the Americans to define successful governance to an ancient country with a rich history like Iran?

---

2 "Mike Wallace Interview with the Shah of Iran in 1976," BBC News, 8 April 2012. https://www.bbc.com/news/av/world-us-canada-17650516

In fact, the Shāh's complaints about America's democracy would sound right at home with many American voters today, on both the right and the left. What's more, before the Vietnam War and the Watergate scandal, his skepticism about democracy in Iran was shared by most American elites. The times may have changed in America, but Iran, one of the most ancient polities in the world, remained stubbornly resistant to such change—especially change imposed upon them by soft-headed, preening Western journalists with only a superficial understanding of the way the world worked.

Like the members of the Eisenhower administration and the Churchill government who had assisted him in the 1953 coup against Mohammad Mossadegh, the Shāh himself worried about how democracy in Iran would weaken his country and stunt the rapid progress his regime had made toward modernization. Wallace and other elites of the sullen post-Vietnam era in the United States gleefully ignored the hard-fought wisdom of those who came before them, like Eisenhower. America's painful experience in Vietnam had clearly eradicated any appreciation of the sacrifices made by Americans who had come before Wallace's generation of elites. American democracy, according to the diatribes of the time, was broken. Rather than address that problem at home, many Western elites sought to impose an unrealistic—and superficial—standard of democracy upon other countries—even when that absurdly high standard harmed American interests.

For starters, Mike Wallace's view of democracy had conflated elections, freedom of expression, and women's rights with democracy itself. In fact, these are merely byproducts of healthy democracies. Such elements are norms in a democratic society. They are not, however, *prerequisites* for democracy. Such democratic norms cannot be imposed either from above or outside—especially in traditional societies that have little experience of either democracy or modernity. And these democratic evolutions cannot arise until the institutions supporting a stable rule of law have been created. Democracy evolves and adapts to suit the needs of the culture embracing it.

This is why no two democracies are identical in their makeup. Since the end of the Cold War, though, Western elites have fetishized democracy to the point that it has become a noose wrapped around America's neck.

How is allowing for anti-American Islamists to arise and take power in a strategically vital territory, like the Middle East, good for American interests?

Democracy has become a secular religion that has lost all of its meaning. It is, today, unmoored from what it once was. If America must deal with the morass of Mideast politics, then it should try to find regimes there that are complimentary to its interests. And when it does, whether that regime is a secular autocracy or a medieval monarchy, Washington must work with those regimes as they are, rather than wish for them to become democracies that inevitably will be weak and susceptible to manipulation by well-organized Islamist movements inimical to the United States and religiously opposed to Western values.

Just look at the first pangs of democracy that appeared in Iran in 1905: it was brought about by the conservative clerics and the business community. It was *not* imposed by the Shāh. Further, the proto-democracy that grew in Iran following the 1905 constitutional revolution did not last very long once the highly influential clerical establishment abandoned it in the wake of Reza Khan's incessant impositions upon that constitutional order.

Much like the old Ottoman sultans, the various special interest groups in Iran, like the clerics or business community, favored a form of consultation with other political entities as well as the Shāh to come to a democratic consensus. The Iranian consultation process was similar to the way other democracies in the world functioned, yet it was still a distinctive feature of democracies that were forming in the Islamic world.[3] So the first phases of Iranian democracy came out of the conservative Shiite establishment. In the West, while Christianity influenced

---

3 Joseph Liu, "Islam and the West: A Conversation with Bernard Lewis," Pew Research Center, 27 April 2006. https://www.pewforum.org/2006/04/27/islam-and-the-west-a-conversation-with-bernard-lewis/

society and the democracies that eventually formed there, its impact was different. Inevitably, most Western democracies would insist upon some degree of compartmentalization between the dominant Christian faith and government. This was born, at least theoretically, out of Christ's command to "render unto Caesar what is owed Caesar and render unto God what is owed God." Islam's impact on Iran's early democracy was not only far more direct, but integration of religion and state was openly encouraged by most Iranians who had sought democratic reforms.

The expectation that Iran needed to be pressured into embracing Western democratic norms when so much about Iran was in flux was not just absurd, but in this author's opinion, downright obscene. Frankly, the standard imposed upon Iran and other nations by the West was cultural imperialism. In this way, then, we must refer again to the arguments regarding Western imperialism as it came to Iran. While I maintain that modern Iran has been far more impacted by Iranians, irrespective of the country's interaction with foreign entities like the British, Russians, or the Americans, the fact remains that American elites *did* put great pressure on the Shāh to alter the way he was governing the country. This did impact the Shāh's decision-making process in the dark days of the revolution in 1979—and not for the better.

The Western elites who berated the Shāh may have meant well. But these Western elites contributed significantly to the downfall of the oldest governing institution in Iran's history, the monarchy. They also paved the way for the rise of a radical theocracy that poses an existential threat to America's interests and allies today. Whereas the 1953 coup simply strove to restore the ancient monarchy of Iran—the actual legitimate head of state in Iran—the Western obsession with rapid democratic change in Iran was doomed to fail from the start because it had little support from Iranian culture.

The 1970s was a crisis of confidence in Western polities.[4] Vietnam

---

4 CBS News, "CBS News Archives: Carter's Famous 'Malaise Speech,'" John Dickerson, 1:46 (2011), YouTube. https://www.youtube.com/watch?v=0tGd_9Tahzw

and Watergate had shattered the post–World War II consensus (and many illusions that Americans had of their own country). Riots and cultural upheaval plagued most Western states. Mike Wallace's cringe-worthy and condescending interview with the autocratic Shāh provides historians with an interesting dichotomy. At a time when most Americans had simply lost faith in their own democracy, they berated critical allies, like Iran, for their lack of democracy. They did this to an important ally because it had not lived up to the impossibly high standards *that not even the United States could meet—a point the Shāh had delighted in making to Wallace's face.*

Iran had not broken any Western notion of democratic norms, for Iran *was not* a traditional Western power, no matter how much the Shāh desired to embrace Western technology, style, and practices. Why else would the Shāh have insisted on honoring the legacy of Darius, whose pre-Islamic dynasty nearly conquered the Greeks and came close to ending Western civilization just as it was starting 2,500 years earlier? The Shāh had simply behaved as all Iranian (formerly Persian) rulers had behaved. In fact, his modernization programs, while too ambitious for his own good, did achieve their basic goals in the end: by the time he was overthrown in 1979, the country was modern, and its standard of living had been elevated as well.

There is another point of contention to be had with Western theorists who argue that Iran suffered from a "resource curse." A resource curse, or the "paradox of plenty," refers to "countries that underperform economically, despite benefiting from valuable resources." What's more, it occurs when "a country focuses all of its production means on a resource-dependent sector." Over time, despite whatever modernization the development of that resource may have supported in the country (in this case, Iran), a limit will be reached in how much more development can be achieved by relying on the one commodity that allowed the modernization of the state to occur in the first place.[5]

---

5 Jason Fernando, "Resource Curse," Investopedia, 22 October 2020. https://www.investopedia.com/terms/r/resource-curse.asp

The narrative of the resource curse is reminiscent of a Greek tragedy. It is less a sober academic assessment of reality than a dramatic narrative initially furthered by Marxist theorists in the West.[6] Under the Marxian dialectic that pervaded mid-twentieth century academia, the West, specifically the United States and Britain, was wholly to blame for most of the ills found in the world. The claim has been unquestioningly embraced by at least three generations of theorists in the West. The popularity of this narrative among some of our most prominent academics proves how corrupted by ideological fads the modern academy has become.

It's not that foreign influence didn't have an impact on Iran's development. Of course it did. The reality is, however, that the resource curse narrative implies causation for the decrepit state that Iran—and the wider developing world—has found itself in since the twentieth century, but no causation exists.

Western academic literature is laden with diatribes about the tragedy of resource wealth. However, it should be noted that without oil—and Britain's need for that precious commodity—Iran would have *never* developed into the relatively modern state that it is today. The resource curse isn't really accurate. A resource is neither a curse nor a blessing.

Instead, a resource is just a fact of life for some countries, with positives and negatives—like all other aspects of life. What matters is how indigenous rulers whose lands are "cursed" with a vital resource, like oil, adapt their states for surviving—and thriving—in the modern world. Internal politics, more than resources or the foreigners who yearn for them, remains the key determinant of whether a state "cursed" with a vital commodity prospers or not. For Iran, the biggest factor in determining the country's viability in the modern era was the influence of its clerics, as well as its tumultuous history with its fellow Muslim neighbors.

As Peter Kaznacheev of the CATO Institute has astutely argued, "a combination of secure property rights, a favorable tax regime, minimal

6 Jonathan Di John, "Is There Really a Resource Curse?" *Global Governance,* 17, no. 2 (2011), 167–184. https://www.jstor.org/stable/23033728?seq=1

red tape, and a strong entrepreneurial culture"—essentially, strong and healthy domestic institutions—are far more important for determining the success or failure of resource-rich nations than whether they're cursed with resources or not.[7] Rarely are these internal factors fully controlled by the interference or influence of foreign powers on a resource-rich country. Nevertheless, the amount of scholarship supporting the resource curse narrative is far greater than the research conducted into alternative explanations that have more merit.

Had the Shāh remained in power, he might have managed to push Iran's standard of living much higher too. We will never know what possibilities might have been realized for Iranians today had the Shāh—as autocratic as his reign was—been kept in power. What we do know is that what came after the Shāh was quantitatively worse than what had come before, not just for America or the wider Middle East, but for ordinary Iranians today.

Strangely, though, the dreary-eyed elites who ruled the West insisted on forcing their idealistic—and impossible—version of democracy on other states in the Middle East. Washington chose to engage in a social engineering project in Iran, a country whose survival as an American ally was essential for America's overall Cold War strategy. Rocking that boat would generate far too many geopolitical waves for America's own good, or so the Western elites who had built the world order after the Second World War believed.

What's more, the boat itself could capsize through all of the rocking. Yet the Western elites of the 1970s were reckless. The proverbial boat ultimately did capsize and, as you will read, it happened precisely because Washington kept meddling in things it did not completely understand. But it sure made those Western elites feel good! Today, we might call this "virtue-signaling." Whatever you want to label it as, it's utterly stupid.

---

7 Peter Kaznacheev, "Curse or Blessing? How Institutions Determine Success in Resource-Rich Economies," CATO, 11 January 2017. https://www.cato.org/publications/policy-analysis/curse-or-blessing-how-institutions-determine-success-resource-rich

As a man who led a large nation bordering the Soviet Union, the Shāh fully understood the threat Moscow and its communist ethos posed to his country. He knew that if a democracy arose in Iran, it would be divided and fractious. Such division would weaken Iran, making it a tempting target for the communists, who were better organized and disciplined than Iranian democrats were. This pattern had been seen earlier throughout the developing world in the Cold War, and it explains why so many nations, large and small, were unable to resist the totalitarian pull of communism. More than anything, the Shāh was a fierce anticommunist and a dedicated Cold Warrior.

Pressuring him at such a tenuous time for the United States on the world stage (and at home) was a terribly inept thing to do. Yet that is precisely what the West did. And Western leaders would thoughtlessly continue doing so to its other autocratic allies, from that point until the present. In future chapters, you will read how Western policymakers' utopian vision of democracy—from both political parties—has led to such disasters as the Iraq War, the Libyan campaign, and the insanity currently plaguing Syria.

13

AMERICA'S MALAISE AND

THE SHĀH'S IDEOLOGICAL HAZE

MIKE WALLACE'S 1976 TRIP to Tehran was a mere prelude to the greater spectacle to come. After all, Jimmy Carter was elected to the presidency in the same year as that fateful interview. The Vietnam War that had eviscerated American politics was followed on by the tumultuous presidencies of Richard M. Nixon and, later, Gerald R. Ford. Not only had Nixon presided over the economic disruptions of the early 1970s, but he had also been forced out of office due to his complicity in the Watergate scandal.

Gerald Ford, Nixon's vice-president, assumed office after Nixon resigned because of the Watergate scandal. Ford entered the presidency when the office was at its weakest point. Ford was thus hamstrung by congressional investigations. He was unpopular among the American people after his decision to pardon his predecessor, Nixon, for his involvement in Watergate. For their part, most Americans had tired of the Cold War—as well as the economic uncertainty of the era. Therefore, Americans ultimately voted for Jimmy Carter when he ran against Ford in 1976.

Jimmy Carter, who had been the Democratic governor of Georgia, was the least experienced candidate to run for the presidency in years. Carter campaigned on a populist message and used his relative inexperience in national politics as a symbol that he was uncorrupted, unlike his last three predecessors (Democrat Lyndon B. Johnson and Republicans Richard Nixon and Gerald Ford), all of whom had been creatures of both the Democratic and Republican Party establishments. Also, Carter's devout Southern Baptist faith helped him achieve the image of incorruptibility that he had painstakingly cultivated. Few among America's political elites took Jimmy Carter's candidacy seriously. His victory shocked many political experts in Washington—and sent chills down the spines of the leaders of America's autocratic allies, like the Shāh of Iran.

Carter had spent time as a nuclear engineer in the United States Navy, serving aboard submarines. He was a protégé of the legendary submariner Admiral Hyman Rickover, and most people who knew Jimmy Carter—including his wife, Rosalynn—assumed that the thirty-ninth American president would have risen to become an admiral in the United States Navy. In fact, this had been Carter's ambition for most of his career.

But Carter was compelled to resign from the Navy in order to help his aging parents' peanut farming business in his home state of Georgia. He abandoned a very promising career in the Navy to run that family business, much to the chagrin of his colleagues as well as his wife, Rosalynn, who fancied herself as an admiral's wife. Eventually, the compounding scandals of the LBJ, Nixon, and Ford administrations pulled the Southern Baptist back into national affairs. Carter first became governor of Georgia and then challenged the embattled Republican incumbent, Gerald Ford, for the presidency.

Ford, despite his lack of popularity, was still seen as a moderate and reasonable leader by many Americans. Carter eschewed running against Gerald Ford directly in the campaign. Instead, he ran against the nation's unhappy memories of Richard Nixon. The strategy ultimately worked. Ford was forgettable, but Nixon was the archvillain of American politics at that time, much as George W. Bush or Donald J. Trump would be in their times. By running against the memory of Nixon, Carter's strengths as an incorruptible outsider and a populist appealed to the weary American voters.

Despite his relative inexperience in national politics, voters admired Carter's personal faith and appreciated that he was unlike any other politician who had run for the presidency in their lifetimes. Carter spoke in flowery language about America's role and reminded people of how John F. Kennedy, whose memory in death shone brighter than his actual record, had spoken about the country. Carter warned voters about the threat that America's newfound dependency on foreign oil posed, a common concern echoed by many presidential candidates even to this day. Jimmy Carter's background in nuclear engineering gave his prognostications about the future of energy in the United States an air of credibility that his opponents lacked. And after the oil shocks in 1973, many Americans were eager to find ways to wean the nation off its dependency on foreign sources of oil.

More importantly, Jimmy Carter openly campaigned on a promise to make human rights a key tenet in US foreign policy if he were elected.[1] This resonated deeply with Americans. After all, Americans at that time were just learning about certain abuses that America's intelligence community had committed in the country's name, purportedly to fight the Soviet Union in the Cold War. No American wanted the nation to be

---

1 Nigel Hamilton, *American Caesars: Lives of the Presidents from Franklin D. Roosevelt to George W. Bush* (New Haven: Yale University, 2010), p. 319.

seen as either imperialist or villainous. Yet thanks to actions taken by a succession of American presidents in the Cold War, that was precisely how many people globally viewed the United States. The struggle for human rights, therefore, made Carter popular with many people.

Many Americans believed that the arrogance of the country's politicians had misled the nation into the wildly unpopular Vietnam War and created the various scandals that had come to dominate the intelligence community. How many of their loved ones might have still been alive if America's leaders not been so corrupt or ignorant? Could Vietnam have been avoided altogether if a greater focus on human rights had been at the center of postwar US foreign policy?

A succession of America's Cold War leaders from both parties, had made compromises between American ideals and what those leaders considered tough, though necessary actions to fight the Cold War. Particularly, the voters had been turned off by Richard Nixon's and Gerald Ford's *realpolitik* in foreign policy. The amoral tenets of *realpolitik,* many believed, had caused the grotesque excesses that were being revealed daily by congressional investigators throughout the 1970s.[2]

Carter's focus on human rights was a shot across the bow, not only to the Soviet Union, which was birthed in blood, but also to many of America's Cold War partners. From Latin America to Saudi Arabia to the Shāh's regime in Iran, the United States had routinely supported dictators over democracy. Washington had understandably feared the spread of communism. As you read in earlier chapters, American leaders worried that new democracies would be too weak to resist the totalitarian

2 *Realpolitik* is defined by Britannica as "politics based on practical objectives rather than ideals." However, this definition hardly does the movement justice. As Henry C. Emory elaborated, the concept finds its origins from turn of the twentieth-century German political thought. In fact, it is more closely synonymous with political realism, and Emory warns of the danger that this realism can easily slide into materialism, which is ultimately self-defeating, since there is always a spiritual and idealistic component to human beings that should be respected. Dr. Henry Kissinger, who served as national security adviser and secretary of state to Richard Nixon as well as the secretary of state to Gerald Ford, is the most famous modern person associated with this school of thought in the United States. In fact, he popularized it throughout his storied career.

pull of the Soviet Union. Rather than risk supporting unstable young democracies and, by extension, human rights, the leaders of the United States often favored the stability of autocrats, such as the Shāh.

All of that would change under Jimmy Carter. Realism would be replaced by idealism. The stability and strength of autocracy would be replaced with the hopeful promise of democracy throughout the world. The Cold War would morph into a hot peace. Or, at least, this was what Carter envisioned. As those who lived through the Carter administration will remember, Carter's vision outstripped his ability to implement such a daring plan.

Jimmy Carter's election was as much a negative reaction by American voters against US foreign policy as it was a reaction to the domestic uncertainty and perceived corruption of Watergate. It is true, however, that Carter paid lip service to the importance of the Shāh's leadership in Iran, just as his predecessors had done. However, it should be noted that Carter's crusade for human rights in US foreign policy essentially baked the Shāh's overthrow into the proverbial cake. It is unclear if Jimmy Carter fully understood the implications of his chosen crusade in US foreign policy. As you will see, however, evidence has come to light that casts doubt on whether Carter's Iran policy was caused by simple incompetence or something more nefarious (possibly a combination of both?)

While on a multination tour, President Carter and his wife decided to spend New Year's Eve in 1977 with the Shāh of Iran. In a glitzy, star-studded evening in Tehran, the American president toasted the Iranian autocrat, even though his human rights violations should have made him a great enemy of the Carter foreign policy. Despite Carter's campaign rhetoric, however, he gleefully declared that the Shāh's Iran was an "island of stability" in an increasingly chaotic Middle East.[3]

In fact, Carter had envisioned getting the Shāh's help on the three major policies that he had campaigned on. First were investments

---

3 Peter L. Hahn, "How Jimmy Carter Lost Iran," *The Washington Post,* 22 October 2017. https://www.washingtonpost.com/news/made-by-history/wp/2017/10/22/how-jimmy-carter-lost-iran/

into viable alternative energy, such as solar power and nuclear energy. Carter also needed assistance on resolving the Israeli-Palestinian conflict. Finally, he wanted the Shāh to help create a nuclear arms treaty with the Soviet Union.

There was something more ominous, though, about Carter's "island of stability" speech. Carter had cultivated his saintly image well. And an American public weary of scandal and corruption was all too happy to believe the image of Carter as an unsullied man seeking power only to do the bidding of the people, rather than the special interests his predecessors had served. Yet politics was still politics. Even a politician as inexperienced as Carter does not reach the highest office in the land *without* patrons of his own special interests and loyalists expecting a return for their support of his unlikely political rise.

The "Georgia Mafia" was the name that *Time* used for the coterie of close Carter advisers who had risen from obscurity in Georgia politics and entered the White House with Jimmy Carter.[4] Whatever these young liberal guns lacked in experience, they more than made up for in ambition. They were fiercely loyal to Carter. They also had little compunction in engaging in corruption of both a professional and personal manner. The Georgia Mafia believed in Carter's vision of post-oil world. These political operatives, though, were still political operatives. In their minds, there was no reason why they couldn't be idealists, remain loyal to Carter's agenda, and still get a cut of the financial action of any nuclear energy deal the Carter administration brokered with the Shāh.

One notorious area of engorgement at the public trough was the bipartisan banquet line that had formed at the Shāh's palace over the years. According to Copley, Carter's "Georgia Mafia" wanted in on that particular action, just as the courtiers of every White House from Truman to Carter had desired. Oil was not the only commodity in Iran. The Shāh's commitment to modernization meant that Iran needed an

---

4 "The Nation: The President's Boys," *Time*, 6 June 1977. http://content.time.com/time/magazine/article/0,9171,914991,00.html

assortment of materials and services from the West. One technology that the Shāh desperately wanted to build was nuclear energy. Brown Boverie, a highly respected Swiss energy company, entered into a nuclear energy development deal between the Swiss company, the Atomic Energy Organization of Iran, and the Shāh.[5]

Copley, a former adviser to the Shāh, recalled that like the last few American presidents, Carter expected the Shāh to cut members of his inner circle in Washington a favorable slice of the deal. Yet when Carter's "Georgia Mafia" met with the Shāh to ask for a cut of that deal, the Shāh declined to help them. As the Shāh explained at the time to Copley, the Brown Boverie deal had already been concluded before Carter's associates had expressed an interest in it. What's more, according to the Shāh, the deal was not as large as the so-called "Georgia Mafia" had been led to believe.

It wasn't long after these events that Carter's support for the Shāh soured. This event was a portent of the disaster that was already taking shape in Iran. At the same time as these events, Soviet-backed Marxist guerillas in the Mujahedin-e Khalq (MEK) and the Fadā'iān-e Kalq (FEK) were agitating the people against the Shāh's reign—precisely when the economy in Iran was beginning to slow.

The Shāh had monitored Jimmy Carter's bid for the presidency closely in 1976. When Carter was elected president, the Shāh knew he had to make some concessions. President Carter was not going to drop the human rights platform he had campaigned on. And the Shāh, even though annoyed with the Americans, could not drop his alliance with them. The Shāh wanted to curry favor with the new American president, so he slowly started to grant political concessions to his detractors and opponents in Iran.

In the run-up to Carter's visit to Tehran, the Shāh began releasing some political prisoners. Further, he allowed Western human rights

---

5 US Embassy Tehran to Department of State, ERDA HQ Washington D.C., 11 May 1977. https://nsarchive2.gwu.edu/nukevault/ebb268/doc14b.pdf

organizations to have a *small* presence in Iran. As Christian Caryl describes, "Activists quickly took advantage of the chink of freedom to establish high-profile [human rights] campaigns. New political groups formed, and lawyers and writers signed declarations criticizing the government." According to Caryl, during this period a West German-backed cultural institute in Tehran "sparked a series of public demonstrations that show-cased the dissatisfaction of the middle-class intellectuals."[6]

In this morass, the Marxist guerillas—with the full backing of the Soviet Union—began piling on, attempting to galvanize a real over-throw of the Shāh. Slowly, the clerics began getting involved. Soon the streets were filled with middle-class intellectuals who were dissatisfied with the slow pace of democratization, Marxist as well as Islamist stu-dents, workers who'd lost their jobs, and a variety of other dispossessed groups in Iranian society. As Lenin once quipped about revolutionary Russia, in Iran, the power was running in the streets, just waiting for someone to pick it up. Would it be the Marxist guerillas or the Islamists?

Carter became increasingly uncertain about the Shāh's reign. The Shāh had given an inch to his political opponents in order to curry favor with the Carter administration. As a result, the Shāh had effectively validated the expiration date that so many had tried to stamp on his regime. What the Shāh believed would be a trickle of political reforms that would allow his regime to continue its modernization drive proved to be an unstoppable flood of revolution.

With the Islamist revolution gaining momentum in Iran, the Shāh would be asked by foreign reporters if he was worried about the religious revolt against his reign. The Shāh understandably fixated on the Marxist threat to his regime. Not only was the Shāh a committed anticommunist, but he also understood that the MEK and FEK communist guerillas in his country were far better organized and much more committed to his overthrow than the religious establishment was. Even though people like

---

6 Christian Caryl, *Strange Rebels: 1979 and the Birth of the 21st Century* (New York: Basic Books, 2013), p. 138.

Khomeini opposed the Shāh's reign, the doctrine of Shiite quietism was still strong at the start of the revolution, and many clerics recognized the greater threat that the Marxists posed to Iran.

When asked about Khomeini, the Shāh answered a French broadcaster that the Khomeinist challenge to his rule was "not serious." Watching the Shāh, one would get the impression that he had believed that he was truly untouchable. Of course, he was quite insecure at that moment—not just because his enemies were climbing over the gates, but because he was very sick.

In 1973, Iran's ruler had been diagnosed with lymphatic cancer. This was partly the reason for his expedited and expansive modernization drive. The Shāh was uncertain of when he would die, so he wanted to leave his country in as good of a condition as he could before he ultimately passed. No one seemed to consider how the economic and social reforms that the Shāh was rapidly implementing would make democratization a dangerous prospect for the long-term stability of the country and survival of his regime.

In addition, according to one of his former advisers, Gregory Copley, the Shāh's wife helped to obscure just how severe the Shāh's illness was. In fact, as the revolution erupted, the Shāh was increasingly medicated on a potent cocktail of drugs that effectively made him passive and unable to focus. It was as though history itself was conspiring to oust the besieged Shāh.[7]

A year after his visit to Tehran, during which the newly elected American president heralded Iran under the Shāh as an "island of stability" and after the Shāh had denied the "Georgia Mafia" access to the Brown Boveri deal in Iran, President Jimmy Carter met with other world leaders in Guadalupe, Spain. By this time, the protests in Iran had devolved into outright street battles between the Shāh's well-armed

---

7 Amir Rosen, "How One Man's Illness May Have Changed the Course of Middle Eastern History," *Business Insider,* 13 October 2014. https://www.businessinsider.com/how-the-shahs-cancer-may-have-changed-history-2014-10

forces and the far greater numbers of ordinary Iranians who had risen up against the monarch.

When the subject of the Shāh arose in conversation between President Carter and French President Valéry Giscard d'Estaing, Carter quipped that "the Shāh was through."[8] From that moment onward, the Shāh's rule was effectively over. Without the support of the Americans, the Shāh would be overthrown; it only was a question of "when" and by "whom." Was Carter planning to betray a man he had heralded as an "island of stability" just one year before the meeting in Guadalupe? Recently declassified evidence suggests that, yes, Carter was at the very least amenable to ousting the Shāh and replacing him with none other than the Ayatollah Khomeini!

---

8 Jean-Michel Vecchiet, "Iran: The Hundred Year War," 1:00:10-13 (2008), Amazon Prime.

14

CARTER'S "PLOT" TO

OVERTHROW THE SHĀH

TEN MONTHS INTO THE REVOLUTION, the Shāh had become paranoid and isolated. Iran's ailing monarch did not know who to trust. The Iranian ruler saw plots behind every door in his palace. The Shāh had ignored the increasingly desperate pleas from his military leadership to let them take sterner measures against the Islamists and Marxist groups who were terrorizing the streets of Iran.

In a strange turn of events, the two most powerful elements of the revolution in Iran were not only the communists that the Islamists had spent years decrying but ultimately the Islamists themselves. In fact, these two groups had been working together to multiply the impact of their revolutionary activities.[1] Revolutions make strange bedfellows indeed!

The Shāh, who was fully aware of how vulnerable his reign was, certainly thought it was necessary to protect his regime. Yet the Shāh believed that President Carter's commitment to human rights abroad imposed serious limitations on him. At such a precarious moment, Iran could not risk alienating its major American ally by killing its citizens in the streets. Until the Americans and British offered a plan to ensure the Shāh's reign, as they had in 1953, he could not countenance moving on his own.

The Shāh believed that the Americans would swoop in to save him in the eleventh hour, as they had done during the 1953 coup against Mohammad Mossadegh. Back then, the Shāh had fled the country, leaving it to Mossadegh. Had it not been for the CIA's intervention, the Shāh would have never returned to power in 1953.

Of course, as you've read, the Iranian military was as supportive of the Shāh during the 1953 coup as the British and the Americans were. In fact, the British and, later, the Americans had simply piggybacked onto the Iranian military's effort to secure the Shāh's status in Iran during the 1953 coup. Without the Iranian military's support in 1953, the Shāh would have never returned to power.

During the 1979 Iranian revolution, the Shāh's military was desperate to stamp out the protests rampaging through the streets. Remember that throughout Iran's history, whether it be the 1905 constitutional revolution or during the 1953 coup, protests—often violent ones—were a common occurrence. They did not necessarily presage an overthrow. But they could be the harbinger of an overthrow if the regime did not move to contain the protests and if the religious leadership in Iran got behind the protest movement. Had the Shāh acted when his military advisers wanted to, at the start of the crisis, not only would he have secured his position in Iran, but the loss of Iranian life would have likely been minimal.

1 Abdolrahim Javadzadeh, "Marxists into Muslims: An Iranian Irony," (2007), FIU Electronic Theses and Dissertations, pp. 91–125. https://digitalcommons.fiu.edu/cgi/viewcontent.cgi?article=1051&context=etd

Despite what many Americans were led to believe about the infamous 1953 coup, the CIA had not spearheaded the painstaking planning for the coup against Mossadegh. It was Britain's MI6, as well as the Iranian military, that planned the successful covert operation.[2] The CIA, led by former President Theodore Roosevelt's grandson Kermit Roosevelt, simply piggybacked onto the fully developed British plot to keep the Shāh in power—and then quickly claimed all of the credit, much to London's chagrin at the time. This is important because by 1978, the British had all but abandoned the Shāh out of the "cold calculation of the national interest" and had started working closely with the Khomeinists.

In fact, the British would continue working with the new Iranian regime for many years after the overthrow of the Shāh. Margaret Thatcher's government sold tanks and arms to the Khomeinist regime. She had believed that the Islamists would be a vital bulwark against Soviet expansionism. Meanwhile, British military advisers would help to train the post-Shāh Islamist military of Iran and provide critical intelligence the theocracy needed to exterminate the last bits of communist opposition within Iran by 1982.[3]

As it would soon turn out, President Carter, a devout Southern Baptist who had his own problems with the Shāh, was also willing to work with Khomeini and his Islamists. Just as Thatcher viewed Khomeini at first, Carter believed that Islamism could be a vital shield against Soviet adventurism in the Middle East. According to many sources, not only did Carter hold these positive views of Khomeini and his Islamist movement, but there is also evidence suggesting that Khomeini sought—and received—audiences with the Carter administration, in which he offered himself as a replacement for the unpopular Shāh.[4]

---

2 Ralph Fiennes, *Coup 53,* Taghi Amirani, (2019; London: Amirani Media), film.

3 Mark Curtis, "Britain and the Iranian Revolution: Expediency, Arms, and Secret Deals," Middle East Eye, 1 February 2019. https://www.middleeasteye.net/opinion/britain-and-iranian-revolution-expediency-arms-and-secret-deals

4 Kambiz Fattahi, "Two Weeks in January: America's Secret Engagement with Khomeini," BBC, 3 June 2016. https://www.bbc.com/news/world-us-canada-36431160

Shockingly, Carter was amenable to this scenario as long as Khomeini prevented any harm to American interests in Iran. In fact, the strategy of aligning US interests in the region with Islamist movements was nothing new. The Carter administration had already implemented this policy during the covert war against the Soviet Union in Afghanistan, which occurred around the same time as the Iranian revolution.

The Americans were in the hotseat during the Iranian Revolution. As you've read thus far, Jimmy Carter led the United States with a completely different view of the world—particularly the Middle East—than his pre–Vietnam War predecessors, such as Dwight D. Eisenhower, had. The British had bailed on the Shāh and were beginning to forge links with his rivals in anticipation of his overthrow. Carter seemed open to doing the same.

The Americans were utterly undependable during the Islamic Revolution in Iran. On the one hand, American representatives constantly spoke approvingly of their alliance with the Shāh. However, behind closed doors, elements of the Carter administration were making secret deals with Khomeini and other opponents of the Shāh. It was a desperate time, and desperate people were in charge everywhere, making bad calls in the heat of the moment, based on incomplete information and even less understanding of the region.

In essence, the situation was bleak for the Iranian monarchy. Neither the Shāh nor his reputed allies in the West were offering direction. There was only paralysis. Revolutions, as the character Tom Zarek in the 2009 series *Battlestar Galactica* reminds audiences, rarely "hinge on some grand operatic idea or 'the will of the people.' [Revolutions] hang on cumulative moments, each one building on the next, and *it can be lost with the slightest hesitation!* [emphasis added]"[5]

The Shāh waited in vain, watching as the situation in his country deteriorated all around him, as it had in 1953. The key difference was

---

5 *Battlestar Galactica,* Episode 13, "The Oath," John Dahl/Mark Verheiden/Richard Hatch, January 13, 2009, SyFy Channel.

that the Americans had not been forthcoming in their assistance for the Shāh as they had been in 1953. The Shāh was right to be paranoid. At the very least, the Carter administration did not have the appetite for assisting Iran's military in suppressing the revolt and securing the monarchy. Many around the Shāh feared that Carter and the British were doing more than resting on their laurels: they were actively working with Khomeini to depose the Shāh before the far scarier communists in Iran could overthrow the monarchy and make Iran a conduit for Soviet power in the region.

The Shāh was simply stunned that the United States responded to the revolutionary threat as lazily as it had. Despite the power that Khomeini wielded over the masses protesting in Iran, the Shāh was still more worried about the Marxist threat. There had to be a reason for American intransigence, beyond Carter's baffling obsession with human rights over his own national interests.

How could Washington fail to plan an operation to protect their stalwart ally in Tehran? Did the Americans not realize how much damage Iran's fall would cause to their network of global alliances? It was believed that a failure to come to the Shāh's aid would cast doubt in the minds of America's other partners in the Cold War about the worth of those alliances.

Soon the Shāh became convinced that an American covert action was underway in Iran. However, unlike in 1953, the Shāh came to believe that the CIA was plotting a coup *against* him, similar to the 1967 coup against Greece's King Constantine. Recently declassified material, as well as the firsthand experiences of people who were advising the Shāh at the time, indicate that President Carter wanted to replace the old Iranian monarch with Khomeini.

The Carter foreign policy team was divided. The official narrative even today is that Washington simply did not see the revolution coming. Certainly, most policy experts in Washington, DC were numb to the needs and wishes of ordinary Iranians. At the same time, though, it is unlikely that it would have taken almost two years for the Carter administration to recognize the threat posed to their Iranian ally.

After all, one of the biggest gripes about Carter as the nation's chief executive was that he was a martinet. One might say it was the curse of an engineer: viewing everything and everyone as one might view a nuclear reactor on a submarine. In the formulation of Nigel Hamilton, "The president, like Captain Queeg, refused to listen to his crew, however, and the chaos in the White House grew only worse."[6]

If Carter was as controlling and committed to his ways as historians and even many of Carter's contemporaries have claimed, how could Carter have missed the threat to the Shāh for so long? How could Carter not have formulated some backup plan for dealing with a post-Shāh Iran?

Maybe the Shāh's suspicions about Carter were correct. According to people in the Shāh's orbit I spoke with, that is precisely what they believed. The domestic opposition to the Shāh provided Carter with a chance to change the situation in a way that would favor both his supporters in Washington, who wanted a greater cut of all of the new deals being made in Iran, and Carter's overall human rights agenda. *It was a classic two-fer.*

WILLIAM SULLIVAN THINKS THE UNTHINKABLE IN IRAN (AND GETS IT WRONG)

Enter Ambassador William Sullivan, a colorful figure with a long and somewhat sordid history in the world of covert affairs. During the Vietnam War, Sullivan had served as the US ambassador to Laos.

His tenure there ran concurrently with the infamous CIA covert operations program that was waging war upon suspected communists in both Laos and Cambodia. Both those countries were involved in the Ho Chi Minh Trail, the network of trails linking North Vietnam to South Vietnam. The popular image is that US ambassadors are always in conflict with their CIA counterparts, but Sullivan was a proponent of the covert war in Laos and Cambodia. His passion for covert operations

6 Hamilton, 315.

never left him, even after he had left Indochina.[7]

Although Sullivan had helped to negotiate the secret accord between the United States and the Soviet Union that barred foreign fighters from taking refuge in Laos, the North Vietnamese did not abide by those terms. They had set up at least 10,000 of their fighters in the country and gave generous support to the Pathet Lao communist insurgency in Laos. In turn, the American covert war in Laos expanded exponentially—with Sullivan's assistance.[8] While there were strategic reasons for waging that war, the covert campaign in Laos and Cambodia not only destabilized the local governments but also paved the way for the rise of new regimes in Indochina that were pro-communist.

The covert wars fought in both Laos and Cambodia are generally viewed as failures by most historians.[9] What's more, they were illegal. The results were devastating for the region. In fact, Sullivan was involved in some of the worst excesses of those covert wars in Indochina. As various congressional investigations were uncovering these abuses throughout the 1970s and early 1980s, these bloody and illegal covert wars turned many American voters against the whole Cold War—thus allowing Jimmy Carter's human rights campaign to be such a hit with the Cold War–weary American voter when he campaigned for the presidency.

Despite his controversial background, however, Sullivan found himself as the US ambassador to Iran. The silver-haired ambassador who had presided over the messy covert wars in Indochina was now present for the revolution in Iran. His flair for the dark arts of espionage,

7 William Branigan, "William H. Sullivan Dies at 90; Veteran Diplomat Oversaw Secret War in Laos," *The Washington Post,* 22 October 2013. https://www.washingtonpost.com/world/william-h-sullivan-dies-at-90-veteran-diplomat-oversaw-secret-war-in-laos/2013/10/22/f13e628c-3b2f-11e3-b6a9-da62c264f40e_story.html

8 Tim Weiner, *Legacy of Ashes: The History of the CIA* (New York: Anchor Books, 2008), p. 291.

9 Fredrik Logevall, "Laos: America's Lesser Known Human and Political Disaster in Southeast Asia," *Washington Post,* 2 February 2017. https://www.washingtonpost.com/opinions/laos-americas-lesser-known-human-and-political-disaster-in-southeast-asia/2017/02/02/a98c7368-dcc9-11e6-918c-99ede3c8cafa_story.html

assassination, and regime change—to say nothing of simple foreign intrigue—had not been lessened by the monumental failure of America in Vietnam. In typical Washington fashion, in fact, Sullivan viewed his experiences in Indochina favorably and was keen on applying to Iran the lessons he learned in Indochina. As Brad Pitt's character quipped to Robert Redford's character in the great 2001 film *Spy Games*, the US government has "some f-cked up barometer for success."

Sullivan was the embodiment of that broken barometer. Like the Bourbons of France, he learned nothing and had forgotten nothing of his time in Indochina. In the opening phases of the Iranian revolution, when it looked like nothing more than your usual demonstration of aging clerics and bitter student activists, Sullivan assured the Carter White House that there was nothing to worry about. However, within a year of making such wrongheaded assurances, Sullivan was frantically telegraphing the White House from the US embassy in Tehran, insisting that they make contact with anti-Shāh elements—notably the Grand Ayatollah Khomeini—to prepare for the end of the Shāh's rule.

From Sullivan, Carter likely got the idea that removing the Shāh and replacing him with the aging Shiite cleric would be an acceptable risk. Carter's own vision for Iran and the Middle East, his inherent distrust of the Shāh, and his idealistic view of himself as the great emancipator of the world combined with his ambassador's obsession with covert action. It was a sort of geopolitical hemlock that the Americans gleefully downed, with predictably disastrous results that still resonate today. For most American policymakers, much like the Shāh, their primary concern was preventing a communist takeover of Iran. They believed that Khomeini posed a minimal threat to American interests. After all, the *mujahideen* in neighboring Afghanistan were proving to be a strategic ally against the perceived Soviet push into the Greater Middle East.

Thanks to these mistaken calculations and ignorant suppositions, the hideousness of the Ayatollah was visited upon the desperate Iranian people—and the world. Carter believed that Khomeini represented a more stable future. As time progresses, history will continue to be unkind to Mr. Carter's time in office, his personal faith and commitment to helping others in his post-presidential life notwithstanding.

Carter's assumption that Khomeini's movement was not harmful to American interests was helped along by Khomeini himself. Ever the manipulator of naïve and ignorant Western leaders, the ayatollah had sent multiple letters to Carter, assuring the American president that his country's interests would be preserved in Iran. In fact, because Khomeini was considered an "object of emulation" in the Shiite faith, so many assumed that he was more popular than the Shāh. Carter's team was, therefore, open to replacing the unpopular Shāh with the far more popular ayatollah. The ayatollah insisted that under him, things in Iran would be even better for Americans than they were under the Shāh (who was known for acting independently from Washington at crucial periods throughout their relationship).

On November 8, 1978, Sullivan cabled Washington that the Shāh's rule could not be maintained. In his view, the law of diminishing returns was at play. How long would the Americans continue propping up such a feckless and corrupt regime that was so unpopular with the Iranian people? The telegram, titled "Thinking the Unthinkable," called for Carter to pressure Iran's elite Imperial Guards divisions, who were fiercely loyal to the Shāh, to abandon their king and embrace Khomeini.

The "Thinking the Unthinkable" memo went beyond simply outlining the facts on the ground as Ambassador Sullivan saw them. He advocated a strategy wherein Washington would get the Shāh and his hardline military leaders out of Iran. With the fiercely loyal top Iranian military leadership gone from the country, Sullivan urged Carter—with himself as the middleman—to broker a deal between the mid-level Iranian military leadership who would remain in the country and the ayatollah.

Because the Iranian military had deep ties with the United States armed forces, Sullivan, and others in Washington, believed that by brokering a deal between the Iranian military and the Islamists, they could keep a check on any of Khomeini's crazier ideas. The arrogance and ignorance of Sullivan and the Carter team continue to astound, as there was simply no way that the Americans would be able to control the events on the ground once the Shāh was forced from the Peacock Throne. Yet Washington believed it was the true puppet master, pulling the strings of all the local yokels in Iran.

According to a BBC report on the matter from 2016, President Carter was "displeased" with his ambassador for writing such an inflammatory cable (after all, that document would become a part of the public record on the Iranian revolution). Carter believed that Sullivan had overstepped his authority. Despite Carter's anger with Sullivan for the cable, the official claim that Carter stood by the Shāh until the bitter end is simply false. We know from recently declassified diplomatic cables from the time that the Carter administration took a far more nuanced approach to Khomeini than the official history currently describes.

Two months after the infamous Sullivan memo, for example, Carter changed his mind. He may have still been angry with Sullivan for the "Thinking the Unthinkable" memo, yet he ultimately embraced the memo in principle. In January of 1979, the American president began entertaining the notion of removing the Shāh and replacing him with the ayatollah. On January 3, 1979, the American president decided to "subtly encourage" the Shāh and his entourage to abandon their position in Iran.

Carter believed that the Shāh could quietly leave Iran under the guise of coming to the United States for a vacation in California—and then simply never return. It is even reported that Carter told his foreign policy team, "A genuinely non-aligned Iran need not be viewed as a US setback." For all of his intelligence, education, and erudition, Jimmy Carter was *utterly clueless* about how dangerous the Khomeinist revolt was, not only for the United States and the region, but for the oppressed Iranian people as well.

On January 4, 1979, Shapour Bakhtiar, a moderate who had previously served in Mohammed Mossadegh's short-lived democratic government, officially became Iran's prime minister. He was chosen by the Shāh because he was fiercely anti-Islamist and anticommunist. At issue for Bakhtiar was that he had made enemies of all three major camps in Iran: the communists, the Islamists, and the monarchists. He never had a mandate. Ambassador Sullivan insisted that Bakhtiar was deeply unpopular and would never overcome the opposition to his leadership. Sullivan continued to encourage Carter to make a deal between the generals in Iran and Khomeini.

Despite his opposition to the monarchy, Bakhtiar had aligned with the pro-Shāh generals in Iran and allowed them to close the Tehran airport in January. This happened because word had reached Tehran that the Grand Ayatollah Ruhollah Khomeini was planning a triumphant return from Paris. Both Bakhtiar and the pro-Shāh generals understood that allowing Khomeini into the country would tip the precarious balance of power in favor of the Islamists. With the Shāh leaving the country, as he had done shortly before the 1953 coup, the generals understood that preventing Khomeini from returning to Iran was their only hope of keeping power.

When Carter learned that Bakhtiar and the generals commanding the elite Imperial Guards were planning to shut down the Tehran airport, he deployed US Army General Robert E. Huyser, deputy commander of all US forces in Europe, to meet with the Iranian generals. There was mounting evidence that Bakhtiar and the generals were planning to fight to the death to defend their beloved Shāh from the rabblerousing Khomeinists and Marxists who had been terrorizing the streets *en masse.* The Carter administration feared a civil war inside Iran and wanted to prevent one at all costs.[10]

A civil war would not only put American military advisers in the country at-risk, but it would also risk letting sensitive American military technology to be poached—which could ultimately end up in the hands of the Soviets. What's more, a civil war would disrupt the vital

---

10 Andrew Scott Cooper, "Declassified Diplomacy: Washington's Hesitant Plans for a Military Coup in Pre-Revolution Iran," *The Guardian,* 11 February 2015. https://www.theguardian.com/world/iran-blog/2015/feb/11/us-general-huysers-secret-iran-mission-declassified?fbclid=IwAR3-1RSLXfuw0nIR hpahrjSFWEOR7N0l8Toug1rA4veIwPz1WevprGzloJ8

flow of oil from Iran and would probably destabilize the greater region. Washington feared that a civil war in Iran was precisely what Moscow wanted, and that prospect was their greatest concern, not the notion of a mad ideology, like Islamism, taking power in Iran.

Beyond that, Washington viewed the Iranian military as the most important institution in the country. It was the direct military-to-military links between the United States and Iran that served as a back-stop against the excesses and instability of the political and religious leadership of the country. The Americans reasoned that if they could ensure their chosen military leaders retained power and entered into the power-sharing agreement with Khomeini and his Islamists, they could check the radicalism of Khomeini and his followers.

A similar calculation was made by President Barack Obama during the ill-fated 2011 Egyptian revolution that catapulted the Islamist Muslim Brotherhood into power there. Obama and his people assumed they could work with the "democratically elected" Muslim Brotherhood leader, Mohamed Morsi, while backstopping his extremism by supporting Egypt's military, which was traditionally far friendlier to the United States than any other institution in that country.

In both instances, these assumptions would prove disastrous. Thankfully, the Egyptian military had far more institutional capacity to resist the imbecilic calls to Islamism after the 2011 revolution. Ultimately, Morsi and the Muslim Brotherhood were deposed from their positions of power in Egypt, despite what the Obama administration had wanted. In Iran in 1979, however, the country's military needed direct American support to accomplish a feat similar to the one that Egyptian military would carry out against rabid Islamists decades later—or similar to the 1953 coup against Mohamed Mossadegh, which was planned by the Iranian military but supported and led by the more powerful American and British intelligence services.

Because the Carter administration refused to offer such support, the Iranian military was unable to stand against Khomeini and his thugs. The Carter administration's actions (or inaction) would prove catastrophic for US foreign policy in the region. In Iran, the military could not survive without the Shāh. Had the military and internal security service been used—and given the support of their American and British allies—they would have likely managed to quell the uprising.

Whether or not the Shāh would have remained in power over the long term remains doubtful. His age and his struggle with terminal cancer at the time of the coup would have probably necessitated his abdication. However, it could have been done when the chaos in the streets had been quelled to ensure an orderly succession of power.

Instead, Carter dithered at a critical moment during the Iranian government's reaction to the revolution. The military did not support Bakhtiar anymore than they had supported Mossadegh in 1953. They were monarchists, not democrats. However, they preferred Bakhtiar to Khomeini or a Marxist for obvious reasons. President Carter had deployed General Huyser to Iran in January 1979 to ensure that the Shāh's generals stayed their hand and did not "jump into a coup against Bakhtiar" (as part of a larger strategy of making open war upon the Islamist and Marxist guerillas rampaging throughout the streets against the Iranian military's beloved Shāh). All throughout this period, Sullivan continued calling for Carter to include Khomeini in any post-Shāh regime, believing that Bakhtiar had little credibility with or support among most Iranians.

As Huyser romped around Iran, uninvited and unannounced, giving unsolicited advice to Iranian military officials, attempting to ensure that Bakhtiar was given a chance to lead Iran, the State Department had no faith in Bakhtiar as a reliable American partner. Not only was the Carter administration dithering at a key moment in the revolution, but classic Washington bureaucratic warfare was taking place just below the surface. The US military supported the Iranian military and desperately wanted to ensure that Bakhtiar had a chance to rule, even if only as a figurehead. Meanwhile, the State Department opposed these designs.

At the same time, the White House National Security Council, led by Zbigniew Brzezinski, hoped that the military of Iran would overthrow Bakhtiar and make a deal with Khomeini. This was their stance even after Brzezinski in particular had spent much time during the Iranian Revolution fighting to maintain the Shāh's power. Ever the anticommunist and seeing the writing on the wall, Brzezinski and his NSC staff were now advocating that Khomeini should be brought in from the cold, mainly because they believed that Islamism would be an effective counterweight to Marxist revolution in the region.

Within the Carter administration, a war over the revolution was taking place. Of course, disagreements among advisers during tense moments is nothing new for any administration. Yet the manner in which the multisided conflict erupted within the Carter administration undoubtedly contributed to the confusion and navel-gazing that Washington embraced at key moments during the Iranian Revolution. Most notably Brzezinski and Cyrus Vance, the secretary of state, were at loggerheads over whether or not to support a coup. The former wanted to support an immediate coup led by the Iranian military, whereas Vance wanted to avoid a coup at all costs.

For his part, Sullivan kept cabling Washington and undercutting Bakhtiar, causing chaos and confusion in the nation's capital every time he cabled back and complained about the "quixotic" Iranian prime minister or about how the Iranian military "would fold" like a chair if revolutionaries actually directly challenged it. Sullivan's running commentary was not helpful either in substance or form. He'd often tell colleagues, even Bakhtiar himself, one thing about what he believed was happening in Iran or how the United States should proceed while cabling the exact opposite statements to Washington.

In-fighting governed the American response to the situation, with President Carter making clear his intention to avoid a coup at all costs, while Bakhtiar and the generals could not muster an adequate defense of the regime from the Islamists. The Shāh's abdication did not ameliorate the dire situation in Iran, as many in Washington had hoped. And without the head of state, the regime did not have legitimacy in the eyes of the Iranian people. Instead, they increasingly looked at the crowds gathering in the streets and believed that the Islamists were preferable to the Marxists. Because Iran's military leaders could not strike fast and hard against the protesters, thanks to General Huyser telling them to stand down, the fate of the regime was sealed.

Bakhtiar formed a moderate government in January 1979 and attempted to govern. All of that ended a month later, when the Grand Ayatollah Khomeini returned to Tehran from Paris. His arrival marked the beginning of the end of a secular, liberalizing regime in Iran. And despite Khomeini's multiple promises to the West, a radical, bloody-minded clerical regime was about to begin.

15

THE GREEN REVOLUTION

TURNS RED

FOR THE MONTH OF JANUARY 1979, the Grand Ayatollah and his top aides met with representatives of the United States. After an exchange of correspondence between himself and the White House, Khomeini had at least enticed the Americans. Publicly, as noted earlier, the Americans did not openly abandon either the Shāh or the Bakhtiar democratic regime that briefly followed. But behind the scenes, both the Americans and British were already making calculations to keep Iran out of civil war and away from the Soviet Union's influence at all costs.

The recently declassified documents detailing the Carter administration's outreach to Khomeini are simply extraordinary. In one letter from Khomeini to Carter, the aging cleric declared, "You will see that we are not in any particular animosity with the Americans." Khomeini, downplaying his vengeful state of mind (despite his repeated threats in broken Farsi that were routinely played throughout Iran on loudspeakers to his throngs of followers) vowed that his proposed Islamic Republic would be a "humanitarian one, which will benefit the cause of peace and tranquility for all mankind." These words likely resonated with a panicked Carter, who strove to maintain American influence over Iran while not abandoning his utopian vision of a human rights–based US foreign policy that promoted an impossibly fetishized version of "democracy" around the world.

Khomeini insisted that he viewed America's role in Iran as essential to countering their shared foe, the Soviet Union. More importantly, Khomeini—like most Iranians of his generation—loathed the British and thought that America could keep the British from exerting undue influence in a post-Shāh Iran. Of course, as you've read, from 1979 until 1982 Khomeini's Islamic Republic had no qualms about taking British military aid and intelligence assistance to squelch Marxist elements in their country. Still, old hatreds die hard, and the Iranians never forgave the British for their role in Iranian domestic politics during the nineteenth and early twentieth centuries.

Although the British Empire was gone by the late 1970s and early 1980s, replaced with an amorphous commonwealth of mostly Western states and some island nations in the Caribbean Sea, southern Atlantic, and South Pacific Oceans, Iranians always believed that Britain's imperial ambitions were a continuing threat to them. In 2007, for example, the Islamic Republic of Iran would infamously capture a small boat full of British military commandos who had gotten lost while on patrol in Iraqi territorial waters. Subsequently Iran would spend much time humiliating the British soldiers until they were ultimately repatriated to the United Kingdom. Iran did this to the British sailors not because they posed a threat to Iran—they did not—but because they were an easy target and their capture in 2007 allowed for Iran's embattled regime to remind their oppressed people of the purported historical evils the British had once visited upon their land.

Playing on Carter's heartstrings, Khomeini insisted that he wanted to lead Islam in Iran to cooperate closely with the world's other great religions, notably Christianity and Judaism, to counter the threat that atheistic communism posed to them all. This statement resonated deeply with both America's Cold War national security establishment and the Southern Baptist American president. Here again, Khomeini played on Western ignorance and, specifically, American naivete to manipulate the more powerful foreign actors into allowing him and his cadre to return to Iran from abroad and assume control there.

In January of that same year, the political counsel for the US embassy in Paris, Warren Zimmerman, was chosen by President Carter to meet with Khomeini's righthand man, Ebrahim Yazdi. Over the course of the month, the two men discussed the possibility of Khomeini's return to Iran and how that would impact American interests there. In one of their covert meetings, Yazdi stated that, "You can tell the American Jews not to worry about the Jewish future in Iran." That, like so many of the Khomeini's promises to the West, would prove to be yet another manipulative lie.

The language and actions that Khomeini and his followers took when dealing with the West worked as well as they did because, like most "marks" during a con job, Western leaders desperately wanted to believe. In the wake of the human rights abuses and the failures of US foreign policy during the Vietnam era, America had elected a leader who conflated the Christian call to atone for one's personal sins with his professional objective of preserving America's national interest. Khomeini understood who he was dealing with. He also understood that, despite appearances to the contrary, America and its Western allies were weak during this time period and were looking for a way to extricate themselves from the ugliness of their support of the Shāh.

Betraying the well-understood notion of "better the devil you know," Carter and many Western foreign policy elites cried, "go away, Devil!"

and rid themselves of the Shāh, not realizing that he would be replaced by a greater evil—a more vicious and longer-lasting tyranny. That was waiting in the form of a man so many postmodern elites assumed was just another New Age mystic; a gentle old man living in France who only sought to return home and ensure that his religion lived peacefully with other faiths.

For the Islamists who followed Khomeini, they could not believe their luck. As Zimmerman met with Yazdi, a well-educated physician with a home in rural Texas, the Khomeinist revolutionaries were keenly aware of their limitations. Namely, the gravest threat to their nascent revolution was the Iranian military. Even as the Shāh left Iran on his indefinite vacation, the military's leaders remained loyal to his regime and were fiercely anticommunist and anti-Islamist. Yazdi and his leader, Khomeini, knew that the Americans had the most sway over the military. What's more, they were aware of General Huyser's mission to meet with the military leadership in Tehran, which stoked fear among the Islamists living in exile in Paris that Washington was preparing for another coup, either to restore the Shāh or to simply crush the Islamists and place the militarists in power.

Amazingly, the American representatives not only met with Khomeini's people, but they included Khomeini's concerns in the larger American response to the unrest in Iran. Huyser was urging the Iranian military leaders to avoid launching a coup until it was absolutely necessary, and Sullivan was declaring the end was nigh for every faction other than the Khomeinist one. As the top foreign policy leaders of the Carter administration were at loggerheads, with the British already moving away from the Shāh and his chosen successor, and Carter clearly enamored of the prospect of an Islamist Iran, Khomeini's complex strategy for lulling the West into a false sense of security was working. The Qur'an calls this "al-Taqiyya," or dissimulation.

Again, Khomeini and his fellow Shiites were harkening back to their history as a minority within the Sunni-dominated Islamic world to manipulate foolish and vain unbelievers to do their bidding. During the seventh century, when the succession crisis after Mohammad's death between the Sunni and Shiite factions tore the Islamic community apart, Shiites had to hide their religious beliefs from vengeful Sunnis. *Taqiyya,* better understood as "deception," was a matter of survival for Shiite Muslims living under Sunni rule, particularly in the immediate aftermath of Abu Bakr's defeat at the Battle of Karbala.[1] Khomeini and his followers understood they could not reveal their true plans for Iran to the Americans and their Western allies. So they lied. Khomeini relied on Western ignorance while Yazdi, using his American heritage, manipulated the Carter administration into opening the front door for the return of Khomeini and his entourage.

The deception worked.

In February, as the riots reached their critical level in Iran, Khomeini and his entourage were flown from Paris to Tehran, where Khomeini made his triumphant return. The already weakened Bakhtari government collapsed soon thereafter. The military, having heeded General Huyser's warnings, stood down and essentially allowed Khomeini and his people to have free rein in the streets. Yet Khomeini did not have the calming effect on the masses that the Americans had hoped—and that Khomeini had promised he'd have. The exact opposite happened. Once their "object of emulation" had returned to fill the power vacuum left by the absence of the Shāh (who had abdicated, in part, because Carter had clearly abandoned him), the Islamists were worked into frothy rage.

Thinking the Americans had managed to broker a power-sharing agreement between the Iranian military and Khomeini, the Islamists began an instant bloodletting once Khomeini had asserted his control over the revolution. Khomeini had never been comfortable with the pro-Shāh military, even though the Americans, thanks to Ambassador Sullivan and General Huyser, had essentially cowed them into submission. As soon as Khomeini took power, his Islamic revolutionaries began

---

1 "Taqiyya, the Art of Terrorist 'Deception,'" France 24, 14 March 2013, https://www.france24.com/en/20130313-taqiya-france-islam-deception-favoured-terrorists-jihad

a massive purge against the most powerful military leaders.[2] They worked their way from the Shāh's military leaders to other undesirables. The historian Paul Johnson assessed:

> In the first two years of [the Islamic Republic's existence] it executed over 8,000 people, convicted in Islamic courts of being "enemies of Allah." The Khomeini terror moved first against the former regime, slaughtering twenty-three generals, 400 other Army and police officers and 800 civilian officials; then against supporters of rival Ayatollahs, 700 of whom were executed; then against its former liberal-secular allies (500) and the Left (100). From the start it organized the execution and murder of leaders of ethnic and religious minorities, killing over 1,000 Kurds, 200 Turkomans, and many Jews, Christians, Shaikhis, Sabeans and members of dissident Shi'ia [sic] sects as well as orthodox Sunnis. Its persecution of the Bahais was particularly ferocious. Churches and synagogues were wrecked, cemeteries desecrated, shrines vandalized or demolished. The judicially murdered ranged from the Kurdish poet Allameh Vahidi, aged 102, to a nine-year-old girl, convicted of "attacking revolutionary guards."[3]

Today the Islamic Republic of Iran teaches a very different, sterile version of its revolutionary origins. Whenever it admits bloodshed occurred, Tehran routinely downplays or downright lies about the grand ayatollah's role in the mass executions—or even that mass executions happened. But happen they did. The early days of the Islamic Republic, when the Khomeinists feared both the militarists and the Marxists, were especially bloody.

---

2 Yasmin Khorram, "Op-Ed: The Iranian General I Never Knew," CNBC, 13 January 2020. https://www.cnbc.com/2020/01/13/op-ed-my-grandfather-was-an-iranian-general-who-was-killed-in-the-revolution.html

3 Paul Johnson, *Modern Times: The World from the Twenties to the Nineties* (New York: Harper Perennial, 1991), p. 713.

And in the decade thereafter, the aging Khomeini, increasingly fearful of his regime's survival, intensified the bloodletting. When reading of post-revolutionary Iran, one cannot help but see the chaos and mania that had gripped post-revolutionary France in 1789 and post-revolutionary Russia in 1917. It was a fearful time, made all the worse by the fragility of the regime, its brutality, and the violence that pervaded the streets.

In fact, Khomeini personally encouraged and ordered his followers to kill as many undesirables in Iran as possible. Even after taking power, Khomeini and his people were dangerously weak. Militarists, monarchists, and Marxists—to say nothing of the Americans and the British—all threatened the survival of Khomeini's nascent Islamic Republic, the first of its kind in the region, once these groups realized that Khomeini meant business. The Islamists were dug in like a tick on a bull's ass.

One promise after another was broken as Khomeini asserted his power over revolutionary Iran. For example, on March 11, 1979, about a month after Khomeini's triumphant return to Iran (thanks to the Americans and French), Khomeini turned his ire on the 55,000-strong historic Jewish community that had called Iran home for centuries. Fearing that the Americans and the Israelis would strike against his regime when it was weak and also being virulently anti-Semitic, Khomeini immediately abandoned the promises his second-in-command, Yazdi, had made to the Carter administration's representatives. The Jews of Iran would not be spared by the Islamists, any more than the Israelis will be once the Iranians and their proxies believe they are within striking distance of the tiny Jewish democracy in the Middle East.

16

THE BROKEN PROMISES AND

SHATTERED DREAMS OF THE

ISLAMIC REVOLUTION

HABIB ELKANIAN, a noted industrialist, was a prominent leader of the Jewish community in Iran. One of the first acts of the Islamist revolutionaries in Iran was to arrest him and five other non-Muslim figures. According to reports from the time, Khomeini personally called for and approved Elkanian's arrest and subsequent execution. The Khomeinist government accused Elkanian of having "Zionist ties."

Aside from his heritage as a Jew and a prominent figure of the 55,000-strong Jewish community, there was no evidence that Elkanian had operated in any capacity as an Israeli agent or as someone seeking to foment unrest against the rising Khomeinist regime because of his

Jewish faith. Yet this did not matter to Khomeini and his followers. They were firmly ensconced, from the start of their regime, in the strange cult of anti-Semitism that has come to define Iran's leadership today.

When Khomeini approved the arrest warrant of Elkanian, he explicitly stated that the move was "a warning to American and Zionist agents in Iran." Elkanian was subjected to a show trial that took place over the course of a twenty-four-hour period. He was permitted no legal representation and was tried in an Islamic court (which, due to his Judaism, was already biased against him). Elkanian was taken to the courtyard of the prison where he was being housed and executed by a firing squad.

As the *Jewish Telegraphic Agency* (JTA) reported at the time, "The State-controlled radio and television used the occasion of Elkanian's execution to launch violent attacks against Israel and vowed that the campaign to root out 'Zionism' in Iran would continue."[1] One of the three struts undergirding the Islamic Republic was being established: anti-Semitism. Soon the other two components, anti-Americanism and anti-Sunnism, would be enshrined through Iranian actions alongside the Islamic Republic's stifling anti-Semitism.

It is no surprise that so many Jewish leaders around the world fear the Iranian regime. Its track record has proven to be similar that of Hitler's of Nazi Germany toward Europe's Jewish diaspora. The case of Elkanian example is a tragic example of what awaits the world's Jews if Iranian power is allowed to spread throughout the region and if the regime becomes "normalized" through an ill-fated nuclear weapons deal and whatever trade deals corrupt American and European politicians can concoct.

What should have been clear to those fickle observers in the Carter administration was that the grand ayatollah and his regime should not have been trusted. Yet Carter dithered more. At any time, the United

1 "Report Execution Elkanian Personally Approved by Khomeini," *Jewish Telegraphic Agency,* 11 March 1979. https://www.jta.org/1979/05/11/archive/report-execution-of-elkanian-personally-approved-by-khomeini

States could have exerted itself and attempted to stabilize the situation. Carter, increasingly committed to his utopian vision of US foreign policy and the hallowed—though entirely amorphous—Western elite definition of "democracy," chose not to be involved in the situation in Iran and simply hoped for the best.

In October 1979, the American embassy in Tehran sent a desperate cable to Washington informing them the situation on the streets of Tehran was deteriorating and the embassy was poorly defended. In February 1979, the embassy had already been broken into, which had resulted in the deaths of American embassy staff members. The embassy staff believed the security gaps remained in October.

The Carter administration ignored their pleas for greater security or evacuation, worried that any overt actions might incite the Islamic Republic against the United States. The larger view in Washington was that they could not afford to turn away from Iran as a strategic lynchpin for America's Cold War strategy of containment. All of these careful formulations would prove useless. At the same time, the embassy in Tehran was cabling their understandable security concerns to Washington, the Shāh, who had settled in Mexico, needed serious medical treatment that he could only receive in the United States.

Most gallingly, Carter, even after urging the Shāh to leave his home in Iran, was now ignoring the Shāh's desperate pleas for medical treatment. The dying and deposed Iranian monarch would have been left out in the cold by Carter. Through the lobbying of an unlikely group of saviors, former Nixon administration official Dr. Henry Kissinger, David Rockefeller, and John McCloy, the Carter administration did admit the Shāh into the United States for medical treatment.

Initially, the Shāh was supposed to be welcomed to the United States with open arms. Yet after he fled Iran, the Shāh decided to spend weeks traveling around the Middle East. Khomeini had even encouraged the Americans to embrace the Shāh upon the monarch's escape from Iran. The Shāh's refusal to fly immediately to the United States and to hang around the region instead complicated things. The longer he stayed close to Iran, the more fearful Khomeini and his followers became that the Americans were planning to oust the Islamists and reinstate the Shāh. Once the Shāh had finished his tour of the Middle East and was ready to come to the United States to live out the remainder of his life, he found the State Department opposed to his return.

Warning indicators were blaring in Washington after the Shāh's departure. Tehran was still very much in the throes of its revolutionary moment. And revolutions are uncertain, fickle, and bloody affairs. Since the 1950s, the CIA had maintained a network of highly sensitive listening posts along Iran's border with the Soviet Union. These posts, designated TACKSMAN sites along the Elbourz Mountains, "provided clear electronic line-of-sight coverage of the Soviet intercontinental missile test ranges. Intelligence from these sites not only allowed the United States and its allies to follow critical developments in the Soviet strategic missile forces, but they later provided data essential to verify arms control agreements with Moscow."

Already on Valentine's Day in February 1979, street protesters had attacked and briefly occupied the American embassy in Tehran. Meanwhile, toward the end of February, Ambassador William Sullivan was in serious negotiations to gain the release of groups of CIA officers who had been captured by radicals while performing their duties at the TACKSMAN sites along the Elbourz Mountains.[2]

Later, Secretary of State Cyrus Vance would argue that admitting the Shāh into the United States would be "inflammatory." Ambassador Sullivan wholeheartedly agreed with Vance's conclusion. More importantly, Carter's national security adviser, Brzezinski, concurred with Vance and Sullivan's conclusion that the Shāh should not be admitted into the United States, unless the administration wanted to risk the ire of the increasingly unpredictable Iran. However, Brzezinski agreed

2 William J. Daugherty, "Jimmy Carter and the 1979 Decision to Admit the Shah into the United States," *American Diplomacy*, April 2003. https://americandiplomacy.web.unc.edu/2003/04/jimmy-carter-and-the-1979-decision-to-admit-the-shah-into-the-united-states/

reluctantly and admitted to having severe "personal repugnance" about his support for these conclusions.

For his part, President Carter seemed interested in both moving beyond the Shāh and ratcheting down tensions with the new Islamist regime in Tehran. Yet Carter was ultimately swayed by the Shāh's call for mercy so he could be seen by American medical professionals in the twilight of his life as his cancer was worsening.[3] Interestingly, as Dr. William J. Daugherty would note in a 2003 article, Carter was never presented with medical proof that the Shāh truly needed the lifesaving measures he claimed were essential.

There had been repeated provocations from the Islamists in Iran against Americans still inside their country. Yet there is little doubt that Carter's ultimate decision to allow the Shāh to enter the United States and receive medical treatment played heavily into the events of the horrifying Iran hostage crisis that lasted from 1979 until 1981. Carter had expressed an unwillingness to allow the Shāh into the United States in June of 1979. However, he quickly reversed course because of the significant pressure that Kissinger's trio of Republican notables were applying on him.

In Daugherty's 2003 article, it is evident that Carter's sudden reversal was caused less by a change of heart and more by the timing of the critical Strategic Arms Limitation Talks (SALT II) between the Carter administration and the Soviet Union. Carter would need the support of Republicans in the United States Senate to ratify this treaty. Carter had viewed the success of SALT II as critical to both his legacy as president and his reelection campaign.

According to Brzezinski, Kissinger had implied that he'd use his leverage with the GOP to sink the SALT II ratification process unless the Carter administration changed its mind about the Shāh's entry into the United States. Kissinger denies this ever happened. And even

---

3 "The Shah's Health: A Political Gamble," *New York Times,* 17 May 1981. https://www.nytimes.com/1981/05/17/magazine/the-shah-s-health-a-political-gamble.html

Carter's personal lawyer, Lloyd Cutler, had denied this occurred. But it seemed obvious to many on Carter's foreign policy team that Kissinger would complicate their lives unless Carter admitted the Shāh.

Ultimately, Kissinger testified before the Senate in favor of the SALT II talks. A few months thereafter, on October 24, 1979, the Shāh was admitted to a New York hospital for treatment. His medical diagnosis was muddied. While the Shāh was in Mexico, his Mexican doctor suspected that the deposed Iranian monarch had come down with malaria. The Shāh had requested a second opinion, and David Rockefeller had deployed his friend, Dr. Benjamin H. Kean, chief of tropical medicine at New York University Hospital.

Kean discovered that the Shāh suffered from jaundice; he was skeptical that the underlying condition was simple malaria and concluded that cancer was the likely culprit. Of course, the Shāh could have been treated anywhere in the United States. Yet because of Rockefeller and Kean's involvement, the Shāh wound up in New York City.

Washington had cabled the American embassy in Tehran and had asked them to put feelers out to the Islamist regime. Representatives from the embassy met with then-Prime Minister Mehdi Bazargan and Foreign Minister Ebrahim Yazdi. The Americans sought assurances from the Iranian leadership that the embassy in Tehran, which had already been overrun, would be unmolested during the Shāh's treatment, but Bazargan's response was nonchalant. The Americans had made it clear that they sought to maintain positive relations with the Khomeinist regime of Iran and were only allowing the Shāh into the United States on humanitarian grounds.

According to reports from the meeting as detailed by Daugherty, the American-trained physician Yazdi made four forceful points to his American interlocutors. The first was that the Shāh should have been treated anywhere other than the United States because it would be inflammatory for Washington allow the Shāh to receive treatment there. The second point was that if the Shāh did receive medical treatment in the United States, it should not be in New York City.

When pressed to explain why, Yazdi exhibited the anti-Semitism that was already endemic of the Islamic Republic: New York was the "center of Rockefeller and Zionist influence," according to Yazdi. The third point that Yazdi made to his American audience was that he wanted doctors loyal to the Khomeinist regime to examine the Shāh and to report the veracity of the Shāh's claims. Finally, Yazdi wanted assurances that the Shāh would not engage in any political activities whatsoever while in the Big Apple.

Yazdi made another comment that American diplomats apparently failed to include in their report to Washington. Yazdi argued that few Iranians would believe that the Shāh was genuinely ill. According to Yazdi, most Iranians, who were still incensed by the Shāh's behavior during his reign, would "import a far more sinister meaning to the event." Again, the false specter of American covert interference in Iranian affairs hung over them. But the Americans had no such designs. In fact, it was obvious that the Carter administration in particular had to be dragged into allowing the Shāh into New York at all.

More importantly, contrary to what Carter administration officials have since insisted to the public, there was no actual reporting from the American representatives who met with Bazargan or Yazdi indicating that the two Iranian leaders were willing to provide protection for the American embassy. In effect, the Carter administration made assumptions about the willingness of the Khomeinist regime to play nice with the Americans that they should not have made. However, as you will soon see, Bazargan himself would attempt to end the inevitable standoff between the Americans and the Islamists of Iran during the early phases of the Iranian hostage crisis. But neither Bazargan nor Yazdi made *promises* that they would deploy Iranian forces to defend the embassy from attack. How could they? The mobs were out of control, and the Khomeinists were adding to the confusion by massacring anyone they deemed an ideological deviationist!

On November 4, 1979, a week after the Shāh was allowed to seek treatment in New York, the Iranian hostage crisis erupted. This was a seminal event in the affairs of Iran and the United States, for it would define US-Iranian relations from that point until today. In just the first few months after Khomeini's return, it was estimated that upwards of 200 Iranians were murdered either by the grand ayatollah or his fanatical followers.

But, as you will soon see, that would merely be sauce for the goose. The worst was yet to come. All of Khomeini's manipulations and lies to the rest of the world and his false promises of a peaceful transition of power from the unpopular and autocratic Shāh to a more beneficent and egalitarian regime under the grand ayatollah were being drowned in blood, spilled on behalf of Khomeini and in defense of his radical new regime.

It wasn't only the Jews of Iran or the monarchists and Marxists who were in for a rough time under the Khomeinist regime. The liberated women of Iran would be sent back to the seventh century under shariah law. What's more, it was the very principles that the grand ayatollah had claimed to believe in when he was in exile in Paris.

Remember, Khomeini had won more than just the support of Islamists in Iran, although he vowed retribution and vengeance upon those who had betrayed Islam and sold out Iran to foreigners while he was in exile during the Shāh's reign. Khomeini had not only told the Americans, French, and British that he wanted to be a more egalitarian leader of Iran, but the grand ayatollah had also made many promises to the more liberal elements of Iran.

One man in particular, Abolhassan Bani-Sadr, the son of a Shiite cleric and a noted economics professor, was an early devotee of Khomeini. Based on personal assurances from Khomeini, the future first president of the Islamic Republic had thrown in with Khomeini while in exile in Paris because the grand ayatollah supported democracy, women's rights, and several other ideals that Abolhassan had devoted his life to. According to Abolhassan, though, Khomeini "abandoned" those concepts the moment he deplaned from the 747 jumbo jet they had all taken from Paris to Tehran in February 1979. At that point, again according to Abolhassan, the mullahs of Iran had gotten their ideological hooks into Khomeini.

Upon Abolhassan's election as the first president of the Islamic Republic in 1980, he became incensed by the increasing radicalism of the Khomeinist regime. Abolhassan had ventured to the holy city of Qom, where Khomeini made his home (before Khomeini's exile, this was also his home). Abolhassan challenged his old friend Khomeini on the fact that he was breaking many of the promises he had made to both the West and his followers while living in Paris. Without much concern for Abolhassan's protests about what was clearly an abandonment of some of Khomeini's strongest promises—particularly about respecting women's liberation in Iran—the Iranian "supreme leader" casually explained that he had said "many things in France that were convenient, but that he was not locked into everything he had said there and if he felt necessary to say the opposite he would."[4]

Abolhassan's feelings are understandable. Yet it is inaccurate to blame the more radical mullahs for turning or manipulating Khomeini into a totalitarian theocrat. Clearly Khomeini, ever since his early associations with Naavab Safavi, the Muslim Brotherhood–inspired Islamist who was put to death by the Shāh in the early 1960s, was himself an Islamic radical. He was also extremely utilitarian in his political affiliations and, as an Islamist, took liberties with the Koranic concept of *taqiyya* in order to fill the power vacuum that had formed in Iran in 1979.

Far from being the egalitarian revolution that Abolhassan and many others—including Jimmy Carter—had hoped for, the Green Islamist Revolution in Iran in 1979 was drowned in blood. This was in large part thanks to the backward-looking ideology of Islamism coupled with the violent and totalitarian impulses of the self-described "supreme leader" of that Islamic revolution, the Grand Ayatollah Ruhollah Khomeini.

---

4 John Irish and Michaela Cabrera, "Iran's First President Says Khomeini Betrayed 1979 Islamic Revolution," Reuters, 4 February 2019. https://www.reuters.com/article/us-iran-revolution-anniversary-banisadr/irans-first-president-says-khomeini-betrayed-1979-islamic-revolution-idUSKCN1PT1IR

17

444 DAYS OF HELL

THE ISLAMIC REVOLUTION in Iran did not happen in a vacuum. At the same time that Khomeini and his followers were establishing themselves in Shiite-dominated Iran, the entire Middle East was ablaze with Islamist fervor. Khomeini and his fellow revolutionaries, like Lenin and the first generation of Bolsheviks, were not content to simply remain within their country's borders. They envisioned spreading their Islamist revolution to all corners of the Islamic world and, perhaps, beyond. But first, the young Islamist regime had to secure itself at home.

Whether ordered to or not by the grand ayatollah, his young, radical followers took to the streets to demand what they perceived as justice.

Scores of young Islamist revolutionaries clamored for the Americans to return the Shāh to face justice in an Islamic court—possibly a grander version of the show trial that Elkanian, the notable Jewish-Iranian industrialist, had been subjected to earlier that year. The young radicals, many of whom were idealistic college students, would brook no compromise.

For the young revolutionaries who composed the ranks of the Islamic Revolution, any delay in their version of justice was not just wrong but also implied that those delaying justice were complicit in those crimes. In this case, the Americans were blamed. Foreign Minister Yazdi's warnings to the American diplomats came true. Fears abounded among the Islamists in Iran that Washington would replicate the 1953 coup.

Of course, that notion was ridiculous, as was shown earlier in this work, the 1953 coup only happened because pro-monarchy Iranian generals organized it. No such organization or movement was ready when the Islamists were demanding the return of the Shāh for trial. The only real threat to the Khomeinist regime came from the Soviet-backed Marxists who, ultimately, were too disorganized to achieve their ambitious goal of making Iran a Soviet-style state. Interestingly, the Marxists were aligned with Khomeini and his revolutionaries on some key issues, ranging from Israel to the United States, and both groups wanted the Shāh to stand trial.

Once it became clear that the Americans were not going to force the Shāh to go back to Iran and had in fact, given the Shāh refuge, all bets were off. Very quickly, a band of radical Marxists sealed off the streets leading into the American embassy in Tehran. Pressure was building in the chaotic streets just beyond the beige-colored walls of the American embassy. Soon the Marxist guerillas were replaced by Islamist revolutionaries looking to force the Americans' hand on the matter of returning the Shāh.

On November 4, 1979, panicked calls between the American embassy and Washington concluded with phrases like, "they're coming over the walls," and "they're inside the building now." Young Islamist revolutionaries, tired of what they considered stalling on the part of the United States, clambered over the poorly defended walls of the compound and stormed inside. Among the radicals climbing the gates of the American embassy were people like Mahmoud Ahmadinejad, a controversial future president of Iran (though, as 2021 would show, he would hardly be the most radical future president of Iran). However, it should be noted that Ahmadinejad's role as a hostage taker has been disputed.[1] While he was a student leader who organized outside the embassy, most sources indicate that he did not take part in the capture and terrorizing of American hostages.[2] Still, when Ahmadinejad ran for the presidency of Iran, he allowed his followers to exaggerate his role in the embassy siege to Iranian voters.

On that day, a 444-day hostage crisis would start. The crisis would test both the resolve of the shaky Islamist regime in Iran and that of the Carter administration. Inevitably, the hostage crisis would harden the extremism of the Islamist regime while basically overthrowing the Carter administration and ushering in what many believe was a conservative revolution in the United States, led by the 1980 Republican Party presidential candidate, Ronald Reagan.

The hostage crisis occurred at a critical moment in the formation of the Islamic Republic. Torn between Marxist radicals, who were still terrorizing the streets, and hardline Islamist clerics, the Khomeinist regime was unable to resolve the crisis in short order. The young people who had stormed the embassy were also inspired by the harsher rhetoric of the more conservative clerics. These were the same clerics that Iran's first president, Abolhassan Bani-Sadr, claimed had coopted Khomeini as soon as he stepped off the plane from Paris at Tehran's international airport.

President Carter had tried to resolve the crisis through negotiations

---

1 Ramita Navai, "New Iranian President's Role as Hostage-Taker Discounted," *The Irish Times*, 2 July 2005. https://www.irishtimes.com/news/new-iranian-president-s-role-as-hostage-taker-discounted-1.463175

2 "Ahmadinejad's Role in the Hostage Crisis Disputed," NPR, 1 July 2005. https://www.npr.org/templates/story/story.php?storyId=4725806

444 DAYS OF HELL

almost immediately but could not. The Americans imposed harsh sanctions on Iran: they refused to purchase billions of dollars' worth of oil
from Iran (denying Iran funds that the Khomeinists needed to prop up
their young regime). Washington also got the United Nations to side
with it in a series of diplomatic actions that ultimately turned Iran into
a pariah state. Then, the US government froze much-needed funds that
were destined for the empty coffers of the Islamic Republic.

Iran's Prime Minister Mehdi Bazargan insisted that Khomeini and
the clerics should allow him to order the release of the hostages just a few
days after the embassy had been captured. Whether Khomeini wanted
to hand over the hostages to the Americans or not remains unclear.
What is clear, however, is that there was a great power struggle within
the new regime.

The hardliners wanted to keep the hostages and make an example
of the Americans. And there is reason to believe that Khomeini himself
approved of the hostage-taking and refused to call for the release of the
Americans. After all, this historic event was happening on the heels of
Khomeini's murder of Elkanian, and we know from official sources
that the Iranian-Jewish industrialist was murdered specifically because
Khomeini and his agents wanted to "send a message" to Israel. Here,
with the hostage crisis, another message could be sent to the other great
Iranian bugaboo, America, against any intervention in Iranian politics.

18

MANIPULATING THE GENTLE

AMERICAN GIANT

YET AGAIN, Khomeini's brilliant use of *taqiyya* was on display. The Carter administration had, at least in part, facilitated the safe return of Khomeini and his cadre to Iran. The British were supporting Khomeini in his battle against the Marxists—and would until 1982. Instead of seeking more amicable relations with the West, though, Khomeini had implicitly allowed the capture of the American embassy.

This was an act that even the pliable Carter would be unable to ignore. As *Britannica* coolly describes, "It soon became evident that no one within the virulently anti-American atmosphere of postrevolutionary

Iran was willing, or able, to release the hostages."[1] In fact, after meeting with Khomeini and urging him to release the American hostages so the Islamic Republic would not be considered a rogue regime in its infancy Bazargan resigned his position as prime minister on November 6, 1979, in protest of the regime's unwillingness to end the hostage crisis. Thus, Khomeini's complicity in this heinous act was clear.

Even before the hostage crisis, the Islamists of Iran routinely referred to the United States as the "Great Satan." Israel quickly became known as "Little Satan." This was an addition to the traditional antipathy between the Shiite Muslims of Iran and the Sunnis of the region, who were considered "apostates." Almost immediately upon his arrival, then, Khomeini negated every promise he had made to the West. For 444 days, Islamists held fifty-two Americans from the US embassy in Tehran in captivity; the Islamists terrorized them for the entirety of their stay. It was obvious to anyone on the receiving end of this treatment—even many early officials of the Islamist regime—that Khomeini and his followers truly loathed the Americans.

In fact, Khomeini's real intentions and the true nature of his Islamic Republic cannot be found in the flowery rhetoric he and his cadre espoused from their posh redoubt in the Parisian suburbs. Khomeini's true ambitions can be seen in his days of exile in Iraq, before he decamped and sought refuge in Paris (when a young Saddam Hussein offered to disappear the radical cleric for the Shāh). And we know that Khomeini's intended to keep the hostages because his prime minister, Bazargan, ultimately resigned in protest shortly after the prime minister's pleas to release the hostages went unheeded by Khomeini.

This was not the first time that Bazargan feuded with his leader, Khomeini. In 1978, while Khomeini was still in exile in Iraq, Bazargan had advised the grand ayatollah not to attack the Americans too loudly. In fact, Bazargan had initially urged Khomeini to allow "the institution

---

1 "Iran Hostage Crisis," Britannica, Accessed on 18 January 2021. https://www.britannica.com/event/Iran-hostage-crisis/Conflict-and-resolution

of the monarchy to continue" while still calling for the Shāh's removal from power for his abuses.

When it came to the Americans, Bazargan advised Khomeini to "moderate his attacks on American 'imperialism,' since the new Iran would still be reliant on help from the United States and other Western countries." Further, Bazargan urged Khomeini to oppose "a clerical monopoly of the leadership of the [revolutionary] movement, since the ulema lacked adequate political experience ... Khomeini ... did not take the advice. He maintained his attacks on the shah and the Americans and continued to stress that Islam was the guiding force of the revolution."[2]

Anti-Americanism and anti-Semitism were the pillars of the Islamic Republic. Khomeini was not just some doddering old man or a mere figurehead. Instead, he was the intellectual driving force—and spiritual leader—of the revolutionary political movement. And the rigid Islamism that has defined Iran until the present day was entirely distilled from Khomeini to his followers.

This was why so many early members of the Khomeinist revolution, who were swayed to join Khomeini by the grand ayatollah's ambiguous language, flowery promises of an egalitarian future, and his phenomenally good press in the West, ultimately resigned in protest during the first decade of the Islamic Republic's reign. These people, whether they realized it or not, likely understood that Khomeini was not the man he had pretended to be. And his revolution was not the color of Islam, green. It was blood red—and Khomeini intended to bathe the country and the region, possibly even the world, in the blood of unbelievers and political rivals alike (one and the same, in Khomeini's view).

The Iran hostage crisis, like the revolution itself, was entirely avoidable. It was the apotheosis of decisions, good and bad, as well as indecision from the key players, both within Iran and outside of the country, that led the world to the terrible place of blood-spilling Islamist revolution in 1979. Although Khomeini had initially encouraged

---

2 Caryl, *Strange Rebels*, p. 140.

the Americans to take the Shāh in as a political refugee, where the deposed monarch could live his last days out of sight and—out of mind, Khomeini and his devoted followers had changed their minds and demanded that the Shāh be returned to Iran for what would have been an unfair trial and a grisly end.

19

WE WON'T LEAVE THE

LIGHTS ON FOR YOU

EVEN THOUGH THE AMERICANS had initially promised the Shāh safe harbor, the monarch's own headstrong behavior after leaving Iran made it politically impossible for Washington to accept him. In fact, President Carter was reticent to even allow the Shāh to receive medical treatment in New York. When he had decided to allow that, Carter instructed his representatives at the American embassy in Tehran to give the new Islamic Republic a head's up—something that Washington was not required to do.

That's what made the 444-day hostage crisis so galling. Carter attempted to negotiate with the hostage takers, but they did not want to hear from him. They wanted the Shāh's blood. But this was not possible after the hostages were taken because the hostage takers had put Carter in a politically untenable situation—especially as the contentious 1980 presidential election was getting underway in the United States.

At the same time, Carter did not think a military response was warranted. He believed in the power of his words and thought that cooler heads could prevail. At no point after the crisis in Iran began in 1978 did Carter fundamentally understand what was at play there. Thus he was never able to craft realistic or reliable strategies for preserving American interests in Iran during those tense years.

The hostages were tormented to varying degrees by their captors. Many were made to endure mock executions; they were trotted out for the world to see as part of an endless ideological tirade by the Islamic Republic against purported American imperialism. The hostage takers demanded the Shāh's return, and each time the United States refused, they got angrier. In the event of the negotiations not working, Carter authorized the creation of a backup plan involving the United States Special Forces.

A COMEDY OF ERRORS

While Carter became increasingly consumed with negotiations, the Pentagon created a detailed, highly complex military rescue plan that used helicopters from the United States Navy and deployed teams of Army Delta Force operators. Eight helicopters would depart from an aircraft carrier in the Indian Ocean and travel 700 miles north, in the dead of night, to land in Iran's Great Salt Desert. Once there, the helicopters would pick up the DELTA Force operators who had been deployed to that location—designated Desert One—by six C-130 transport airplanes belonging to the Air Force earlier that evening.

While highly complex, this sort of mission is relatively easy for the US military to perform today. What made the mission so difficult in April 1980 was that it was one of the first times the highly specialized U.S. Army Delta Force elements had operated jointly with the Navy and Air Force. Furthermore, never before had such a stealthy mission, using so many different moving parts, been attempted—especially when the stakes were so very high.

President Carter had ordered the mission to go ahead, thinking that negotiations had dragged on far too long and that the situation for the hostages was deteriorating (as was Carter's campaign for reelection against Ronald Reagan). One of the eight helicopters had to drop out of the mission early on the way to the Great Salt Desert rendezvous point because of a blade failure. The seven other helicopters continued onward. As the helicopters got nearer to the rendezvous point with the Delta Force, a sudden sandstorm clouded their path.

Disoriented and only a few hundred feet from the desert floor, one of the Navy helicopters turned around and returned to the aircraft carrier. The others pressed on. The worst was yet to come for the units who continued toward their objective.

At Desert One, the rendezvous point, Delta Force operators detected an incoming busload of people on a dirt road that passed near their landing zone. The American Special Forces operators disabled the bus. Shortly thereafter, the Americans sighted another set of headlights approaching their location.

An anti-tank weapon was used on the vehicle. As soon as the American anti-tank weapon found its target, it caused a massive explosion—far more massive than it should have been. Very quickly, the Americans on the ground realized that they had exploded an Iranian fuel truck full of gasoline. The darkness of the desert night sky was punctuated by the blistering flames of ignited gasoline—all while a busload of Iranians looked on from their disabled vehicle.

The mission, which depended on being conducted by covert warriors with the utmost secrecy in the dead of night, had just placed a massive signal light on its position. The Delta Force operators knew it was only a matter of time before Iranian authorities saw the flames from afar and came to investigate. Still, the Americans resolved to press on to save their fellow countrymen in Tehran.

"Welcome to World War Three," quipped Colonel "Chargin'"

Charlie Beckwith, a hardnosed Army special forces warrior, as he saw the flames rising from the exploded gasoline truck.

That World War III reference was *not* mere in-the-moment hyperbole on the part of "Chargin'" Charlie Beckwith. These were *always* the stakes. Iran was and is at the epicenter of global politics, and under its Islamist regime, it is a danger to the region and the world. Throw in the anti-Americanism that has defined the regime since its beginning—as evidenced by the hostage crisis—and it is a question of "when" not "if" Iran initiates a great power conflict. This moment in the Great Salt Desert was one such precarious moment when another great-power war could have come about due to Iran's malicious behavior.

When the helicopters arrived at the Desert One landing site, another had experienced mechanical failure and was no longer operational. This meant that only five helicopters were available for the mission. The minimum requirement for the mission to press onward from Desert One to the American embassy in Tehran was six. The mission had to be aborted. Four C-130 transport planes had landed in the desert with the Delta Force operators. As they readied to evacuate the Delta operators, one of the remaining Navy helicopters crashed into the wing of the C-130, creating a massive inferno. Eight Americans would die that night, and the Americans from both the downed C-130 and remaining Navy helicopters would have to be evacuated on the three Air Force planes that remained.

At the start of the mission, four CIA operatives had been secreted into Tehran to surveil the captured American embassy. Unaware of the chaos in the Great Salt Desert and expecting the Delta Force team to arrive at the embassy and save the day, one of the CIA operatives radioed his supervisors and calmly assured them that the pending rescue mission would be, "a piece of cake" for the Americans because the Iranians holding the embassy personnel hostage appeared to be so hapless.

As the "piece of cake" call was being made by CIA operatives in Tehran, the bodies of the dead Americans at Desert One had to be abandoned by their brothers in arms. If the Americans at Desert One did not escape at that moment, they knew the Iranian military would arrive at their location soon, and something far more terrifying than a darkly comical failure in the desert would have occurred. The abandoned helicopters could not be destroyed by Delta Force operators before their escape because the fuel in the helicopter's tanks would have produced an explosion that could have threatened the remaining American C-130s.

Ultimately, the disaster in the desert became a propaganda victory for Khomeini and his regime. The Islamist regime proclaimed that Allah was truly on their side. The once-mighty Americans were feckless and corrupt; America was being humiliated for all to see because of its corruption. Khomeini and his followers became convinced that they could dictate terms to the Americans and that they had made the right decision in capturing the embassy.

For his part, the fiasco at Desert One would spell the end of Jimmy Carter's presidency. He would appear incompetent, and his inability to resolve the Iran hostage crisis, the embarrassing failure of the operation to rescue those hostages, and an assortment of other domestic problems Carter faced proved to be his undoing. But it must be noted that the enduring humiliation of the hostage crisis and the failure of the rescue attempt were the most likely reasons why Carter failed to win a second term.[1]

After all, with the exception of JFK, who was assassinated before he could run for reelection, no American president had failed to secure a second term in the post-World War II era. Carter, who had been elected because he vowed to ratchet down global tensions while also crafting a smarter, less vicious foreign policy, had been taken down by the failure of his military and foreign policies in Iran. Thus, a country that most in Washington considered to be a minor power displayed the potential to fundamentally destabilize US foreign policy.

---

1 Brandon J. Weichert, "Jimmy Carter: The Indecisive Hawk," The Weichert Report, 31 August 2018. https://theweichertreport.wordpress.com/2018/08/31/jimmy-carter-the-indecisive-hawk/

2 0

FREEING THE HOSTAGES:

MATCHING MYTH TO REALITY

IT WOULD BE ANOTHER EIGHT MONTHS before the hostages were freed. This would happen because Ronald Reagan outwardly threatened the nascent regime with brutal reprisals if they did not return the hostages by the time he was inaugurated. Behind the scenes, however, the truth is far more complicated than many Reagan supporters are comfortable with admitting.

In fact, it is very likely that the painful negotiations between Carter's team and Khomeini's representatives paved the way for the hostages to be freed on the very day that Reagan became the fortieth president of the United States. However, it is also quite likely that the Iranians wanted to conclude a deal with the Carter administration because Reagan had already indicated that not only would his administration make no deals with Iran for the hostages, but he wouldn't even continue the negotiations if they did not end during Carter's presidency.[1]

Hoping to get something as opposed to possibly nothing—or worse an actual competent American military response to their provocations—the Iranians endeavored to make a deal with Carter. Because Carter was the American president when the Islamic Revolution occurred, though, there was a special hatred of Jimmy Carter in the minds of most Iranians. (If only they knew how helpful Carter was in getting their revered grand ayatollah into power!) The Iranian negotiators hoped to humiliate Carter, extract as many concessions from his administration as possible, and then help to push him out of power.

All three of these happened.

First, the Iranians played hardball until the bitter end—especially after the failed rescue attempt. Second, the Iranians wanted an end to sanctions, and they wanted the money that Washington had frozen at the start of the crisis to be unfrozen. Third, the Iranians waited until Carter was officially an ex-president to agree to the deal, in order to allow for the new Reagan administration to make the announcement.

Their hatred of Carter ensured that Iran would not allow Carter to have a victory and claim credit for the release of the hostages. In fact, when Carter did finally fly to Germany to meet with the hostages after 444 days of miserable captivity and a complete failure to rescue the hostages from what most believed to have been a haphazard, undisciplined, poorly resourced enemy, most of the freed hostages did not want to see or hear from Carter.

Many conspiracy theories have circulated about Reagan's involvement in the freeing of the American embassy hostages. The American left has long believed that Reagan had a hand in delaying their release

---

1 Amanda Taub, "The Republican Myth of Ronald Reagan and the Iran Hostages, Debunked," Vox, 25 January 2016. https://www.vox.com/2016/1/25/10826056/reagan-iran-hostage-negotiation

by Iran until after he was sworn in as the fortieth US president. In fact, it is likely that Reagan had little to do with the timing of the end of the negotiations. Several negotiators, both from the Carter side and the Iranian side, have claimed that Reagan campaign adviser William Casey contacted the Iranians and urged them to delay the signing of the deal until after Carter's presidency had ended.

As author Mark Bowden has shown, though, Casey's calls *had no impact* on the progress of the negotiations. In fact, Casey's calls likely increased the Iranians' desire to conclude the negotiations favorably by the end of Carter's presidency. Iran's leadership feared having to deal with someone they believed was a tougher, less-restrained American president, like Reagan.[2]

The hostage crisis ended with Iran looking tougher and getting richer, and it created a complete regime shift in the United States. This is not a polemical statement. In fact, Carter, although unpopular, had many advantages in running for reelection as an incumbent, but he was unable to exploit them because he had become so mired by the hostage crisis.

Yet Carter bizarrely eschewed doing even the most rudimentary activities that all presidential candidates are required to do to "press the flesh" on the campaign trail. Instead, Carter engaged in what his critics derisively (and aptly) described as his "Rose Garden campaign." Carter argued that he avoided engaging in traditional political campaigning required to win the presidency so he could dedicate his time to negotiating with Iran for release of the hostages.

This strategy, as many political strategists would agree, was suicidal for Carter's reelection bid. Without Carter's abject failure to resolve the Iranian hostage crisis in a meaningful and timely way, it is likely that Reagan would have had a much more difficult time in the 1980 presidential election. After all, incumbents often have significant advantages when

---

2 Mark Bowden, *Guests of the Ayatollah: The Iran Hostage Crisis: The First Battle in America's War with Militant Islam* (New York: Grove Press, 2006), pp. 469–590.

the electorate believes that everything is going well under their leadership.[3]

Given the turgid economy at the time, it's possible that Reagan would have still won. Nevertheless, Iran had become such a global flashpoint that it totally undermined the image of the United States as a superpower. Because of this, the Islamist regime was able to essentially effect a regime shift in America's domestic political order in ways that few other foreign powers have managed to do either before or after the tumultuous events of 1979.

More importantly, the abject failure of the most powerful military in the world to rescue a handful of hostages from an angry mob in the midst of a revolution—with the very public disaster that was the Desert One fiasco—forced major changes in the structure of the United States military. Never again would the United States suffer the indignity that the Iranian hostage takers had subjected the country to.

Lessons learned from the Desert One fiasco proved to be critical in making lasting and important changes to America's post–Vietnam War military structure. In fact, this was one of the earliest examples in the Revolution in Military Affairs (RMA) that would define the modern US military. The idea of seamless joint operations conducted in hostile territory, far removed from friendly areas on the map, was too enticing for Washington policymakers to pass up. The lessons learned from the debacle in the Great Salt Desert on that fateful night would pave the way for the methods and practices that define America's Special Forces today.

In 1979, the world was subjected to one of the most damaging events in recent international politics, a revolution whose effects are still being felt today. The United States was made to appear weak and impotent in the face of rag-tag band of religious zealots. An American presidency was cast aside because of this action. The American way of war, because of this failure, was also completely changed (for the

---

3 Aaron David Miller, "The Power of the Incumbency: Four Two-Term Presidents in a Row?" Carnegie Endowment for International Peace, 15 October 2019. https://carnegieendowment. org/2019/10/15/power-of-incumbency-four-two-term-presidents-in-row-pub-80072

better). More importantly, because of the apathy or short-sightedness of the Carter administration and their British allies, the Islamist genie was loosed from its ideological bottle with the rise of Khomeini. From this moment onward, the path to a Third World War, not between capitalism and communism but between Islamism and the West, would first be forged.

21

DOMINOS FALLING:

AFGHANISTAN TO IRAN?

WHEN RED ARMY TANKS came smashing across the USSR's border with Afghanistan in an effort to support the Marxist-Leninist government of Kabul in December 1979, policymakers in Washington went mad. Fear-filled scenarios were concocted in the minds of Washington leaders about the Soviet's real ambitions in taking Afghanistan. Just as today, Afghanistan in the late 1970s was a proverbial backwater. The country was torn asunder by fighting between the forces of modernity and tradition, just as today. The Soviets supported the minority communist groups in Afghanistan, while the Islamists were increasingly opposed to the ethos and objectives of the communists.

Since Afghanistan borders Iran and because the Islamist revolution was raging in Iran, the great fear of American leaders was that the Soviet Union's ultimate goal in invading Afghanistan was to threaten Iran. At the time, as you've read previously, the streets of Iran were plagued by riots and violence. The Shāh's regime worried more about the Moscow-supported Marxist elements than the Khomeinist elements. This view was shared by Washington. In the fearful minds of Western leaders, it looked as though the Soviets were poised to take Afghanistan as a base of operations for the Red Army to charge into neighboring Iran.

If the Marxist groups of Iran had prevailed in the revolution against the Shāh, then it was probable that the Soviets would take Iran and not only have access to its vast oil wealth there but also lay claim to the warm-water ports of Iran. Taking the warm-water ports would have given the Soviet Navy the ability to project power beyond their borders in ways they historically could not. What's more, such a move by the Soviets would effectively end the decades-long strategy of containment that the West had embraced since the late 1940s. Few in the West believed the events on the streets of Iran were unconnected to the Soviet invasion of Afghanistan.

Six years before the Soviet invasion of Afghanistan, the Red Army had "carried out an ambitious exercise of its ability to invade Iran," and when the Soviets invaded Afghanistan, all those concerns came flooding back into Washington. In response, the Carter administration created the Rapid Deployment Force, which would evolve into the United States Central Command (CENTCOM) that manages American military efforts in the Middle East today. Again, this was another US military evolution that was sparked over fears about Iran's collapse and its conquest by the Red Army.[1]

---

1 Michael R. Gordon, "1980 Soviet Test: How to Invade Iran," *New York Times,* 15 December 1986. https://www.nytimes.com/1986/12/15/world/1980-soviet-test-how-to-invade-iran.html

Speaking at the time, Carter declared:

An attempt by any outside force to gain control of the Persian Gulf region will be regarded as an assault on the vital interests of the United States of America, and such an assault will be repelled by any means necessary, including military force.[2]

Carter made this declaration during his 1980 State of the Union Address. It led to one of his most far-reaching foreign policy moves, one that continues to damage US foreign policy today. Carter, looking for a foreign policy victory as the situation in Iran deteriorated, believed that intervening in Afghanistan was a good move. The Carter Doctrine would help him to justify aiding the Islamist Afghan *mujahideen* fighters that were terrorizing the invading Soviet Army in Afghanistan. Sending aid to the Afghan fighters was popular among the voters, and Carter believed this would aid his ailing reelection campaign.

Alongside Carter's creation of the Rapid Deployment Force for the Middle East was his administration's decision to expand America's arsenal of smaller nuclear weapons that could be used to hit highly specific targets. Interestingly, Carter had moved away from his previous antipathy toward nuclear weapons and the prospect of nuclear war and embraced the concept of limited nuclear warfare. All of this happened in the context of the growing threat in the Middle East and the Soviet intervention there.

It is within this context that Carter's decision was made to allow Khomeini to return to Iran, to take the mad grand ayatollah at his word rather than stand by the Shāh, and to empower the Islamist movement in neighboring Afghanistan. There does seem to be a real strategy at play, but it was inevitably doomed to fail from the start. A superficial understanding of political Islam was all that the Carter policymakers had

---

2 "The Carter Doctrine," *Air Force Magazine,* 1 April 2010. https://www.airforcemag.com/article/0410keeperfile/

to work with, and it showed. Ultimately, the decision to look the other way while Khomeini returned to Iran and to initiate support for the "fiercely independent and deeply religious people" of Afghanistan would lead us to the current impasse the United States is enduring with Iran, as well as, in the case of Afghanistan, the horrific events of the September 11, 2001, terrorist attacks on New York City and Washington DC.

Further, as Steve Coll assessed in his magnificent book *Ghost Wars,* in truth the Soviet incursion into Afghanistan was far less threatening to the United States than the policymakers in Washington had assumed. In fact, the real purpose behind the Soviet invasion of Afghanistan was their fear of losing their communist proxy in Afghanistan to an Islamist insurgency. The Soviet Union (like its modern successor the Russian Federation) had (and still has) a large (and growing) Muslim population. Moscow feared that an Islamist insurgency along their southern periphery could trickle northward and agitate the large number of Muslims living in the atheistic Soviet Union. The last thing Moscow wanted was an Islamist insurgency within its own territory.

Long after Jimmy Carter left the Oval Office, his eponymous doctrine has endured. American policymakers from both parties have labored under the assumption that it would be a strategic weakness to allow another power to dominate the flow of oil and natural gas out of the Middle East. Reagan actually expanded his much-maligned predecessor's doctrine by adding the so-called "Reagan Corollary," which fully "committed Washington to defending the free export of Gulf oil against threats from within the Middle East as well."[3]

In his writings, Andrew J. Bacevich has been highly critical of the Carter Doctrine. He believes that many of the worst excesses of the last forty years of American policy can be traced back to the assumptions behind the Carter Doctrine's formulation. Bacevich challenges

---

3 Hal Brands, Steven A. Cook, and Kenneth M. Pollack, "RIP the Carter Doctrine, 1980–2019," *Foreign Policy,* 13 December 2019. https://foreignpolicy.com/2019/12/15/carter-doctrine-rip-donald-trump-mideast-oil-big-think/

notions that there were real differences between liberal Democrats and conservative Republicans in the presidencies that ran America between 1980 and 2001. Essentially, the United States needed access to cheap, abundant fossil fuels. Few Americans were willing—or able—to reduce their consumption of energy. So without either reducing American consumption of energy produced by fossil fuels or creating sustainable alternative forms of energy, America would inevitably become more invested in the Middle East than it had ever been.[4]

The Carter Doctrine, in Bacevich's formulation, "represented a broad, open-ended commitment, one that expanded further with time. As subsequent events made clear, the Carter Doctrine applied to areas well beyond the Persian Gulf per se [that also] encompassed local [threats], such as Iran, Iraq, and lesser entities referred to as 'terrorists.'" Bacevich observed also that the "successful implementation of the Carter Doctrine was going to require something more than mere *containment*. Ensuring that Americans and America's allies would not want for oil required that the United States impose order on the Persian Gulf and its environs." For all intents and purposes, the Carter Doctrine "implied the conversion of the Persian Gulf into an informal American protectorate."[5]

This is the true legacy of the Carter Doctrine. It created a pretext for America's present expansive role in the Middle East. The twin shockwaves of the Khomeinist revolution in Iran as well as the *mujahideen* resistance to the Soviet invasion of Afghanistan served as the midwife for an increasing American presence and commitment to a region that had, before 1979, been viewed as a proverbial backwater unworthy of much commitment of American time, blood, or treasure. My, what a difference forty-two years makes!

4 Andrew J. Bacevich and Stephen Kinzer, "Matters of Choice," *Boston Review*, 4 April 2016. http://bostonreview.net/us/andrew-j-bacevich-interviewed-stephen-kinzer-war-greater-middle-east

5 Andrew J. Bacevich, *America's War for the Greater Middle East: A Military History* (New York: Random House, 2016), pp. 28–9.

As was noted at the start of the book, it *is* in America's interest to maintain a position of influence over the energy flows from the region, especially as America's new great rival, China, expands its own presence in the region and increases its demand for Mideast oil. However, Mideast energy is no longer as essential to US economic and national security as it once was. Between the advent of increased domestic energy production and alternative energy innovation, the Middle East is simply no longer as important as it was when the Carter Doctrine and Reagan Corollary were formulated. Therefore, a greater balance is needed in US foreign policy toward the Middle East, irrespective of whether or not China and other great powers are exploiting the region.

It was fear of Soviet expansionism that prompted the United States to support the *mujahideen* in Afghanistan. Fear of Soviet designs on both the oil wealth of Iran and its fortuitous geographical position helps to explain why Carter did little to stop the rise of Khomeini and his Islamist regime in Iran. Because of its bad decision-making during the growth of Islamism in the Mideast, the United States has been bogged down in the region—even when it is no longer as dependent on Middle Eastern energy supplies as it once was.

The Americans helped to create today's Islamist threats to better fight yesterday's Communist foes. It was a Faustian bargain that I'm not entirely convinced was worth it. This is especially true because Iran, in particular, has a proven track record of disrupting international order. Iran would have never become the major disruptive influence to US foreign policy had the Khomeinist revolution in 1979 not been given Washington's tacit support over America's long-term ally, the Shāh, thanks to Jimmy Carter.

22

SADDAM VS. KHOMEINI

THE IRANIAN REVOLUTION OF 1979 was a catalyzing event in the Greater Middle East. It shattered the thin veneer of Western style "modernization" that had gripped the minds of many of the region's leaders throughout the twentieth century, notably the mind of the Shāh. More than that, it expedited the shift away from the West and toward something else entirely, something less recognizable to Western eyes. The shift was ushered in by the Islamists, who had for decades yearned for a return of the caliphate of old.

Most would have assumed the change would have occurred in the Sunni world. It did not. However, the rise of Islamist governance in

Shiite-dominated Iran spurred many events in the region—the consequences of which continue to shape our world today.

At the same time the revolution in Iran occurred, as you've read, the Soviet-Afghan War was breaking out. The year 1979 was also important because Islamists in Saudi Arabia then seized the Grand Mosque at Mecca and attempted to engineer the downfall of the ruling House of Saud in an attempt to replicate in the Sunni-dominated Kingdom of Saudi Arabia the same kind of Islamist revolution that successfully swept aside the Shāh of Iran (more on this later). Meanwhile, Saddam Hussein's Baathist regime in Iraq opted to make a bold play for Iran's oil-rich southern territories, which bordered Iraq.

The Iran-Iraq War was ostensibly fought over oil rights. But it was so much more. It was a war between Islamist Iran and Arabist, Baathist Iraq. The war was a fight for regional supremacy by a wannabe Stalinist, Saddam Hussein, and a totalitarian religious fundamentalist, the Grand Ayatollah Khomeini. Saddam had far greater military power than Iran did when the Iran-Iraq War began. Saddam also had more powerful friends, such as the United States. Yet after a decade, the Iranians had won that fight, and Saddam's regime was on the path to destruction.

In the words of Andrew J. Bacevich, the Iran-Iraq War should really have been called the "First Persian Gulf War," since it was merely the start of a series of conflicts that would ultimately draw in outside powers, such as the United States, with increasing levels of commitment.[1] In fact, Iran serves as the connective tissue that explains America's involvement with Iraq. Had Saddam won the Iran-Iraq War or if he had never initiated the conflict at all (which might have occurred if the Carter administration had more forcefully supported the Shāh against the revolutionaries in 1979), it is highly unlikely that either Desert Storm (the Second Persian Gulf War, using Bacevich's formulation) or the Iraq War in 2003 (the Third Persian Gulf War) would have transpired at all.

This is a very important point because America's deepening

---

1 Bacevich, *America's War for the Greater Middle East*, p. 88.

involvement not only against Iran but inevitably also against Iraq would shatter whatever order had existed in the region by 2003. A butterfly effect had begun in the region from the moment that the Carter administration allowed the Shāh to be deposed by Khomeini and his band of Shiite Islamist zealots. The perceived weakness of Khomeini's regime in the aftermath of the revolution induced his Baathist neighbor, Saddam, into gambling on a war against Iran. When one looks back at the history of the region, one can find a straight line connecting the thirty years' disaster that eventually became US-Iraqi relations and the Iranian revolution in 1979.

Weakness begat weakness in that part of the world. Iraq believed Iran was weak after its revolution and thus attacked. After Iraq failed to defeat Iran, Iraq was weakened. In an attempt to rehabilitate itself after the disastrous Iran-Iraq War, Saddam's Iraq would inevitably attempt to annex neighboring Kuwait, sparking the events of Desert Storm. After his humiliating defeat by an American-led coalition in 1991, Saddam would be placed into a "box," if you will, by the world's great powers: he'd not be toppled but kept in a weakened condition. Inevitably, in order to appear strong to his neighbors, Saddam would bluff the world into believing the absurdity that he had reconstituted his programs for weapons of mass destruction—specifically his nuclear weapons program—which would spur the Americans after 9/11 to invade Iraq and ultimately depose the Baathist regime.

And once the Americans toppled Saddam and became bogged down in the Islamist insurgency there, Iran would be made stronger because its regional—and even its American—rivals would be made weaker from the fighting.

What's more, the American intervention against Iraq in 2003 was motivated, in part, by a desire on the part of some US policymakers to use Iraq as a springboard for an invasion of Iran.[2] So these two states are connected. One affects the other. Attempting to isolate and hone

---

2 Joe Conason, "Seven Countries in Five Years," Salon, 12 October 2007. https://www.salon.com/2007/10/12/wesley_clark/

into one at the expense of the other only empowers the country not being targeted. In this case, Iran would survive its bloody ten-year war with Iraq and outlast Saddam Hussein's regime, thereby complicating US foreign policy in the region immensely.[3]

As for the Iran-Iraq War and America's role in that bloody conflict, Washington and many of its allies happily supplied Saddam's forces with critical intelligence and diplomatic support. Further, the Americans looked the other way as Saddam's forces used chemical weapons against the Iranians in battle—a clear violation of international legal norms. The Iraqis were, after all, attacking an Iranian regime that was essentially birthed in anti-Americanism and considered harming any and all US interests in the region a holy imperative. So while Washington was unwilling to get its hands dirty in a major Persian military intervention, it was more than happy to encourage the bombastic, fascistic regime of Saddam Hussein to do the job.

If one were to look at the two sides in the war on paper, it would seem clear that Iran had been laid low by years of Islamist revolution followed on by Western sanctions. It was assumed that Saddam's bristling military junta would have little problem sweeping aside the fanatical but poorly equipped and trained Iranian defenders and toppling the regime. Furthermore, Saddam's willingness to serve as a partner on the ground for the United States gave US policymakers hope that an Iraqi-dominated Iran would be preferable to one controlled by either the Islamists or the communists.

For Saddam's part, he was simply following the formulation of Lee Smith that Arab leaders abide by the stronger horse principle. Whoever is viewed as weak in the region will get attacked by the nations that are believed to be more powerful. Saddam believed—as did most of the rest of the world—that he was more powerful than his Iranian neighbors and pounced when he thought it was easy pickings.

---

3 Suzanne Maloney, "How the Iraq War Has Empowered Iran," Brookings Institute, 21 March 2008. https://www.brookings.edu/opinions/how-the-iraq-war-has-empowered-iran/

Yet as the work of Kenneth Pollack proves, Arab armies of the modern era are historically inept. They are very efficient in cracking down on domestic threats to their autocratic regimes. They can also be useful in combating terrorism (whenever Arab regimes decide to crackdown on terrorists).

Historically, however, when they engage in war with external threats, Arab armies—no matter how well equipped and funded—rarely perform well. While many scholars have emphasized that Arab armies in the twentieth century came to rely upon Soviet military technology and doctrine, which could be a potential weakness, Pollack argues that the embrace of Soviet technology and doctrine likely helped Arab armies. The real weakness was the autarkic political systems and the unique culture that Arab armies, in this case, Saddam's army, were spawned from.[4]

Evoking Bacevich again, "When Saddam sent his Soviet-equipped army plunging into Iran on September 22 [1980], he envisioned a brief, satisfying land grab."[5] In 1980, Saddam wanted to extend Iraq's control into southern Iran. The Iran-Iraq War would replicate a pattern that has historically pervaded the Greater Middle East before and after this conflict: territorial conquest in order for one side to dominate both natural resources, like oil and natural gas, as well as control over vital territory. In this case, Saddam wanted the Shatt al-Arab waterway that separates southern Iran from Iraq. This tiny, though vital, waterway forms the lynchpin of the Tigris-Euphrates river networks. Once the two ancient rivers fuse into the Shatt al-Arab waterway, the water then flows into the Persian Gulf.

The Shatt al-Arab is also one of the few points of egress for Iraq to potentially extend its naval power, as the desert country is almost entirely landlocked. Although Iran has other points of entry from its territory into the seas beyond, the Shatt al-Arab waterway was also a zone where a

---

4 Kenneth Pollack, *Armies of Sand: The Past, Present, and Future of Arab Military Effectiveness* (New York: Oxford University Press, 2019), pp. 510–24.

5 Bacevich, *America's War for the Greater East*, pp. 89.

considerable volume of Iranian oil exports traveled to reach the Persian Gulf. Further, the Shatt al-Arab waterway was a natural source of conflict because it constituted the "cultural line between Persians and Arabs."

As the authors of a report for the Environment, Conflict, and Cooperation (ECC) project at the Adelphi Institute assessed:

> This boundary illustrates the many fault lines between Iran and Iraq: Shi'a vs. Sunni Government; heir of the Persian Empire vs. heir of the Ottoman Empire; Fundamentalist/Secular Government. The delimitation of the Shatt al-Arab River's borders has been a point of contention between Ottomans and Persians for centuries and both empires have sought to control it [after] the dissolution of the Ottoman Empire, the dispute shifted to an Iran-Iraq conflict.[6]

Because of the confluence of historical animosity over this particular strip of territory, Saddam wanted total control rather than shared control and access of this vital waterway. What's more, the ideological distinctions, as well as the ethnic and religious differences between Saddam's Baathist regime and the Khomeinist regime of Iran, implied that war would come sooner or later. Beyond the Shatt al-Arab waterway, Saddam's ultimate objective with initiating hostilities was to dominate the Khūzestān Province in southern Iran.

Khūzestān, nestled astride the ancient Zagros Mountains separating Iran from neighboring Iraq, can be "divided into two regions, the plains and mountainous regions." The Karun River, Iran's largest riverway, flows nicely into this region along with two other major rivers, whose waters are used by the locals to irrigate the lush and fertile agricultural lands of the historic province. Not only is the region a historically important area, rich in farmland and diverse in ethnic groups, but this region sits atop of large concentration of oil wealth in Iran's south.

---

6 "Iraq-Iran: From Water Dispute to War," ECC Platform Library, Accessed on 9 February 2021, https://library.ecc-platform.org/conflicts/iraq-iran-water-dispute-war

Located in this region is the oil-rich island of Abadan. Saddam wanted Abadan as part of his push into Iran. The region is also home to a large Arab population. When Saddam invaded Iran, he believed the Arabs of Khūzestān would rise up behind Iranian lines and help to hand Iraq's army a key victory. Saddam miscalculated terribly. Most of the region's Arabs sided with the Iranian defenders, and many even joined the ranks of the Iranian military to help repulse the Iraqi invaders. When the Khūzestāni Arabs did not rise up and join the proto-separatist movement that Saddam's military had fostered, the Iraqi military went on a rampage in the area, raping and killing countless women, children, and men in the region as retribution for their failure to align with their fellow Arabs in neighboring Iraq.

In fact, the entire city of Khorramshahr was decimated in 1982 during the epic battle fought there. During Saddam's invasion of this region, the critical Iranian oil refinery at Abadan was destroyed by Iraqi shelling. This incapacitated an important component of Iran's oil economy for the course of the war. Once the hellish conflict ended, however, the region was restored as Iran's oil-producing dynamo. Today, the massive Karun-3 dam generates vast amounts of hydroelectric power from the Karun River flowing through the region to help propel the region's economic dynamism.[7]

The military historian Edward N. Luttwak has asserted that war is not entirely a destructive act. While terrible, warfare is more of an act of creative destruction. It can weaken states and potentially lead to their downfall. Yet it can also strengthen states.[8]

Saddam and his American backers assumed the war against Iran would be quick, short, and decisive. Washington believed it could back

7 "Province of Khuzestan," Iran Chamber Society, Accessed on 9 February 2021. http://www.iranchamber.com/provinces/15_khuzestan/15_khuzestan.php

8 CinnovationGlobal, "Edward Luttwak at Creative Innovation 2010—'How War Can Bring Peace,'" YouTube, 8:58–15:24, 13 November 2012. https://www.youtube.com/watch?v=XTTruD9WTvc&t=55s

Saddam's butcherers in order to squelch the religious maniacs in Tehran and then mop up whatever messes remained in the region. Instead, the Iran-Iraq War ended up eviscerating Saddam's regime and strengthening the Khomeinist government. The bloodbath that defined the frontlines of the Iran-Iraq War broke Saddam's army but empowered the outwardly weaker Iranian forces to overcome the odds and sweep aside their opponents.

More dangerously for the Americans, the Iran-Iraq War empowered the Islamist regime in Tehran. During the conflict with Iraq, the Islamist regime conscripted young men to fight Saddam's army. Few were given adequate training or arms to effectively combat the Soviet-equipped Iraqi forces. Instead, the young men—many of them children—were given a green-colored *Qur'an,* a key to wear around their bodies, so their eternal souls could unlock the gates of Paradise when they died, and a blessing from the grand ayatollah.[9]

The Iranians engaged in human-wave attacks against the entrenched Iraqi positions. Many of these young Iranians between the ages of twelve and seventeen donned red headbands with the words *"Sar Allah,"* meaning "Warriors of God" in Farsi. Many military historians have likened the fighting between Iraqi and Iranian forces during this time to the horrible trench warfare that defined the European battlefields of the First World War.

The grand ayatollah, while his hands had been bloodied during the mass executions of his political enemies during the Islamist revolution that catapulted him to power in 1979, was not a military strategist. He viewed victory in terms of body count—if more Iraqi soldiers died than did Iranian, then he was winning. "To Khomeini, so long as the math worked and his fighters were sufficiently motivated by religious fanaticism

---

9 Terrance Smith, "Iran: Five Years of Fanaticism," *New York Times,* 12 February 1984. https://www.nytimes.com/1984/02/12/magazine/iran-five-years-of-fanaticism.html

and revolutionary spirit, he could push all of the way to Baghdad."[10]

Much to Saddam's chagrin, the poorly armed and trained young Iranian attack force was able to swamp the lines of his armies. Khomeini's assumption that his soldiers needed only religious fervor and revolutionary gumption appeared to be more correct than anyone outside of Iran had estimated. Inevitably, Iraq was defeated, in large part by these bloody though effective tactics. The takeaway from these events in Iran was that Allah was on Iran's side. Some undoubtedly did blame the Khomeinist regime for the loss of their loved ones.

Yet, for the most part, the Khomeinist regime was never more popular than after the Iran-Iraq War—especially because they played up the victim card. (Saddam had, after all, attacked Iran.) As noted, Saddam's regime in Iraq was running on borrowed time from the moment it withdrew from Iran. Luttwak's postulation about the real nature of war, therefore, holds true: warfare helped to gut Saddam and empower Iran. Warfare, whether desired or not, really is the ultimate method of state-building. And the Iran-Iraq War had the exact opposite effect on the region from Saddam's and the Americans' intentions. It weakened Iraq, which was not a direct threat to the United States, and it empowered Iran, which has proven to be the most consistent threat to US strategic interests in the region since 1979.

---

10 Blake Stillwell, "The Horrifying Way Iran Used Kids to Clear Mines," We Are the Mighty, 5 February 2021. https://www.wearethemighty.com/mighty-history/iran-iraq-war-child-soldiers-mines/

23

NUCLEAR DAY-DREAMIN'

WHEN THE SHĀH still ruled Iran, he dreamed of modernizing the country. Part of his modernization drive was to diversify his country's economy away from oil. He would continue pumping oil and natural gas from Iran, but he did not want that to be the only product his country produced.

This was partly because the Shāh believed throughout the 1970s that the world had reached peak oil. Therefore, if Iran's only major commodity was oil and the world was slowly running out of it, Iran would be left behind when the world eventually weaned itself off oil. It would be better to get a jump on the coming change by investing significantly in alternative energy, notably nuclear power, or at least that was the Shāh's thinking.

The Iranian nuclear program today really does have its origins in a desire for Iran to spearhead peaceful development of nuclear energy. As you've read in previous chapters, Western firms like Brown Boveri were interested in developing an Iranian nuclear capability for civilian energy production. France was also intimately involved in supplying the Shāh with nuclear reactors. In fact, the origins of Iran's present nuclear weapons program can be traced back to President Dwight D. Eisenhower's "Atoms for Peace" program in the 1950s.

Immediately after the Second World War, there was a wave of interest globally in developing nuclear energy. Iran also wanted to develop this budding new industry. The Shāh built Iran's nuclear program courtesy of the West. After the Shāh was deposed, however, the Islamists were initially uninterested in the program. That all changed once it became clear that the United States was inimical to the Islamist regime—especially after the hostage crisis and the humiliation of Carter's Desert One rescue mission.

During the Reagan administration, the situation between Iran and the United States only worsened. During this time, Iran's revolutionaries were on a high. The Islamist movement in Iran was fervently committed to spreading its revolution beyond its borders during the 1980s. One of their first international alliances was formed with the Lebanese Shiite terrorist organization Hezbollah. Together, Iran and Hezbollah forged a bloody path of Islamist uprising in Lebanon during the horrific events of the multisided ethno-religious civil war in Lebanon. American troops were stationed in Beirut to try to bring peace to the region—only to be murdered by Iranian agents seeking to exacerbate the chaos and strife of the civil war in Lebanon.

Iranian agents terrorized Israel and took Americans hostage throughout the 1980s. Infamously, Hezbollah took the Beirut CIA station chief William Buckley hostage and tortured him to death. During the course of Buckley's torturous, nineteen-month ordeal with Hezbollah that ended when Buckley suffered a fatal heart attack around October 4, 1985 while in Iranian captivity, Iran's government assessed that Buckley had divulged "200 to 300 sensitive names of people and over 400 pages of debriefing."[1]

Meanwhile, Iranian agents took other Americans hostage, which prompted President Reagan to trade arms for the hostages. This resulted in the Iran-Contra Affair, which almost led to Reagan's impeachment and resulted in the removal of key Reagan administration foreign policy advisers. Reagan had experienced the death that Iranian-backed terrorism could bring when Hezbollah bombed the Marine barracks in Beirut. He then saw what Iran was willing to do to spread their variant of Islamism to the wider world—and the threat that posed to the United States.

The Iranian threat was so outsized that it created the risk of toppling Reagan's presidency during the Iran-Contra affair. If that had happened, yet another American presidency—the second in a row, actually—would have been toppled, thanks to Iran's perfidy. Yet the Iranian threat grew stronger. Tehran believed it was in a spiritual struggle against unbelievers in the United States and against America's allies in the Jewish state of Israel and the Sunni Arab states. Iran did not want to become a normal country in the Middle East. Iran wanted to take over the Middle East—and purify the lands of their Prophet by killing all of the unbelievers and preparing to release the twelfth imam from his occlusion.

THE MAD MULLAHS AND THE BOMB

That is why the Islamist regime in Iran reconstituted the Shāh's old nuclear program. While the Khomeinist regime continued propagating the old talking points of the Shāh regarding Iran's nuclear program (that it was for peaceful purposes), the truth was that Iran wanted nuclear weapons. This became especially apparent after how close the Iraqis came to destroying the nascent Islamist regime of Iran during their

1 Jack Andersen and Dale Van Atta, "CIA Official Tortured to Death, Gave Secrets," *Deseret News*, 28 September 1988. https://www.deseret.com/1988/9/28/18779491/cia-official-tortured-to-death-gave-secrets

ten-year war. Plus, the Iranians knew the Israelis had nuclear weapons since 1969.[2] Tehran believed it was only a matter of time before the Sunni Arab states built their own nuclear weapons arsenal

Then in May of 1998, the Sunni Islamic state of Pakistan test-detonated their first atomic weapon shortly after Pakistan's great rival India had exploded its own atomic weapon. India's test caught the world—notably US intelligence—totally by surprise. Fears abounded that an Indo-Pakistani nuclear war would soon occur. Meanwhile, Iranian leaders began worrying that Pakistan would start sharing their own nuclear weapons technology with fellow Sunni states, like Saudi Arabia. In fact, in 2009, reports emerged that the Kingdom of Saudi Arabia had placed an order for nineteen nuclear weapons from Pakistan, as a stopgap in case the Iranians built their own reliable nuclear weapons arsenal.[3]

When President Barack Obama crafted the Joint Comprehensive Plan of Action (JCPOA), the agreement between the United States and the Islamic Republic of Iran in 2015, he and his advisers believed they were bringing peace to the region by normalizing relations with Iran. Since 1979, as you've seen, the United States has striven to contain Iran. Obama's team believed that normalizing relations with Iran would force it to play by international rules and make Iran comport with international standards.

As previous chapters have shown, Iran does not aspire to play within the rules of international norms. They want to reimagine the conditions for life in the Middle East. Iran's leaders want to make the region more conducive to the interests of Iran's Islamist regime, not to make Iran more palatable to American, Israeli, and Sunni Arab tastes.

Iran views nuclear weapons as a necessary cudgel to deter American military intervention. They also believe it is a necessary check against

---

2 "Fact Sheet: Israel's Nuclear Arsenal," Center for Arms Control and Non-Proliferation, 31 March 2020. https://armscontrolcenter.org/fact-sheet-israels-nuclear-arsenal/

3 Mark Urban, "Saudi Nuclear Weapons 'On Order' from Pakistan," BBC, 6 November 2013. https://www.bbc.com/news/world-middle-east-24823846

Israel and even potentially the Sunni Arab states. Yet Iranian plans for the bomb are not merely defensive. They have offensive designs for these weapons as well.

Further, Iran's close-knit relationship with Hezbollah and other terrorist proxies indicates an asymmetrical threat posed to the United States, Israel, and the wider world. The Obama nuclear deal allowed Iran to follow a legal pathway to gaining nuclear capabilities—while enhancing the Iranian regime through greater normalization of trade. This would have done little to reduce the threat Iran poses to American interests. In fact, it would have likely empowered Iran to further threaten and degrade American interests in the region.

Even if Iran was sincere in their desire to have nuclear weapons simply as a check against Sunni Arab or Israeli aggression, there is little that would stop them from handing off nuclear weapons to their terrorist proxies. We have already seen how dangerous Hezbollah has been not only for the region but for the Americans. And we know that Hezbollah has sent its agents far afield to do the bidding of Iran—with many of their agents and affiliated organizations entering the United States.

Here is what the director for the US National Counterterrorism Center said after the arrests of Hezbollah agents Ali Kourani and Samer el-Dabek in 2017: "It's our assessment that Hezbollah is determined to give itself a potential homeland option as a critical component of its terrorism playbook."[4] Now imagine if Iran handed off nuclear materials to its Hezbollah proxies to use against its foes.

The Obama-era nuclear agreement was forged with the belief that allowing Iran to have the same opportunities and capabilities as its neighbors would effectively bring stability to the region.[5] What the

---

4 Matthew Levitt, "Hezbollah Isn't Just in Beirut. It's in New York, Too," *Foreign Policy*, 14 June 2019. https://foreignpolicy.com/2019/06/14/hezbollah-isnt-just-in-beirut-its-in-new-york-too-canada-united-states-jfk-toronto-pearson-airports-ali-kourani-iran/

5 Stephen M. Walt, "How Not to Contain Iran," *Foreign Policy*, 5 March 2010. https://foreignpolicy.com/2010/03/05/how-not-to-contain-iran/

Obama team never understood was that Iran was the key agent desta-bilizing the region. Iran's very history and political system meant that it was at war with its neighbors unless those neighbors swore fealty to Tehran—and to the Shiism particular to Iran's leadership—which Iran's neighbors would never do of their own volition. Even as the Obama administration went about drawing down American forces in Iraq and as Obama had slowed the tempo and size of the US forces deployed to Afghanistan in his second term, Iran used that as an excuse to expand their footprint in the region.

While it might seem comforting to note that the United States and Iran were actually aligned against the ISIS threat in the region, clearly Iran had no intention of leaving when and if their preferred proxies defeated ISIS and similar groups in Syria, for example. In fact, Iran's support for Syria's embattled strongman, Bashar al-Assad, is all part of a larger scheme to threaten Israel and push American influence farther back. Thanks to their alliance with Assad and the compliance of the friendly Shiite-dominated post–Saddam Hussein regime in Iraq, Iranian forces and goods have been able to move freely back and forth from Iran through Iraq into Syria and down into Lebanon.

Letting Iran get the bomb while American forces leave the region *en masse* will have unintended consequences. It will spur the Sunni Arabs to fulfill their desire to acquire nuclear weapons. Further, Israel will likely be goaded into launching a preemptive nuclear strike on Iran to prevent them from acquiring a functional nuclear weapons arsenal.[6] Under such conditions, the United States, along with China and Russia, would be drawn into a much greater fight in the region—one in which the great powers may be threatening nuclear war against each other in response.

The myth of stability is part of the nuclear day-dreaming that has enchanted Western policymakers as much as it has enraptured the

---

6 Judah Ari Gross, "Likud Minister Warns Israel Could Attack Iran Nuclear Program if US Rejoins Deal," *Times of Israel,* 13 January 2021. https://www.timesofisrael.com/likud-minister-warns-israel-could-attack-iran-nuclear-program-if-us-rejoins-deal/

Islamists of Iran. The Iranian regime is inherently expansionistic and revolutionary. Even though the grand ayatollah died in 1989, his successors have proven to be just as fiery in supporting their brand of Shia Islam. And his successors have had greater longevity than he did. Iran's regime cannot be trusted with nuclear weapons. Heck, Iran's regime cannot be trusted, period.

The Obama administration's great error was believing that Iran was akin to a recalcitrant child who could be manipulated with kind words and the turning of a blind eye to their hostility toward their neighbors and the United States. In fact, Iranian hostility is part and parcel of the regime. If the regime were allowed to acquire nuclear weapons and its status were "normalized," Iran would abuse that position and overrun the region. Or, more likely, Iran would spark a world war, as the Sunni Arabs and Israelis, possibly even the Turks, would all start balancing against or cooperating with Iran. Over time, the Americans, Chinese, and Russians would rally against each other in the region as well.

As for Iran's trustworthiness, there is a clear history of malintent. Think about it this way: the JCPOA gave money, time, materials, and prestige to an Islamist regime in Iran that lacked all of these things in 2015. What did Iran do with these gifts? Did Obama's great concession to Iran placate the mad mullahs? Did the JCPOA make Iran more amenable to American interests? Certainly not.

Here's what Suzanne Maloney of the left-leaning Brookings Institute had to say to the House Committee on Foreign Affairs Subcommittee on the Middle East and North Africa in 2015:

> Iran will be unshackled from the preponderance of the sanctions regime that halved its oil exports, crashed the value of its currency, and cost the country tens of billions—at least—in lost revenues and additional costs over the course of the past five years. The United Nations Security Council measures, which served as a platform for most of the actions undertaken by the rest of the world against Iran, will vanish with a few notable exceptions pertaining to conventional arms and ballistic missiles.

The totality of European Union sanctions, including the embargo on Iranian oil and prohibitions on energy investment, will evaporate. And nearly all of the American measures that had effectively severed Iran's economy from the international financial system will be waived, permitting somewhere in the realm of $100 to $150 billion in Iranian assets that had been held in overseas accounts to flow back into Iran.

The agreement also provides for the effective cessation of a number of American measures that were predicated on the full range of concerns about Iranian policies, re-opens a loophole that permits U.S. corporations to trade with or operate in Iran via foreign subsidiaries, and carves out a wider array of permissible U.S. business with Iran than at any time since the comprehensive embargo was put in place twenty years ago. Like the release of Iran's frozen assets, these new openings in the American sanctions architecture will go into effect immediately after Tehran's initial nuclear constraints have been certified.

This wide-ranging sanctions relief incorporated in the JCPOA has elicited considerable angst among some here in Congress, as well as other U.S. policymakers and allies. The sense of affront at the appearance of rewarding Tehran after decades of bad behavior is magnified by the irony that Washington is being forced to cede the most effective instrument in its policy toolbox, at the very moment when its efficacy has finally been confirmed, even as some of the most strategically relevant aspects of the Iranian challenge remain unabated. That inescapable reality underscores the importance of identifying and implementing new mechanisms for addressing Iran's problematic regional policies.[7]

As Maloney pointed out, Iran's ballistic missile program is as troubling to the United States and its allies as Iran's nuclear program. Even without nuclear weapons, Iran's growing arsenal of ballistic missiles and precision munitions, coupled with their forward operating bases in

7 Suzanne Maloney, "Major Beneficiaries to the Iran Deal: The IRGC and Hezbollah," Brookings Institute, 17 September 2015. https://www.brookings.edu/testimonies/major-beneficiaries-of-the-iran-deal-the-irgc-and-hezbollah/

Yemen, Iraq, Syria, and Lebanon, can threaten the United States, the Sunni Arab nations, and Israel with disturbing consistency. In fact, in November 2020, shortly after the assassination of Mohsen Fakhrizadeh, the godfather of Iran's nuclear weapons program, Iranian leaders threatened the Israeli port city of Haifa.

Hezbollah and its masters in Tehran believe Haifa is the "economic heart of the Israeli regime." Hezbollah has announced "five vital arteries of Israel that are within the range of Hezbollah's Iranian missiles: the port of Haifa, a petrochemical complex, an electricity company, the Matam Hi-Tech and Business Park, and a railway network."[8] Remember, shortly after the Beirut blast in the summer of 2020, Hezbollah's leader, Hassan Nasrallah, threatened to blow up the port of Haifa using "ammonium nitrate" that would be "like a nuclear explosion."[9] Given the presence of Iranian precision-guided munitions in neighboring Lebanon, this is not something to take lightly.

According to Maloney's 2015 testimony, Iran's ballistic missile and conventional arms were to remain under sanctions even according to the terms of the JCPOA. Yet, as you've seen, Iran has not been deterred from developing these weapons. Why assume that Iran would act differently in nuclear weapons development?

And what of Iran's undying support for terrorism? Surely the retinue of gifts that the Obama JCPOA handed to the mullahs gave the Iranians pause in supporting Hezbollah and other extremist groups around the world?

Well, as Suzanne Maloney described, Iran's egregious support for terrorism beyond its borders has continued, whether the country faced pressure from the Americans or not. Addressing whether or not increased pressure on Iran in the form of sanctions has lessened the Iranian penchant for terrorism, Maloney testified:

8 Emily Judd and Yaghoub Fazeli, "Why Is Iran Threatening Israel's Haifa? Experts Explain," Al-Arabiya English, 30 November 2020. https://english.alarabiya.net/features/2020/11/30/Why-is-Iran-targeting-Israel-s-Haifa-Experts-explain

9 Seth J. Frantzman, "Nasrallah Threatens to Blow Up Israel with Same Chemicals as Beirut Blast," *The Jerusalem Post*, 8 August 2020. https://www.jpost.com/middle-east/nasrallah-threatened-to-blow-up-israel-with-same-chemicals-as-beirut-blast-637582

These same trends have held over the course of the past decade, as externally-imposed economic pressures on Tehran, as a result of both sanctions and the more recent decline in oil prices, reached or even surpassed the heights of the hardships during the war. These pressures provided no remedy to Iran's efforts to extend its influence through nefarious activities and allies, or its substantial investment in fueling and fighting conflicts in Iraq and Syria. Even since 2010, when the world has applied unprecedented financial pressure on the regime including measures that have directly targeted the institutions and assets related to Iran's regional power projection and its support for terrorist proxies beyond its borders, there is little evidence that sanctions impeded Iran's most destabilizing policies.

The relative consistency of Iran's relationships with terrorist organizations and extremists across the region makes it impossible to discern much, if any, remedial relationship between the economy and the adoption of more responsible regional policies. This is in part a function of the relatively low funding threshold for these activities; the expense associated with sustaining Hezbollah's massive rocket arsenal or fueling Bashar Al Assad's barrel bombs is relatively easily absorbed even at times of relative scarcity. More importantly, the persistence of these policies is further confirmation that they tend to reflect opportunism on the part of Iranian leaders rather than budget priorities.[10]

Let's get this straight: The West gives up all its leverage over a pernicious state sponsor of terrorism in exchange for airy promises that Iran won't pursue nuclear weapons before the JCPOA allows them to get them? This doesn't sound like a deal so much as a concession. And it's almost as though supporting terrorism and destabilizing the region were baked into Iran's ideological cake!

What of the parts of the deal that former President Obama and current President Biden promise us will prevent Iran from acquiring nuclear weapons?

---

10 Maloney, "Major Beneficiaries."

The original 2015 deal had sunset clauses written into it. The restrictions that Iran had agreed to that limited the number of centrifuges needed for uranium enrichment went away automatically by 2025. By 2030, any remaining limitations on uranium enrichment activities automatically expire.[11] If President Biden does what he said he would while campaigning in the contentious 2020 presidential election, then Iran will have a reliable nuclear weapons capability by the end of the decade.

In 2019, Iran began to break free of any remaining constraints on their nuclear weapons program. Iran's leaders said it was because President Trump had abrogated the Obama-era JCPOA. What's more likely is that the Iranians had continued amassing the resources needed to break free from the JCPOA constraints, before, during, and after the JCPOA. This is what's known as a "surge capacity." The Iranians have no intention of ending their nuclear weapons program. Instead, they're simply stockpiling resources so they can break free of the JCPOA constraints, all while trying to gain economic relief and strategic advantage over their regional foes.

NUKES FOR ALL!

Western policymakers also forget that the situation in the region is not dyadic. It is not just the United States and Iran. Notions that nuclear parity can create stability have arisen from America's experience in the Cold War, when the two nuclear-armed superpowers stared down each other and dared the other side to blink.

A degree of stability was created from that situation, for neither side wanted to start nuclear Armageddon first. Yet, unlike the Cold War dynamic, in the Middle East today there are multiple ideologically charged tribal groups who compete for dominance. Between Iran, Israel, and the Sunni Arab states, the situation in the region is, at the very least,

---

11 John Haltiwanger, "Here's What's in the 2015 Nuclear Deal with Iran That Trump Abandoned and Biden Pledged to Restore," *Business Insider,* 2 December 2020. https://www.businessinsider.com/iran-nuclear-deal-explained

tripolar. The situation is particularly tenuous if the United States does as the last two presidents have said they wanted to do: disengage from the region. Removing the American security umbrella from the region, while ultimately desirable, will lead to disaster if the proper forces are not empowered to enhance stability in the region.

Tripolar power dynamics are inherently unstable. One side of the triangle will always be weaker and feel left out, creating the possibility of war. Throwing nuclear weapons into that situation will ensure that instability reigns—especially if one or two sides of the triangle are left without nuclear weapons. In that situation, a race will occur to acquire these weapons in order to rebalance the equation. This process of endless rebalancing in a tripolar system creates the greatest likelihood for war.

And what does Iran hope to accomplish with nuclear weapons?

Iran's Islamists are keenly aware that their Shiism is a minority in a region of mostly Sunni Muslim states. Iran's leadership seeks to redress this imbalance with nuclear weapons. Iran's military has an offensive doctrine of expansion. Nuclear weapons coupled with an American withdrawal from the region will create the very conditions American leaders are hoping to avoid. American leaders, with the exception of former President Trump, have both underestimated and misunderstood Iran's threat.

Whether it was Jimmy Carter encouraging the return of the grand ayatollah or Barack Obama being amenable to Iranian nuclear weapons development, American actions have only allowed Iran's threat to the world to grow. It's a fantasy that Iran's current regime can be trusted with nukes, just as it is a fantasy that letting the Saudis get nuclear arms would be acceptable. Yet if Iran does officially get nuclear weapons, the Saudis will get them as well. And this fantasy will become an atomic nightmare very quickly once Tehran becomes a true nuclear power.

24

OIL WAR!

PART OF IRAN'S DIZZYING ATTEMPTS to pressure the United States and its allies is to target the critical oil supply from the region, which passes through the vital Straits of Hormuz and even the Bab el-Mandeb. Iran first deployed this strategy against the Americans during the 1987 "Tanker War" that happened during the Iran-Iraq War. Iran began targeting oil shipments passing through the Strait of Hormuz.

The oil-producing Gulf states were most negatively impacted by Iran's attacks and demanded greater action from the United States to protect their oil shipments. After the USS *Stark*, an American frigate, was accidentally attacked by an Iraqi Exocet missile that was meant to target Iranian naval forces in the Straits, the Americans began escorting oil shipments through the Strait of Hormuz.

Clashes occurred between US Navy and Iranian naval forces. In one seminal instance, the Iranians mined the USS *Samuel B. Roberts* and American forces sank Iranian frigates in response. This was, by all measures, an oil war. However, it should be noted that the "Tanker War" did not lead to the closing of the Straits of Hormuz, nor did it significantly impact oil exports from the Gulf or result in sustained increases in the price of oil. According to some estimates the combined anti-shipping campaigns of both Iran and Iraq never disrupted more than two percent of ships in the Gulf."[1]

The idea that Iran could disrupt the world's oil flows, however, never died. Over time, Iran would craft bold strategies meant to threaten the stability of the world's oil supply with the hope of visiting another oil shock upon the Americans—something not endured since the 1970s. Interestingly, in 2018 the Iranians attempted to stoke the fires of an oil war with the West when they captured a British tanker passing through the strait. Ultimately, the tanker was released after two months. In 2019, Iran threatened to close down the Straits of Hormuz in response to the Trump administration's decision to end the waivers in the Obama-era nuclear deal that allowed Western companies to do business in Iran.[2]

And now that the tiny country of Yemen, along the Gulf of Oman, has been entirely destabilized by civil war—the bloodiest in the world—Iran has moved its forces into the beleaguered country to support the Houthi rebels. Meanwhile, the Saudis are leading the Sunni Arab states in military action in Yemen directed against the Houthis and, by extension, Iran. Thanks to Iran's influence over the Houthi rebels in Yemen,

---

1 Martin S. Navias, "The First Tanker War," *History Today,* August 2019. https://www.historytoday.com/history-matters/first-tanker-war

2 Amanda Macias, "Japanese Oil Tanker Owner Disagrees with US Military That a Mine Caused a Blast Near Iran," *CNBC,* 14 June 2019. https://www.cnbc.com/2019/06/14/oil-tanker-owner-disagrees-with-us-that-mine-caused-a-blast-near-iran.html

though, Tehran is now able to attack Saudi Arabia with their increasingly accurate missiles and drones. Iran can also threaten shipping in the Gulf of Oman and the Strait of Bab el-Mandeb, which is to Saudi Arabia's south.

Over the summer of 2019, ten drones were launched from Yemen that bombarded sensitive targets in Saudi Arabia's Eastern Province (which is also home to Saudi Arabia's largest Shiite Muslim population). The attack was designed to disrupt Saudi Arabia's oil production capabilities. One of Saudi Arabia's largest oil fields, known as Hijra Khurais, and Saudi Arabia's Abqaiq crude stabilization facility—the largest facility of its kind in the world—were struck by the Iranian-built drones.

Hijra Khurais produces 1.5 million barrels of crude oil per day, and Abqaiq helps to produce up to 7 million barrels a day. While the Houthi rebels officially took credit for the attack, it was clearly done with Iranian drones and ultimately served Iranian interests.[3] Despite its destruction, the Iranian-backed Houthi attack had minimal impact on the global price of oil.

This was partly because the Saudis effectively contained the massive fires that had erupted in a timely manner. It was also because, at the time, the United States was steadfastly committed to expanding and modernizing its natural gas and oil production in North America. Due to this, America had more oil than it needed and could export some.

Further, as energy analyst Richard Mallinson said in 2019, "slower global economic growth and [the] trade war between the US and China," meant that the supply was greater than demand. When the Iranian-backed Houthis attacked the Abqaiq crude facility and the Hijra Khurais oil fields in Saudi Arabia's Eastern Province, it had a minimal impact on the global price of oil. Iran's sustained commitment to stoking an oil war with the West remains a key tenet of their national strategy for gaining regional dominance.

Not only did Iran threaten international oil supplies during the aforementioned Tanker War in 1987 and in the last few years, but

---

3 Weichert, "Iran Keeps Asking for It." https://spectator.org/iran-keeps-asking-for-it/

Iran has used its growing cyberwar capabilities to attack Saudi oil firms. Shortly after Israel and the United States launched the infamous "Stuxnet" cyberattack against Iran's nuclear weapons program, Iran retaliated with a cyberattack against Saudi ARAMCO computers.

All of these actions—the threats against the Strait of Hormuz and other critical oil transit chokepoints, the increasing threat to oil production facilities in neighboring Saudi Arabia, and the growing Iranian threat in cyberspace—are proofs of concept. The Iranians are perfecting their asymmetrical warfare capabilities. These unconventional strategies are meant to complicate life for the United States and its allies and to prepare the future battlefield between Iran and the United States in Iran's favor.

The Iranians envision attacking these energy assets in ways that cause the price of oil to spike as high as $200 a barrel! In so doing, Tehran believes not only that they will increase the pain of ordinary energy consumers in the West—and create friction between American leaders and their voters—but that Iran itself could also benefit financially from the increased price of oil. Although it remains under sanctions, Iran does sit atop one of the most abundant sources of oil in the world. Tehran has been desperate to get out from under Western sanctions so it can sell its product on the wider market.

As it stands, only countries like the People's Republic of China purchase Iranian oil. Other countries do as well, but the Iranian ability to make a profit off its oil supplies is complicated by US foreign policy. Even if the sanctions weren't removed but Iran successfully attacked international oil supplies (and Iran's attacks have been growing more complex and diffuse), the resultant spike in prices would still give the regime the life-breath it needs. Iran already uses those funds to support its growing, global terrorist network.

Imagine what might happen if Iran used a nuclear device against these assets. Or if Iran attacked international oil production in the region at the same moment Hezbollah used an Iranian bomb against any of their enemies, even possibly the United States?

In 2010 Condoleezza Rice, former Bush administration national security adviser and, later, secretary of state, told an audience that if Iran did anything with nuclear weapons against the United States or its allies, Tehran would be "turned into a parking lot." Surely that cannot be the threshold for responding to Iranian malfeasance. And it is probably easier said than done. While America does possess the means—far more than Iran does—retaliating with nuclear arms would evoke responses, likely hostile ones, from both China and Russia, to say nothing of the response from America's allies in Europe and beyond. What's more, this very high threshold for direct American retaliation against Iranian perfidiousness has not prevented Iran from acting in its routine malign fashion.

Thankfully, Iranian attempts to spike the price of oil have thus far fallen flat. However, their continued commitment to the project implies that they believe it will inevitably work. This is especially the case today as the Biden administration seeks to return to the Obama-era JCPOA nuclear agreement with Iran—thereby reducing sanctions—and as the Biden team cancels vital energy production projects here in the United States, such as the Keystone XL pipeline. These reductions in supply increases Iran's ability to create spikes in the price of oil globally.[4]

Again, many pro-Iran nuclear deal advocates believe that removing the sanctions on Iranian oil sales and integrating them into the world economy would not only help to keep the price of oil low but might make Iran "buy into" the status quo.

This is not so. It is true that in the aftermath of signing its nuclear agreement with the United States, Iran adhered to the framework of the agreement. Yet this was more likely because the JCPOA gave Iran what it wanted: stable, open, and free trade with the rest of the world and a legal pathway to acquiring nuclear weapons—without the risk of a wider war with the United States. When the Obama administration was followed

---

4 Matthew Brown, "Keystone XL Pipeline Nixed after Biden Stands Firm on Permit," AP News, 9 June 2021. https://apnews.com/article/donald-trump-joe-biden-keystone-pipeline-canada-environment-and-nature-141eabd7cca6449dfbd2dab8165812f2

by the Trump administration, however, that framework changed.

Initially, the Trump administration respected the JCPOA while making minute changes, such as imposing renewed sanctions on Iran or refusing to grant waivers to Western businesses that wanted to conduct transactions there. By 2018, the Trump administration had fully abandoned the JCPOA after news broke that the Iranians were enriching uranium again and exceeding the stockpile of heavy water allowed under the terms of the JCPOA.[5]

In fact, once the Obama administration entered into the Iranian nuclear agreement, Tehran took that as a green light to shore up their hold in post-Saddam Iraq and to expand their presence in Syria and Lebanon. The Iranians are building a corridor connecting their power along the Shia Crescent in order to gain access to the eastern Mediterranean Sea, to buttress their clients in Syria and Lebanon, and most importantly to threaten Israel while outmaneuvering the Saudis and their Arab allies. So, yes, the Americans got Iran to sign on the dotted line of the nuclear agreement. Obama's team *did not* get Iran to give up its quest for the bomb in any meaningful way—nor did Obama's team do much to assuage the concerns of the Arabs or Israelis.

It should be clear by now that Iran has ulterior motives. Give the Iranians an inch, and they'll turn it into a mile. The oil war that Iran hopes to wage is merely a part of Iran's overall strategy for attacking the United States and its allies, thus ensuring that Iranian interests in the region are preserved above all others. While the JCPOA was hailed by its advocates in the Obama and now the Biden administrations as paradigm-shifting, they were merely an acknowledgment of Iranian ambitions for the region—ambitions that Iran has held for centuries, notably since the Carter administration allowed the grand ayatollah to return during the revolution in 1979. The deal did not preserve

---

5 "Assessing the Risk Posed by Iran's Violations of the Nuclear Deal," *Arms Control Association*, vol.11, issue 9, 29 January 2020. https://www.armscontrol.org/issue-briefs/2019-12/assessing-risk-posed-iran-violations-nuclear-deal

American interests in the region. How could it? It basically granted the Islamist regime in Iran wealth and nukes.

Some of you may be old enough to remember the halcyon days of the Nixon administration, when Dr. Henry Kissinger and former President Richard M. Nixon defied expectations and crafted an historic deal with Mao's Communist China. At the time, its proponents proclaimed that the action would bring peace to the world and that it would end the Cold War with the stroke of a pen rather than a nuclear conflict because the move divided the communist bloc against itself. Nearly fifty years after that agreement, China has become a juggernaut with regional and global ambitions to become the world's preeminent superpower—at the expense of the United States and the West.

All of that was made possible by Nixon's initial diplomatic forays into China. Once China was enmeshed into the world economy, there was no going back. This was precisely the outcome the Iranians hoped for in their dalliance with former President Obama.

When President Obama signed the JCPOA with Iran, his supporters likened it to Nixon's outreach to China, as though that was a positive. Strengthening American rivals while weakening the United States appears to be a hallmark of the foreign policy "experts" who populate Washington, DC, and control the major parties. How else could such bad moves not only happen in the first place but be encouraged with other malign actors again? If you ask me, we'd be better off with non-experts at the helm of US foreign policy at this rate.

At best, the Biden administration's commitment to the Obama-era JCPOA will create a China-like threat in the Middle East when we don't need that kind of a threat there. At worst, it will only encourage the Iranians to act more boldly in other areas, such as in the energy arena, where they have already been very active.

Don't be fooled; an Iranian oil war could be a serious problem for the United States, especially as President Biden returns the United States to the JCPOA, stunts America's robust domestic energy production in the name of "climate change," and encourages the world to become more, not less, dependent on Mideast oil. In the fall of 2021, for example, as the Biden administration was canceling major pipelines that helped the United States become energy independent, Secretary of Energy Jennifer Granholm begged the Saudis and other OPEC states to pump more oil so as to lower what had become extremely high global prices of oil.[6] Just ten months into Joe Biden's presidency, the world was becoming more, not less, dependent on Mideast oil. Therefore, the US is increasingly exposed to the kind of attacks on Mideast oil supplies that Iran wants to conduct. That in turn increases the attractiveness of attacks on those assets by the Iranians. It is a question of "when," not "if" the Iranians figure out how to make an oil war as effective as they need it to be.

---

6 Matt Clinch, "The U.S. Energy Secretary Has a Message for OPEC: Boost Oil Supply So People Don't Get Hurt This Winter," *CNBC*, 5 November 2021. https://www.cnbc.com/2021/11/05/granholm-opec-message-increase-oil-supply-so-people-dont-get-hurt.html

25

IRAN'S CYBERWAR

IN 2010, as Iran was attempting to enrich another round of uranium, the strangest thing occurred. The centrifuges that spin at extremely fast speeds to make weapons-grade uranium spun out of control. An entire batch of this sensitive material was destroyed. The Iranians had to shut down their centrifuges, which effectively halted their nuclear weapons program until they could figure out what happened. Inevitably, it was discovered that a strange new computer virus that attacked the industrial switches of the Siemens-built equipment had been introduced to the Iranian uranium enrichment programs and caused the destruction of the valuable uranium.

The computer virus became known as "Stuxnet." Questions abounded as to how this could have happened because Iranian computers used in their uranium enrichment program were not connected to the internet. It was eventually discovered that a programmer at the facility in Iran had accidentally uploaded the virus from the internet onto the computer system. Once inside, the virus spread and targeted the industrial switches of the Iranian enrichment facility. The only problem for the world was that the virus got out into the World Wide Web—and continues to be there today.

Computer experts have some concern that the virus, which was programmed to target the industrial switches of Siemens-built equipment, might eventually target civilian systems in other parts of the world, for the German-based company provides industrial switches to many companies in many places. This has not yet happened.

It is now widely believed that the United States and Israel were behind the Stuxnet cyberattack. Approved in the final days of the George W. Bush administration and carried over by Barack Obama, the hack was intended to set the Iranian nuclear weapons program back further than where it had been. One will never know if a President John McCain, rather than a President Barack Obama, would have gone beyond the Stuxnet attack to completely debilitate Iran.

However, it's probable, given McCain's rendition of The Beach Boys' "Barbara Ann" on the 2008 campaign trail.[1]

Instead, the Obama administration used the Stuxnet attack to create a setback in Iran's nuclear weapons program that would make the JCPOA more palatable to the Iranians. And given how many concessions the Obama administration made in the JCPOA to Iran, it was already quite palatable.

For a multitude of reasons, many cyber experts have lamented that the Stuxnet attack was the equivalent of opening up Pandora's box.

---

1 The Progressive Magazine, "McCain Sings 'Bomb, Bomb, Bomb, Bomb Iran,'" YouTube, 20 April 2007. https://www.youtube.com/watch?v=U7s5pT3Rris

The first reason is that the Stuxnet virus, as previously noted, remains in existence, floating free on the World Wide Web, and could attack civilian systems globally at any moment. The other problem is that it signaled to the world's powers, including Iran itself, that this form of electronic warfare was acceptable. Sure enough, Iran began ramping up its own threats to the United States and its allies in cyberspace.

Between 2011 and 2013, a group of Iranian hackers are believed to have targeted several American banks and a dam in upstate New York with distributed denial of service (DDoS) attacks. These attacks overwhelm computer networks and, in the case of the bank attacks, prevented countless numbers of Americans from accessing their money. The Iranian hackers also attacked the New York Stock Exchange (NYSE). What was particularly worrying to American cybersecurity experts was that the Iranian cyberattack on the New York dam was clearly intended as a "dry run."[2]

Ultimately, the dam the Iranians targeted was not considered a vital component of America's infrastructure. Yet just as with Iranian attacks on the world's oil flows, strong evidence suggests that these Iranian cyberattacks have merely been dry runs. Iranian hackers were probing America's networks, figuring out methods to get inside the networks and to stay inside, and seeing how American security experts would respond.

In 2013, the Jewish-American casino magnate Sheldon Adelson appeared at a convention in New York in which he suggested that the United States demonstrate its willingness to curb Iranian nuclear ambitions by detonating a nuclear bomb in the middle of the Iranian desert. Adelson, who died in 2020, was a staunch supporter of conservative politicians and causes both in the United States and Israel. His comments gained international media attention, and Iran took note, given Adelson's influence over powerful elements in both the United States

---

2 "Seven Iranian Hackers Indicted over Alleged Cyber Attacks Targeting US Banks and NY Dam," Trend Micro, 29 March 2016. https://www.trendmicro.com/vinfo/de/security/news/cyber-attacks/seven-iranian-hackers-indicted-over-attacks-on-banks-ny-dam

and Israel, the two countries Iran calls "Big Satan" and "Little Satan," respectively.[3] In early 2014, Iranian hackers successfully broke into Adelson's Sands Casino in Las Vegas and caused the storied casino over $40 million in damages.[4]

Iran has perfected—and continues perfecting—this new form of warfare that can have devastating effects on the United States and its allies. Presently, Iranian cyberattacks merely pose a nuisance. But their targets and methodology indicate Iran's willingness to try, learn, and adapt for the time when Tehran believes it must use such unconventional warfare tactics to greater effect. Tehran has not only tested these new methods on the United States, which has thus far managed to rebuff Iranian probes of its cyber networks, but it has gone after both the Saudis and the Israelis in cyberspace.

In 2020 alone, Israeli security firms claimed that there were at least five major Iranian hacks of Israeli firms. Specifically, there was an Iranian attempt to hack Israel's water infrastructure. Targeting potable water sources for Israel's civilian population has long been a tactic that Iran and its terrorist proxies, such as Hezbollah, have favored in the event of a war. Beyond that, there were a series of attacks on Israeli companies that specialized in "freight movement, logistics, and custom clearance." It was reported that the attack on these firms raised concerns that it would delay the release of some "shipments to Israel, in both private and business sectors." In fact, it has been reported that Israel and Iran have been engaged in an escalating cyberwar for years.[5]

---

3 Alyza Sebenius, Kartikay Mehrotra, and William Turton, "Iran's Cyberattack on Billionaire Adelson Provides Lesson on Strategy," Bloomberg, 5 January 2020. https://www.bloomberg.com/news/articles/2020-01-05/iranian-attack-on-adelson-provides-lesson-on-cyber-strategy

4 Russell Brandom, "Iran Hacked the Sands Hotel Earlier This Year, Causing over $40 Million in Damage," The Verge, 11 December 2014. https://www.theverge.com/2014/12/11/7376249/iran-hacked-sands-hotel-in-february-cyberwar-adelson-israel

5 Stuart Winer and the TOI Staff, "Cyberattack Hits Israeli Companies, with Iran Reportedly the Likely Culprit," Times of Israel, 13 December 2020. https://www.timesofisrael.com/israels-supply-chain-targeted-in-massive-cyberattack/

Could this be a prelude to a larger Iranian offensive against Israel, both in the realm of cyberspace as well as in the real world, possibly a coordinated strike with Iran's precision-guided munitions from Lebanon coupled with a ceaseless wave of cyberattacks against critical Israeli infrastructure to sow confusion in the tiny country? And should this, in fact, be Iran's ultimate strategy how would this ensnare the Americans? Would Iranian attacks be limited only to targets in the Middle East? Or would they also expand to include American and European targets? How would Washington respond? With Biden in charge, the world cannot be certain.

Iran will not be deterred. It will not back down. The country can only be contained and strangled by a more powerful American-backed regional alliance of Sunni Arab states and Israel. What's more, Iran will continue to expand its arc of aggression to achieve its grand strategic objective: the restoration of the influence and power that it once held in the Middle East during the Safavid Dynasty—only with the mullahs at the top of the power structure rather than a monarch.

Many in the West think that mitigating the nuclear threat through the restoration of the Obama-era nuclear agreement will end the threat posed to the United States. In fact, it will merely give the Iranians the license they seek to engage in greater acts of aggression. The Iranian nuclear weapons threat is serious enough. But as recent chapters have shown you, Iran is very much invested in asymmetrical forms of warfare meant to complicate and confuse America and its regional allies. Cyberattacks, oil wars, and terrorism appear just as effective as conventional attacks in the grand war on the West and its regional partners, such as Israel and Saudi Arabia.

26

IRAN'S EXOTIC TECHNOLOGY:

FROM EMPS TO DRONES

IN 2010, Iran's religious leadership declared that it had mastered a "shariah-approved" nuclear weapons attack.[1] Under the current Islamic guidelines that rule Iran, the Iranians are barred from engaging in a first-strike nuclear attack against their enemies. Of course, little prevents the Iranians from handing over nuclear weapons to their terrorist proxies. In addition to that, the Iranians are believed to have an electromagnetic

---

1 James Woolsey and Peter Pry, "A Shariah-Approved Nuclear Attack," *The Washington Times,* 18 August 2015. https://www.washingtontimes.com/news/2015/aug/18/jams-woolsey-peter-pry-emp-a-shariah-approved-nucl/

pulse (EMP) weapons capability. This asymmetrical threat to the United States and its allies is troubling to many security experts.

An EMP blast is generated right before a nuclear weapon explodes. These pulses can completely destroy all electronic equipment in a given blast area. After the 1962 Starfish Prime EMP test in the upper atmosphere, American as well as Soviet scientists began working on a way to weaponize the blast *without* having to engage in nuclear war. Recognizing that an EMP could knock out a modern army or a country's infrastructure without directly killing people, both the United States and the Soviet Union realized this could be potentially effective if hostilities broke out between the two superpowers.

As former CIA director R. James Woolsey and Peter Vincent Pry reported in *The Wall Street Journal*, "Rogue nations, such as North Korea (and possibly Iran) will soon match Russia and China and have the primary ingredients for an EMP attack: simple ballistic missiles such as Scuds that could be launched from a freighter near our shores; space-launch vehicles able to loft low-earth-orbit satellites; and simple low-yield nuclear weapons that can generate gamma rays and fireballs."[2]

As I reported in 2020, Iran's space program is a direct threat to the United States; I believe it is a cover for Iran not only to test ballistic missiles but also to potentially place EMP weapons in orbit.[3] Placing EMP weapons in orbit would allow Iran to hold the world hostage, threatening to attack or destroy critical American and allied satellite systems. Or worse, Iran could detonate an EMP above the continental United States and knock out the American power grid.

The United States would be debilitated under such conditions. It would be unable to retaliate or respond. What's more, America's allies

---

2 R. James Woolsey and Peter Vincent Pry, "The Growing Threat from an EMP Attack," *Wall Street Journal*, 12 August 2014. https://www.wsj.com/articles/james-woolsey-and-peter-vincent-pry-the-growing-threat-from-an-emp-attack-1407885281

3 Brandon J. Weichert, "Iran's Space Threat is the Problem," American Greatness, 27 April 2020. https://amgreatness.com/2020/04/27/irans-space-threat-is-the-problem/

would be vulnerable to attack. Without the American security umbrella, these nations could be obliterated by an Iranian strike. It would also fundamentally alter the world order and would likely empower other American rivals, such as China and Russia. If America goes down and its allies are being pushed around, unable to respond effectively, the world system would forever be upended.

No longer would we be living in an American-centric world. Instead, we would be living in a world ruled by authoritarians and religious fanatics. Or, more probably, we'd be living in a world that had become nothing more than an irradiated husk of its former self. And the United States would be left without power, thrown back to a nineteenth century-level of existence—the stuff of nightmares, pretty much. There will be a straight line from the President Biden's restoration of the ill-advised Obama-era JCPOA to such a nightmarish post-American world.

IRAN'S SATELLITE THREAT

America is threatened not only in the domain of exotic EMP weapons, which very much are part of the Iranian repertoire for hitting Uncle Sam and his allies. As I noted in my first book, *Winning Space: How America Remains a Superpower,* Iran's space program allows the country to increase its intelligence, surveillance, and reconnaissance (ISR) capabilities. Furthermore, an Iranian space program allows Tehran to acquire advanced nuclear command, control, and communications (NC3) capabilities that would improve their nuclear weapons threat by giving those weapons a longer reach with greater precision.

In the summer of 2021, for example, President Joe Biden met with Russian President Vladimir Putin. While at that meeting, Biden urged his wily Russian counterpart not to sell an advanced Russian-built surveillance satellite to Iran's military. If the sale had gone through, Iran's ability to track and target US forces operating in the region, as well as to threaten both Saudi and Israeli targets, would have been advanced by a generation.

For his part, Putin denies that such a sale was set to take place. Given the Russian military's close relationship with Iran, though, it is likely that this sale was set to occur. And the transaction may yet happen because Moscow greatly values its alliance with Tehran and wants Iran to continue being a perennial thorn in America's side.

IRAN'S DRONE ARSENAL

Consider again how Iran's precision-guided munitions have evolved. Since at least 2016, as you've read, Iran has thrown many resources into their precision-guided munitions capability. Thanks to this consistent investment, Iran's capabilities have increased so much that today Tehran can give its technology to Hezbollah, who can in turn threaten Israel with it. When Iran first began investing in this capability, it was inconsequential. Over time, it has become a very serious threat to Israel, the United States, and the Saudis. The same pattern of development holds true for the Iranian use of cyberwarfare, as you've read, and drone technology.

In fact, when it comes to Iran's growing arsenal of advanced drones, we can thank former President Obama's strategic malfeasance for that. In 2011, an advanced RQ-170 drone was flying over Iran as part of a covert CIA reconnaissance mission. While passing through Iranian airspace, the drone, according to official Pentagon reports, suffered a bizarre systems failure. Once the drone failed, it effectively crash-landed in the desert.

American intelligence tracked the drone as it glided down to the desert floor below and could have easily destroyed the drone on the ground as no retrieval mission could have been mounted. Instead, Obama opted to publicly request that the Iranian government return the RQ-170. Naturally, Iran said "no." They put the downed drone on display in the museum that commemorates their regime's commitment to anti-Americanism and anti-Semitism and celebrated the downing as a great victory.[4]

Rumors abounded at the time that Iranian cyberespionage actually downed the RQ-170. That has never been proven, although in 2019, it

---

4 CNN News Wire Staff, "Obama Says U.S. Has Asked Iran to Return Drone Aircraft," CNN, 12 December 2011. https://www.cnn.com/2011/12/12/world/meast/iran-us-drone/index.html

was revealed that Iran had perfected the capability to track and possibly hack America's growing fleet of drones that were buzzing around the Middle East. The Iranian Revolutionary Guards Corps (IRGC) insists that they can control American drones operating in or near their territory. It has been confirmed that the Iranians can hack into those drones and see what those drones are observing. That alone is troubling.[5]

Since the capture of the RQ-170, Iran's rudimentary drone fleet has been expanded and modernized. David Hambling of *Forbes* assessed that Iran "may not be good at original [drone] designs, but Iran is the world leader in copying its enemies' drones." Iran's most ambitious drone pirating exercise was done with the RQ-170, according to Hambling.[6]

The capture of the RQ-170 was not the only time when Iran managed to get their hands on an advanced American drone. In fact, it happened again a year later. Iran captured a US Navy Scan Eagle drone in 2012. In 2013, the Iranians unveiled the *Yasir,* an exact copy of the advanced Scan Eagle, and, according to *Forbes,* even gave a copy of it to the Russian Air Force. The *Yasir* has been transferred to Iranian-backed militants fighting in Syria, handed over to Hezbollah fighting in Lebanon, and given to Iranian militants in Iraq. What's more, the *Yasir* was converted into a suicide drone in 2015.

As Iran's space program becomes more advanced and increases its satellite capabilities, whether Tehran has placed EMP weapons in orbit or not, the fact remains that greater satellite capabilities will allow Iran to have greater strategic depth in drone operations and nuclear warfare. This is why Israel has invested so much in their small but strong space program; it gives them strategic capabilities that many of their hostile neighbors lack.

5 Nick Waters, "Has Iran Been Hacking U.S. Drones?" Bellingcat, 1 October 2019. https://www.bellingcat.com/news/2019/10/01/has-iran-been-hacking-u-s-drones/

6 David Hambling, "Clone Wars: Why Iran Will Copy Captured U.S. Global Hawk Drone," *Forbes,* 16 July 2020. https://www.forbes.com/sites/davidhambling/2020/07/16/clone-wars-why-iran-will-copy-captured-us-global-hawk-drone/?sh=44b6b7567540

The same reasoning explains why India has spent years investing in their budding satellite program and why the United States has for decades invested in these capabilities. Iran has learned from the best. Their education has matured, and the Iranian leadership is now applying those lessons learned in real time. Eventually the regime will be able to deploy an entire arsenal of combat-effective unconventional weapons—married to asymmetrical warfare doctrines that the Americans and their allies are not prepared to endure.

In September 2021, the Director of the National Counterterrorism Center, Christine Abizaid, testified to Congress that Iran-backed Hezbollah maintained a "high threshold for conducting attacks in the [American] Homeland." Seated at the hearing alongside Abizaid was FBI Director Chris Wray who added onto her testimony that, "FBI arrests in recent years of alleged Iranian and Hezbollah operatives in the United States suggest the Government of Iran and Hizballah [sic] each seek to establish infrastructure here, potentially for the purpose of conducting operational or contingency planning."[7] In October of 2021, Seth J. Frantzman of *The Jerusalem Post* reported that, "Iran conducted a complex and coordinated attack on US forces in Syria" a week before his piece appeared. The Iranian attack was complex because it "used up to five armed drones to strike at the Tanf garrison, a lonely US outpost in Syria near the Jordanian and Iraqi border."[8]

Despite knowing about the attack ahead of time, the US decided to remove 200 of its troops by C-130 transport plane from the Tanf base rather than mount an active defense. More ominously, as Frantzman reported, the Iranian attack was not only intended as a warning to

---

7 Joseph Haboush, "Iran, Hezbollah Planning Attacks on US Homeland to Retaliate for Soleimani Slaying: Officials," *Al Arabiya English*, 21 September 2021. https://english.alarabiya.net/News/middle-east/2021/09/21/Iran-Hezbollah-planning-attacks-on-US-to-retaliate-for-Soleimani-slaying-Officials

8 Seth J. Frantzman, "Could the Iran Drone Attack on US in Syria Be Message to Israel? – Analysis," *The Jerusalem Post*, 26 October 2021. https://www.jpost.com/middle-east/iran-news/could-the-iran-drone-attack-on-us-in-syria-be-message-to-israel-683127

Americans but also as a signal to the Israelis and the Saudis: Iran can launch increasingly complex, hard-to-disrupt drone attacks on any target of their will. The reason was because the US military will need to deploy larger anti-drone systems, like Israel's Iron Dome, to defend against the kinds of drones that Iran is increasingly using against American, Israeli, and Saudi targets. Sadly, the US military only possesses two of such systems—and both are deployed to Guam, to defend against a potential Chinese attack on the American-held island in the Indo-Pacific.[9] The kind of drones that Iranian-backed Houthi Rebels in Yemen are using against Saudi targets are "basically large flying tubes with wings, which can be backed with explosives so that the drone is a kind of Kamikaze device, not so different than a German V-1 [rocket] World War II," according to Frantzman's reporting.

But if the directors of the FBI and National Counterterrorism Center were correct in their warnings to Congress in September 2021 about Hezbollah's desire to create the infrastructure needed to launch devastating attacks on the American homeland, then what's stopping Hezbollah from moving drones within range of the mainland United States to launch the same kind of complex attacks on targets in America that Iran routinely conducts on targets in the Mideast—drone attacks against which the United States presently lacks reliable defenses, especially in the mainland United States?

As time progresses, Iran will enhance this dangerous capability and will use any advantage—such as a sophisticated offensive drone system—to force their enemies into a more conciliatory position.

---

9 Judah Ari Gross, "Israel Ships 2nd of Two Iron Dome Batteries to US, Hopes to Sell More," *The Times of Israel*, 3 January 2021. https://www.timesofisrael.com/israel-ships-2nd-of-two-iron-dome-batteries-to-us-hopes-to-sell-more/

27

DEATH TO AMERICA!

WHAT DOES IRAN WANT from the United States? Western proponents of stabilizing relations with the Islamic Republic insist that in spite of their blood curdling cries of "Death to America," the Iranians just want to be left alone. Iran's Islamists don't just want to be left alone. Iran's rulers want vengeance for what they view as historical injustices perpetrated upon them by a host of actors. They drank their own Kool-Aid.

And they're ferocious fighters.

Just go back to the chapter that covers Saddam's invasion of Iran. By all accounts, it should have been a simple and quick war for Saddam's relatively modern and well-funded forces. It wasn't. Iran's ideological fervor drove them to perform extraordinary acts. It is the height of Western naivete to believe we can do business with this regime in any meaningful way.

First, Iran wants revenge upon the Sunni Arabs for the murder of Husayn and his compatriots at Karbala—along with all of the subsequent wrongs perpetrated upon the Shiites over the generations. This is a centuries-old grudge we're talking about. The next target on Iran's hit list is Israel, which is a strange turn of events because as late as 1987, Israeli leaders like Yitzhak Rabin were calling the Islamists in Iran "Israel's best friend."[1] Nevertheless, since the 1990s, the Islamists in Tehran have considered Israel's very existence an affront.

Despite what Rabin and other Israeli leaders may have thought about Iran in the 1980s, earlier chapters described how the grand ayatollah and his followers were consistently antisemitic from the start of their revolution. Surprisingly, the same naivete about the Islamists of Iran that pervades American strategic thinking today apparently dominated Israeli strategic thinking back then. Historically, Western societies underestimate authoritarian societies with revanchist territorial goals at their own peril. At least the West is playing to type when it comes to Iran.

Then there's Iran's special animosity for Britain. This animus explains why the Iranians delighted in capturing British sailors in 2007.[2] In fact, because of Britain's history of imperialism in Iran, many Iranians today still think that British perfidy is behind many of their country's problems.

The Great Satan, the United States, is Iran's main target. The reasoning for this is convoluted. On the one hand, Iran blames the West

---

1 David B. Green, "From Friends to Foes: How Israel and Iran Turned into Arch-Enemies," *Haaretz*, 8 May 2018. https://www.haaretz.com/middle-east-news/iran/MAGAZINE-how-israel-and-iran-went-from-allies-to-enemies-1.6049884

2 Aref Mohammed, "Iran Seizes 15 British Marines and Sailors in the Gulf," Reuters, 23 March 2007. https://www.reuters.com/article/us-iraq-iran-britain/iran-seizes-15-british-marines-and-sailors-in-gulf-idUSCOL33182120070323

for the perceived damage their country suffered in the colonial era. As the most powerful Western nation, the United States has become the mullahs' primary target. On the other hand, the event that most Western academics believe incurred the wrath of the Iranian people, American support for the 1953 coup, does not factor that heavily into the ideological framework of the Iranian regime. Yet channeling anti-Americanism in the streets on a daily basis has served the Islamists' interests in Iran. The hate distracts many Iranians from the misery the Islamist regime has subjected them to for decades.

We do know that Iran has almost half a century of demonstrated hostility directed against these targets—and that hostility is growing in scope and lethality precisely when the United States is seeking to play nice with Iran. The Iranians are not going to play nicely just because America turns a blind eye to their nuclear weapons and regional ambitions. They will take that largesse (or decadence as Tehran views it) and use it as a cudgel against their perceived foes—especially the United States.

ISLAMISM IN IRAN

The problem with Iran's regime is the ideology that guides them—Islamism. While a broad term for various groups found in both the Sunni and Shiite interpretations of Islam, there's connective tissue linking the ideas of these groups together across time. Islamism's earliest roots can be traced back to the nineteenth century in the Middle East, when the region was grappling with Enlightenment ideals as well as European colonialism. The printing press became available in the region during this time as well. There was a flowering of radical and extremist thought during this era.

When Europeans began arriving in the region *en masse,* the region suffered ontological shock. At one period of time in Islam's history, it was the purveyor of an advanced society. After Europe had entered a period known as the Dark Ages, Islam was a conduit for mathematics, spoken language, and cultural attainment. By the nineteenth century, however, that had flipped. Islamic society, when measured against the arriving Europeans, was seen as stagnant and backward. China also experienced something similar when Europeans began arriving in the Asian country around this time.

Muslims were shocked to discover their European Christian rivals were now more advanced than the Islamic cultures were. While Islamic societies, Sunni and Shiite alike, wanted to embrace the advanced technology of the West, they feared that the Christian Europeans would usurp Islam. Remember that for centuries, Muslim and Christian armies had clashed in the Crusades that stretched from central Europe down to Jerusalem. The Crusades had ended with Muslim armies successfully pushing Europeans out of the Middle East. When the nineteenth century rolled around, however, highly advanced European armies were arriving—and bringing with them not only Christianity but also the ideas of irreligious Enlightenment thinkers. Islam was under pressure from all sides. To compound matters, most Islamic governments of the time were viewed as corrupt and inefficient.

Interestingly, the introduction of the printing press allowed the *Qur'an* to be mass printed throughout the region. Literacy rates also rose in the region. But as literacy rates rose, the traditional role of trained Islamic scholars—*'ulamā*—was reduced, and an explosion of scriptural literalism occurred. The scriptural literalism led to the creation of radical Islamic thinking.

THE INFLUENCE OF THE MUSLIM BROTHERHOOD IN IRAN

Groups of Islamic scholars began propagating the idea that Islam needed to become more rationalist, just as the European philosophers had demanded of Christian Europe since the Enlightenment. Meanwhile, other Islamic thinkers preached the need to return to a purer form of Islam in order to make Islamic society more competitive with the Europeans. The Salafist sect of Sunni Islam became most associated with these notions. Today, Salafist ideas, along with Wahhābīst thought, inform the core ideologies of Sunni Islamist groups like al Qaeda and ISIS. Alongside this development was the belief that Islam promotes modernity and prosperity, which eventually led to the formation of the Muslim Brotherhood in Egypt in 1928 under the leadership of Hassan al-Banna.[3]

The Muslim Brotherhood did not begin as the mothership of Islamic terrorism that it would ultimately become. It initially started as an Egyptian grassroots movement. The Muslim Brotherhood promoted social welfare, economic development, and mass education for Egypt's newly liberated population. Eventually, the Muslim Brotherhood became violently opposed to British imperial influence over Egypt, and because it was such a well-organized group, the Muslim Brotherhood became the hub of Islamic resistance to foreign influences over the Islamic community and the rule of local apostates.

Soon the Muslim Brotherhood radicalized. It had initially supported Egyptian General Abdel Nasser and his coup against Egypt's king in 1952. But Nasser was no Islamist. He was an Arabist who yearned to create a secular, modern socialist society in Egypt and the wider Middle East. The Brotherhood could not support Nasser's ideology or rule. Thus, the autocratic Arabist General Nasser soon committed his regime to suppressing the Brotherhood and its members—which was large, growing, and devout.

At the same time on the Indian subcontinent, the Muslim League was pushing for the creation of a secular government in what would become Pakistan. An ideological split occurred between those who wanted secular governance in the new territory and those who wanted a stricter Islamist regime. Abū al-Ala al-Mawdūdī led the fight against the Muslim League in Pakistan. He believed that the purpose of any government's rule was to perpetuate God's sovereignty, apply the tenets of Islam—specifically Islamic law, shariah—and create a heavenly utopia on Earth. Secularism, according to Mawdūdī, was a disease that would lead Islamic countries to destruction. This explains why Islamists view secular regimes, Arabist rulers, and non-Muslim governments alike as blood enemies to be destroyed.

---

3 Adam Zeidan, "Islamism," *Encyclopedia Britannica*, Accessed on 20 February 2021. https://www.britannica.com/topic/Islamism

SAYYID QUTB'S CONNECTION TO THE
ISLAMIC REVOLUTION IN IRAN

The Muslim Brotherhood in Egypt imported Mawdūdī's ideas of Islamic governance. Specifically, the Muslim Brotherhood ideologue Sayyid Qutb, a scholar who had spent time studying in the United States, shared similar ideas. But Qutb took it a step further. Qutb argued that current Muslim society was not nearly as devout as it should be. He believed that any Muslim, such as Nasser, who opposed the true purification of Islamic society was subject to death. Qutb helped to popularize the notion of *jihad* as a form of physical combat.

Sayyid Qutb had an outsized influence on the development of Islam as a political force in the postwar Middle East. He was ultimately arrested by Egypt's military and executed by hanging in 1966. Before his arrest and death, however, Qutb made many friends throughout the region who spread his ideas. One notable relationship was his friendship with the Iranian firebrand Navvab Safavi—a close friend of Ruhollah Khomeini. Safavi served as a conduit between Qutbist thought that was rising to prominence in the Sunni Islamic world and the Shiite Islamic community.[4]

Beyond that personal connection, Qutb influenced the Shiite Dawa Party in Iraq. Khomeini himself would ultimately find a safe haven among Iraq's Shiite community when the Shāh exiled him from Iran. Three years after Qutb was hanged in Egypt, Khomeini wrote his most important book, *The Islamic Government,* which echoes Qutb's own prolific writings. Qutbist thought inspired Khomeini to envision an Islamic government for Iran.

This is the regime the naïve Jimmy Carter would help to usher in during the 1979 revolution; the same regime today gleefully chants "Death to America!" in the streets of its major cities and has waged an

4 Mohammed Amr, "Iran's Islamic Republic and the Muslim Brotherhood," European Eye on Radicalization, 5 July 2019. https://eeradicalization.com/irans-islamic-republic-and-the-muslim-brotherhood/

unremitting campaign of aggression against the United States. This is the same regime that the former Obama administration and the current Biden administration believes can be trusted with atomic weapons, a technology that even though eighty years old is still the most physically destructive weapon ever built by humankind.[5]

Sayyid Qutb imparted the radical notions that dominate today's Islamists, both those in Sunni extremist groups like al Qaeda and those who rule Iran. The idea that Islam cannot exist alongside atheist societies; that the world is divided between the "House of Peace" (Islam) and the "House of War" has been emphasized by Qutbist thought. What's more, the Iranian Revolutionary Guards Corps—the branch of the Iranian military that Qassem Soleimani was part of—has integrated Qutbist teaching into their ideological training for new recruits.

The very notion of dealing with Iran is absurd. Tehran has a radical objective. Iran's leaders will neither slow down nor deviate from the warpath the grand ayatollah himself placed them on. Qutbist (and therefore Khomeinist) thought is uncompromising. Even when the power imbalances between the United States and the Islamic Republic of Iran were glaring, as they were when the regime took over the American embassy in 1979 or when Hezbollah killed those American Marines in 1983, the Iranians moved decisively in the direction of war. The world was given a preview of what Iran would do with the reprieve they were given when the Obama administration first negotiated the JCPOA with the mullahs: Iran doubled down on its aggressive policies in the Mideast.

The nature of regimes and the personality of their leaders count when seeking to do deals with regimes like the theocracy of Iran. As you've read, Hassan Rouhani, the supposed moderate president of Iran from the Obama years until the beginning of the Biden administration, was a fanatic. Rouhani's harder line replacement, Ebrahim Raisi, was not

---

5 "Why Sayed Qutb Inspired Iran's Khomeini and Khamenei," Al-Arabiya English, 3 September 2018. https://english.alarabiya.net/features/2018/09/03/Why-Sayed-Qutb-inspired-Iran-s-Khomeini-and-Khamenei

just known for being a strict interpreter of Sharia law while he served as the chief justice of Iran's supreme court. At the age of 21, the all-black-clad, dark-bearded, young, and scowling Ebrahim Raisi had risen to the position of chief prosecutor in the Iranian city of Hamadan. Raisi was possessed of ambition and cruelty, two factors that would ensure his ultimate rise to power as Iran's president in 2021.

In his teens, Raisi had linked up with the Khomeinist revolt that ultimately overthrew the Shāh. During his revolutionary exploits, he became close personal friends with Ali Khamenei, who would eventually succeed the grand ayatollah after his death in 1988. Once in Khomeini's old job, Khamenei would maintain the close friendship with Raisi that the two had forged as street revolutionaries during the seminal days of the Khomeinist overthrow of the Shāh. This relationship would serve Raisi well throughout the remainder of his career.

While Raisi is known as a devout, hardline believer in the Khomeinist revolution, he is also known as a "butcher" to many Iranians. When he was a fearless and taciturn prosecutor in Hamadan, the Marxist groups that the Khomeinists had originally aligned with, had realized that the Khomeinists meant to monopolize power in the post-Shāh Iran. The Marxist groups, such as the MEK, waged war on the Khomeinists. As you've read, the 1980s in Iran were defined by the bloodletting of dissidents inside Iran. Raisi was one of the young Khomeinist movement's chief high executioners and most effective torturers. At his core, Raisi was more than a true believer. He was one of its fiercest ideological warriors.

In fact, Raisi was renowned for delighting in the gruesome torturing of pregnant women suspected of being MEK sympathizers. Farideh Goodarzi was 21 and nine-months pregnant when she was arrested for reading an MEK newspaper in Hamadan. Throughout 1981, Farideh was subject to Raisi's merciless tortures. Raisi would order his guards to beat the heavily pregnant Farideh with electrical cables, their fists, and any other implement they could in order to extract a confession from the young, expectant mother. According to Farideh, "In [Raisi's] speech, in his eyes, in his every manner, you could see the vengeance that he had for all MEK members and supporters." Raisi is like a villain from a Victor Hugo story—only without any of the sympathetic qualities of a Javert or Frollo that Hugo had imbued in those villains.

Since the 1980s, Raisi's reputation has only ever been tied to massive political bloodshed in service to the regime. During the particularly contentious Iranian presidential election in 2021, despite his history with violence, many opponents of Raisi took the streets chanting, "Ayatollah-e ghatl-e ām!" Or "The ayatollah of massacre!" Regardless of what the people of Iran had wanted, the mullahs—specifically Raisi's old friend, Ayatollah Khamenei—wanted Raisi for the presidency. And so, it was. Khamenei has been recorded as referring to Raisi as "Hezbollah's young government."[6]

The Islamist regime has reached its horrific apex in Iran with the rise of Ebrahim Raisi. Make no mistake, with the two personalities of Ayatollah Khamenei and President Ebrahim Raisi at the helm of Iran, there is no hope for the nuclear talks between the West and Iran. What's more, there is no hope for peace in our time so long as this Iranian regime gets what it wants: nuclear weapons tied to an expansionistic Islamist regime. Many in the West believe that the Islamist regime in Iran is on its last legs. Yet, that should not comfort anyone—especially considering what the Biden administration has in store for Iran.

By giving Iran's regime legitimacy and allowing for it to acquire nuclear weapons whether it be in a few months or by the end of the decade, it will ensure that a regional war erupts. This is especially true if the regime really is about to collapse. What would stop the true believers ruling the Iranian regime from trying to take down as many unbelievers with them as their regime implodes under its own internal contradictions?

---

6 David Patrikarakos, "The Life of the Islamic Republic's Most Fundamentalist President Mirrors the Story of the State Itself," *New Line Magazine*, 16 December 2021. https://newlinesmag.com/reportage/a-malign-embrace-ebrahim-raisi-and-iran/

There is a direct line between the rise of Islamism in Iran and destabilization of the entire Middle East. The revolutionary ethos that gave birth to the Khomeinist movement in Iran is alive and well among Iran's leaders today. The regime is not seeking stability in the region. It is seeking supremacy. Because Shiites are a minority in the region and the Sunnis will *never* accept Shia supremacy—nor will the Israelis—war is the only likely path forward. And such a war will involve nuclear weapons and will drag the United States back into the region at a time when Washington must focus its efforts on other parts of the world.

28

HISTORY REPEATS:

CARTER, OBAMA, AND BIDEN

PRESIDENT JOSEPH R. BIDEN, Obama's former vice president, agrees with the Carter and Obama view of Islamism. In February of 2021, Jake Sullivan, the Biden administration's national security adviser, told CNN that he believed "[right now] may be the best chance" for the United States to reenter the 2015 JCPOA that former President Trump had abandoned in 2018.[1]

Why?

---

1 CNN, "Biden Nat Sec Adviser: This May Be the Best Chance at Iran Deal," YouTube video, 8:32, February 20, 2021. https://www.youtube.com/watch?v=vl6bboPHgW8

Sullivan asserted that Iran had been moving beyond the constraints the 2015 nuclear deal imposed upon Iran's nascent nuclear weapons program. Iran started doing this in 2019. The original agreement, as you've read, kept Iran's nuclear weapons program constrained only until 2025—just a few years away from when the Biden team wants to reenter the 2015 agreement.

One way or the other, in the next decade Iran will have nuclear weapons, and that will be a catastrophe for the region. Since the death of the Prophet Muhammad and the succession crisis that soon followed, Persia (present-day Iran) has struggled with its role in the Middle East. It has always existed as a part of the wider region, yet it was also consistently apart from it. Ethnically and religiously, it differs greatly from the Sunni majority countries. What's more, it has a long and rich history predating Islam that many in Iran still remember and revere.

Shiite extremists, in particular, assume that they are the true followers of Muhammad. Since they were the followers of Ali, Muhammad's grandson who was murdered at Karbala in 680 CE, the Shiites of Iran are stubbornly convinced that they are the only ones who were right in this ancient feud. The Shiites of Iran are certain that they should be at the top of the power pyramid in the Middle East. All others should be subordinated to them. Those who refuse to acknowledge the rightful heir of Muhammad's reign on earth must either submit—or be destroyed.

The United States of America is wholly unable to match such an ancient idea and power. There is no point in American leaders trying to convince the Iranian regime of something other than what they believe. Those neuronal pathways are too far ingrained in the minds of the elites in Tehran. Furthermore, the United States simply doesn't have the bandwidth to try what will basically be a strategy of appeasing a truly evil regime in Iran. Appeasement will not work. It cannot. At every turn, as you've seen throughout this work, Iran has viewed the United States as the "Great Satan," and it has acted accordingly.

Meanwhile, a succession of American leaders—specifically, presidents belonging to the Democratic Party—have acted on the assumption that Iran can be reasoned with, that if Iran were allowed to slowly develop nuclear weapons, inevitably, it would be as rational an actor as Israel has proven to be. In fact, these presidents have assumed Iran's possession of a nuclear weapon would balance whatever threat the Democratic presidents think Israel's regional monopoly of nuclear weapons poses to the region.

But just look at Iran's leaders over the years. Whether it be the truly insane President Mahmoud Ahmadinejad or the purportedly moderate Hassan Rouhani; whether it be the founder of the Islamic Republic, the Grand Ayatollah Ruhollah Khomeini, or his successor, Ayatollah Ali Khamenei, Iran's rulers have made clear their strategic ambitions. Either the Islamic Republic of Iran will become the regional hegemon, or they'll burn the whole place down.[2]

The Islamists believe they have a mandate from their deity to wage a holy war against the unbelievers and apostates. It makes little sense to engage them when the Islamists in Iran have been so clear and consistent in their opposition to the United States. At the same time, the United States has made one blunder after another in the region—all serving the interests of Tehran.

First, Carter encouraged the Khomeinist revolution, believing the grand ayatollah was a gentler person than the Shāh and that Islamism would be a more potent bulwark against Soviet expansionism than Iranian nationalism. Second, Ronald Reagan retreated in the face of Iranian provocations. Reagan even encouraged Saddam Hussein to press on with his bloody war against Iran in the 1980s, which resulted in the destruction of Iraq as a viable counterweight to Iran's growing power. Third, a succession of US presidents, beginning with George H. W. Bush, began waging war on Saddam Hussein. Bill Clinton then put Saddam's Iraq in a box throughout the 1990s. Then came George

---

2 TOI Staff and Agencies, "Khamenei: If We Wanted Nukes, Nobody, including 'Zionist Clown,' Could Stop Us," *Times of Israel,* 22 February 2021. https://www.timesofisrael.com/khamenei-if-we-wanted-nukes-nobody-including-zionist-clown-could-stop-us/

W. Bush who finally ended Saddam's rule—only to hand over Iraq to the Iraqi Shiites and the Iranians! Finally, Barack Obama made a point of empowering Islamists in the Sunni Arab world, from Libya to Egypt to Syria, while constantly attacking our allies in the region and courting the crazies in Iran.

For his part, Joe Biden appears intent on reviving and following Barack Obama's failed Mideast legacy.[3] Not only has Biden insisted on restoring the Iran nuclear agreement, but his secretary of state, Anthony Blinken, is enthusiastic about ousting the Assad regime in Syria.[4] While Bashar al-Assad is a butcher and a stooge for both Russia and Iran, in fact the only viable forces arrayed against him in Syria are jihadist terrorists. Aligning with these elements, as Obama did and it seems as though Biden wants to do, to push Assad out will only further weaken America's stance in the region. The Syrian Civil War *is a distraction.* Any significant investment of American manpower into ousting Assad will distract the United States at a time when its resources are stretched to the breaking point.

What we should do in Syria is to place it in the wider context of America's Little Cold War with Iran. The United States has reliable allies geographically close to Syria that can help contain whatever problems Iran poses to the wider region. Keeping the Syrian conflict frozen serves America's interests. There can be no victor there. Assad's regime is Alawite; it is a minority sect of the minority Shia Islamic faith in a majority Sunni Muslim country.

With Russia and Iran pouring endless resources into the Syrian war and with Israel unwilling to grant Iran a secure foothold in Syria, it will continue being a frozen conflict that serves no purpose and helps no one.

---

3 The Dispatch Staff, "The Morning Dispatch: Biden Courts Iran," *The Dispatch,* 22 February 2021. https://morning.thedispatch.com/p/the-morning-dispatch-biden-courts?utm_source=kw&utm_campaign=Sept_promo&kwp_0=1875715&kwp_4=5451157&kwp_1=2336582&fbclid=IwAR06961u7_BlqqDGunDiW4s1tikt5276_DuCnfyjNykwsRvVts6v7W5oGsc

4 Brandon J. Weichert, "Biden's Foreign Policy," DefCon One's Newsletter, 9 November 2020. https://defcon1.substack.com/p/bidens-foreign-policy

It's a waste of Washington's time to get too involved there, as Biden's team clearly wants to do. If it cooperates more fully and consistently with its Israeli and Sunni Arab allies, America can prevent the Syrian civil war from serving Iranian geostrategic ambitions. But so long as America's feckless political class insists on keeping some forces, mostly private military contractors and special forces, in Syria and neighboring Iraq, they will continue being targets of Iranian-backed militias.

On February 15, 2021, Iranian-backed militias operating in Syria launched a missile targeting an American base in Erbil, the capital of the Kurdish enclave in northern Iraq. The rocket attack killed an American private military contractor and wounded several members of the coalition forces operating there, including one American service member and several American private military contractors.[5] After that Iranian-backed attack on American and coalition forces operating in Iraq, Iranian forces followed it up with an additional rocket attack directed against the Green Zone in Baghdad. It is believed that the rockets were intended for the massive American embassy in Baghdad, but they fell short of their target. No injuries or fatalities were reported from that fusillade.

A few days later, on February 25, the United States responded. According to Fox News, "Multiple facilities [in Syria] were struck by American F-15 fighter jets that targeted Iraqi border-based Shia militia groups, [Kateab] Hezbollah and [Kateab] Sayyid al Shuhada." A Biden administration official explained after the attacks that the air strikes were a "shot across the bow" and part of a larger Biden administration "defensive strategy, intended to deter Iran and its militia from launching rockets at US forces in the region, like the recent attacks in Iraq."[6]

---

5 Anthony J. Blinken, "Rocket Attacks in Erbil," U.S. Department of State, 15 February 2021. https://www.state.gov/rocket-attacks-in-erbil/

6 Caitlin McFall and Jennifer Griffin, "US Launches Airstrike Against Iranian-Backed Forces in Syria," Fox News, 25 February 2021. https://www.foxnews.com/politics/us-hits-iranian-backed-forces-in-syrian-in-defensive-airstrike?fbclid=IwAR2yIokJff5i_f6qMn3aVP62t671BkcsCEsGZlT7tusyFfazu0c0ZMCLn3I

Some of you might be inclined to quibble with my assessment that the Biden administration is intent on handing the region over to the lunatic Islamists in Iran. Let's place this move in the wider context, shall we? For starters, if you'll remember, former President Obama had no qualms about launching the devastating Stuxnet cyberattack against Iran's nuclear centrifuges.

Obama looked like quite a hero when it became obvious that his administration had taken part in the attack. Then, a few years thereafter, what'd Obama do? Did he follow that up with another devastating attack on Iran's nuclear weapons program?

No.

Obama entered into the Iran nuclear deal. Placed in its proper context, Obama's chest beating against Iran in 2009 and 2010 was only a feint to get his "deal" (read, concession) with Iran signed by 2015. Remember that in 2009, a wave of protests rocked Tehran after those youthful protesters believed a rigged election put a hardliner, Mahmoud Ahmadinejad, into office.

These protests looked to be a true threat to the survival of the Islamist regime in Iran. As a newly elected president, a man who campaigned on the narrative of "hope" and "change," Obama could have supported the democratic protesters in the streets of Tehran in 2009. Yet he chose to remain quiet. Obama explicitly stated that he would not seek to intervene in the internal affairs of Iran.[7] Reading between the lines, it seems the reason is that Obama always planned on making his deal with Iran and believed that agitating the protests against the Islamists would jeopardize his moment to claim victory in getting that deal.

The Biden administration is doing precisely what Obama ended up doing with Stuxnet. The February 2021 air strikes are not part of a larger military move against Iran. On his social media page, my colleague Brad Blakeman voiced his support of the Biden move, believing

---

7 Eli Lake, "Why Obama Let Iran's Green Revolution Fail," Bloomberg, 24 August 2016. https://www.bloomberg.com/opinion/articles/2016-08-24/why-obama-let-iran-s-green-revolution-fail

it would "check" Iran. I believe the move was calibrated to encourage Tehran to meet with Biden administration negotiators and reenter the 2015 JCPOA that Trump abandoned in 2018. Biden's team was trying to imply to Iran's leaders that if they didn't deal diplomatically with the Biden White House, then more pain would follow. Iran doesn't read the situation like this, though. They know that Biden is posturing and that his team is intent on a deal at any cost, which is why Iran keeps engaging in hostile behavior.

If anything, the Biden air strikes against the Iranian militia in Syria are part of a larger move against Bashar al-Assad in Syria; in this case, Iranian militia rocket attacks against American targets in neighboring Iraq provide a pretext for expanding America's military footprint in Syria. The words of Biden's national security adviser, Jake Sullivan, clearly betray the strategic intent of the forty-sixth American president: he aims to "make peace" with an Iran that yearns for bloody war against all the forces that the Islamists in Tehran believe have wronged their cause over the centuries.

Cornelius Adebahr of the German Foreign Policy Council (DGAP) believes that "the window of opportunity [to reinstate the Iran nuclear agreement] is short. We are talking about only three or four months, max, where we need to have some kind of accord to reinstate the old agreement, and then go on to some follow-on negotiations. So, this is really an issue of urgency."[8] Jake Sullivan and other members of the Biden administration clearly believe that dealing with Iran is preferable to dealing with America's traditional allies, the Sunni Arabs and Israel.

And Americans should keep an eye on these movements as we approach the important 2022 midterm elections in the United States. During the Obama administration, Democrats believed that the Iranian JCPOA deal was as important for their political fortunes as the passage

---

8 DW News, "Iran and the US: Can Joe Biden Renegotiate the Nuclear Deal?" YouTube, 26:08, 25 February 2021. https://www.youtube.com/watch?v=4MA7fRXd10w

of Obamacare.[9] Similarly, Democratic lawmakers looking to gain votes for their foreign policy are probably hoping to have at least a tentative deal with Iran ready by 2022.

Even if the United States was willing reenter the Iran nuclear deal soon, Iran would return to the negotiating table only if the United States ended all, or most, of the economic sanctions directed against Iran. While sanctions certainly can have unintended consequences, the fact remains that only the American sanctions on Iran have kept the Islamists in Tehran even mildly at bay. Once sanctions are removed, it becomes increasingly difficult to reimpose them—especially with the Europeans so eager to have greater trade relations with oil-rich Iran.[10]

Short of threatening overwhelming military force (which Iran does not believe the Americans will ever resort to), the sanctions provide the only real leverage that Washington has over Tehran. Why give that up for a deal that essentially allows Iran to acquire nuclear weapons in the next few years—and also empowers the Islamist regime in Iran by giving the country sweetheart trade deals with Europe, Canada, and the United States?

Voiding the sanctions just to get Iran to the negotiating table, where they will stonewall and strongarm American negotiators, is a bad move. However, I have no doubt that the Biden administration desperately wants to get the proverbial ball rolling on negotiations with Iran—so Biden's negotiators might be willing to give away the store just to claim that they've reentered the 2015 nuclear deal. Biden is a career politician, like Obama. Like Obama, Mr. Biden believes that having a deal—*any deal*—provides political capital that he and his party can use against their Republican opponents at home.

---

9 Rich Lowry, "The Iran Deal Is the New Obamacare," Politico, 5 August 2015. https://www.politico.com/magazine/story/2015/08/the-iran-deal-as-obamacare-121058/

10 John O'Donnell and Jonathan Saul, "European Allies Pushed Back When Trump Sanctioned Iran's Banks," Reuters, 1 December 2020. https://www.reuters.com/article/iran-germany-sanctions-banks-exclusive/european-allies-pushed-back-when-trump-sanctioned-irans-banks-idUSKBN28B59T

Thus far, the Biden plan for Iran is the conclusion of a long arc that began with Jimmy Carter and was carried forward over many decades by many Democratic Party presidents. It is a conclusion based on the flawed notion that the Iranian regime, whether it is armed with nuclear weapons or not, is capable of behaving as a rational actor. It assumes the regime will work as a responsible stakeholder of the wider regional order that the United States helped to create after the Second World War.

Working Iran into the regional framework would militate against the interests of the other players. This plan will spur nuclear proliferation among the Sunni Arab states. Such a move might even precipitate a desperate Israeli nuclear first strike against Iran if Jerusalem believes it is being left out in the cold by its American ally. American policymakers, sitting comfortably in the White House situation room or at Foggy Bottom, might feel they can afford to roll the dice by legitimizing the Islamist regime in Iran.

But the Israelis, who live under constant threat of annihilation from Iran and its terrorist proxies, are not willing to hope for the best when it comes to trying to make Iran a normal country. The Islamist ethos that rules Iran implies that it, in its present form, is *not* just another country. It is a radical, revolutionary power seeking to export its particular millenarian brand of Shia Islam to the world—just as the early Bolsheviks of the Soviet Union strove to export their communist ideals to the countries surrounding Russia.

Should Israel decide that leaving Iran alone is more dangerous than risking a preemptive war with Tehran, the United States will be left holding the bag. The Americans will be forced to intervene in a war that will have begun at a time not of its choosing—and its only reliable partners in that war, Israel and the Sunni Arab states, may have been decimated in its opening phases. In other words, the Americans would have to go it alone, with their backs up against a proverbial wall, and fight a crazed adversary possessing nuclear weapons in Iran.

Many analysts in the West remain unconvinced that Iran seeks to attack, let alone destroy, Israel with nuclear weapons. After all, the conventional wisdom is that such a strike would end in a massive American retaliation against Iran. Yet, few remain convinced that the United States would dare risk a larger war—nuclear war, no less—in the Middle East for an ally, even one as close to America as Israel. And with the Biden administration in charge, it is likely that this assumption is closer to the truth than many would care to acknowledge.

While stifling anti-Semitism within the Islamist regime of Iran explains a large part of Iran's desire to make Israel burn, there is another reason: sending a message to the Sunnis. Here, history comes back into play. The tiny state of Israel has, since its founding, withstood massive attacks from larger Arab armies belonging mostly to the Sunni side of the Middle East. Each war, Israel has dominated its Sunni Arab enemies—so much so that now many Arab Sunnis entertain notions of normalizing relations with Israel. But if Shiite Iran could blast Israel as Tehran routinely threatens, removing it as a force in the region, it would send a chilling message to the Khomeinists' real enemies in the Sunni Arab states: we decimated a country that your combined forces could not topple in multiple wars throughout the twentieth century. Do not mess with us.

Consider these recent events. After the American airstrike against Iranian targets in Syria on February 25, 2021, an Israeli transport ship transiting the Gulf of Oman (near Yemen's shores) exploded. No one was reported killed or injured, thankfully. Israeli intelligence suspects that the explosions were the result of "asymmetric activity by Iranian military" directed against Israeli targets. It is theorized that this was an Iranian attempt to "create leverage over Washington" to get the Biden administration to grant the Iranians relief from sanctions, as well as to punish Israel for its ongoing talks with several Sunni Arab states to create a multilateral defensive alliance designed to contain Iran's growing power in the region.[11] It's only a matter of time before the situation in the region

---

11 Shahar Klaiman, "Explosion Hits Israeli Cargo Ship in Gulf of Oman," *Israel Hayom,* 26 February 2021. https://www.israelhayom.com/2021/02/26/explosion-hits-israeli-cargo-ship-in-the-gulf-of-oman/

gets out of hand. It's already almost there, in my opinion.

At the end of November in 2021, representatives from multiple nations, notably from Iran, gathered in the historic capital of Austria, Vienna. Since June of that year, representatives from Europe, the United States, the United Kingdom, Russia, China, Iran, and several other nations had been negotiating the restoration of the Obama era Joint Comprehensive Plan of Action, the executive nuclear agreement that former US President Donald Trump had abandoned in 2018. The Iranians wanted two things: wider sanctions relief and a clear, legal pathway to nuclear weapons. The Biden administration, while thumping their chests at Iran's leaders by threatening greater sanctions if Tehran did not return to the JCPOA, want only one thing: the restoration of Obama's nuclear deal with Iran—no matter what.

This became evident when, during the seventh round of negotiations in Vienna in December, representatives from the European Union and the United States accused Iran's hardline delegation of reneging on promises they had made to the West during the first and second rounds of the Vienna talks in June. While these talks bore on, reports were disseminated to the press that the Israelis, who had no faith whatsoever in the Vienna talks yielding anything than an even more aggressive Iran that threatened Israeli security, were planning a massive strike on Iran once the talks failed. But most experts understand that Israel lacks the military capability to successfully conduct such a mission—and even if it did have that capability, it would need to coordinate closely with Washington, and the Americans are unlikely to approve of such a strike.[12] Just when it seemed like Israeli leaders would be proven correct; that the talks would indeed implode under the weight of their own absurd goals, representatives from Moscow apparently pressured Iranian delegates to uphold their initial promises. This, as tensions between Moscow and Washington

---

12 Yaniv Kubovich, "Israel Preps to Strike Iran Nuke Sites. It Will Take Years to Materialize," *Haaretz*, 9 December 2021. https://www.haaretz.com/israel-news/.premium-like-an-arrow-through-the-heart-idf-prepares-for-military-action-against-iran-1.10451436

flared over a potential Russian military buildup against Ukraine.

For their part, according to my colleague at the *Asia Times*, David P. Goldman, the Israelis were "pondering a Pax Sinica". Jerusalem, fully aware that Washington's leaders wanted peace at any price with the theocrats in Tehran, believed that China held the true sway over Iran's leaders. According to Goldman, "China has been Iran's main trading partner for more than a decade, taking advantage of Western sanctions on Iran to dictate usurious terms of trade. But China needs Saudi Arabia, Iran's strategic rival, more than it needs Iran." In Goldman's assessment, "China may use its ties to exercise pressure on the United States, but it does not want Tehran to dominate the Gulf." The brilliant Goldman, who wrote under the pseudonym "Spengler" for many years, attested that he had "heard a presentation under the auspices of [Sino-Israel Global Network and Academic Leadership] by a Chinese scholar explaining how China carefully calibrates its missile sales to Iran and Saudi Arabia to maintain the regional balance of power." As Goldman's *Asia Times* report suggested, during the fateful breakdown between the US-European negotiating team and Iran, China exercised an unspecified amount of influence over the Iranian delegation that "saved" the Vienna talks.[13]

The problem is that now both Russia and China have an unspecified, very potent hold over Iran—and by extension American allies, like Israel and Saudi Arabia. Representatives from Beijing and Moscow may very well have "saved" the disastrous nuclear talks in Vienna but that may be the problem. The talks themselves are setting a new geopolitical paradigm wherein Iran, Israel, and the Sunni Arab states are all balancing against each other, with the United States, China, and Russia maneuvering against each other in the background. Yet, this high stakes tripolar paradigm that's being established in the Middle East will not lead to peace. As you read earlier: historically, tripolar systems

---

13 David P. Goldman, "Israel Ponders a Pax Sinica," *Asia Times*, 19 December 2021. https://asiatimes.com/2021/12/israel-ponders-a-pax-sinica/

are inherently unstable and will collapse into warfare. And as tensions between Washington and Moscow flare over Russian brinkmanship in Ukraine or between Beijing and Washington over Chinese irredentism against Taiwan, both China and Russia will happily use their ties with Tehran to "exercise pressure on the United States" in the Mideast to prevent Washington from responding to whatever crises either China or Russia are ginning up elsewhere in the world.

America pushing its traditional allies away, giving a strategic opening to its great power rivals, China and Russia, all while empowering a nuclear Iran with a revanchist policy in the Mideast will not bring peace to the Middle East. It will trigger greater instability. Containing Iran and using Israel and the Sunni Arab states to enforce that containment is the easiest path for the West. Yet, it's the one path that Washington refuses to take.

There's still time to change this. But the Biden administration does not appear to be well suited to the challenge. Joe Biden, a man who spent decades in the Senate, is a creature of habit—and his habits were formed by a political establishment that has completely mismanaged US foreign policy in the Mideast generally, especially in relation to Iran. It's almost as if he were the perfect choice if one wanted to ensure that nuclear conflict in the Middle East broke out. If trends persist, it surely will.

29

SETTLING THE ISRAEL-PALESTINE

CONFLICT ISN'T WORTH

AMERICA'S TIME

JARED KUSHNER SEEMS like an unlikely person to be mentioned in a foreign policy book. After all, he is a Manhattan real estate magnate who is politically moderate. Yet it was Kushner, along with former Secretary of State Mike Pompeo—with the blessing of Kushner's father-in-law, former President Donald J. Trump—who helped to create one of the most important diplomatic success stories in the annals of US foreign policy in the Middle East. Representing President Trump, Kushner orchestrated the Abraham Accords, the first attempt at bringing together the Sunni Arab states with Israel.

Throughout 2020, multiple Sunni Arab countries hopped aboard the Abraham Accords and normalized relations with the Jewish state of Israel. Meanwhile, the Kushner plan allowed Israel to claim up to 30 percent of the West Bank, including all settlements and the Jordan Valley. Detractors argued that this plan was the end of the Palestinian cause; that it represented a complete, official siding with Israel in the decades old Israel-Palestine conflict; and that it ran counter to the traditional American diplomatic policy of trying to broker a fair end to that conflict.[1]

The detractors were correct in their worries but were wrong about the result. By refusing to become involved in the Israel-Palestine conflict, the Trump administration moved the diplomatic ball forward as never before. Since the 1950s, American diplomats and policymakers from both political parties have attempted to navigate the Middle East by linking everything back to the Israel-Palestine conflict. Kushner and his cohort rightly perceived this as wasteful.

After all, Israel is a tiny country, and Palestine is not really a country at all. Both Israel and Palestine exist on the periphery of the Middle East. Why was the United States spending such an inordinate time on this issue? Besides, the Palestinians have been given more than one chance to end the conflict and create an equitable peace between themselves and the Israelis. Each time, however, a succession of Palestinian leaders opted for continued conflict rather than peace. The longer this dynamic endured, the less that the Americans would be able to get done in the region.

What the Trump administration recognized was that Israel was an actual country and Palestine was not. Further, Israel is—and has been—an American ally. It makes no sense for Washington to besmirch its ally, Israel, when it needs as many allies in the Middle East as it can get.

What's more, Israel's primary enemies in the region, Islamist radicals in both the Sunni and Shiite camps, also happen to be America's greatest

1 Lahav Harkov, "The Abraham Accords Domino Effect Will Lead to More Peace Deals," *Jerusalem Post*, 1 January 2021. https://www.jpost.com/middle-east/the-abraham-accords-domino-effect-will-lead-to-more-peace-deals-653940

threats. And the biggest threat of them all is the Islamic Republic of Iran. Previous American administrations fixated on Israel's actions in Palestine. What they should have focused on was the important role that Israel played in helping to secure American interests in the wider region, specifically as they related to the US-Islamist war. Palestine does little to preserve or enhance US regional interests.

The Trump administration recognized the importance of Israel. In fact, the Trump administration attempted to bring Palestinian leaders into the fold. In the first few years of the Trump administration, Kushner led an effort to offer economic aid to Palestine. In the summer of 2019, Jared Kushner "outlined a $50 billion Middle East economic plan that would create a global investment fund to lift the Palestinian and neighboring Arab state economies and fund a $5 billion transportation corridor to connect [the] West Bank and Gaza."

Kushner named it the "Peace to Prosperity" Plan. It included "179 infrastructure and business projects." In 2019 Reuters dubbed the plan "ambitious." The plan would have seen half the $50 billion "spent in the economically troubled Palestinian territories over 10 years while [the] rest [would have been] split between Egypt, Lebanon, and Jordan." What's more, according to Kushner himself at the time, "Some of the projects [would have been] in Egypt's Sinai Peninsula, where investments [would have benefited] Palestinians living in adjacent Gaza, a crowded and impoverished coastal enclave."[2]

The Palestinians refused to partake in the program, claiming that the plan was one-sided in favor of Israel. For Kushner, it was a tangible effort to bring the Palestinians to the table without throwing America's ally, Israel, under that table. The Israel-Palestine peace process has been stalled for decades because Washington essentially wanted to hit the

---

2 Matt Spetalnick and Steve Holland, "Exclusive: White House's Kushner Unveils Economic Portion of Middle East Plan," Reuters, 22 June 2019. https://www.reuters.com/article/us-israel-palestinians-plan-exclusive/exclusive-white-houses-kushner-unveils-economic-portion-of-middle-east-peace-plan-idUSKCN1TN0ES

reset button on a key international development: the founding—and recognition—of Israel as a sovereign nation-state. That particular ship had sailed, though, decades earlier in 1947, when the international community—specifically, the United States government—recognized Israel as a free and independent state.

Since then, the Arabs of Palestine have tried to end Israel's existence. A succession of wars have been waged between Israel and its Arab neighbors. Israel won every one of those wars (which the Arabs all started). Just when it seemed as if the Arab states were coming around to the fact that Israel was going to stay, Iran became an Islamist state that took up the mantle of Palestinian resistance. Here's the thing, though; at every turn, Israel has attempted to stabilize its relationship with its Palestinian Arab neighbors. And every time Israel attempts to make peace with them, the Palestinian leaders—most of whom are both radical and beholden to foreign regimes, like Iran, that are intent on annihilating Israel—refuse to make a deal.

Palestinian leaders have for decades argued that they merely wanted a state of their own. The Israelis have consistently supported the two-state solution at every turn. The Palestinians have repeatedly rejected Israeli overtures. Instead, Palestinian leaders favored pushing for the total destruction of Israel as an independent Jewish state. By the 1980s, the Palestinians finally decided to abandon their dream of returning to territories once held by the Palestinians and instead favored creating a separate state for themselves beside Israel.

Yet they couldn't agree on the particulars—who would get what parts of the territory. As the debates raged, the radicals kept inciting Israel with terrorist attacks. Each attack prompted Israel to react militarily. And every time Israel reacted militarily, it usually gained more territory. In spite of these developments, however, Israeli leaders have consistently offered Palestinians a separate state. *Palestinian leaders don't know how to say "yes."*

American leaders, meanwhile, have gotten lost in the policy weeds. Fancying themselves as the great peacemaker, a succession of

American presidents have attempted to achieve peace between Israel and Palestine by essentially downplaying their intimate role in the creation of Israel (President Harry Truman was an ardent supporter of Israel) as well as trying to rationalize with radical elements of Palestine's leadership. For decades, the peace process had been stalled because the world's most powerful country, the United States, was trying to force the parties on the ground to play by the fantasies of American statesmen in Washington.

The Trump administration cut through these fantasies and recognized the reality: Israel was a free and independent state entitled to defend itself against all foes. Israel had also proven itself to be a consistent ally in the shared fight against Islamist terrorism. And that fight was far more important to the United States than any attempts to end the ongoing conflict between Israel and Palestine. The Kushner plan attempted to give the Palestinians a viable path forward—with money in hand—to begin developing their proto-state while also giving Israel the space it needed to secure itself while rededicating its energies to containing the growing Iranian threat.

Of course, the Palestinians didn't go for it. Although individual Palestinians may be ready for the fighting to be over with Israel, their leaders are not. The Kushner proposals were lambasted by the "experts" in the West. But these are the same people who've spent entire careers steeped in solving the Israel-Palestine conflict, and the only thing they have ever accomplished was pushing Israel away from the United States and empowering the craziest elements of the Islamic world.

Kushner's instincts were right. You don't get a do-over on Israeli sovereignty. That debate was settled more than seventy years ago. This was why the Trump administration worked as hard as it did to ensure that Jerusalem was made the official capital of Israel, a promise that every American president for forty years had made, but a promise that none except Trump kept.[3]

---

3 Brandon J. Weichert, "Trump's Jerusalem Gambit Recalls Harry Truman," American Greatness, 10 December 2017. https://amgreatness.com/2017/12/10/trumps-jerusalem-gambit-recalls-harry-truman/

Israel's sovereignty was not just established by an official act of the United States and the entire international community in 1947. Its sovereignty was reaffirmed each time Arab armies attempted to push the Israelis into the Mediterranean Sea and ended up getting their rear ends handed to them by the Israeli Defense Force. At the same time, everyone—including the Israelis—believed that Palestine needed to be its own state, separate from the Jewish democracy of Israel. The issue was figuring out how to get there.

What Kushner did was offer incentives to the Arabs while, as the most powerful country in the world, the Trump administration backed Israeli sovereignty unapologetically. It was a decisive signal to the region that the most powerful country, the United States, was standing firmly behind its allies in the region. It was a symbol of unity that was meant to inspire all of the other powers in the region to get on board America's new Mideast policy train before it left the proverbial station.

If the Palestinians wanted to come along, a boatload of cash was waiting for them. That $50 billion investment deal Kushner proposed was just the opening bid. Had the Palestinians played fairer with the West, they probably would've walked away in a much more tenable position than they presently have.

Palestinians yet again chose obstinance. They replicated the same pattern that every generation of Palestinian leadership has displayed since Israel's rise in 1947. Because of their own intransigence, the Palestinians will continue to be marginalized. Either way, the United States has much bigger problems to concern itself with in the region than worrying about an obscure ethno-religious blood feud between Palestinian Arabs and Jewish Israelis, especially since Israel has decisively won its independence—time and time again.

The Kushner plan that former President Trump pushed for was a deliberate, realistic plan that addressed *America's strategic needs first.* For the first time in decades, Washington was thinking about what it needed from the region rather than what the region needed from it. Before President Trump's time in office, there was an old joke about the State Department's (and the wider foreign policy establishment's) inability to look at things through the lens of actual American interests.

Essentially, the State Department has a desk that specializes in understanding the needs of every country in the world—except the needs of the United States. Perhaps Foggy Bottom should create an America desk, so things can start moving in a direction that benefits the United States, the way US foreign policy has benefited the rest of the world!

The Trump and Kushner plan for the Middle East was momentous precisely because it didn't attempt to restore the region to its state before the rise of Israel in 1947. It accepted the situation in the region as it was. And it tried to work within the confines of reality to best secure America's interests in the region. In addition, because the United States is the strongest country operating in the region today, the other countries in the Mideast—especially the Arab states—all took note that Washington was decisively using its power to shape the region *without invading or bombing any more Muslim countries.* They followed America's lead.

Every expert told the world that the Trump administration's Mideast plans were reckless. They told us that the Arab states would *never* get on board with what Kushner was proposing. It was all considered a gigantic waste of time. Every single one of those experts was wrong.

By the time Kushner got the proverbial ball rolling on his plan, multiple Muslim countries signed up. Israel went from being a pariah in the region to having its status normalized by many Sunni Arab states. The United Arab Emirates, Bahrain, even African Muslim states like Sudan, all recognized Israel.

Kushner's big prize, though, was the Kingdom of Saudi Arabia. Before President Trump left office under a cloud of controversy in January 2021, there were strong signals coming from Riyadh that the Saudi regime was at last going to recognize Israel and move closer to Israel militarily. As of the summer of 2021, Saudi Arabia has not recognized Israel.[4] However, it has used its influence as the center of the Sunni Arab world to pressure almost every other Sunni Arab state, including nuclear-armed Pakistan, to "normalize normalization" with Israel. Not all Sunni Arab states have normalized relations with Israel, but many have. For Pakistan to normalize ties with Israel would be almost as important as Saudi Arabia's normalizing ties with Israel. As this is written in the summer of 2021, it remains to be seen whether Pakistan will do this. There is a political dogfight on the issue within Pakistan's uneven domestic politics.

Many have speculated that Pakistan-Israel relations will be determined by the outcome of the war in Afghanistan. In December of 2020, it was reported that senior officials from an unidentified large Muslim country traveled to Israel to conduct high-level talks with the Israeli government regarding recognition. For months thereafter, it was assumed that these were representatives from Pakistan. The Pakistani government has issued strident denials.

In July 2021, the Biden administration began a rapid drawdown of US forces in Afghanistan, leading to a massive resurgence in the fortunes of the Islamist Taliban. At that time both Pakistan and India were vying for influence with the Taliban, a group both governments believed would be the future leader of Afghanistan. Because the Taliban are rabid Islamists and virulent anti-Semites, Pakistan was concerned that earlier reports of their previous outreach to Israel might harm their capability to keep the Taliban under their sway and away from their Indian rivals. Thus, it seems likely that the Taliban will play a key role in whether Pakistan ultimately recognizes Israel.[5]

It is key to understand Saudi Arabia's important role in getting

---

4 Hussein Ibish, "Why Saudi Arabia Is Now in No Rush to Recognize Israel," *Haaretz*, 7 July 2021. https://www.haaretz.com/middle-east-news/.premium-why-saudi-arabia-is-now-in-no-rush-to-recognize-israel-1.9976034

5 Kunwar Khuldune Shahid, "The Taliban Will Decide if Pakistan Recognizes Israel," *Haaretz*, 30 June 2021. https://www.haaretz.com/israel-news/the-taliban-will-decide-if-pakistan-recognizes-israel-1.9953445

other Sunni states to recognize Israel. According to Mideast expert and *Washington Post* columnist David Ignatius, "Mohammed bin Salman would tell people, 'I see a Middle East that's going to include Israel. I'm prepared to recognize Israel; have trade relationships with Israel.'"[6] Even two years ago, this was called an impossibility by Middle East experts in the West.[7]

All of this happened so that the region's powers could contain the growing Iranian threat—a threat that blundering American policies had helped to create. The Sunni Arab states must now, more than anyone, live with the disastrous results of such ignorant US foreign policies. With Donald Trump's loss in the 2020 election, though, the momentum his administration's policies in the Mideast generated is being lost. The Biden administration is committed to going back to the bad old days in the Mideast, when American power was wasted on vanity projects like resolving the intractable Israel-Palestine conflict or going to war against Sunni Arab states for democracy and human rights—and recognizing the crazies who run Iran. We're now back to square one, unfortunately.

6 Martin Smith, "Transcript: The Crown Prince of Saudi Arabia," PBS Frontline, December 2018. https://www.pbs.org/wgbh/frontline/film/the-crown-prince-of-saudi-arabia/transcript/

7 Kunwar Khuldune Shahid, "How Saudi Arabia Is Pressuring Pakistan to Recognize Israel," *Haaretz*, 22 November 2020. https://www.haaretz.com/middle-east-news/.premium-how-saudi-arabia-is-pressuring-pakistan-to-recognize-israel-1.9315768

30

SAUDI ARABIA:

AN IMPERFECT ALLY

IN 2017, comedians around the world had great fun talking about the hilarious image of then-President Donald J. Trump standing shoulder-to-shoulder with the leaders of the Arab world at a conference in Riyadh, Saudi Arabia. Trump, the king of Saudi Arabia and an assortment of other Arab leaders were all standing together for a photo op in which they were touching a glowing orb. Many people joked that it looked as if they were touching one of the orbs that Saruman, the corrupt wizard in *Lord of the Rings,* used to communicate with Sauron, the main villain in that series.[1]

---

1 "What Was That Glowing Orb Trump Touched in Saudi Arabia?" *New York Times,* 22 March 2017. https://www.nytimes.com/2017/05/22/world/middleeast/trump-glowing-orb-saudi.html

In fact, that photo op was one of the most momentous images taken of an American leader in the Middle East. That image was the apotheosis of the strategic shift that the Trump administration was engineering in the region. Under President Obama, the Sunni Arab states—notably Saudi Arabia—were punished by their strongest ally, the United States. They were punished for not being liberal enough (though no one other than Israel is as liberal as the West in that part of the world). They were punished by Obama for lacking a strong human rights record (again, it's the Middle East; Westerners should lower their expectations).

These two issues, by the way, were strangely intertwined with the Obama administration's bizarre support for Islamist organizations like the Muslim Brotherhood.[2] After all, for the various secular autocracies of the Sunni Arab world, Islamist groups were the primary enemies their regimes faced. The autocratic regimes often used undemocratic means to wage war upon the Islamist organizations in their midst. But the same Islamist groups that undemocratic regimes suppressed in places like Saudi Arabia or Egypt were the same Islamist groups that were at war with the United States and Israel.

Emphasizing democracy and human rights, therefore, only benefited the same Islamist groups that were at war with the United States. Yet, the Obama administration made clear its preference for supporting Islamist groups over the secular autocratic regimes in the Sunni Arab community of nations.[3] The result was the proliferation of Islamist terrorism coupled with the explosion of Iranian Islamist power in the region.

The Trump administration did away with all of that. Whereas Obama was skeptical of a Sunni Arab-Israeli military alliance aimed

2 Egypt Today Staff, "Leaked Emails: Obama Administration's Support to Muslim Brotherhood to Dominate Media," *Egypt Today,* 12 October 2020. https://www.egypttoday.com/Article/1/93011/ Leaked-emails-Obama-administration's-support-to-Muslim-Brotherhood-to-dominate

3 Anne R. Pierce, "US 'Partnership' with the Egyptian Muslim Brotherhood and Its Effect on Civil Society and Human Rights," *Society,* 18 December 2013. https://www.ncbi.nlm.nih.gov/pmc/articles/ PMC3882524/

at containing Iranian power, President Trump fully embraced it.[4] The image of Trump and the Sunni Arab leaders holding the glowing orb was meant to signify that the Americans were *finally* understanding that, in the Islamic world, they had no better ally than those despotic regimes that Obama, and even George W. Bush, had despised.

Trump intuitively understood what the former US ambassador to Israel and top-ranking Democratic Party foreign policy aficionado Martin Indyk said about former President Obama's lack of understanding about the Middle East. Obama, according to Indyk, did not grasp that "It takes three to tango in the Middle East—an Israeli leader and an Arab leader who are ready to take risks and an American president who is willing to invest his time and prestige to convince them that he will support them if they take the risks."[5]

Speaking to an anxious audience of the Arab world's leaders, Trump proudly proclaimed that:

> America will not seek to impose our way of life on others, but to outstretch our hands in the spirit of cooperation and trust. ... Our goal is a coalition of nations who share the aim of stamping out extremism and providing our children a hopeful future that does honor to God.[6]

During his Riyadh speech, Trump also proclaimed the creation of a new Global Center for Combating Extremist Ideology, which would be located in Saudi Arabia, the land of Muhammad's birth. Trump announced the adoption of "principled realism," which he described as distinct from George W. Bush's "freedom agenda," which sought

---

4 Martin S. Indyk and Nahum Barnea, "What Obama Doesn't Understand About Israel and the Middle East," *Brookings Institute,* 28 May 2012. https://www.brookings.edu/on-the-record/what-obama-doesnt-understand-about-israel-and-the-middle-east/

5 Indyk and Barnea, "What Obama."

6 "Transcript of Trump's Speech in Saudi Arabia," CNN, 21 May 2017. https://www.cnn.com/2017/05/21/politics/trump-saudi-speech-transcript

to replace undemocratic regimes, like Saddam Hussein's Iraq, with democratic ones—even if those new democratic regimes were inimical to American interests, as the Shiite-dominated government of Iraq today often is. Trump also sought to make "principled realism" different from the Obama approach to the Middle East, which explicitly empowered Islamist movements like the Muslim Brotherhood so long as they opposed the secular autocracies of the region—secular autocracies that were, in many cases, closely aligned with the United States.[7]

As part of his "principled realism" approach to the region, Trump vowed that:

> Our friends will never question our support, and our enemies will never doubt our determination. Our partnerships will advance security through stability, not through radical disruption. We will make decisions based on real-world outcomes—not inflexible ideology. We will be guided by the lessons of experience, not the confines of rigid thinking. And, wherever possible, we will seek gradual reforms—not sudden intervention.[8]

Finally, the United States had a leader who would *listen* to America's allies in the region. This American president would accept the facts on the ground rather than try to impose the lofty idealism of neo-Marxist Western academicians who are more beholden to their ideological worldview of how Mideast ought to be rather than how it really is. Trump emphasized his point when he coolly stated that, *"We must seek partners, not perfection—and to make allies of all who share our goals* [emphasis added]."[9]

---

7 "Transcript of Trump's Speech."

8 "Transcript of Trump's Speech."

9 "Transcript of Trump's Speech."

Trump further elucidated a point that was music to the ears of most Americans, who were tired of the Middle East and the way conflicts there consumed the national discourse. The forty-fifth American president stated that "Muslim nations must be willing to take on the burden, if we are going to defeat terrorism and send its wicked ideology into oblivion." Trump then listed what every Muslim-majority country has contributed to the fight against Islamism, whether it be against al Qaeda, Al Nusra, or Iranian-backed groups, such as Hezbollah or the Houthi rebels in Yemen.[10]

What's more, Trump announced the formation of another counterterrorism venture with Saudi Arabia, the Terrorist Financing Targeting Center. More than any other joint endeavor in the Global War on Terror, this should prove to be the most decisively damaging program to Islamists everywhere. After all, if you cut off their cash flows, the global *jihad* will grind to a halt.[11]

President Trump continued in this way for an hour, and the audience of Arab rulers and assembled Saudi notables were rapt by the speech. This was not simply pandering to the leader of their most powerful ally, the United States. People I've spoken with who were present at the speech said most people listening were sincerely stunned by Trump's words.

Never before had they heard such a practical and wise speech come from the mouth of an American president—especially one as gonzo as Donald Trump! Whatever Trump's political legacy will be after the tumultuous events that followed the November 2020 election, the years leading up to those fateful weeks at the end of 2020 and the start of 2021 were punctuated by the most insightful foreign policy choices, especially when it came to the Middle East, that any American leader had made in years.

---

10 "Transcript of Trump's Speech."

11 Juan C. Zarate, *Treasury's War: The Unleashing of a New Era of Financial Warfare* (New York: Public Affairs, 2013), pp. 15–44.

During that famous summit in Riyadh, President Trump negotiated a historic arms deal with the Saudis.[12] Trump was apparently the only American leader who recognized that Saudi Arabia was taking the fight to Iran in Yemen. In 2015, when the Obama administration was making its ill-advised nuclear concession to Iran, Mohammed bin Salman (MBS), the Saudi defense minister at the time, called for a massive air campaign against Iranian-backed Houthi rebels in Yemen.[13] The Saudi military was designed to do two things: fight Islamist terrorists at home and secure the regime's rule. It had to change gears and become a more traditional fighting force—if it was going to believably stand up to Iran's growing threat in the region, with or without the assistance of the United States.

Because Saudi Arabia is relatively inexperienced in conducting more conventional military actions, its air war over Yemen has proven to be one of the gravest human rights disasters in modern history.[14] With nearly 18,400 civilian deaths in six years and the world's worst food security crisis affecting around 20.1 million people, the Yemen civil war is considered to be far more devastating on a human scale than even the ongoing Syrian civil war.[15] That's a sobering statistic.

What many Western policymakers and pundits view as malign action on the part of Saudi Arabia in Yemen is simply the result of the Saudis' inexperience in waging this kind of military campaign outside

12 Javier E. David, "US-Saudi Arabia Seal Weapons Deal Worth Nearly $110 Billion Immediately, $350 Billion over 10 Years," CNBC, 20 May 2017. https://www.cnbc.com/2017/05/20/us-saudi-arabia-seal-weapons-deal-worth-nearly-110-billion-as-trump-begins-visit.html

13 Reuters Staff, "Kerry Stresses Need to End Syria, Yemen Conflicts in Talks with Saudis," Reuters, 11 March 2016. https://www.reuters.com/article/us-usa-kerry-saudi/kerry-stresses-need-to-end-syria-yemen-conflicts-in-talks-with-saudis-idUSKCN0WD26J

14 John R. Allen and Bruce Riedel, "Ending the Yemen War Is Both a Strategic and Humanitarian Imperative," Brookings Institute, 16 November 2020. https://www.brookings.edu/blog/order-from-chaos/2020/11/16/ending-the-yemen-war-is-both-a-strategic-and-humanitarian-imperative/

15 Kenneth Roth, "Yemen: Events of 2020," Human Rights Watch, Accessed on 26 February 2021. https://www.hrw.org/world-report/2021/country-chapters/yemen

of their territory. It's sad, but it is true. As the prospect of regional great power war inches closer, especially because the Biden administration seems intent on erasing the gains made during the Trump years by returning to the Iran nuclear agreement and distancing the United States from Israel and the Sunni Arab states, Riyadh has no choice but to improve its conventional warfighting capabilities—which are behind the curve, to say the least.

Should the Americans under President Biden prove unable or unwilling to aid Saudi Arabia against Iranian military aggression, then Riyadh must have reliable defensive capabilities of its own. In a sick way, Yemen is a proving ground for Saudi Arabia's forces. Thus far, Saudi Arabia's military has proven effective in stunting the gains of the Iranian-backed Houthi rebels in Yemen. Even though it owns a suite of advanced American and European weapons, the Saudi war machine still leaves much to be desired—especially in light of the human rights catastrophe Riyadh's intervention in Yemen has caused. The Saudis still need more work to become a reliable check against Iran's growing power. But ceding the region to Iran over the next four years or abandoning Saudi Arabia at this point will do little to protect American interests in the region.

Furthermore, had the Obama administration not spent so much time punishing its Arab partners and courting Iran, it is unlikely that Saudi Arabia would have engaged the Iran-backed Houthi rebels in Yemen as it has. As former Obama Secretary of State Hillary Clinton once noted, everywhere Saudi Arabia looked in the Middle East, they saw Iran's hand acting against their interests.

If left unchecked, Iranian power in Yemen will grow. This Iranian influence will directly threaten Saudi Arabia. These facts, more than anything else, explain the wild Saudi military intervention in the Yemen civil war.

You have already seen how Iran has used the Houthi rebels to launch devastating drone attacks on critical Saudi infrastructure. Iran has also striven to separate the Shiite-majority Eastern Province of Saudi Arabia from Riyadh's control. Iran tried this first in 2011, when the mullahs supported an attempted uprising against the Sunni Khalifa family that rules Bahrain. (Bahrain is a majority Shiite country as well.) Saudi Arabia deployed its military to secure the Khalifa family's reign and to curb Iran's growing influence in that tiny nation so close to Saudi Arabia's borders. Once the Yemen civil war got underway, Iran sensed that it had a new opportunity to threaten Saudi Arabia's territorial integrity.

Because of the human toll that Saudi Arabia's airstrikes have taken on the people of Yemen, most Western leaders were not willing to treat Saudi Arabia as an ally. During the Obama administration, Washington sought to distance itself from the Kingdom much as Washington under various Democratic Party administrations has attempted to push Israel away over the years. Obama's distancing from Saudi Arabia happened at a time when Iranian power was spreading at breakneck speed throughout the region.

The Saudis needed new arms deals with the United States. They needed to be seen as trusted partners of the world's sole remaining superpower to remain a viable center of resistance to Iranian power. Until Trump came along, though, deals with the Saudis were facing increased scrutiny because of perceived human rights abuses by the Kingdom. Under the Biden administration, these deals are threatened yet again.[16]

None of these moves by well-meaning Western liberals helped the cause of stopping Iranian aggression. In June 2018, Senator Patrick Leahy (D-VT) attempted to use the National Defense Authorization Act (NDAA) as a venue to virtue-signal his moral superiority to the world. The so-called "Leahy Law" prevents the United States government from providing military assistance to countries with an unsavory record. Leahy wanted to apply this counterproductive provision to America's vital relationship with the Kingdom of Saudi Arabia when Iranian power was fully on the march.

---

16 Patricia Zengerle and Mike Stone, "Exclusive: Biden Team Considering a Halt to 'Offensive' Arms Sales for Saudis," Reuters, 26 February 2021. https://www.reuters.com/article/us-usa-saudi-arms/exclusive-biden-team-considering-a-halt-to-offensive-arms-sales-for-saudis-idUSKBN2AQ2J6

I critiqued the Leahy Law at the time by arguing that:

Should the United States fully adhere to the Leahy Law and only support democratic regimes, it would find itself losing out in the grand, geopolitical game. Or worse, it might end up supporting the very same regimes it must protect itself from (as former President Obama briefly did when he supported the Muslim Brotherhood's takeover in Egypt during the Arab Spring).[17]

Naturally, Senator Leahy didn't like my take on his signature legislation. He wrote a snippy response in the pages of *The American Spectator* in which he claimed I was exaggerating the case against the Leahy Law. According to Leahy, his eponymous law was "targeted" and meant to "enhance the professionalism of our partners, which helps build their legitimacy and ensures that the U.S. is not associated with such acts."[18]

Yes, Senator Leahy, we will deny the militaries of our allies the weapons they need to basically fight America's enemies for us, so as to enhance their professionalism! Just so you understand, Senator Leahy is an ancient member of the Democratic Party's establishment. He is a contemporary of President Joe Biden. These men think in very similar terms. And they are consistently wrong.

This is not some freshman senator from an obscure state. Leahy is practically a Senate institution unto himself. Even though Leahy has since retired, there remain plenty of other Liberal dinosaurs in the Senate (and even many of the younger members leave much to be desired when it comes to dealing with the realities of the Greater Middle East). These are the purportedly serious—*very senior*—people helping to craft America's foreign policy in the Middle East. It's no surprise, then,

---

17 Brandon J. Weichert, "Repeal the Leahy Law," *The American Spectator,* 11 June 2018. https://spectator.org/repeal-the-leahy-law-2/

18 Patrick Leahy, "Reader Mail: Senator Patrick Leahy Responds to Brandon Weichert," *The American Spectator,* 22 June 2018. https://spectator.org/reader-mail-senator-patrick-leahy-responds-to-brandon-weichert-2/

that America keeps finding itself bogged down in *multiple* inconclusive wars in the Mideast—while Iran, its primary geostrategic rival in the region, continues to be empowered.

We can all tell ourselves that we're morally superior to a people who exist in what many consider to be one of the deadliest regions of the world—as we sit in our posh homes in Northern Virginia, get free airtime on international news, and go to work in taxpayer-funded cars in one of the most storied buildings in the history of democracy, the United States Capitol Building. When one is in the sandbox, it's an entirely different affair. Because ensuring the stable and easy flow of oil from the region to the rest of the world continues to be in the American interest, and because most Americans understandably do not want to send their loved ones to fight in endless Mideast wars, Washington must find willing and able partners in the region to do its bidding. The Saudis, like the Israelis, have consistently proven to be such a force—even if their military is not yet as competent as America's.

Saudi Arabia *is* an imperfect ally. As is Israel. But these two countries remain America's best friends in a troubled, though important, region. And you can bet that the Saudis and Israelis feel the same way about us Americans.

Fact is, we Americans just don't get the Middle East. Thanks to the presence of nations like Israel and Saudi Arabia in the Mideast, nations that want to do the fighting (and dying) for the United States, *we don't have to get it.* But we do have to get out of their way. In our decadence, we persist in involving ourselves in situations we will never fully understand to try to create impossible outcomes.

Putting any distance between the United States and Saudi Arabia or Israel now ensures that Iran, Russia, and China will quickly become the powers that rule this strategically vital region. In fact, in August 2021, it was confirmed that the Islamic Republic of Iran had been officially invited to join the Shanghai Cooperation Organisation (SCO) by China and Russia. The SCO is considered to be both China and Russia's answer to the US-led NATO alliance. By incorporating Iran into this alliance of Eurasian autocracies, Beijing and Moscow are signaling their intention to expand their influence through Iran and into the wider world.[19]

Even though Americans do not get a majority of their oil from the Middle East anymore, much of the rest of the world—especially many of America's closest partners in Europe and Asia—do. Should Iran, Russia, and China become the powerbrokers in the region, you can rest assured that America's allies in Europe and Asia will be forced to break away from the United States and hew much more closely to the whims of Iran, Russia, and China.

This would swing the global balance of power away from the United States and toward China, Russia, and Iran. It should be American policy to avoid such an outcome at all costs.

---

19 "Iran to Join the Shanghai Cooperation Organization," *Tehran Times,* 11 August 2021. https://www.tehrantimes.com/news/464001/Iran-to-join-Shanghai-Cooperation-Organization

31

JAMAL KHASHOGGI'S MURDER

WAS GROSS. IRAN'S THREAT IS

MORE DANGEROUS.

EVEN THE STARTLING EXAMPLE of Jamal Khashoggi's murder by agents of Saudi Arabia has more to it than the Western media reports. While it's true that Khashoggi's murder was gruesome, it is also true that Khashoggi had been dancing around this horrific outcome with his actions in the years leading up to his murder. Khashoggi had spent decades as the ultimate insider to the Saudi royal family.

In fact, Khashoggi was a close friend and confidant of Saudi Prince Turki al-Faisal, the Svengali of the Saudi royal family; a man whose secrets had secrets, for Faisal had been the Saudi intelligence chief for twenty-five years (before he suddenly quit the job immediately after

9/11). You should think of Khashoggi as a Saudi spy who pretended to be a Saudi journalist.

As the ultimate insider to the Saudi regime for decades, Khashoggi was a staunch nationalist. For instance, Khashoggi was described by PBS Frontline's Martin Smith in 2018 as "the most ardent supporter of the Yemen campaign." Defending what some of the elder members of the Saudi royal family described as Mohammed bin Salman's "rash" decision to take Saudi Arabia to war against the Iranian-backed Houthi rebels, Khashoggi explained that:

> If Saudi Arabia waited for Mr. Obama to approve an intervention in Yemen, Yemen would have gone and lost a long time ago. It would be controlled by the Iranians and the Houthis. So we did not wait for Mr. Obama's approval. And I think that empowers Saudi Arabia.[1]

In an interview with Martin Smith conducted before he turned on the Saudi regime, Khashoggi described Saudi Arabia as facing "a 1939 moment." He continued, correctly, by explicitly comparing the Islamist regime in Iran to the Nazis, adding "We either accept Iranian hegemony, control over Yemen and over our destiny, or freedom." On the issue of Crown Prince Mohammed bin Salman as the future king of Saudi Arabia, according to Martin Smith, Jamal Khashoggi "was especially enthusiastic about MBS [bin Salman] when he talked about the need for reform [in Saudi Arabia]." During one interview with Smith, Khashoggi said that both Saudi youth and he himself viewed bin Salman as a "savior."

KHASHOGGI, MBS, AND REFORM IN SAUDI ARABIA

Once given the power to run Saudi Arabia's daily operations by King Salman, his father, Mohammed bin Salman did make several reforms.

---

1 Martin Smith, PBS Frontline. https://www.pbs.org/wgbh/frontline/film/the-crown-prince-of-saudi-arabia/transcript/

He allowed young people to gather in public and listen to music. The young Saudi ruler insisted that women be allowed more freedoms, such as the right to drive vehicles without men. Like every Saudi ruler since the 1960s, bin Salman yearned to diversify Saudi Arabia's economy away from oil. Yet, unlike every other Saudi ruler, bin Salman had both the incentive and vision to do this quickly.

From 2014-2020, the global price of oil was at relative lows. That fact, coupled with chronic high unemployment for Saudi Arabia's young people, prompted MBS to devise a brilliant plan—Saudi Vision 2030—wherein Saudi ARAMCO, Saudi Arabia's national oil company, would be taken public. Mohammed bin Salman stated that Saudi ARAMCO's IPO had an initial valuation of nearly $2 trillion.

With funds taken from the sales of percentages of the ownership of Saudi ARAMCO, the Saudi government would reinvest that money into building out Saudi Arabia's version of Silicon Valley. Mohammed bin Salman dreamed of making Saudi Arabia more modern and more open, and he wanted the Kingdom no longer to be considered an oil producer. Instead, MBS envisioned Saudi Arabia becoming the high-tech innovation hub of the Middle East.

It was an ambitious and bold strategy—one that Khashoggi wholly supported. However, as a public intellectual, Khashoggi could not wrap his head around the election of Donald J. Trump.

Fearing that Trump would promote chaos in the region and that chaos was Saudi Arabia's worst enemy going forward, Khashoggi publicly prodded the young Saudi ruler to distance the Kingdom from Trump and to diversify its partnerships with other world powers, until the results of the unpredictable Trump foreign policy could be discerned at a later date. Mohammed bin Salman, who was latching onto the new Trump administration as a vehicle for solidifying both his rule at home and for completing his modernization plan, did not want anyone—Khashoggi in this case—getting between himself and President Trump. Khashoggi was asked to stop making public appearances, to stop writing publicly about politics, and to stop tweeting.

Over time, this muzzling understandably did not sit well with a man like Khashoggi who had become used to being a public intellectual. He fled Saudi Arabia after his family had distanced themselves from him because he had become too socially and politically toxic for them. Khashoggi arrived in Washington, DC and eventually began writing for *The Washington Post.* His first article was entitled, "Saudi Arabia Wasn't This Repressive. Now It's Unbearable."[2] Strange that this ultimate insider would have taken such an outsider route, especially when he was initially so enthusiastic about MBS' potential reign as Saudi Arabia's next king.

MBS VS. MBN (AND KHASHOGGI)

Interestingly, MBS was not always perceived as the heir apparent to the Saudi throne. He faced stiff competition from his cousin, Mohammed bin Nayef (MBN), a man who served as the Saudi deputy prime minister and before that, the interior minister. Mohammed bin Nayef helped to lead the Kingdom's wildly successful war against al Qaeda in the Arabian Peninsula (AQAP) from 2003 to 2014.[3] Because of his brutal and effective leadership during that campaign, bin Nayef had many supporters inside the CIA.

Had Hillary Clinton won the 2016 presidential election instead of Donald Trump, it is likely that bin Nayef would have easily been the heir apparent to the aging King Salman (although rumor had it that King Salman had believed bin Salman had greater vision and more gumption than his cousin bin Nayef).[4] The Trump administration,

---

2 Jamal Khashoggi, "Saudi Arabia Wasn't This Repressive. Now It's Unbearable," *Washington Post,* 18 September 2017. https://www.washingtonpost.com/news/global-opinions/wp/2017/09/18/saudi-arabia-wasnt-always-this-repressive-now-its-unbearable/

3 Thomas Small and Jonathan Hacker, *Path of Blood: The Story of Al Qaeda's War on the House of Saud* (New York: Overlook, 2015), pp. 46–51.

4 Amélie Zaccour, "Saudi Arabia: How MBS Deposed His Cousin Mohamed bin Nayef as Crown Prince," *Africa Report,* 11 February 2021. https://www.theafricareport.com/64599/saudi-arabia-how-mbs-deposed-his-cousin-mohammed-bin-nayef-as-crown-prince/

however, favored bin Salman. This created friction not only at the highest levels of the Saudi royal family but also between the institutional stakeholders at the CIA and the controversial forty-fifth president. Remember that at this time, President Trump was essentially at war with the CIA because of the Russia collusion investigation, which Trump insisted was a "witch hunt."

JAMAL KHASHOGGI, THE MAN, THE MYTH
Jamal Khashoggi had been a servant of elements within the Saudi royal family affiliated with bin Nayef. It is likely that once Khashoggi had been muzzled by bin Salman, he soon found himself thrown in the middle of the internecine fight between bin Salman and bin Nayef for control of the Saudi throne. In light of that fight, and Khashoggi's background as the ultimate Saudi insider, his days were numbered.

More importantly, Khashoggi had close associations with the Islamist world. No, he wasn't a head-chopper or a suicide bomb maker. He was a dignified and eloquent gentleman who liked to put cardamom in his lightly roasted coffee made with *al-Mokha* beans from Yemen.[5] But Khashoggi *was* a fellow-traveler of Islamists. He was a chimera; traversing the more respectable world of absolute power, as defined by the Saudi royal family and Washington DC or London. With his affiliations to the Islamist wing of the Middle East, though, Khashoggi could enmesh with a much murkier nexus of people—ranging from shady financiers to radical preachers to terrorist masterminds, like Usama bin Laden.

According to Robert Fisk, who had known Khashoggi for years, Khashoggi was a "sincere believer—woe betide anyone who regards his round spectacles and roguish sense of humor as a sign of spiritual laxity." Fisk met with Usama bin Laden in Khartoum, Sudan, in 1993. It was Fisk's good friend, Jamal Khashoggi, who arranged that meeting. While introducing Fisk to Bin Laden, Khashoggi "put his arms around [bin

---

5 Martin Smith, PBS Frontline. https://www.pbs.org/wgbh/frontline/film/the-crown-prince-of-saudi-arabia/transcript/

Laden]. Bin Laden kissed [Khashoggi] on both cheeks, one Muslim to another, both acknowledging the common danger they had endured together [during the Soviet invasion of] Afghanistan."[6]

For his part, Jamal Khashoggi's sincere belief in a purer form of Islam—certainly no crime in and of itself—drove him to sympathize with bin Laden and other Saudis who volunteered to fight for the United States against the Soviet invasion of Afghanistan. While he was not a foreign fighter in Afghanistan, Khashoggi was brought to Afghanistan at the request of a young bin Laden to profile the Saudis who had gone there to fight the Red menace. Khashoggi was "clearly sympathetic to [bin Laden's cause] and shared Bin Laden's passion for it."[7] He became a great promoter of the Islamists who fought against the Soviet Union and of bin Laden himself. However, Khashoggi was supposedly never sanguine about bin Laden's plans for Afghanistan after the Soviets withdrew in 1989—and he certainly did not agree with bin Laden's plans to wage armed *jihad* against the Americans.

Why would he? Ultimately, Khashoggi was an agent of the Saudi royal family, most of whom wanted nothing to do with bin Laden or his Islamist notions.

Much to Khashoggi's credit, he apparently had a falling out with bin Laden in 1995, when Khashoggi pleaded with his old friend to desist from making war against the Americans. When bin Laden refused, Khashoggi ended their friendship immediately. This is why I described Khashoggi as a "fellow traveler" with the Islamist movement, rather than a true believer in their methods.[8]

---

6 Robert Fisk, *The Great War for Civilisation: The Conquest of the Middle East* (New York: Vintage Books, 2007), pp. 5–7.

7 Rahul Kalvapalle, "Missing Saudi Journalist Jamal Khashoggi's Ties to Osama bin Laden Explained," Global News, 13 October 2018. https://globalnews.ca/news/4545784/jamal-khashoggi-osama-bin-laden/

8 Lawrence Wright, *The Looming Tower: Al-Qaeda and the Road to 9/11* (New York: Vintage Books, 2006), pp. 69-96.

After all, one can be an Islamist and not be a terrorist, just as one could have been a member of Ireland's Sinn Fein political party and not have taken part in the terrorism of the Irish Republican Army (IRA). Nevertheless, one hand always washed the other—even if its members strove to remain apart from each other in public.[9]

Jamal Khashoggi was a complex man from a complicated region, at a time when simplicity and clarity were needed from all the major players in that part of the world. Khashoggi's failure to understand how the fickle political sands of the region were shifting beneath his feet is, in part, the reason why he ran afoul of the Saudi regime, as led by the Crown Prince Mohammed bin Salman—and why Khashoggi was ultimately murdered in such a brutal way. This is not a justification for the grisly end he met. But Khashoggi's death, much like his life, was more complicated than it seemed.

For example, Lawrence Wright's masterpiece, *The Looming Tower: Al-Qaeda and the Road to 9/11,* clearly identifies Jamal Khashoggi as a card-carrying member of the Muslim Brotherhood in his youth, along with bin Laden and Abdullah Azzam—the two men who would create al Qaeda from the *mujahideen* during their war against the Soviets in Afghanistan.[10] Wright, a friend and defender of Khashoggi, even states that bin Laden and Khashoggi shared a desire to create "an Islamic state anywhere." These men believed that the first Islamic state could have a "domino effect which would reverse the history of Mankind."[11]

9 A. Richards, "Terrorist Groups and Political Fronts: The IRA, Sinn Fein, the Peace Process and Democracy," *Terrorism and Political Violence,* December 2001, 13(4): 72–89. https://www.researchgate.net/publication/233239643_Terrorist_Groups_and_Political_Fronts_The_IRA_Sinn_Fein_the_Peace_Process_and_Democracy

10 AW Staff, "The Looming Tower: Jamal Khashoggi's Little-Known Past Comes to Light," *The Arab Weekly,* 15 October 2018. https://thearabweekly.com/looming-tower-jamal-khashoggis-little-known-past-comes-light

11 Wright, *The Looming Tower,* p. 78.

KHASHOGGI, AN OLD INSIDER, AND
ABDULAZIZ, A YOUNG OUTSIDER

As Khashoggi's dalliance with the world of Saudi activism grew, he came into contact with Omar Abdulaziz. The young Abdulaziz is a Saudi activist and is very opposed to Mohammed bin Salman. He hosts one of the most popular YouTube channels that consistently attacks bin Salman and the Saudi regime. Abdulaziz fled Saudi Arabia after bin Salman started cracking down on dissidents and found himself living as a political refugee in Montreal, Canada. He belongs to the National Assembly Party, a dissident Saudi political party composed mostly of political exiles like himself. The global consulting firm McKinsey & Company named Abdulaziz as one of Saudi Arabia's top social media influencers in an internal report.

Abdulaziz's popularity among the Saudi youth attracted both Jamal Khashoggi and bin Salman. In fact, according to the 2020 documentary *The Dissident* by Bryan Fogel, bin Salman's people attempted to coopt the headstrong and idealistic Abdulaziz. In response to bin Salman's "total infiltration of Twitter in 2015," Abdulaziz attempted to build his own Twitter army of hacktivists who would do the exact opposite online as what the pro–bin Salman Twitter army was doing. Abdulaziz had passion and intelligence. But he needed funding. While he had maintained contact with Khashoggi since 2017, in 2018 Khashoggi gave Abdulaziz a small amount of money to create his own anti–bin Salman Twitter army.

As the Bryan Fogel film entertainingly details, Abdulaziz assembled his rag-tag Twitter army—what he called his bees—and waged unremitting cyberwar upon bin Salman's Twitter army. It was hugely embarrassing for the young ruler of Saudi Arabia. And Abdulaziz did great damage to the public relations campaign that bin Salman was waging in order to gin up global support for his Saudi Vision 2030 initiative. Infuriated, Mohammed bin Salman learned through his spies who had hacked Abdulaziz's phone that Khashoggi was not only a key adviser to Abdulaziz but was the primary funder of Abdulaziz's Twitter army campaign.

I believe that Khashoggi's role in this event precipitated his murder. Before his alliance with Abdulaziz, Khashoggi was a nuisance to the Saudi regime. Although disgraced, he still was a revered figure among the elite because of his decades of service to the royal family. Had Khashoggi not involved himself with Abdulaziz, a man that bin Salman is clearly threatened by, and had Khashoggi not assisted Abdulaziz in humiliating bin Salman in such a public way, it is likely that Jamal Khashoggi would still be alive today, publishing for the *Washington Post*.

Khashoggi's role as a long-time insider to the Saudi royal family, his close associations with bin Salman's rivals both at home and abroad, and Khashoggi's sinecure at the *Washington Post* likely also became far too threatening to bin Salman. Khashoggi was a man who knew where the Saudi royals had buried all of the bodies—both metaphorical and probably literal. His newfound alliance with young, popular hacktivists, like Abdulaziz, elevated Khashoggi's threat to bin Salman.

Thus, after Khashoggi gave his initial tranche of cash to Abdulaziz, he traveled to Turkey to wed his fiancée. In a final text message to Abdulaziz, Khashoggi vowed to give the young hacktivist another infusion of money. Of course, Khashoggi would not return.

JAMAL KHASHOGGI'S MURDER

Khashoggi needed a marriage certificate from the Saudi consulate. When he arrived looking for it, the consulate, in a state of shock that this enemy of the crown would so brazenly show up, told him to wait three days. The Saudi consulate general then phoned Riyadh about Khashoggi's sudden appearance in Turkey and his plans to return to the consulate three days later. A team of assassins was assembled in Riyadh and flown to Turkey. One of the assassins, according to *The Dissident,* was bin Salman's personal bodyguard. Among the assassination team was a military coroner who specialized in dismemberment.

When Jamal Khashoggi entered the Saudi consulate in Turkey, he was confronted by the consulate general, an old colleague of his. The two men argued. Khashoggi was then led down to a windowless room, where Turkish investigators believe Khashoggi was drugged, placed on the floor before a webcam that may have been broadcasting the scene live to Riyadh; and was summarily dismembered while still alive. Khashoggi's body parts were then hustled over to the nearby home of the Saudi consulate general in Turkey.

The assassins had ordered pounds and pounds of meat from a nearby kebab restaurant. Clay Tandoori ovens at the consulate general's residence were fired up, and it is believed that Khashoggi's dismembered body was incinerated in the ovens, the assassins using the smell of cooked kebab meat to mask the stench of burning human flesh. Turkish investigators believe that Khashoggi's incinerated body parts were then gathered into bags and lowered into a deep well beneath the garage of the Saudi consulate general's residence in Turkey.

SAUDI VISION 2030 GETS MURDERED TOO (ALONG WITH JEFF BEZOS'S MARRIAGE)

In response to the international outcry about Khashoggi's disappearance and possible murder, bin Salman's signature modernization plan, Saudi Vision 2030, was derailed as his involvement in the assassination could not be ignored or covered up. Jeff Bezos, the founder and CEO of Amazon, was set to headline the international conference in Riyadh where bin Salman would announce the start of Saudi Vision 2030, with Bezos as a key player in that program. After the Khashoggi slaying, though, Bezos backed out, as did many other notable tech entrepreneurs from the West. Saudi Vision 2030 stalled, and bin Salman was further humiliated.

Mohammed bin Salman had grown personally close to Bezos—to the point that the two had exchanged personal cell phone numbers and emails. The two men had apparently communicated regularly via the What's App cellphone application until the Khashoggi murder. Because of his access to Bezos's personal data, though, bin Salman was able to turn his digital army against Bezos for the perceived insult of Bezos backing out of the Saudi Vision 2030 program.

Shortly after these tumultuous events, the international tabloids would gain access to Bezos's personal texts between himself and Lauren Sanchez, which revealed that Bezos was engaged in a long-time extra-marital affair with Sanchez. These revelations would ultimately split Bezos from his wife and create an international scandal in the business and gossip columns. Given bin Salman's potential involvement in the scandal, it also proved to be a big story on the national security beat.

We know this about bin Salman: he's young, brash, and possesses vision. Further, he's power hungry. Therefore, bin Salman is highly defensive about his standing in the Saudi power structure. Despite the missteps he has taken over the years, whether it be overcommitting himself to a poorly planned air war in Yemen or murdering Jamal Khashoggi, none of what he did is as bad as what the Islamists of Iran have planned for the region.

At the start of bin Salman's rise, Jamal Khashoggi was his supporter. As noted above, Khashoggi agreed with bin Salman's belief that Iran's threat to the kingdom was akin to the threat Nazi Germany posed to Europe in 1939. What's more, the Saudis are scared of two things: that the Americans are about abandon them under President Joe Biden's leadership and that the Biden administration is going to allow Iran to become a major regional *nuclear* power.

The Saudis share these fears with the Israelis. The Biden administration has idiotically begun distancing itself from Israel while it also demands that the Saudis "sideline" Crown Prince Mohammed bin Salman.[12] Consequently, Israel, Bahrain, Saudi Arabia, and the United Arab Emirates are "exploring the possibility of creating a four-nation defensive alliance" against Iran.[13]

The Americans under President Biden, unlike under former

---

12 CNN, "US Sidelines Crown Prince in 'Recalibration' with Saudi Arabia," YouTube, 6:08, 17 February 2021. https://www.youtube.com/watch?v=oVYpHzAGRHc

13 ILH Staff, Ariel Kahana, and Neta Bar, "Israel Reportedly in Talks on Defense Alliance with Gulf States," *Israel Hayom,* 25 February 2021. https://www.israelhayom.com/2021/02/25/israel-reportedly-in-talks-on-defense-alliance-with-gulf-states/

President Trump, appear completely out of touch with the realities on the ground yet again. As the situation deteriorates because of American mismanagement under the Biden administration, the chance of catastrophic conflict increases—as well as the chance that America's allies, such as Saudi Arabia and Israel, will simply move on from the United States and make better deals with China and Russia.

The Trump administration's Mideast policy was entirely distinct from what came before and, judging from early Biden administration moves, what is coming after. The region, the United States, and the world are less safe because of this. Biden, like Jimmy Carter and Barack Obama before him, has a naïve commitment to human rights even at the expense of US national interests. It will lead to America losing the Middle East. And it might lead to a nuclear war. Or, almost just as bad, it might produce a new world order in which China, Russia, and Iran set the standard and the United States is completely isolated and alone.

32

DANCING WITH THE ONES

WHO BROUGHT YOU

"I SUSPECT we ought to lighten our hand in the Middle East," said the terse memo that then-President Ronald Reagan's special envoy to the region, Donald H. Rumsfeld, had written. The laconic report by the former (and the future) Republican secretary of defense continued, "We should move the framework away from the current situation, where everyone is telling us everything is our fault and angry with us, to a basis where they are seeking our help. *In the future we should never use US troops as a peacekeeping force* [emphasis added]."

Rumsfeld's prescient "snowflake" to Reagan accurately assessed, "We're too big a target. Let the Fijians or New Zealanders do [the peacekeeping]. And [Americans should] keep reminding [themselves] that it is easier to get into something than it is to get out of it." Reflecting on his tour of the Middle East, Rumsfeld personally promised that "you will never hear out of my mouth the phrase, 'the US seeks a just and lasting peace in the Middle East.' There is little that is just and the only things that I've seen that are lasting are conflict, blackmail, and killing."[1] These words were written by Rumsfeld on November 23, 1983, in a memo entitled "The Swamp."[2]

Donald Rumsfeld had been appointed to the position of special envoy to the Middle East by his old friend, then-Secretary of State George Schultz in response to the horrific Iran-backed Hezbollah terror attack on the US Marine Corps barracks in Beirut, Lebanon, in October 1983. The United States had deployed its forces to Lebanon as part of an international coalition in an attempt to pacify what was then a brutal multisided civil war—with foreign actors, like Iran, the former Soviet Union, Israel, and many others involving themselves as well.

After a period of time, Hezbollah built a truck bomb and drove it into the Marine barracks, murdering 220 Marines and 21 other US military service members. Approximately 1,800 US Marines were stationed at the Beirut barracks at the time of the attack.[3] As you've read, this was the largest loss of Marines in a single day since the Second World War.

At the time, it was assumed that President Reagan would retaliate militarily against Hezbollah in Lebanon. Ultimately, however, Reagan

---

1 Donald Rumsfeld, "The Swamp," Department of State Information Memorandum, 23 November 1983. https://papers.rumsfeld.com/library/default.asp?zoom_sort=0&zoom_query=The+Swamp&zoom_per_page=10&zoom_and=0&Tag+Level+1=-1%7E0&Tag+Level+2=-1%7E0

2 The Swamp is a metaphor. When people drain a swamp, they are eliminating predatory species and bugs that spread disease. As used by Rumsfeld, the phrase was meant to convey the murky geopolitical conditions that a power foreign to the region, like the United States, faces. It was also meant to evoke a sense of danger and was, in fact, a reference to the Vietnam War, which in 1983 was less than a decade old.

3 "Beirut Marine Barracks Bombing Fast Moving," CNN, 6 October 2020. https://www.cnn.com/2013/06/13/world/meast/beirut-marine-barracks-bombing-fast-facts/index.html

opted to remove all US forces from the country and maintain a relatively small US military footprint from then on. Rather than invade Lebanon and bog the United States down in an intractable tribal conflict—while still trying to resist the Soviet threat globally—Reagan deployed Rumsfeld to ferret out what, precisely, was occurring in the region. Reagan hoped that Rumsfeld's assessments would allow him to make better policy choices in the Middle East.

It was a vain hope, apparently. Two more decades of bad policies from both Democratic and Republican presidents would compound the mistakes of the past. They would also set the United States up for a catastrophe—one even greater than what Americans have thus far endured in the Middle East—that I fear is coming soon as Iran inches closer to nuclear weapons.

A BROKEN CONSENSUS AFTER 9/11

The Washington consensus about the Middle East was necessarily broken by the 9/11 attacks. That was a good thing. Unfortunately, the new consensus was still wrong. Washington's elites, namely those in the Republican Party's foreign policy establishment but also eventually those in the Democratic Party's foreign policy intelligentsia, assumed that America's detachment from the region allowed the geopolitical "swamp" of the Mideast to grow out of control, thus allowing 9/11 to happen.

Their solution was to do the exact opposite of what they had done before 9/11. Whereas America withdrew and ignored the Middle East after the Beirut bombing in 1983, because of 9/11, America would now become engaged and invade the region—imposing its will and preferences upon everyone there, friend and foe alike. What Washington's elites failed to understand was that any consensus that relied solely upon Washington to find a solution to the problems of the Middle East would not work.

Neither the Reagan-era solution of withdrawing from the region nor the Bush era solution of "sweeping it all up, things related and not" worked. In both cases, the policy resulted in the same outcome: strategic defeats for Americans. Further, these actions missed the point.

Go back to Beirut. Who was the culprit? The Iranian-backed Shiite Lebanese terrorist organization Hezbollah. Why did they attack the Marines? *Because since 1979, the Islamist regime of Iran has been at war with the United States.*

When the Americans cut and ran from the region after the 1983 Hezbollah attacks, Iran was empowered. Similarly, when George W. Bush declared his "Global War on Terrorism" after the 9/11 attacks and invaded Sunni Muslim countries like Afghanistan and Iraq, Shiite-dominated Iran was given a great reprieve: its sworn ethnic and religious rivals, the Sunni Arabs, were being weakened by American actions.

What's needed, therefore, is a *lighter* American hand in the region, as Rumsfeld argued in his 1983 memo to Reagan. Yet at the same time, the Americans need to hand off the region to forces that generally share American objectives: partners whom Washington can ultimately influence at appropriate times from afar. As you've read, the policies advanced by Jimmy Carter, then Barack Obama, and today, Joe Biden, as they relate to Islamism generally and Iran specifically, have weakened the United States in this critical region and empowered the forces that seek to harm Americans.

One cannot simply run away and ignore the threats to the United States emanating from the Middle East—not as long as the world still uses Mideast energy supplies and has major trading hubs cutting across the region. Remarkably, the regional policies advanced by Donald Trump, a man we were told was completely unfit for the presidency, were far better suited to the challenges of the Middle East than anything his purportedly wiser presidential predecessors had ever concocted. Had Trump gotten a second term, I believe, the Abraham Accords would have served as the basis for a truly historic shift in Mideast politics, one that would have secured America's interests while allowing the United States to pivot away from the region and to entrust daily security there to reliable partners in Israel and the Sunni Arab states. With Iran having been contained by the Abraham Accords and its economy strangled by

Trump's "maximum pressure," with no reprieve in sight, I believe the second Trump term (that, sadly, never was) would have seen the forty-fifth president having the leverage necessary to get Iran's leadership to actually negotiate in good faith with the West. And, failing that, the regime would have been overthrown due to the economic hardship imposed upon it by a united alliance of the United States, Israel, and the Sunni Arab nations.

The Abraham Accords remain viable, even under the Biden administration, if only Biden would have the political courage to follow through with what his maligned predecessor began.

Therefore, a new condition for the United States in the Middle East would be one that elevates local actors into the driver's seat of regional politics. Most importantly, this new paradigm would allow Americans to return to their preferred role of merely being an "offshore balancer." In the excellent formulation of Stephen M. Walt, one of the doyens of American realism, offshore balancing is a "realist grand strategy, and its aims are limited," making clear—as Rumsfeld did in 1983—that "promoting peace, although desirable, is not [an aim of offshore balancing]." Further, according to Walt, "the United States would calibrate its military posture according to the distribution of power in the three key regions [Europe, the Mideast, and Northeastern Asia]."

Walt states an offshore balancing approach would allow Washington to "turn to regional forces as the first line of defense" for preventing the rise of a power or grouping of powers that could challenge America's interests in the region. An offshore balancing strategy does not preclude the US military from wading ashore to help its regional partners when an enemy proves too tough for them. However, the purpose of the offshore balancing plan is to "remain offshore as long as possible."[4]

WHAT ARE AMERICA'S INTERESTS?

---

4 Stephen M. Walt, "The Case for Offshore Balancing," *Foreign Affairs*, July/August 2016. https://www.foreignaffairs.com/articles/united-states/2016-06-13/case-offshore-balancing

At its core, America's interest in the region remains the stable and consistent flow of oil. But the Mideast is no longer the primary exporter of the world's energy needs. Today, there are other major producers of oil outside of the Middle East. Beyond that, the goal of every American statesman must be to ensure the creation of a pro-American balance of power. Therefore, America must contain Iran and empower the Sunni Arab states and Israel.

As the Saudis, other Sunni Arab states, and Israelis stand up, America can slowly stand down. We will remain involved, but just over the horizon. The Middle East is not inconsequential, but it's just not the priority any longer. But if the Americans get their Iran policy wrong, it could prevent the United States from leaving the Middle East safely.

If the Biden administration reverses its attack on America's domestic energy production and does not cede the region to Iran, the Middle East will not consume all of America's foreign policy bandwidth.[5] After all, the stable flow of oil and natural gas from the region is a far greater concern to Europeans and Asians than it is to Americans.[6] Americans are sitting atop an oil shale and natural gas revolution (all while receiving many more oil imports from nearby Canada and Mexico than the Middle East). Of course, the Biden administration is doing everything in its power to stunt that oil shale and natural gas revolution in America.

This is to say nothing of the alternative energy revolution that is coming as the twenty-first century progresses. For example, by 2030 electric vehicles are predicted to compose 20 percent of annual vehicle sales in the United States, up from a mere 7 percent of all vehicle sales in the

---

5 Leyland Cecco, "Alberta Leader Says Biden's Move to Cancel Keystone Pipeline a 'Gut Punch,'" *The Guardian,* 27 January 2021. https://www.theguardian.com/environment/2021/jan/27/alberta-leader-says-bidens-move-to-cancel-keystone-pipeline-a-gut-punch

6 Julian Lee, "Which Oil Buyers Have the Most at Stake as Mideast Tensions Rise," Bloomberg, 26 June 2019. https://www.bloomberg.com/news/articles/2019-06-26/which-oil-buyers-have-most-at-stake-as-mideast-tensions-rise

United States in 2018.[7] By 2030, it is also believed that 24 percent of the energy produced to power these new vehicles will come from renewable resources (solar, wind, nuclear), up from 17 percent in 2018.[8]

Electric vehicle use and alternative energy consumption in the United States are only slated to increase in the decades to come. Given this, the real concerns for America in the Middle East will likely be keeping the vital trade routes open through the use of the US Navy and maintaining a high degree of influence in the region to prevent the Chinese (and their Iranian friends) from dominating the area. Therefore, the Americans should reassess their commitment to the Mideast accordingly.

Yet the Biden administration appears committed to expanding the American war in Syria. As previously noted, President Biden wants to distance the United States from the countries that former President Trump spent much time and political capital courting—countries that are traditional American allies in the region—and Biden wants to hand the region off to a nuclear Iran.

A nuclear Iran will not stabilize the region as so many two-dimensional international relations theorists in the West believe. It will inspire a frantic race for nuclear arms. The Saudis will seek their own nukes. And as I wrote in the *American Spectator*, because of the presence of so many Islamist radicals in Saudi Arabia—and the precarious position the pro-American royal family finds itself in—allowing the Kingdom to acquire nuclear weapons is a really bad idea.[9] What should be done, on top of enhancing the conventional military capabilities of the Sunni Arab states and making clear that there is no daylight between

7 "EEI Celebrates 1 Million Electric Vehicles on US Roads," Edison Electric Institute, Accessed on 27 November 2020. https://www.eei.org/resourcesandmedia/newsroom/Pages/Press%20Releases/EEI%20Celebrates%201%20Million%20Electric%20Vehicles%20on%20U-S-%20Roads.aspx

8 "Renewable Energy," Center for Climate and Energy Solutions, Accessed on 27 November 2020. https://www.c2es.org/content/renewable-energy/

9 Brandon J. Weichert, "Don't Let Saudi Arabia Get Nukes," *The American Spectator*, 2 November 2018. https://spectator.org/dont-let-saudi-arabia-get-nukes/

the United States and Israel, is that the United States should extend its nuclear umbrella over Saudi Arabia and the other Sunni Arab states to defend against threats from Iran. This simple act not only will reassure America's allies but will deter Iran. It would also prevent an accidental nuclear war. (American nuclear command-and-control functions are far better than anything the Saudis will rely on.)

What's more, the presence of a nuclear and aggressive Iran will not allow the United States to extricate itself from the toxic miasma of daily Middle East politics. On the contrary, it will ensure that the United States is bogged down in a far deadlier war with a far more lethal Iranian enemy. The tragic thing here is that the United States still has the leverage it needs to deter Iran without losing its primary position in the region. It can still curb the hegemonic fantasies of Iran, chase down terrorists as needed, and stunt the growth of Chinese and Russian influence in the Middle East if it follows through on what the Trump administration was attempting to do in the region.

Sadly, in today's America "Orange Man Bad" is the ruling ethos among our political class. Anything that President Trump touched or supported is automatically suspect. The day when Joe Biden was inaugurated was essentially Year Zero in American politics, as far as a large segment of America's ruling class was concerned. The Great Reset is upon us. Everything will have to be rethought—especially any successful initiatives that Donald Trump took, such as the Abraham Accords and the concept of "principled realism"—simply because America's ruling class hates Trump.

It would be nice if America's leaders could learn the timeless lesson that the Middle East has taught other great powers seeking to meddle in the affairs of that region: there are no good options there. Dealing in this region is a lose-lose proposition. The question Americans must ask themselves is: Do we want to lose little or lose bigly?

Joe Biden's answer, apparently, is to lose bigly. We might soon wake up to a Mideast that's engulfed in a regional war in which nukes have been popped off like firecrackers on the Fourth of July, Iranian terrorists have launched waves of lethal surprise terrorist attacks against their enemies, and America must step in militarily to stop the madness. And if America does this, the Chinese and Russians would likely intervene against the Americans. This scenario has the makings of a third world war. And like the First World War, this conflict is entirely avoidable, but only if American statesmen and women recognize the limits of American power in the Middle East. It'd be great if America's leaders recognized the opportunities that an alliance with less-than-savory actors in that messy region would afford Washington.

Already momentous changes have washed over the unstable region. As noted at the start of this book, Ebrahim Raisi, a notorious hardliner, was made the new president of Iran. His first actions were to reassert Iran's right to nuclear weapons and to increase the proliferation of deadly weapons, like long-range precision-guided missiles, to Yemen and Lebanon. The Islamist regime may have even tried to send them to Nicolas Maduro's embattled regime in Venezuela. Raisi has made it clear that Iran under his leadership (and the leadership of both the mullahs and the IRGC) will not be deterred from its dangerous actions without some kind of pushback from the United States. Invading Iran is not the right answer. Empowering Washington's regional allies, like Israel and the Sunni Arab states, as the Abraham Accords sought to do, is the viable pathway for Washington secure its interests as they relate to Iran without risking a wider war. For the Iranian regime, the imperative to dominate its part of the world is as historic as it is religious. Any American compromise with this regime will not favor US national interests.

Meanwhile, tumult has reigned in Israel. Benjamin Netanyahu is out. Yet, the Israeli government is divided. Netanyahu's successor, Naftali Bennett, lasted barely a year in power. His successor, Yair Lapid, is a centrist who desires stronger relations with the Sunni Arab world. Although, it remains to be seen if Lapid can hold onto power anymore than Bennett could. And hanging like a Damocles Sword over the whole Israeli political system is Benjamin Netanyahu, who senses an opportunity for him to return to power soon. Whether it be

Naftali Bennett, Yair Lapid, or Benjamin Netanyahu, Israeli leaders are united in opposition against Iran's rise and they seek closer relations with Iran's other enemies, the Sunni Arabs, as part of a plan to contain Iran's threat. Given how unsupportive of Israel's Iran policies the Biden Administration is, however, any Israeli leader may soon be forced to launch preemptive strikes against Iranian targets...and such attacks would inevitably suck the United States back into the region at a time when it cannot afford yet another large-scale Middle East war.

The Saudis, too, are divided. When Trump was in office, it was obvious that Mohammed bin Salman was orchestrating the regional commitment to the Abraham Accords. Now that Trump is gone and Joe Biden is in charge, the Saudis are seeking greater conciliation with the Iranians, and they want to distance themselves from Israel yet again. At the same time, the Saudis are not stupid. They understand how Iran's leaders view the world. They consider the Sunnis apostates, and Iran's mad quest for nukes is partly born out of the Shiites' historical and religious resentment of the Sunnis. Therefore, the Saudis will seek to hedge their position by acquiring their own nuclear weapons capability—while also moving closer to both the Russians and Chinese.

As for Washington, confusion and ambivalence reign supreme. With Trump gone, the United States has returned to its decades-long commitment to ineffectual policy in the Middle East. The Biden administration has weakened the Abraham Accords and distanced the United States from Israel and the Sunni Arabs—all to placate an Iran that will not be placated. The political instability in the region and within the United States mirrors the political changes that happened in Europe in the decade leading into the First World War. No one in charge seems willing or able to make the necessary changes to avoid this destructive course.

America must dance with the ones who brought us—in this case, the Sunni Arab states and Israel. Or America must be prepared to fight nuclear-armed Iranian Islamists. Hoping that Iran will suddenly about-face and embrace the Americans as friends and partners is not realistic. The regime is programmed to its core to be rabidly anti-American and viciously anti-Semitic and anti-Sunni. For their part, neither the Israelis nor Sunni Arabs are inclined to take Iran at its word that it comes in peace. As soon as the United States reenters the Iran nuclear deal, as President Biden has stated he intends to do, the countdown to nuclear war in the Mideast will have begun.

This situation is entirely avoidable, simply if the United States restores and maintains the confidence of its traditional allies. Washington must stop playing footsie with an Islamist regime in Iran that cries "Death to America!" on a daily—sometimes even hourly—basis. And the United States must simply dance with the ones who brought us. For more than half a century, Washington has supported and built up the Sunni Arabs and Israelis as allies. Whatever their eccentricities (most of which come from belonging to different religions and cultures), these two groups have ensured that American power in the region is preserved.

Rather than rolling the dice by letting the Iranians in through the front door, America must steel itself against Iran's aggression and do its best to build a regional security alliance that preserves American interests while allowing the United States not to be as involved in the daily operations of the region. The United States must also ensure that nuclear proliferation does not take hold throughout the region. If it does, the unintended consequences could be too terrible to consider. Ultimately, by standing with its traditional regional allies to curb Iranian aggression, Washington will likely prevent a catastrophic regional conflict that could become a major nuclear world war.

These are the stakes. The next decade in the Middle East will be a pivotal time in the world's history. The time for talking with the enemy is over. The time for standing with our friends—no matter how imperfect they may be—is here. Otherwise, we will surely witness the rise of a Middle East that is in the throes of an uncontrolled nuclear arms race, where Islamism is ascendant, and where the Americans will have to come rushing back in but will no longer enjoy the kind of regional dominance they once did.

EPILOGUE

BIDEN ABANDONS AFGHANISTAN

AND OPENS THE DOOR FOR JIHAD

AS I WAS SITTING in my living room on Sunday, August 15, 2021, I decided to switch over to the news to see if anything was going on. I am a news junkie, which is one of the reasons I chose policy as my profession. It was quiet. My kids were preoccupied. And my wife was working from home. I expected to see another banal story about Scarlett Johansson's lawsuit against Disney or another segment about the woes of cancel culture, since weekends typically are slow for news—especially weekends in the dead of summer. At the very most, I thought I might see another story about how the COVID-19 Delta variant was ravaging unvaccinated people in the United States.

Much to my surprise, a breaking news story appeared on the screen. There were reports that the Taliban were arriving in the outskirts of Kabul, the capital city of Afghanistan.[1] Soon images showed white-and-gray State Department Chinook twin-rotor helicopters appearing in the skies over Kabul, frantically flying over increasingly chaotic streets, landing on the roof of the $2 billion US embassy there, and ferrying people over to the Hamid Karzai International Airport. As the helicopters flew, they dropped dazzling flares. I knew that such flares were dropped only when the helicopter pilots feared that their aircraft would be attacked by heat-seeking surface-to-air missiles.

The time in Kabul is eight hours and thirty minutes ahead of the East Coast of the United States. Over the course of several hours, the news became consumed with stories of chaos at the airport, the last place from which Americans and their allies could leave Afghanistan. Everyone was surprised by what was transpiring. Not only did the media appear shocked but, more frighteningly, the Biden administration appeared to be caught completely flat-footed by the Taliban's rapid advance from the frontier of Afghanistan into the capital. Most intelligence assessments had indicated that it would take weeks, possibly months, for the Taliban to make their way to the capital.[2]

In fact, just forty-eight hours before Kabul fell, John Kirby, the Biden administration's Pentagon spokesperson, explicitly told the world that "Kabul was not in any imminent danger" of being overrun by the Taliban.[3] Without a doubt, the fall of Kabul is the worst intelligence failure since the invasion of Iraq in 2003, when no weapons of mass

---

1 Ahmed Seir, Rahim Faiez, Tameem Akhgar, and Jon Gambrell, "Taliban Sweep into Afghan Capital after Government Collapses," AP News, 15 August 2021. https://apnews.com/article/afghanistan-taliban-kabul-bagram-e1ed33fe0c665ee67ba132c51b8e32a5

2 Nomaan Merchant and Zeke Miller, "Misread Warnings Helped Lead to Chaotic Afghan Evacuation," AP News, 18 August 2021. https://apnews.com/article/joe-biden-evacuations-32bb6a22846f649b626a3130f8c5dffb

3 "Kabul Not in 'Imminent Threat' Environment: Pentagon," Reuters, 13 August 2021. https://www.reuters.com/video/watch/idOVEQ4CELB

destruction were discovered. That the disaster in Kabul could have been avoided is the most shocking part of the Afghanistan debacle.

What few appeared to understand was that as soon as the Biden administration began its drawdown of US forces in Afghanistan in May of 2021, the purportedly 300,000-strong Afghan National Army (ANA), which Washington had spent $88 billion training and equipping over twenty years, effectively collapsed in about ninety-six hours.[4] This collapse left the roads into Kabul open. To compound matters, several weeks before the Taliban began showing up in Kabul, the Americans had surreptitiously removed all their forces from the once-mighty compound known as Bagram Airbase.[5]

Unbeknownst to their Afghan allies, American forces were pulling out in the dead of night. When the ANA commander of the base awoke in May of 2021, he found the Americans and their equipment all gone. At that point, the collapse of the Afghan National Army as an effective defense for Kabul was a foregone conclusion—even if the Biden administration didn't realize it.

Hours of chaos in Kabul turned into days. Thousands of Taliban fighters stormed the streets of the mostly undefended city and began setting up checkpoints.[6] The hardened Taliban fighters, now armed with the advanced American weaponry that the ANA forces had abandoned when their army completely collapsed, controlled the capital of Afghanistan. By taking the streets of Kabul, the Taliban effectively cut off upwards of 15,000 American civilians from the Karzai International Airport that was still nominally under the control of the US military and their allies.

---

4 Brandon J. Weichert, "The Afghan National Army was Never Meant to Fight Alone," The Weichert Report, 21 August 2021. https://theweichertreport.wordpress.com/2021/08/21/the-afghan-national-army-was-never-meant-to-fight-alone/

5 Kathy Gannon, "US Left Airfield at Night, Didn't Tell New Commander," AP News, 6 July 2021. https://apnews.com/article/bagram-afghanistan-airfield-us-troops-f3614828364f567593251aaaa167e623

6 Matt Stevens, "Scenes from Kabul as Taliban Tightens Control," New York Times, 17 August 2021. https://www.nytimes.com/live/2021/08/17/world/kabul-afghanistan-video-photos

A few observers, such as this author, fretted about the reasoning for this move: Were the Taliban and their allies in the Haqqani Network possibly preparing to kidnap or kill Americans attempting to escape to the airport *en masse*?[7] That the Americans trusted the Taliban either to honor their initial agreement with the Trump administration or to ensure the safe exit of all Americans and their Afghan allies is the most disturbing component of this event. As the Taliban seized control, the runways of the only international airport in Afghanistan (barely) under American control were swamped with thousands of desperate Afghans frantic to flee the country on the US military jets lining the runways.[8]

The Biden administration made absolutely no preparation to effectively evacuate the 15,000 American civilians and their thousands of Afghan allies by the August 31, 2021, the deadline for Americans to leave the collapsing country, Although many US personnel were rescued, even the official statements of the Biden administration admit that around a hundred American citizens were left in Afghanistan. Many observers believe the number is much higher. Untold numbers of Afghans who worked for the United States were abandoned.[9]

As I was writing this section, there were reports coming from Kabul that hundreds of Americans were being beaten by Taliban insurgents at the various checkpoints between the US embassy and the airport.[10] The travel papers that allowed Afghans aligned with the United States to leave were confiscated at Taliban-controlled checkpoints. The

---

7 Brandon J. Weichert, "Are Taliban Planning to Massacre Americans?" *Asia Times*, 19 August 2021. https://asiatimes.com/2021/08/are-taliban-planning-to-massacre-americans/

8 Funker530-Veteran Community and Combat Footage, "Afghans Cling to C-17, Fall to Their Death on Takeoff," YouTube, 16 August 2021. https://www.youtube.com/watch?v=x9uxHb5dii4

9 Lucas Y. Tomlinson and Brooke Singman, "US Officials Warn Biden's Aug. 31 Deadline to Withdraw Troops from Afghanistan Will Be 'Challenging,'" Fox News, 18 August 2021. https://www.foxnews.com/politics/biden-deadline-withdraw-afghanistan-troops-challenging

10 Andrew Desiderio, Heather Caygle, and Laura Seligman, "Austin Contradicts Biden, Says Americans Have Been 'Beaten' by the Taliban," Politico, 20 August 2021. https://www.politico.com/news/2021/08/20/lloyd-austin-taliban-america-defeat-506475

Afghans who had documents allowing them and their families to leave Afghanistan were often either beaten or murdered at these checkpoints and the documents were then given to people friendly to the Taliban (or other, scarier elements, like ISIS or al Qaeda).[11]

Several days after the Taliban entered Kabul and seized control, the Biden administration's secretary of defense, Lloyd Austin and the chairman of the Joint Chiefs of Staff, US Army General Mark Milley, took to the airwaves to explain that even though the US military then controlled the airport, they had "no capacity" to leave the confines of the airport and bring in US citizens unable to pass through the Taliban checkpoints outside into the airport.[12] In effect, the United States had to rely on the Taliban, an Islamist terrorist organization, to grant safe passage so US citizens and their Afghan allies could enter the airport.

What's more, it strained credulity to believe that the United States, the world's sole remaining superpower, could not extend its security perimeter beyond the gates of the embattled airport to the streets beyond. The US military most certainly did have that capability. What America's forces lacked was political leadership in Washington with the will to issue that order. President Biden relentlessly defended his decision to withdraw US forces from Afghanistan, even as chaos reigned.[13]

But why did Biden do nothing to prepare for overcoming any obstacles the Taliban might throw in the way of the American evacuation?

Unbelievably, Biden doubled down; he said he'd make the same decision again if he could. He then insisted that the "buck stopped"

11 Hollie McKay, "Taliban Seizing Afghan-American's US Passports outside Kabul Airport," *New York Post,* 20 August 2021. https://nypost.com/2021/08/20/taliban-seizing-afghan-americans-us-passports-outside-airport/

12 Aaron Mehta, "Pentagon Leaders: Not Enough Capacity for Rescue Operations in Kabul," *Breaking Defense,* 18 August 2021. https://breakingdefense.com/2021/08/pentagon-leaders-not-enough-capacity-for-rescue-operations-in-kabul/

13 Shannon K. Crawford and Libby Cathey, "Biden Stands by His Decision, Concedes Taliban Takeover Was Faster Than Expected," ABC News, 16 August 2021. https://abcnews.go.com/Politics/biden-return-white-house-deliver-remarks-afghanistan/story?id=79479724

with him—all while blaming his predecessor and the Afghan National Army and Afghan government for collapsing as quickly as they did.[14]

This, of course, did little to ameliorate the threat that most Americans in Afghanistan were then facing. However, it highlighted a larger strategic issue within the Biden administration. While it was true that Biden's predecessor, Donald Trump, negotiated the deal that would have seen the bulk of all remaining US forces leaving Afghanistan by 2021, it was not a firm commitment.[15]

It was, as always, contingent upon facts on the ground—and whether the Taliban would uphold their end of the agreement. The moment that the Biden administration abandoned Bagram Airbase, the Taliban raced toward the city of Kabul. That alone was a violation of the initial agreement crafted between the Taliban and the Trump administration in Doha, Qatar in February 2020.[16]

Even before the Taliban entered Kabul and began to seize the city, they had violated the original Doha agreement, which most experts believed was a weak framework for actual peace from the start.[17] Yet Biden insisted on respecting the full letter agreement, as though it had been made between two equals who were both operating in good faith. One can understand why both the Trump and Biden administrations sought to negotiate a settlement with the group that had remained intractably opposed to the American presence in Afghanistan for twenty

14 Kathryn Watson, "Biden Says, 'Buck Stops with Me,' and Defends Afghanistan Withdrawal," CBS News, 17 August 2021. https://www.cbsnews.com/news/biden-afghanistan-withdrawal-taliban-decision/

15 Jennifer Hansler, "US and Taliban Sign Historic Agreement," CNN, 29 February 2020. https://www.cnn.com/2020/02/29/politics/us-taliban-deal-signing/index.html

16 Shadi Khan Saif, "Taliban Reject US Charges of Violating Peace Accord," Anadolu Agency, 29 January 2021. https://www.aa.com.tr/en/asia-pacific/taliban-reject-us-charges-of-violating-peace-accord/2127756

17 Matthew Lee and Eric Tucker, "Was Biden Handcuffed by Trump's Taliban Deal in Doha?" *Times of Israel,* 20 August 2021. https://www.timesofisrael.com/was-biden-handcuffed-by-trumps-taliban-deal-in-doha/

years. However, one cannot forgive President Biden for adhering to the Doha agreement crafted by his predecessor when the other party, the Taliban, were so obviously violating it almost from the moment the tentative deal was inked in February 2020.[18]

The Biden administration inherently accepted the Taliban as the ruling regime in Afghanistan, even though President Ashraf Ghani and the regime that the United States had installed in 2001 still ruled Afghanistan. American leaders had always envisaged a power-sharing deal between the Ghani government and the Taliban. Biden's extreme commitment to the Doha Agreement, even in the face of Taliban violations, made that impossible. Once the bulk of US forces were withdrawn and the Bagram Airbase abandoned, the warlords that Mr. Ghani needed to protect his regime switched sides and became Taliban agents.[19]

Any hope for a power-sharing agreement was over. The Taliban took control of Afghanistan, erasing twenty years of American sacrifices. President Biden remained steadfast in his commitment to the flawed Doha Agreement, even as that Islamist government did everything in its power to harm Americans attempting to flee the country.

Now that President Biden has shown his unflinching commitment to dealing with radical Islamist regimes, even at the expense of thousands of American lives, it is essential to look at nearby Iran. As you've read, not only has President Biden viewed the Islamist regime of Iran as the legitimate government of that country, but every Democratic Party president going back to Jimmy Carter has viewed the Islamic Republic of Iran in this way.

Just as President Biden effectively midwifed the restoration of the Islamist Taliban government in Afghanistan, former President Carter

---

18 Pip Murrison, "What Is the Doha Agreement? Has the Taliban Broken Its Promise?" *Express UK,* 17 August 2021. https://www.express.co.uk/news/world/1478134/doha-agreement-explained-Taliban-Afghanistan-ceasefire-evg

19 "Afghan Warlords Give Up to the Taliban with Surprising Ease," *Deccan-Herald,* 15 August 2021. https://www.deccanherald.com/international/world-news-politics/afghan-warlords-give-up-to-the-taliban-with-surprising-ease-1019968.html

presided over the rise of the grand ayatollah's murderous government in Tehran in 1979. As you have read, the Khomeinist regime then gleefully took Americans at their embassy hostage and held them for ransom for over a year.

The Carter administration never wavered in their acknowledgment that Khomeini's regime was the legitimate government of Iran, even as the Islamists of Iran held Americans hostage and humiliated the United States daily. Biden did the same in Afghanistan. It raises the question: What will Biden and the Democratic Party do about Iran's nuclear weapons program?

Clearly, there is an unspoken assumption on the part of a succession of Democratic Party presidents that Islamism is the only legitimate form of popular governance in the Greater Middle East. Whether Islamism is the only political force with durability in the region or not, Washington is not required to embrace these totalitarian theocracies—especially when there are viable alternatives that are friendlier to the United States and its national interests in the region. Even if Washington wants to normalize relations with these regimes, a questionable goal given how untrustworthy they are, allowing them to have untrammeled access to advanced weapons—nuclear or otherwise—and to be integrated into the international trading system are unnecessary concessions unworthy of the world's sole remaining superpower.

And before anyone lays the blame for the situation in Kabul on former President Trump, it is imperative that you understand that Trump never intended to simply abandon Afghanistan to the Taliban. He indeed made a tentative agreement with the Taliban. Yet according to multiple Trump administration insiders, the plan always included a residual force of US military personnel that would remain inside Afghanistan both to conduct counterterrorism operations and to keep an eye on the Taliban.[20] Trump valued flexibility and unpredictability in foreign affairs, whereas Biden clearly prefers rigid conformity to deeply flawed and ambiguous agreements with threatening Islamist regimes. If the Biden administration had not pulled out US forces as rapidly or sloppily as they did in the months before August 2021, it is likely that the Taliban advance would not have reached Kabul as quickly as it did.

President Biden saw no reason to evacuate preemptively the thousands of Americans who were left at the mercy of the Taliban in Afghanistan because of some agreement that was crafted between the Taliban terrorist organization and Washington. Now imagine what the Biden administration might countenance from the rabid Islamists of the far more threatening Iranian regime. We have from the American Left a stunning suspension of disbelief when it comes to understanding the hostile intentions of Islamist organizations.

This pattern of poor decisions by a succession of Democratic Party presidents has destroyed our position in Iran. It has also destroyed America's position in Afghanistan. As time progresses, it is becoming clear that President Biden will do whatever he can to give Iran everything it wants, all for the hope of being able to claim that he made peace with Tehran—while consigning American interests and regional allies to the trash bin.

Therefore, the Biden administration's disastrous handling of the Afghan withdrawal is a frightening portent of how this administration might empower the nuclear-armed Islamists of Iran. Every American outraged over how Biden bungled the Afghanistan withdrawal should be equally unnerved by Mr. Biden's single-minded obsession with handing the wider region over to Islamists in Iran, no matter what they do to harm US national interests, allies, and personnel. The real divide in US policies toward the Middle East is whether Islamists can be trusted to

---

20 Patrick Tucker, "Trump's Pledge to Exit Afghanistan Was a Ruse, His Final SecDef Says," Defense One, 18 August 2021. https://www.defenseone.com/policy/2021/08/trumps-pledge-exit-afghanistan-was-ruse-his-final-secdef-says/184660/

be reliable, stable stakeholders in the US-led international order.

It is patently obvious that none of the Islamists are interested in this. They only want to push the Americans out of their region so that they can implement their radical political agenda for the entire Mideast. Yet from Carter to Biden, nearly every Democratic Party president has attempted to normalize relations with a variety of Islamist groups who seek to destroy the United States.

AND WHAT OF IRAN'S INVOLVEMENT IN AFGHANISTAN?

As was noted in an earlier chapter, 1979 proved to be a seminal year for Islamism throughout the region. In the year when the Shāh was overthrown in Iran, the Soviet-Afghan War began. It was the same year that a massive outbreak of Islamist fervor in the Sunni Arab world began. By the 1990s, the Soviets would be gone from Afghanistan, and the Islamist forces who fought them would be turning against each other and their one-time American allies. At the end of that six-year civil war in Afghanistan, the Taliban would rise to power in Afghanistan and rule with an iron fist. The Taliban were ethnic Pashtuns and Sunni Muslims, at war with all other groups and religions—especially the Shiites who lived in Afghanistan, which meant they were at war with neighboring Iran.

In 1998, Pakistani militants affiliated with the Taliban murdered eleven Iranian citizens in the city of Mazar-i-Sharif, nine of whom were Iranian diplomats. This almost led to a war between the Taliban and the Islamic Republic of Iran. Although war was averted, the animus between the Sunni Taliban and Shiite Iranians ran deep for many years thereafter. In fact, Iran assisted the George W. Bush administration in its efforts to oust the Taliban from power in 2001 and even facilitated contacts between the Northern Alliance and the Americans (the US–Northern Alliance relationship would prove decisive in defeating the Taliban in 2001).[21]

---

21 Barnett Rubin, "A New Look at Iran's Complicated Relationship with the Taliban," War on the Rocks, 16 September 2020. https://warontherocks.com/2020/09/a-new-look-at-irans-complicated-relationship-with-the-taliban/

Yet as time progressed and America's military presence in the region became more pronounced, Iran became an ally for the Taliban and al Qaeda, despite the bad blood and religious differences. The enemy of Iran's enemy was now its friend. Iran no longer believed the Taliban were the greater threat to its security. It was the United States.

When the Americans toppled Saddam Hussein's regime in Iraq in 2003, Iran found itself flanked by two large American armies, one to its east in Afghanistan and the other to its west in Iraq. To counteract this unwanted presence so close to their territory, the Iranians allowed al Qaeda and the Taliban to use their territory as a haven from US military forces.[22] Just as the relationship between the Palestinian Sunni terror organization, Hamas, and Iran grew since 2001, the Taliban have become partners with the Islamic Republic of Iran in their shared resistance to the Americans.

As the Americans were desperately searching for any exit they could find in Afghanistan in August 2021, the Iranian government proudly claimed that their embassy would remain operational in Kabul, as would their consulate in Herat.[23] The Taliban had guaranteed the safety of Iranian holdings in the region. What's more, the previous twenty years had proven far too fruitful for either side to turn away from the other— especially because American sanctions against Iran remained in place, and Tehran desperately needed trading partners.

The Iran–Taliban relationship today is fundamentally different and better than it was in the 1990s and early 2000s. This does not mean that a "new kind of Taliban" is returning to power in Afghanistan. Far from it. What it means is that the Taliban owe Iran much for its survival during the dark years when it looked as though the Americans were in Afghanistan to stay. Some Taliban leaders, in fact, had Iranian military

---

22 Margherita Stancati, "Iran Backs Taliban with Cash and Arms," *Wall Street Journal*, 11 June 2015. https://www.wsj.com/articles/iran-backs-taliban-with-cash-and-arms-1434065528

23 "Iran Says Its Embassy in Kabul Remains Open," Reuters, 17 August 2021. https://www.reuters.com/world/asia-pacific/iran-says-its-embassy-kabul-remains-open-2021-08-17/

bodyguards while the Taliban waged war against the Americans and their allies in Afghanistan.[24]

Although acceptance of the Taliban as an ally is by no means universal among the people or even the leadership of Iran, the fact remains that Iran's Islamist regime is happy to see the Americans out of Afghanistan. They are happier still that the Americans are leaving in such a humiliating and degrading way. And as Central Asia is yet again outside the American sphere of influence, the region's new dominant powers, notably China and Russia, want a cooperative framework with the Taliban. Therefore, Tehran wants a more amicable relationship with the Taliban as well. After all, they all hate America together.

Relying upon agreements crafted between the Taliban and the now-deceased Iranian General Qassem Soleimani, Tehran believes that it will be able to maintain a working relationship with the Sunni Pashtun Taliban now ruling Afghanistan.[25] Again, none of this was a *fait accompli.* It was made possible entirely by the short-sightedness and abject weakness of the Biden administration. It came about, in part, because President Biden and his supporters genuinely believe that Islamist regimes, whether the Taliban of Afghanistan or the Islamic Republic of Iran, are inherently rational actors who can be trusted to uphold deals they make with the United States, a country they describe often as the "Great Satan" or the "infidel."

Throughout this book, you have read how Democratic Party presidents have led America down very dangerous roads by thinking that Islamists could be trusted and treated as rational actors. We have seen this disaster play out in the Iranian hostage crisis and the fallout from the failed rescue attempt in the desert. You have read about it in the horrific example

24 Shelly Kittleson, "Why Iran Will Welcome the Taliban Takeover in Afghanistan," *Foreign Policy,* 18 August 2021. https://foreignpolicy.com/2021/08/18/why-iran-will-welcome-the-taliban-takeover-in-afghanistan/

25 Suadad al-Salhy, "Afghanistan: How Iran and Its Allies are Relying on Soleimani's Deals with the Taliban," Middle East Eye, 20 August 2021. https://www.middleeasteye.net/news/afghanistan-taliban-iran-allies-soleiman-deals-relying-on

of the Biden administration's disastrous pullout from Afghanistan.

If President Biden follows through on his desire to make a comprehensive agreement with Iran, the fallout from this move could be even more damaging than the Kabul collapse. It will lead to the rise of a nuclear-armed Iran that has expanded far beyond its borders, has helped to move China and Russia into the region while pushing the Americans out, and will put Israel's survival at stake while creating a nuclear arms race within the Sunni Arab world.

Even if this worst-case scenario of Israel preemptively launching nuclear strikes against Iran and/or the Saudis surging their own nuclear weapons program forward is avoided, the next worst alternative would be if Israel along with the Sunni Arabs reorient their foreign policies to favor the two nations they believe to be the new powerbrokers in the region: China and Russia. At that point, the United States will be boxed out of what will continue being a geostrategically important part of the world. Being boxed out of the Greater Middle East will ensure that global power shifts away the American-led world order toward a new, Sino-Russian-led order of Eurasian autocracies inimical to the United States.

The Biden administration's fiasco in Afghanistan was entirely avoidable, and it is a snapshot of our near future if Biden gets his way. The only way to avoid this dark but certain future is for the American people and the two political parties to recognize the folly of seeking negotiated settlements with Islamist regimes that grant them greater economic power, political legitimacy, and access to nuclear weapons. There can be no compromise with these entities. They are opposed to US power and interests.

Afghanistan's connection to Iran has not been overlooked by Israel. According to a "right-wing" Mideast analyst, Nahum Barnea, "The conviction in Israel is that Qatar misled [the Trump administration in 2020 about the Taliban's trustworthiness]." Barnea adds, "Israeli officials [believe] that Doha is playing a similar game with [US-Iran negotiations]." Israeli military analyst Alon Ben-David has publicly lamented that Washington's abandonment of its twenty-year commitment in Afghanistan means that it might have similar intentions with Israel as it relates to opposing Iran's nuclear weapons program. According to Ben-David, "[the Biden administration] will refrain from military engagement with Iran, particularly if Tehran gets the bomb, and so Israelis will confront [their] fate alone against Iran."[26]

As we witness the sad reality in Afghanistan, in a way we are also witnessing the future rise of an Iranian empire, armed with nukes and other advanced weapons, that is intent on laying claim to the region—and will risk a world war to achieve that goal. President Biden is completely incapable of handling the Iranian threat. What his administration plans to do with Iran will ensure that a conflict will erupt in the region. If you thought the American evacuation of Afghanistan was a disaster, just wait until President Biden hands the region over to the mad mullahs of Iran. Biden's actions will not ensure the Americans will avoid another major war in the region, as he believes. Instead, they will hasten the start of a greater conflict and ensure that America can never extricate itself from this most unstable region.

---

26 MEE Staff, "Israeli Press Review: Qatar 'Misled the US' in Taliban Negotiations," Middle East Eye, 20 August 2021. https://www.middleeasteye.net/news/israel-afghanistan-qatar-us-misled-taliban-negotiations-press-review

BIBLIOGRAPHY

"1916 Election." The President Woodrow Wilson House. 2021. http://www. woodrowwilsonhouse.org/1916-election

Abrahamian, Ervand. "History Used and Abused." PBS. 19 August 2009. https:// www.pbs.org/wgbh/pages/frontline/tehranbureau/2009/08/history-used-and-abused.html

Afsaruddin, Asma. "Caliph." Britannica. 2020. https://www.britannica.com/topic/caliph

"Afsharid Dynasty (Nader Shah)." Iran Chamber Society. 2020. http://www. iranchamber.com/history/afsharids/afsharids.php

"Afsharid Dynasty." *The Oxford Dictionary of Islam.* 2020. http://www. oxfordislamicstudies.com/article/opr/t125/e60

"Ahmadinejad's Role in the Hostage Crisis Disputed." NPR. 2005. https://www. npr.org/templates/story/story.php?storyId=4725806

Allen, John R. and Riedel, Bruce. "Ending the Yemen War Is Both a Strategic and Humanitarian Imperative." Brookings Institute. 16 November 2020. https://www.brookings.edu/blog/order-from-chaos/2020/11/16/ending-the-yemen-war-is-both-a-strategic-and-humanitarian-imperative/

Ali, Kecia. "Islam and Slavery." The Feminist Sexual Ethics Project at Brandeis University. 2004. https://www.brandeis.edu/projects/fse/muslim/slavery.html

Amadeo, Kimberly. "OPEC and Its Goals, Members, and History." *The Balance.* 10 July 2019. https://www.thebalance.com/what-is-opec-its-members-and-history-3305872

Amini, Hassan. *Decadence and Downfall: The Shah of Iran's Ultimate Party.* 2016. BBC Studios, London. 2016. YouTube. https://www.youtube.com/watch?v=fDhGPYWfKFU&feature=emb_logo

Andersen, Jack and Atta, Dale Van. "CIA Official Tortured to Death, Gave Secrets." *Deseret News.* 28 September 1988. https://www.deseret.com/1988/9/28/18779491/cia-official-tortured-to-death-gave-secrets

"Anglo-Prussian War (1856)." *Encyclopedia.* 2020. https://www.encyclopedia.com/humanities/encyclopedias-almanacs-transcripts-and-maps/anglo-persian-war-1856

"Assessing the Risk Posed by Iran's Violations of the Nuclear Deal." *Arms Control Association.* vol. 11. issue 9. 2020. https://www.armscontrol.org/issue-briefs/2019-12/assessing-risk-posed-iran-violations-nuclear-deal

Axworthy, Michael. *Empire of the Mind: A History of Iran.* New York: Basic Books, 2008.

Axworthy, Michael. *Revolutionary Iran: A History of the Islamic Republic.* New York: Oxford University Press, 2013.

Azhari, Timour. "Beirut Blast: Tracing the Explosive That Tore the Capital Apart." Al Jazeera. 5 August 2020. https://www.aljazeera.com/news/2020/8/5/beirut-blast-tracing-the-explosives-that-tore-the-capital-apart

Babbin, Jed. *In the Words of Our Enemies.* Washington, D.C.: Regnery Publishing, 2007.

Babbin, Jed. *Inside the Asylum: Why the United Nations and Old Europe Are Worse Than You Think.* Washington, D.C.: Regnery Publishing, 2004.

Bacevich, Andrew J. *America's War for the Greater East: A Military History.* New York: Random House, 2016.

Bacevich, Andrew J. and Kinzer, Stephen. "Matters of Choice." *Boston Review.* 4 April 2016. http://bostonreview.net/us/andrew-j-bacevich-interviewed-stephen-kinzer-war-greater-middle-east

Bard, Mitchell. "Israel's Wars & Operations: First Intifada (1987–1993)." Jewish Virtual Library. Accessed on 5 December 20202020. https://www.jewishvirtuallibrary.org/first-intifada

Bassam, Laila and Osborn, Andrew. "Iran Troops to Join Syria War, Russia Bombs Group Trained by CIA." Reuters. 1 October 2015. https://www.reuters.com/article/us-mideast-crisis-russia-syria/iran-troops-to-join-syria-war-russia-bombs-group-trained-by-cia-idUSKCN0RV41O20151002

"The Baghdad Pact and the Central Treaty Organization." U.S. Department of State. Accessed on 5 December 2020. https://2001-2009.state.gov/r/pa/ho/time/lw/98683.htm

Battlestar Galactica. Episode 13. "The Oath." John Dahl/Mark Verheiden/Richard Hatch. 2009. SyFy Channel.

"Battle of Badr." Britannica. 2020. https://www.britannica.com/event/Battle-of-Badr

Bauer, Katherine, Ghaddar, Hanin, and Orion, Assaf. "Iran's Precision Missile Project Moves to Lebanon." The Washington Institute for Near East Policy. December 2018. https://www.washingtoninstitute.org/policy-analysis/view/irans-precision-missile-project-moves-to-lebanon

Beardsley, Eleanor. "In France, the Protests of May 1968 Reverberate Today—And Still Divide the French." NPR. 29 May 2018. https://www.npr.org/sections/parallels/2018/05/29/613671633/in-france-the-protests-of-may-1968-reverberate-today-and-still-divide-the-french

"Beirut Marine Barracks Bombing Fast Moving." CNN. 6 October 2020. https://www.cnn.com/2013/06/13/world/meast/beirut-marine-barracks-bombing-fast-facts/index.html

Ben-Zvi, Abraham. "Biden's Conduct Endangers the Abraham Accords." *Israel Hayom.* 7 February 2021. https://www.israelhayom.com/opinions/bidens-conduct-endangers-the-abraham-accords/

Berman, Ilan. *Iran's Deadly Ambition: The Islamic Republic's Quest for Global Power.* New York: Encounter Books, 2015.

"Biden Will Seek to Re-Enter Iran Nuclear Deal within Months, Former Aide Says." *The Times of Israel.* 8 November 2020. https://www.timesofisrael.com/biden-will-seek-to-reenter-iran-nuclear-deal-within-months-aide-says/

Blinken, Anthony J. "Rocket Attacks in Erbil." U.S. Department of State. 15 February 2021. https://www.state.gov/rocket-attacks-in-erbil/

Borbor, Dariush. "A Comparative Overview of the Iranian Constitutions of 1906–07 and 1979."

Iran & the Caucasus. vol. 10. no. 2. 2006. https://www.jstor.org/stable/4030928?seq=1

Bowden, Mark. *Guests of the Ayatollah: The Iran Hostage Crisis: The First Battle in America's War with Militant Islam.* New York: Grove Press, 2006.

Brandom, Russell. "Iran Hacked the Sands Hotel Earlier This Year, Causing over $40 Million in Damage." *The Verge.* 11 December 2014. https://www.theverge.com/2014/12/11/7376249/iran-hacked-sands-hotel-in-february-cyberwar-adelson-israel

Brands, Hal, Cook, Steven A., Pollack, Kenneth M. "RIP The Carter Doctrine, 1980–2019." *Foreign Policy.* 13 December 2019. https://foreignpolicy.com/2019/12/15/carter-doctrine-rip-donald-trump-mideast-oil-big-think/

Branigan, William. "William H. Sullivan Dies at 90; Veteran Diplomat Oversaw Secret War in Laos." *Washington Post.* 22 October 2013. https://www.washingtonpost.com/world/william-h-sullivan-dies-at-90-veteran-diplomat-oversaw-secret-war-in-laos/2013/10/22/f13e628c-3b2f-11e3-b6a9-da62c264f40e_story.html

Brew, Gregory. "The Collapse Narrative: The United States, Mohammed Mossadegh, and the Coup Decision of 1953." *Texas National Security Review.* Vol. 2, issue 4. November 2019. https://tnsr.org/2019/11/the-collapse-narrative-the-united-states-mohammed-mossadegh-and-the-coup-decision-of-1953/

Brook, Tom Vanden. "Qasem Soleimani: The Pentagon Had Tracked Iranian General for Years before He Was Killed." *USA Today.* 3 January 2020. https://www.usatoday.com/story/news/politics/2020/01/03/us-military-tracked-iran-general-soleimani-years-killed-thursday/2806630001/

Bryen, Stephen. 4 August 2020, 1:22 pm. Twitter.https://twitter.com/stevebryen/status/1290699671174819840

Bucci, Steven. "The Shia Crescent Is Still America's Biggest Middle East Challenge." Al Arabiya. 13 March 2020. https://english.alarabiya.net/en/views/news/middle-east/2020/03/13/The-Shia-Crescent-is-still-America-s-biggest-Middle-East-challenge

Caryl, Christian. *Strange Rebels: 1979 and the Birth of the 21st Century.* New York: Basic Books, 2013.

CBS News. "CBS News Archives: Carter's Famous 'Malaise Speech.'" John Dickerson. 2011. YouTube. https://www.youtube.com/watch?v=0tGd_9Tahzw

Cecco, Leyland. "Alberta Leader Says Biden's Move to Cancel Pipeline a 'Gut Punch.'" *The Guardian.* 27 January 2021. https://www.theguardian.com/environment/2021/jan/27/alberta-leader-says-bidens-move-to-cancel-keystone-pipeline-a-gut-punch

Chuck, Elizabeth. "What Are the Differences Between Sunni and Shiite Muslims?" NBC News. 4 January 2016. https://www.nbcnews.com/news/mideast/what-are-differences-between-sunni-shiite-muslims-n489951

CinnovationGlobal. "Edward Luttwak at Creative Innovation 2010—'How War Can Bring Peace.'" YouTube. 2012. https://www.youtube.com/watch?v=XTTruD9WTvc&t=55s

CNN. "Biden Nat Sec Adviser: This May Be the Best Chance at Iran Deal." YouTube video. 2021. https://www.youtube.com/watch?v=vl6bboPHgW8

CNN. "US Sidelines Prince in 'Recalibration' with Saudi Arabia." YouTube. 2021. https://www.youtube.com/watch?v=oVYpHzAGRHc

CNN News Wire Staff, "Obama Says U.S. Has Asked Iran to Return Drone Aircraft." CNN. 12 December 2011. https://www.cnn.com/2011/12/12/world/meast/iran-us-drone/index.html

Coll, Steve. *Ghost Wars: The Secret History of the CIA, Afghanistan and Bin Laden.* New York: Penguin, 2005.

Conason, Joe. "Seven Countries in Five Years." Salon. 12 October 2007. https://www.salon.com/2007/10/12/wesley_clark/

Cooper, Andrew Scott. "A Tale of Two Oil Shocks, Part I: 1973–1976." PBS. 15 June 2012. https://www.pbs.org/wgbh/pages/frontline/tehranbureau/2012/06/a-tale-of-two-oil-shocks-part-1-1973-76.html

Cooper, Andrew Scott. "Declassified Diplomacy: Washington's Hesitant Plans for a Military Coup in Pre-Revolutionary Iran." *The Guardian.* 11 February 2015. https://www.theguardian.com/world/iran-blog/2015/feb/11/us-general-huysers-secret-iran-mission-declassified?fbclid=IwAR3-1RSLXfuw0nIRhpahrjSFWEOR7N0l8Toug1rA4veIwPz1WevprGzloJ8

Cooper, Andrew Scott. *The Fall of Heaven: The Pahlavis and the Final Days of Imperial Iran.* New York: Picador, 2018.

Cooper, Andrew Scott. *Oil Kings: How the US, Iran, and Saudi Arabia Changed the Balance of Power in the Middle East.* New York: Simon & Schuster, 2011.

"Crude Exports from Iran's Kharg Terminal at 2.2m bpd." *Financial Tribune.* 2018. https://financialtribune.com/articles/energy/86404/crude-exports-from-irans-kharg-terminal-at-22m-bpd

Curtis, Mark. "Britain and the Iranian Revolution: Expediency, Arms, and Secret Deals." Middle East Eye. 1 February 2019. https://www.middleeasteye.net/opinion/britain-and-iranian-revolution-expediency-arms-and-secret-deals

Daneshkhu, Scheherazade. "The Political Economy of Industrialisation in Iran, 1973–1978." London School of Economics. 2020. https://etheses.lse.ac.uk/2794/1/U615743.pdf

Daugherty, William J. "Jimmy Carter and the 1979 Decision
to Admit the Shah into the United States." *American Diplomacy.*
April 2003. https://americandiplomacy.web.unc.edu/2003/04/
jimmy-carter-and-the-1979-decision-to-admit-the-shah-into-the-united-states/

David, Javier E. "US-Saudi Arabia Seal Weapons Deal Worth Nearly $110 Billion
Immediately, $350 Billion Over 10 Years." CNBC. 20 May 2017. https://www.
cnbc.com/2017/05/20/us-saudi-arabia-seal-weapons-deal-worth-nearly-110-billion-
as-trump-begins-visit.html

"Decadence and Downfall: The Shah of Iran's Ultimate Party." The Royal Watcher.
27 February 2017. https://royalwatcherblog.com/2017/02/27/persepolis-1971/

Dehghanpiseh, Babak. "Soleimani Was Iran's Celebrity Soldier,
Spearhead in Middle East." Reuters. 3 January 2020. https://
www.reuters.com/article/us-iran-security-soleimani-newsmaker/
soleimani-was-irans-celebrity-soldier-spearhead-in-middle-east-idUSKBN1Z20C4

De Luce, Dan. "Trump Pressure Will Fail Because Iran Has a 'Ph.D. in Sanctions
Busting, Says Iran's Zarif." NBC.25 April 2019. https://www.nbcnews.com/news/
world/trump-pressure-will-fail-because-iran-has-ph-d-sanctions-n998711

Di Giovanni, Janine. "Why America Isn't Equipped for the
New Rules of War." *MIT Technology Review.* 24 October
2019. https://www.technologyreview.com/2019/10/24/132194/
america-isnt-equipped-for-shadow-war-disinformation-sean-mcfate/

Di John, Jonathan. "Is There Really a Resource Curse?" *Global Governance.* 17. no.
2. 2011. https://www.jstor.org/stable/23033728?seq=1

Duchesne-Guillemin, Jacques. "Zoroastrianism." Britannica. 2020. https://www.
britannica.com/topic/Zoroastrianism/Practices-and-institutions

Dylan-Böhmer, Daniel. "Die explosive Spur führt zur Hisbollah." *Die Welt.* 19
August 2020. https://amp.welt.de/politik/ausland/article213884822/Libanon-Die-
explosive-Spur-fuehrt-zur-Hisbollah.html?twitter_impression=true

Eberstadt, Mary. "How the West Really Lost God: A New Theory of Secularization." The Heritage Foundation. 30 May 2013. YouTube. https://www.youtube.com/watch?v=DcVyz5C3LPY

"EEI Celebrates 1 Million Electric Vehicles on Roads." Edison Electric Institute. Accessed on 27 November 2020. https://www.eei.org/resourcesandmedia/newsroom/Pages/Press%20Releases/EEI%20Celebrates%201%20Million%20Electric%20Vehicles%20on%20U-S-%20Roads.aspx

Embassy of Israel. "The Beautiful Cry of 'Death to America' Unites Our Nation." Twitter 21 November 2014. https://twitter.com/IsraelinUSA/status/535834105150451712

"'Eternal Flames' of Ancient Times Could Spark Interest of Modern Geologists." *Science Daily.* 18 May 2015. https://www.sciencedaily.com/releases/2015/05/150518102031.htm

"Fact Sheet: Israel's Nuclear Arsenal." Center for Arms Control and Non-Proliferation. 31 March 2020. https://armscontrolcenter.org/fact-sheet-israels-nuclear-arsenal/

Fattahi, Kambiz. "Two Weeks in January: America's Secret Engagement with Khomeini." BBC. 3 June 2016. https://www.bbc.com/news/world-us-canada-36431160

"Fedā'iān-e Kalq." *Encyclopædia Iranica.* 7 December 2015. https://www.iranicaonline.org/articles/ fadaian-e-khalq

Fernando, Jason. "Resource Curse." Investopedia. 22 October 2020. https://www.investopedia.com/terms/r/resource-curse.asp

Fiennes, Ralph. *Coup 53.* Taghi Amirani. 2019. London: Amirani Media. *Film.*

Fisk, Robert. *The Great War for Civilisation: The Conquest of the Middle East.* New York: Vintage Books, 2007.

Flynn, Mike T and Ledeen, Mike. *The Field of Fight: How We Can Win the Global War Against Radical Islam.* New York: St. Martin's Press, 2016.

"Four Hellfire Missiles and a Severed Hand: The Killing of Qassem Soleimani."
The Times of Israel. 3 January 2020. https://www.timesofisrael.com/
four-hellfire-missiles-and-a-severed-hand-the-killing-of-qassem-soleimani/

Frantzman, Seth J. "Beirut Explosion Wrapped in Conspiracies, Fueling Online
Sleuths." *The Jerusalem Post.* 11 August 2020. https://www.jpost.com/middle-east/
beirut-explosion-wrapped-in-conspiracies-fuelling-online-sleuths-638125

Frantzman, Seth J. "Nasrallah Threatens to Blow Up
Israel with Same Chemicals as Beirut Blast." *The Jerusalem
Post.* 8 August 2020. https://www.jpost.com/middle-east/
nasrallah-threatened-to-blow-up-israel-with-same-chemicals-as-beirut-blast-637582

Frantzman, Seth J. "Were Suspicious Tunnels Near Beirut Port Discovered
after Blast?" *The Jerusalem Post.* 2020. https://www.jpost.com/middle-east/
were-suspicious-tunnels-discovered-near-beirut-port-after-explosion-638131

Freilich, Chuck. "Hamas is a Distraction for Israel Compared to Hezbollah
and Iran." *Haaretz.* 19 November 2018. https://www.haaretz.com/israel-news/.
premium-conflict-with-hamas-is-hardly-the-main-threat-facing-israel-1.6432549

Galstyan, Areg. "Third Rome Rising: The Ideologues Calling for a New Russian
Empire." *The National Interest.* 27 June 2016. https://nationalinterest.org/feature/
third-rome-rising-the-ideologues-calling-new-russian-empire-16748

Gasiorowski, Mark J. "U.S. Perceptions of the Communist Threat in Iran during
the Mossadegh Era." *Journal of Cold War Studies.* Vol. 21. no. 3. Summer 2019.
https://www.mitpressjournals.org/doi/pdf/10.1162/jcws_a_00898

Gerges, Fawaz A. *Obama and the Middle East: The End of America's Moment?* New
York: Palgrave Macmillan, 2012.

Giambertone, Francesco. "Beirut, l'esperto di esplosivi: «La nuvola arancione e gli
scoppi: ecco perché credo ci fossero anche armi»" *Corriere Della Sera.* 5 August
2020. https://www.corriere.it/esteri/20_agosto_05/beirut-esperto-esplosivi-la-
nuvola-arancione-scoppi-ecco-perche-credo-ci-fossero-anche-armi-6da4a01e-d71b-
11ea-93a6-dcb5dd8eef08.shtml

Glick, Caroline B. "Column One: Mowing the Lawn in Gaza." *The Jerusalem Post.* 18 October 2018. https://www.jpost.com/opinion/column-one-mowing-the-lawn-in-gaza-569775

Goldenberg, Ilan, Heras, Nicholas, Thomas, Kaleigh, and Matuschak, Jennie. "Countering Iran in the Gray Zone." Center for New American Security. 14 April 2020. https://www.cnas.org/publications/reports/countering-iran-gray-zone

Goldman, David P. *How Civilizations Die: And Why Islam is Dying Too.* Washington, D.C.: Regnery Publishing, 2011.

Goldman, David P. "How Fragile is Iran's Regime?" *The Asia Times.* 13 January 2020. https://asiatimes.com/2020/01/how-fragile-is-irans-regime-2/

Gordon, Michael R. "1980 Soviet Test: How to Invade Iran." *New York Times.* 15 December 1986. https://www.nytimes.com/1986/12/15/world/1980-soviet-test-how-to-invade-iran.html

Graefe, Laurel. "Oil Shock of 1978–79." Federal Reserve Bank of Atlanta. 22 November 2013. https://www.federalreservehistory.org/essays/oil-shock-of-1978-79

Green, David B. "From Friends to Foes: How Israel and Iran Turned into Arch-Enemies." *Haaretz.* 8 May 2018. https://www.haaretz.com/middle-east-news/iran/MAGAZINE-how-israel-and-iran-went-from-allies-to-enemies-1.6049884

Green, William C. "The Historic Russian Drive for a Warm Water Port: Anatomy of a Geopolitical Myth." *Naval War College Review.* Vol. 46. no. 2. Spring 1993. https://www.jstor.org/stable/44642451?seq=2#metadata_info_tab_contents

Gross, Judah Ari. "Likud Minister Warns Israel Could Attack Iran Nuclear Program if US Rejoins Deal." *Times of Israel.* 13 January 2021. https://www.timesofisrael.com/likud-minister-warns-israel-could-attack-iran-nuclear-program-if-us-rejoins-deal/

Hahn, Peter L. "How Jimmy Carter Lost Iran." *The Washington Post.* 22 October 2017. https://www.washingtonpost.com/news/made-by-history/wp/2017/10/22/how-jimmy-carter-lost-iran/

Haltiwanger, John. "Here's What's in the 2015 Nuclear Deal with Iran That Trump Abandoned and Biden Pledged to Restore." *Business Insider.* 2 December 2020. https://www.businessinsider.com/iran-nuclear-deal-explained

Hambling, David. "Clone Wars: Why Iran Will Copy Captured U.S. Global Hawk Drone." *Forbes.* 16 July 2020. https://www.forbes.com/sites/davidhambling/2020/07/16/clone-wars-why-iran-will-copy-captured-us-global-hawk-drone/?sh=44b6b7567540

Hamilton, Nigel. *American Caesars: Lives of the Presidents from Franklin D. Roosevelt to George W. Bush.* New Haven: Yale University, 2010.

Harkov, Lahav. "Hezbollah Stockpiled Chemical behind Beirut Blast in London and Germany." *The Jerusalem Post.* 5 August 2020. https://www.jpost.com/middle-east/hezbollah-stockpiled-chemical-behind-beirut-blast-in-london-637578

Harkov, Lahav. "Israeli Minister Warns of War If Biden Returns to Ideal Deal." *The Jerusalem Post.* 5 November 2020. https://www.jpost.com/us-elections/israeli-minister-warns-of-war-if-biden-returns-to-iran-deal-648097?fbclid=IwAR1Ho7lbjhCdsU3Ssjbrgtn8ocw1o4VwkOsxWOh3eTVV4rPAsdLKKbg2aeg

Harkov, Lahav. "The Abraham Accords Domino Effect Will Lead to More Peace Deals." *Jerusalem Post.* 1 January 2021. https://www.jpost.com/middle-east/the-abraham-accords-domino-effect-will-lead-to-more-peace-deals-653940

"Hashd al Shaabi/Hashd Shaabi/Popular Mobilisation Units/People's Mobilization Forces." Global Security. Accessed on 1 November 2020. https://www.globalsecurity.org/military/world/para/hashd-al-shaabi.htm

Hellman, Ziv. "The Second Intifada Begins." My Jewish Learning. Accessed on 2 November 2020. https://www.myjewishlearning.com/article/the-second-intifada-begins/

"Hezbollah Procured Hundreds of Tons of Ammonium Nitrate from Iran, Report Says." *Haaretz.* 2 August 2020. https://www.haaretz.com/middle-east-news/.premium-hezbollah-procured-hundreds-of-tons-of-ammonium-nitrate-from-iran-report-says-1.9087357

"Hidden Imam." Oxford University Islamic Studies Online. Accessed on 19 November 2020. http://www.oxfordislamicstudies.com/article/opr/t125/e838

History.com Editors. "Napoleon Dies in Exile." A&E Television Networks. 2010. https://www.history.com/this-day-in-history/napoleon-dies-in-exile

History.com Editors. "Soviets Announce Withdrawal from Iran." History. 2009. https://www.history.com/this-day-in-history/soviets-announce-withdrawal-from-iran

Hopkirk, Peter. *The Great Game: The Struggle for Empire in Central Asia.* New York: Kodansha USA, 1990.

Iddon, Paul. "In a Third Lebanon War, Israel Will Have to Contend with Increasingly Lethal Hezbollah Missiles." *Forbes.* 27 June 2020. https://www.forbes.com/sites/pauliddon/2020/06/27/in-a-third-lebanon-war-israel-will-have-to-contend-with-increasingly-lethal-hezbollah-missiles/?sh=705682a84b5e

"Iranian Women—Before and After the Islamic Revolution." BBC. 8 February 2019. https://www.bbc.com/news/world-middle-east-47032829

"Iran Hostage Crisis." Britannica. Accessed on 18 January 2021. https://www.britannica.com/event/Iran-hostage-crisis/Conflict-and-resolution

"Iran President Says Iran Responded, Will Respond to Assassination of Soleimani." Reuters. 18 March 2020. https://fr.reuters.com/article/uk-iran-us-soleimani-idAFKBN215124

"Iran to Produce Octogen Explosive Materials to Power Weapons Systems." *Defense World.* 8 April 2016. https://www.defenseworld.net/news/15772/Iran_To_Produce_Octogen_Explosive_Materials_To_Power_Weapon_Systems#.X6BhDi9h3xt

"Iran Protests: All You Need to Know in 600 Words." Al Jazeera. 20 November 2019. https://www.aljazeera.com/news/2019/11/20/irans-protests-all-you-need-to-know-in-600-words

"Iran's Qassem Soleimani: Global Mass Killer." Al Arabiya. 4 January 2020. https://english.alarabiya.net/en/features/2020/01/04/Iran-s-Qassem-Soleimani-Global-mass-killer

"Iran, Russia to Launch Cargo Shipping Line in September." *Tehran Times.* 12 August 2020. https://www.tehrantimes.com/news/451144/Iran-Russia-to-launch-cargo-shipping-line-in-September

"Iraq-Iran: From Water Dispute to War." ECC Platform Library. Accessed on 9 February 2021. https://library.ecc-platform.org/conflicts/iraq-iran-water-dispute-war

Irish, John and Cabrera, Michaela. "Iran's First President Says Khomeini Betrayed 1979 Islamic Revolution." Reuters. 4 February 2019. https://www.reuters.com/article/us-iran-revolution-anniversary-banisadr/irans-first-president-says-khomeini-betrayed-1979-islamic-revolution-idUSKCN1PT1IR

"Israel's Netanyahu Says Hezbollah Has 'Arms Depot' in Beirut." Arab News. 30 September 2020. https://www.arabnews.com/node/1741846/middle-east

Jafarzadeh, Alireza. *The Iran Threat: President Ahmadinejad and the Coming Nuclear Crisis.* New York: Palgrave Macmillan, 2007.

Javadzadeh, Abdolrahim. "Marxists into Muslims: An Iranian Irony." 2007. FIU Electronic Theses and Dissertations. https://digitalcommons.fiu.edu/cgi/viewcontent.cgi?article=1051&context=etd

"Joe Biden Elected 46th President of the United States." *Tampa Bay Times.* 7 November 2020. https://www.tampabay.com/news/florida-politics/elections/2020/11/07/joe-biden-elected-46th-president-of-the-united-states-ap-says/

"John F. Kennedy and the Shah." Radio Farda. 2 June 2017. https://en.radiofarda.com/a/kennedy-sha-visit-iran-alliance/28524785.html

John, Tara, Mecaya, Melissa, Hayes, Mike, et al. "Beirut Explosion Rocks Lebanon's Capital City." CNN. 5 August 2020. https://edition.cnn.com/middleeast/live-news/lebanon-beirut-explosion-live-updates-dle-intl/h_0f646d1827f2f246b9c48701b5c8eac5?fbclid=IwAR2VyQVipSk_jsZwxJguZaTASML5KXcGIA4AL4jugiB-IWXY4r2aVepSkeo

Johnson, Paul. *Modern Times: The World from the Twenties to the Nineties.* New York: Harper Perennial, 1991.

Judd, Emily and Fazeli, Yaghoub. "Why Is Iran Threatening Israel's Haifa? Experts Explain." Al-Arabiya English. 30 November 2020. https://english.alarabiya.net/features/2020/11/30/Why-is-Iran-targeting-Israel-s-Haifa-Experts-explain

Kalvapalle, Rahul. "Missing Saudi Journalist Jamal Khashoggi's Ties to Osama bin Laden Explained." Global News. 13 October 2018. https://globalnews.ca/news/4545784/jamal-khashoggi-osama-bin-laden/

Karkar, Sonja. "The First Intifada—Historical Overview." American Muslims for Palestine. 10 December 2007. https://www.ampalestine.org/palestine-101/history/intifadas/first-intifada-historical-overview

Katouzian, Homa. *The Persians: Ancient, Medieval, and Modern Iran.* New Haven: Yale University Press, 2009.

Kaufman, Robert G. *Dangerous Doctrine: How Obama's Grand Strategy Weakened America.* Lexington: University of Kentucky Press, 2016.

Kaye, Dalia Dassa, Nader, Alireza, and Roshan, Parisa. *Israel and Iran: A Dangerous Rivalry.* Santa Monica: RAND Corporation, 2011. https://www.rand.org/content/dam/rand/pubs/monographs/2011/RAND_MG1143.pdf

Kaylan, Melik. "Was Khomeini's Father a Brit?" *Forbes.* 8 October 2009. https://www.forbes.com/2009/10/08/ayatollah-khomeini-british-ahmadinejad-iran-opinions-columnists-melik-kaylan.html?sh=309a15d21a53

Kaznacheev, Peter. "Curse or Blessing? How Institutions Determine Success in Resource-Rich Economies." CATO. 11 January 2017. https://www.cato.org/publications/policy-analysis/curse-or-blessing-how-institutions-determine-success-resource-rich

Khorram, Yasmin. "Op-Ed: The Iranian General I Never Knew." CNBC. 13 January 2020. https://www.cnbc.com/2020/01/13/op-ed-my-grandfather-was-an-iranian-general-who-was-killed-in-the-revolution.html

Khoshnood, Ardavan. "Iran-Russia Ties Never Better but Maybe Not Forever?" The Middle East Institute. 12 February 2020. https://www.mei.edu/publications/iran-russia-ties-never-better-maybe-not-forever

Kinzer, Stephen. "BP and Iran: The Forgotten History." CBS News. 2010. https://www.cbsnews.com/news/bp-and-iran-the-forgotten-history/

Klaiman, Shahar. "Explosion Hits Israeli Cargo Ship in Gulf of Oman." *Israel Hayom*. 26 February 2021. https://www.israelhayom.com/2021/02/26/explosion-hits-israeli-cargo-ship-in-the-gulf-of-oman/

Klein, Joe. "Hamilton Jordan and Jody Powell: The White House Whiz Kids." *Rolling Stone Magazine*. 19 May 1977. https://www.rollingstone.com/politics/politics-news/hamilton-jordan-and-jody-powell-the-white-house-whiz-kids-64641/

Koss, Maren. "Flexible Resistance: How Hezbollah and Hamas Are Mending Ties." Carnegie Middle East Center. 11 July 2018. https://carnegie-mec.org/2018/07/11/flexible-resistance-how-hezbollah-and-hamas-are-mending-ties-pub-76782

Kotkin, Stephen. *Stalin, Volume I: Paradoxes of Power, 1878–1928.* New York: Penguin Press, 2014.

Kraft, Joseph. "Letter from Iran." *The New Yorker*. 18 December 1978. https://www.newyorker.com/magazine/1978/12/18/letter-from-iran

Kumar, Rajeesh. "What New Declassifications Reveal about the 1953 Coup in Iran." E-International Relations. 7 September 2017. https://www.e-ir.info/2017/09/07/what-new-declassifications-reveal-about-the-1953-coup-in-iran/

Kuo, Lily. "The Worst Thing About Kenya's New Power Plant Isn't That Chinese Workers Are Being Brought in to Build It." Quartz. 28 July 2016. https://qz.com/africa/743461/the-worst-thing-about-kenyas-new-power-plant-isnt-that-chinese-workers-are-being-brought-in-to-build-it/

Lake, Eli. "Why Obama Let Iran's Green Revolution Fail." Bloomberg. 24 August 2016. https://www.bloomberg.com/opinion/articles/2016-08-24/why-obama-let-iran-s-green-revolution-fail

Lallanilla, Marc. "Peak Oil: Theory or Myth?" Live Science. 12 February 2015. https://www.livescience.com/38869-peak-oil.html

Leahy, Patrick. "Reader Mail: Senator Patrick Leahy Responds to Brandon Weichert." *The American Spectator.* 2018. https://spectator.org/ reader-mail-senator-patrick-leahy-responds-to-brandon-weichert-2/

"Lebanon Accuses Israel of Provoking Border Escalation." AP. 2020. https://www.baynews9.com/fl/tampa/ap-online/2020/07/28/ lebanon-accuses-israel-of-provoking--border-escalation

"Lebanon's Army Finds Firework Cache at Devastated Beirut Port." Reuters. 2020. https://www.reuters.com/article/uk-lebanon-crisis-port/ lebanons-army-finds-firework-cache-at-devastated-beirut-port-idUSKCN26A0H8

"Lebanon Explosion: Deadly Fuel Tank Blast Rocks Beirut." BBC. 2020. https:// www.bbc.com/news/world-middle-east-54486402

Lee, Julian. "Which Oil Buyers Have the Most at Stake as Mideast Tensions Rise." Bloomberg. 26 June 2019. https://www.bloomberg.com/news/articles/2019-06-26/ which-oil-buyers-have-most-at-stake-as-mideast-tensions-rise

Leverett, Flynn and Leverett, Hillary Mann. *Going to Tehran: Why the United States Must Come to Terms with the Islamic Republic of Iran.* New York: Metropolitan Books, 2013.

Levitt, Matthew. "Hezbollah Isn't Just in Beirut. It's in New York, Too." *Foreign Policy.* 2019. https://foreignpolicy.com/2019/06/14/hezbollah-isnt-just-in-beirut-its-in-new-york-too-canada-united-states-jfk-toronto-pearson-airports-ali-kourani-iran/

Lewis, Bernard. *The Assassins: A Radical Sect in Islam.* New York: Basic Books, 1967.

Lewis, Bernard. *The End of Modern History in the Middle East.* New York: Hoover Institute Press, 2011.

Lewis, Bernard. *The Middle East: A Brief History of the Last 2,000 Years.* New York: Scribner, 1995

Lewis, Bernard. *What Went Wrong? Western Impact and Middle Eastern Response.* New York: Oxford University Press, 2002.

Linker, Damon. "Why I Miss the Gritty Greatness of the 1970s." *The Week*. 2014. https://theweek.com/articles/448596/why-miss-gritty-greatness-1970s

Liu, Joseph. "Islam and the West: A Conversation with Bernard Lewis." Pew Research Center. 27 April 2006. https://www.pewforum.org/2006/04/27/islam-and-the-west-a-conversation-with-bernard-lewis/

Logevall, Fredrik. "Laos: America's Lesser Known Human and Political Disaster in Southeast Asia." *Washington Post*. 2017. https://www.washingtonpost.com/opinions/laos-americas-lesser-known-human-and-political-disaster-in-southeast-asia/2017/02/02/a98c7368-dcc9-11e6-918c-99ede3c8cafa_story.html

Macias, Amanda. "Japanese Oil Tanker Owner Disagrees with US Military That a Mine Caused a Blast Near Iran." *CNBC*. 2019. https://www.cnbc.com/2019/06/14/oil-tanker-owner-disagrees-with-us-that-mine-caused-blast-near-iran.html

Makdisi, Ussama. "The Mythology of the Sectarian Middle East." James A. Baker III Institute for Public Policy. 2017. https://www.bakerinstitute.org/media/files/files/5a20626a/CME-pub-Sectarianism-021317.pdf

Mallam, Sally. "The Pre-Islamic World." The Human Journey. 2020. https://humanjourney.us/ideas-that-shaped-our-modern-world-section/mohammad-and-the-beginnings-of-islam-mecca-backdrop/

Maloney, Suzanne. "How the Iraq War Has Empowered Iran." Brookings Institute. 2008. https://www.brookings.edu/opinions/how-the-iraq-war-has-empowered-iran/

Maloney, Suzanne. "Major Beneficiaries to the Iran Deal: The IRGC and Hezbollah." Brookings Institute. 2015. https://www.brookings.edu/testimonies/major-beneficiaries-of-the-iran-deal-the-irgc-and-hezbollah/

Mankoff, Jeffrey and Bowen, Andrew. "Russia Doesn't Care if Assad Wins. It's About Russian Power Projection." *Foreign Policy*. 22 September 2015. https://foreignpolicy.com/2015/09/22/putin-russia-syria-assad-iran-islamic-state/

Mann, James. *The Obamians: The Struggle Inside the White House to Redefine American Power*. New York: Viking Press, 2012.

Matthews, Matt M. "We Were Caught Unprepared: The 2006 Hezbollah-Israeli War." U.S. Army Combined Arms Center for Combat Studies Institute Press. The Long War Series Occasional Paper. No. 26. 2006. https://www.armyupress.army. mil/Portals/7/combat-studies-institute/csi-books/we-were-caught-unprepared.pdf

Majidyar, Ahmad. "Iranian Cleric Calls for Arming Palestinians for 'Third Intifada.'" The Middle East Institute. 15 December 2017. https://www.mei.edu/ publications/iranian-cleric-calls-arming-palestinians-third-intifada

McCarthy, Andrew C. *Spring Fever: The Illusion of Islamic Democracy.* New York: Encounter Books, 2013.

McFall, Caitlin and Griffin, Jennifer. "US Launches Airstrike Against Iranian-Backed Forces in Syria.*" Fox News.* 2021. https://www.foxnews.com/politics/us-hits-iranian-backed- forces-in-syrian-in-defensive airstrike?fbclid=IwAR2yIokJff5i_ f6qMn3aVP62t671BkcsCEsGZlT7tusyFfazu0c0ZMCLn3I

"Mike Wallace Interview with the Shah of Iran in 1976." BBC. 8 April 2012. https://www.bbc.com/news/av/world-us-canada-17650516

Milani, Abbas. "The Three Paradoxes of the Islamic Revolution in Iran." *The Iranian Revolution at 30.* Ed. Andrew Parasiliti. Washington, D.C.: The Middle East Institute, 2009. https://library.nwacc.edu/c.php?g=221361&p=1465188

Miller, Aaron David. "The Power of the Incumbency: Four Two- Term Presidents in a Row?" Carnegie Endowment for International Peace. 15 October 2019. https://carnegieendowment.org/2019/10/15/ power-of-incumbency-four-two-term-presidents-in-row-pub-80072

Mirrazavi, Firouzeh. "The Removing of Hijab in Iran." *Iran Review.* 2013. http:// www.iranreview.org/content/Documents/The-Removing-of-Hijab-in-Iran.htm

Mock, Geoffrey. "How the Trauma and Struggles of World War I Helped Shape the Modern World." Duke Today. 2018. https://today.duke.edu/2018/11/ how-trauma-and-struggles-world-war-i-helped-shape-modern-world

Mohammed, Aref. "Iran Seizes 15 British Marines and Sailors in the Gulf." Reuters. 2007. https://www.reuters.com/article/us-iraq-iran-britain/iran-seizes-15-british-marines-and-sailors-in-gulf-idUSCOL33182120070323

Mroue, Bassem, Karam, Zeina, Deeb Sarah El. "Negligence Probed in Deadly Beirut Blast Amid Public Anger." AP News. August 5, 2020. https://apnews.com/article/global-trade-ap-top-news-international-news-middle-east-lebanon-4475998de078a93bbe91b7ac9d43ada2

Muravchik, Joshua. *Making David into Goliath: How the World Turned against Israel.* New York: Encounter Books, 2014.

Naqvi, Saeed. "How the Battle of Karbala Conditions the Iranian Mind on Palestine." *The Citizen.* July 14, 2019. https://www.thecitizen.in/index.php/en/NewsDetail/index/4/17268/How-Battle-Of-Karbala-Conditions-the-Iranian-Mind-On-Palestine

Nasr, Vali. *The Shia Revival: How Conflicts within Islam Will Shape the Future.* New York: W.W. Norton & Company. 2006.

Navai, Ramita. "New Iranian President's Role as Hostage-Taker Discounted." *The Irish Times.* July 2, 2005. https://www.irishtimes.com/news/new-iranian-president-s-role-as-hostage-taker-discounted-1.463175

Navias, Martin S. "The First Tanker War." *History Today.* August 2019. https://www.historytoday.com/history-matters/first-tanker-war

News, DW. "Iran and the US: Can Joe Biden Renegotiate the Nuclear Deal?" YouTube. February 25, 2021. https://www.youtube.com/watch?v=4MA7fRXd10w

"Nuclear Weapons Primer." Wisconsin Project on Nuclear Arms Control. 2020. https://www.wisconsinproject.org/nuclear-weapons/

Nyok, Akol and Thayer, Bradley A. "Takeover Trap: Why Imperialist China Is Invading Africa." *The National Interest.* July 10, 2019. https://nationalinterest.org/feature/takeover-trap-why-imperialist-china-invading-africa-66421

O'Connor, Tom. "Iran Seeks Deals with Russia and China to Build Coalition to Resist U.S." *Newsweek.* July 22, 2020. https://www.newsweek.com/iran-russia-deal-china-agreement-coalition-1519467

O'Donnell, John and Saul, Jonathan. "European Allies Pushed Back When Trump Sanctioned Iran's Banks." Reuters. December 1, 2020. https://www.reuters.com/article/iran-germany-sanctions-banks-exclusive/european-allies-pushed-back-when-trump-sanctioned-irans-banks-idUSKBN28B59T

Ofek, Raphael. "What the Smuggled Archive Tells Us About Iran's Nuclear Weapons Project." The Begin-Sadat Center for Strategic Studies. July 22, 2019. https://besacenter.org/perspectives-papers/smuggled-iran-nuclear-archive/

Osborn, Andrew. "Russia Uses Iran as Base to Bomb Syrian Militants for the First Time." Reuters. August 16, 2016. https://www.reuters.com/article/us-mideast-crisis-russia-iran/russia-uses-iran-as-base-to-bomb-syrian-militants-for-first-time-idUSKCN10R0PA

"Palestinians Meet with Hezbollah Terror Leader to Spark Third Intifada." *Jewish News Syndicate.* January 8, 2018. https://www.jns.org/palestinians-meet-with-hezbollah-terror-leader-to-spark-third-intifada/

Panetta, Grace. "Why Neither Bush nor Obama Killed Iranian Commander Qassem Soleimani, Who the US Took Out in an Airstrike." *Business Insider.* January 4, 2020. https://www.businessinsider.com/why-neither-bush-or-obama-killed-iranian-general-qassem-soleimani-2020-1

Parsi, Trita. *A Single Roll of the Dice: Obama's Diplomacy with Iran.* New Haven: Yale University Press, 2013.

Parsi, Trita. *Losing an Enemy: Obama, Iran, and the Triumph of Diplomacy.* New Haven: Yale University Press, 2017.

Peters, Ralph. "The Stakes in Syria Now Include US-Russia War." *New York Post.* June 19, 2017. https://nypost.com/2017/06/19/the-stakes-in-syria-now-include-us-russia-war/

"Pew Forum on Religion & Public Life / Mapping the Global Muslim Population." Pew Research Center. 2020. https://www.pewresearch.org/wp-content/uploads/sites/7/2009/10/Shiarange.pdf

Pillalamarri, Akhilesh. "This 16th Century Battle Created the Modern Middle East." *The Diplomat.* August 21, 2014. https://thediplomat.com/2014/08/this-16th-century-battle-created-the-modern-middle-east/

Pollack, Kenneth. *Armies of Sand: The Past, Present, and Future of Arab Military Effectiveness.* New York: Oxford University Press, 2019.

"Province of Khuzestan." Iran Chamber Society. October 22, 2021. http://www.iranchamber.com/provinces/15_khuzestan/15_khuzestan.php

Qutb, Sayyid. *Milestones.* New Delhi: Islamic Book Service, 2002.

Rabino, Joseph. "An Economist's Notes on Persia." *Journal of the Royal Statistical Society.* No. 64. Vol. 2. 1901. https://www.jstor.org/stable/2979943?origin=crossref&seq=1

Rafizadeh, Majid. "Iranian Regime Betrays Its Principles with China Deal." Arab News. July 12, 2020. https://www.arabnews.com/node/1703671

Razak, Rowena. "Iran: Cold War Crucible." *History Now.* Vol 68, Issue 3, March 2018. https://www.historytoday.com/archive/feature/iran-cold-war-crucible

Reed, Thomas C. and Stillman, Danny B. *The Nuclear Express: A Political History of the Bomb and Its Proliferation.* Minneapolis: Zenith Press, 2009.

"Renewable Energy." Center for Climate and Energy Solutions. 2020. https://www.c2es.org/content/renewable-energy/

"Report Execution Elkanian Personally Approved by Khomeini." *Jewish Telegraphic Agency.* May 11, 1979. https://www.jta.org/1979/05/11/archive/report-execution-of-elkanian-personally-approved-by-khomeini

Richards, A. "Terrorist Groups and Political Fronts: The IRA, Sinn Fein, the Peace Process and Democracy." *Terrorism and Political Violence.* December 2001. Vol. 13. Issue 4. https://www.researchgate.net/publication/233239643_Terrorist_Groups_and_Political_Fronts_The_IRA_Sinn_Fein_the_Peace_Process_and_Democracy

Riedel, Bruce. *Kings and Presidents: Saudi Arabia and the United States Since FDR.* Washington, D.C.: Brookings Institute Press, 2018.

Rosen, Amir. "How One Man's Illness May Have Changed the Course of Middle Eastern History." *Business Insider.* October 13, 2014. https://www.businessinsider.com/how-the-shahs-cancer-may-have-changed-history-2014-10

Ross, Angus. "HMS Dreadnaught (1906)—A Naval Revolution Misinterpreted or Mishandled?" *The Northern Mariner/le marin du nord.* XX. No. 2. 2010. https://www.cnrs-scrn.org/northern_mariner/vol20/tnm_20_175-198.pdf

Roth, Kenneth. "Yemen: Events of 2020." Human Rights Watch. 2021. https://www.hrw.org/world-report/2021/country-chapters/yemen

Rubin, Michael. *Dancing with the Devil: The Perils of Engaging Rogue Regimes.* New York: Encounter Books, 2014.

Rubin, Shira. "Israel's Netanyahu Walks Out of His Own Corruption Trial." *Washington Post.* 8 February 2021. https://www.washingtonpost.com/world/middle_east/netanyahu-corruption-israel-trial/2021/02/08/108453dc-69ee-11eb-a66e-e27046e9e898_story.html

Rumsfeld, Donald. "The Swamp." Department of State Information Memorandum. 1983. https://papers.rumsfeld.com/library/default.asp?zoom_sort=0&zoom_query=The+Swamp&zoom_per_page=10&zoom_and=0&Tag+Level+1=-1%7E0&Tag+Level+2=-1%7E0

"Safavid Dynasty." Britannica. 2020. https://www.britannica.com/topic/Safavid-dynasty

Safi, Michael. "Iran Admits It Fired Two Missiles at Ukrainian Passenger Jet." *The Guardian.* January 21, 2020. https://www.theguardian.com/world/2020/jan/21/iran-admits-it-fired-two-missiles-at-ukrainian-passenger-jet

Schogol, Jeff. "No, That Mushroom Cloud in Beirut Doesn't Indicate a Nuclear Bomb Went Off." *Task & Purpose.* August 4, 2020. https://taskandpurpose.com/analysis/beirut-explosion-nuclear-blast-debunked

Sebenius, Alyza, Mehrotra, Kartikay, and Turton, William. "Iran's Cyberattack on Billionaire Adelson Provides Lesson on Strategy." Bloomberg. January 5, 2020. https://www.bloomberg.com/news/articles/2020-01-05/iranian-attack-on-adelson-provides-lesson-on-cyber-strategy

"Seven Iranian Hackers Indicted over Alleged Cyber Attacks Targeting US Banks and NY Dam." Trend Micro. March 29, 2016. https://www.trendmicro.com/vinfo/de/security/news/cyber-attacks/seven-iranian-hackers-indicted-over-attacks-on-banks-ny-dam

Shahid, Kunwar Khuldune. "How Saudi Arabia is Pressuring Pakistan to Recognize Israel." *Haaretz.* 22 November 2020. https://www.haaretz.com/middle-east-news/.premium-how-saudi-arabia-is-pressuring-pakistan-to-recognize-israel-1.9315768

Shebaya, Helim. "Where Do Lebanon's Christians Stand on Hezbollah?" Al Jazeera. 30 November 2017. https://www.aljazeera.com/opinions/2017/11/30/where-do-lebanons-christians-stand-on-hezbollah/?gb=true

Slackman, Michael and O'Neill, John. "Hezbollah Chief Leads Huge Rally." *New York Times.* 22 September 2006. https://www.nytimes.com/2006/09/22/world/middleeast/23lebanoncnd.html

Small, Thomas and Hacker, Jonathan. *Path of Blood: The Story of Al Qaeda's War on the House of Saud.* New York: Overlook, 2015.

Smith, Martin. "Transcript: The Crown Prince of Saudi Arabia." PBS Frontline. 2018. https://www.pbs.org/wgbh/frontline/film/the-crown-prince-of-saudi-arabia/transcript/

Smith, Terrance. "Iran: Five Years of Fanaticism." *New York Times.* 12 February 1984. https://www.nytimes.com/1984/02/12/magazine/iran-five-years-of-fanaticism.html

Snow, Shawn. "American Troops Had Only Hours to React to Iranian Ballistic Missile Attack. Here's What They Did." *Military Times.* 21 April 2020. https://www.militarytimes.com/flashpoints/2020/04/21/american-troops-had-only-hours-to-react-to-iranian-ballistic-missile-attack-heres-what-they-did/

Spencer, Robert. *The History of Jihad: From Muhammad to ISIS.* New York: Bombardier Books. 2018.

Spetalnick, Matt and Holland, Steve. "Exclusive: White House's Kushner Unveils Economic Portion of Middle East Plan." Reuters. 22 June 2019. https://www.reuters.com/article/us-israel-palestinians-plan-exclusive/exclusive-white-houses-kushner-unveils-economic-portion-of-middle-east-peace-plan-idUSKCN1TN0ES

"Spirit of 68: French Countercultural Art—In Pictures." *The Guardian.* 23 February 2017. https://www.theguardian.com/artanddesign/gallery/2017/feb/23/spirit-of-68-french-countercultural-art-in-pictures

Staff, AW. "The Looming Tower: Jamal Khashoggi's Little-Known Past Comes to Light." *The Arab Weekly.* 15 October 2018. https://thearabweekly.com/looming-tower-jamal-khashoggis-little-known-past-comes-light

Staff, Dispatch. "The Morning Dispatch: Biden Courts Iran." *The Dispatch.* 22 February 2021. https://morning.thedispatch.com/p/the-morning-dispatch-biden-courts?utm_source=kw&utm_campaign=Sept_promo&kwp_0=1875715&kwp_4=5451157&kwp_1=2336582&fbclid=IwAR06961u7_BlqqDGunDiW4s1tikt5276_DuCnfyjNykwsRvVts6v7W5oGsc

Staff, ILH, Kahana, Ariel, and Bar, Neta. "Israel Reportedly in Talks on Defense Alliance with Gulf States." *Israel Hayom.* 25 February 2021. https://www.israelhayom.com/2021/02/25/israel-reportedly-in-talks-on-defense-alliance-with-gulf-states/

Staff, Reuters. "Kerry Stresses Need to End Syria, Yemen Conflicts in Talks with Saudis." Reuters. 11 March 2016. https://www.reuters.com/article/us-usa-kerry-saudi/kerry-stresses-need-to-end-syria-yemen-conflicts-in-talks-with-saudis-idUSKCN0WD26J

Staff. "Khamenei: If We Wanted Nukes, Nobody, including 'Zionist Clown,' Could Stop Us." *Times of Israel.* 22 February 2021. https://www.timesofisrael.com/khamenei-if-we-wanted-nukes-nobody-including-zionist-clown-could-stop-us/

Stead, Rebecca. "Remembering Israel's 2006 War on Lebanon." *Middle East Monitor.* 12 July 2018. https://www.middleeastmonitor.com/20180712-remembering-israels-2006-war-on-lebanon/

Stillwell, Blake. "The Horrifying Way Iran Used Kids to Clear Mines." We Are the Mighty. 5 February 2021. https://www.wearethemighty.com/mighty-history/iran-iraq-war-child-soldiers-mines/

Strachan, Hew. *The First World War.* New York: Penguin Books, 2005.

Streusand, Douglas E. *Islamic Gunpowder Empires: Ottomans, Safavids, and Mughals.* Boulder: Westview Press. 2011.

Summit, April R. "For a White Revolution: John F. Kennedy and the Shah of Iran." *Middle East Journal.* 58. no. 4. 2004, pp. 560–75. https://www.jstor.org/stable/4330063?seq=1

"Sunni and Shia Muslims Pray Together in Azerbaijan's Heydar Mosque." *TRT World.* 19 November 2019. https://www.trtworld.com/life/sunni-and-shia-muslims-pray-together-in-azerbaijan-s-heydar-mosque-31473

Taheri, Amir. *The Spirit of Allah: Khomeini & the Islamic Revolution.* Bethesda, MD: Adler & Adler, 1986.

Tahmizian Meuse, Alison. "Trump May Be Right about Beirut 'Attack.'" *Asia Times.* 8 August 2020. https://asiatimes.com/2020/08/trump-may-be-right-about-beirut-attack/

Tan, Su-Lin and Nyabiage, Jevans. "Kenya Keen to Renegotiate Debt, Fees with China as Coronavirus Hits Unprofitable Mombasa-Naivasha Rail Line." 3 October 2020. https://www.scmp.com/economy/china-economy/article/3103710/kenya-keen-renegotiate-debt-fees-china-coronavirus-hits

"Taqiyya, the Art of Terrorist 'Deception.'" France 24. 13 March 2013. https://www.france24.com/en/20130313-taqiya-france-islam-deception-favoured-terrorists-jihad

Taub, Amanda. "The Republican Myth of Ronald Reagan and the Iran Hostages, Debunked." Vox. January 25, 2016. https://www.vox.com/2016/1/25/10826056/ reagan-iran-hostage-negotiation

Teitelbaum, Joshua. "The Shiites of Saudi Arabia." *Current Trends in Islamist Ideology.* Vol. 10. 2010. https://www.hudson.org/content/researchattachments/ attachment/1288/teitelbaum.pdf

"The Carter Doctrine." *Air Force Magazine.* 1 April 2010. https://www.airforcemag. com/article/0410keeperfile/

"The Nation: The President's Boys." *Time.* 6 June 1977. http://content.time.com/ time/magazine/article/0,9171,914991,00.html

"The Prophet Muhammad and the Origins of Islam." The Met. 2020. https://www. metmuseum.org/learn/educators/curriculum-resources/art-of-the-islamic-world/ unit-one/the-prophet-muhammad-and-the-origins-of-islam

"The Repeal of Corn Laws and Free Trade." *The British Empire 1815–1914.* 2020. https://www.britishempire.me.uk/freetrade.html

"The Rush of Gurus." The Pluralism Project. 2020. https://pluralism.org/ the-rush-of-gurus

"The Russian Quest for Warm Water Ports." Global Security. 2020. https://www. globalsecurity.org/military/world/russia/warm-water-port.htm

"The Treaty of Turkmenchay between Russia and Iran Signed." Boris Yeltsin Presidential Library. 2020. https://www.prlib.ru/en/history/619048

"The Zand Dynasty." Britannica. 2020. https://www.britannica.com/topic/ Zand-dynasty

Toft, Monica Duffy, Philpott, Daniel, and Shah, Timothy Samuel. *God's Century: Resurgent Religion and Global Politics.* New York: W.W. Norton & Company, 2011.

"Transcript of Trump's Speech in Saudi Arabia." CNN. 21 May 2017. https://www. cnn.com/2017/05/21/politics/trump-saudi-speech-transcript

Traub, James. *The Freedom Agenda: Why America Must Spread Democracy (Just Not the Way George Bush Did)*. New York: Picador, 2008.

Trump, Donald J. Twitter. 2019, 4:19 pm. https://twitter.com/realDonaldTrump/status/1212121026072592384

Trump, Donald J. "Remarks by President Trump on the Killing of Qasem Soleimani." The White House. 3 January 2020. https://www.whitehouse.gov/briefings-statements/remarks-president-trump-killing-qasem-soleimani/

"Underground Shelters Found at Beirut Port Spark Hopes of Unlikely Survivor Stories." NBCUniversal. 7 August 2020. https://news.yahoo.com/underground-shelters-found-beirut-port-162926443.html

Urban, Mark. "Saudi Nuclear Weapons 'On Order' from Pakistan." BBC. 6 November 2013. https://www.bbc.com/news/world-middle-east-24823846

US Embassy Tehran to Department of State, ERDA HQ. Washington, D.C. 11 May 1977. https://nsarchive2.gwu.edu/nukevault/ebb268/doc14b.pdf

"U.S. Officials Rebut Claim by Trump that Deadly Beirut Explosion Resulted from a 'Terrible Attack.'" *Market Watch*. 5 August 2020. https://www.marketwatch.com/story/us-officials-refute-trump-claim-that-beirut-deadly-explosion-resulted-from-a-terrible-attack-2020-08-05

Uskowi, Nader. "The Evolving Iranian Strategy in Syria: A Looming Conflict with Israel." Atlantic Council. September 2018. https://www.atlanticcouncil.org/wp-content/uploads/2019/09/The_Evolving_Iranian_Strategy_in_Syria.pdf

Vatanka, Alex. "Russia, Iran, and Economic Integration on the Caspian." The Middle East Institute. 17 August 2020. https://www.mei.edu/publications/russia-iran-and-economic-integration-caspian

Vecchiet, Jean-Michel. *Iran: The Hundred Year War*. 2008. Amazon Prime.

Walt, Stephen M. "The Case for Offshore Balancing." *Foreign Affairs*. July/August 2016. https://www.foreignaffairs.com/articles/united-states/2016-06-13/case-offshore-balancing

Walt, Stephen M. "How Not to Contain Iran." *Foreign Policy.* 5 March 2010. https://foreignpolicy.com/2010/03/05/how-not-to-contain-iran/

Waters, Nick. "Has Iran Been Hacking U.S. Drones?" Bellingcat. 1 October 2019. https://www.bellingcat.com/news/2019/10/01/has-iran-been-hacking-u-s-drones/

Ward, Vicky. *Kushner, Inc.: Greed, Ambition, Corruption.* New York: St. Martin's Press, 2019.

"Warren Implies Trump Had Soleimani Killed to Distract from Impeachment." *The Times of Israel.* 6 January 2020. https://www.timesofisrael.com/warren-implies-trump-had-soleimani-killed-to-distract-from-impeachment/

Weichert, Brandon J. "Biden's Foreign Policy." DefCon One's Newsletter. 9 November 2020. https://defcon1.substack.com/p/bidens-foreign-policy

Weichert, Brandon J. "Blame Iran for Iran's Problems." Real Clear World. 16 January 2020. https://www.realclearworld.com/articles/2020/01/16/blame_iran_for_irans_problems_255091.html

Weichert, Brandon J. "Don't Let Saudi Arabia Get Nukes." *The American Spectator.* 2 November 2018. https://spectator.org/dont-let-saudi-arabia-get-nukes/

Weichert, Brandon J. "HMX Explosives Present at Beirut Port." The Weichert Report. 5 August 2020. https://theweichertreport.wordpress.com/2020/08/05/hmx-explosives-present-at-beirut-port/

Weichert, Brandon J. "Iran: More Failures from US Intelligence." *The American Spectator.* 23 May 2019. https://spectator.org/iran-more-failures-from-u-s-intelligence/

Weichert, Brandon J. "Iran Keeps Asking for It." *The American Spectator.* 15 September 2019. https://spectator.org/iran-keeps-asking-for-it/

Weichert, Brandon J. "Iran Will Strike Again." *The American Spectator.* 22 September 2019. https://spectator.org/iran-will-strike-again/

Weichert, Brandon J. "Iran's Space Threat is the Problem." American Greatness. 27 April 2020. https://amgreatness.com/2020/04/27/irans-space-threat-is-the-problem/

Weichert, Brandon J. "Jimmy Carter: The Indecisive Hawk." The Weichert Report. 21 August 2018. https://theweichertreport.wordpress.com/2018/08/31/jimmy-carter-the-indecisive-hawk/

Weichert, Brandon J. "Joe Biden's 'Values-Based' Foreign Policy Is a Loser." *The Washington Times*. 5 November 2020. https://www.washingtontimes.com/news/2020/nov/5/joe-bidens-values-based-foreign-policy-is-a-loser/?fbclid=IwAR0-zL4UXrEyU2jiyDGVpN1K3y2NXonJuJ5O0ah7cctodlIgvaMUIAV KOFE

Weichert, Brandon J. "Official Narrative about Beirut Explosion Not Adding Up." The Weichert Report. 8 August 2020. https://theweichertreport.wordpress.com/2020/08/08/official-narrative-about-beirut-explosion-not-adding-up/

Weichert, Brandon J. "Repeal the Leahy Law." *The American Spectator*. 11 June 2018. https://spectator.org/repeal-the-leahy-law-2/

Weichert, Brandon J. "Russia Is Not Going to Change." *New English Review*. September 2018. https://www.newenglishreview.org/custpage.cfm?frm=189386&sec_id=189386

Weichert, Brandon J. "Trump Is Winning the Little Cold War with Iran." *The American Spectator*. 23 June 2019. https://spectator.org/trump-is-winning-the-little-cold-war-with-iran/

Weichert, Brandon J. "Trump's Jerusalem Gambit Recalls Harry Truman." American Greatness. 10 December 2017. https://amgreatness.com/2017/12/10/trumps-jerusalem-gambit-recalls-harry-truman/

Weichert, Brandon J. "Trump Strikes the Right Balance with Iran." American Greatness. 3 January 2020. https://amgreatness.com/2020/01/03/trump-strikes-the-right-balance-with-iran/

Weichert, Brandon J. *Winning Space: How America Remains a Superpower*. Alexandria: Republic Book Publishers, 2020.

Weiner, Tim. *Legacy of Ashes: The History of the CIA*. New York: Anchor Books, 2008.

Weintraub, Bernard. "Their Oil Embargo." *New York Times.* 22 December 1973. https://www.nytimes.com/1973/12/22/archives/shah-of-iran-urges-arabs-to-end-theiroil-embargo-shah-of-iran-urges.html

"What Is Ashura?" BBC. 6 December 2011. https://www.bbc.com/news/world-middle-east-16047713

"What Was That Glowing Orb Trump Touched in Saudi Arabia?" *New York Times.* 22 March 2017. https://www.nytimes.com/2017/05/22/world/middleeast/trump-glowing-orb-saudi.html

"Why Sayed Qutb Inspired Iran's Khomeini and Khamenei." Al-Arabiya English. 3 September 2018. https://english.alarabiya.net/features/2018/09/03/Why-Sayed-Qutb-inspired-Iran-s-Khomeini-and-Khamenei

Williams, Dan. "Seismic Data Suggests String of Blasts Preceded Beirut Explosion: Israeli Analyst." Reuters. 13 August 2020. https://www.reuters.com/article/us-lebanon-security-blast-seismology/seismic-data-suggests-string-of-blasts-preceded-beirut-explosion-israeli-analyst-idUSKCN2591S2

Winer, Stuart. "Cyberattack Hits Israeli Companies, with Iran Reportedly the Likely Culprit." *Times of Israel.* 13 December 2020. https://www.timesofisrael.com/israels-supply-chain-targeted-in-massive-cyberattack/

Wintour, Patrick. "Iran at Breaking Point as It Fights Third Wave of Coronavirus." *The Guardian.* 14 October 2020. https://www.theguardian.com/world/2020/oct/14/iran-at-breaking-point-as-it-fights-third-wave-of-coronavirus

"Women Protest in Iran, Shout 'Down with Khomeini.'" *Washington Post.* 9 March 1979. https://www.washingtonpost.com/archive/politics/1979/03/09/women-protest-in-iran-shout-down-with-khomeini/84d3a780-738a-4dfd-a2a5-c7d4f546323c/

Woodward, Bob. *Rage.* New York: Simon & Schuster. 2020.

Woolsey, James and Pry, Peter. "A Shariah-Approved Nuclear Attack." *The Washington Times.* 18 August 2015. https://www.washingtontimes.com/news/2015/aug/18/jams-woolsey-peter-pry-emp-a-shariah-approved-nucl/

Woolsey, R. James and Pry, Peter. "The Growing Threat from an EMP Attack." *Wall Street Journal.* 12 August 2014. https://www.wsj.com/articles/james-woolsey-and-peter-vincent-pry-the-growing-threat-from-an-emp-attack-1407885281

Wright, Lawrence. *The Looming Tower: Al-Qaeda and the Road to 9/11.* New York: Vintage Books, 2006.

YouTube. CBS News. "Netanyahu Claims Proof of Secret Iranian Nuclear Activities." 30 April 2018. https://www.youtube.com/watch?v=Bmpgaig54-k&feature=emb_logo

YouTube. *The American Conservative.* "The American Conservative's Curt Mills Talks Iran and General Soleimani on Tucker Carlson Tonight." 3 January 2020. 4:42. https://www.youtube.com/watch?v=bvI-5rI2RX8

Zaccour, Amélie. "Saudi Arabia: How MBS Deposed His Cousin Mohamed bin Nayef as Crown Prince." *Africa Report.* 11 February 2021. https://www.theafricareport.com/64599/saudi-arabia-how-mbs-deposed-his-cousin-mohammed-bin-nayef-as-crown-prince/

Zarate, Juan C. *Treasury's War: The Unleashing of a New Era of Financial Warfare.* New York: Public Affairs, 2013.

Zeidan, Adam. "Islamism." Britannica. Accessed 20 February 2021. https://www.britannica.com/topic/Islamism

ACKNOWLEDGEMENTS

No book is an entirely solo affair—especially a nonfiction book based on the messy geopolitics of the Greater Middle East. My first big thanks goes to my friend and colleague, Gregory Copley, who shared much with me about his time working in Iran during the reign of the Shāh. His insights and stories were invaluable in sending me down the necessary paths of research and for avoiding the pitfalls that tend to come with research projects, such as *The Shadow War*.

I would also like to thank some other colleagues for serving as sounding boards for me over the years on this subject as well as several other topics that I spend most of my time writing on. Dr. Robert

Kaufman of Pepperdine University, whose books were greatly inspiring to me as a young man studying international relations theory (and who was gracious enough to provide the foreword to this book). Thomas Lipscomb, former publishing extraordinaire who has spent much time and many phone calls advising me on which projects I should focus on and who I should be talking to—and emulating in my work. I've learned much about actual journalistic reportage from him. My dear friend and fellow contrarian, F.H. Buckley, who I have had the pleasure of knowing for many years now and continues to be a sounding board and inspiration for me. He is always gracious and thoughtful in his interactions with me.

Next, I'd like to express my great appreciation both for the works of Colin Dueck as well as for his willingness to drop everything and provide me with a helpful blurb for whatever project I am working on. It is an honor to be associated with him as his work, like that of F.H. Buckley and Dr. Kaufman's, was so helpful to me as a young student in international relations. Gordon G. Chang and Cleo Paskal also deserve honorable mentions for entertaining my often-radical notions whenever we are together on the lecture circuit. Their work continues to encourage me to push forward as we all strive to protect our liberty from rapacious foreign rivals, such as China, Russia, and Iran.

Although he was not directly involved in this project, I would like to acknowledge Kamran Bokhari of *New Lines Institute*. Bokhari and I have bumped into each other more than once on the lecture circuit and I've found him to be a fascinating subject matter expert and someone with whom I enjoy a cup of coffee, talking about the Mideast. In fact, our last conversation together during a speaking event in California in November of 2021 helped me to refine some elements of this book and to expand on some parts related Iran's overall geopolitical ambitions in the region that I had downplayed.

Seth Leibsohn and John Batchelor, two brilliant radio show hosts separated by geography, radio network, and age, have both spent the last few years letting me on their shows to spend an inordinate amount of time talking about the things that I care dearly about. It is always such a joy to be able to chat with these two gentlemen (Leibsohn on his show in Phoenix and Batchelor on his New York-based program). Both men are excellent interviewers: they give me time to speak and develop my thoughts and are knowledgeable enough about these topics to be able to engage meaningful in our conversations. The various chats I've had on these two programs certainly helped to hone my thinking on certain aspects of the book as I was writing *The Shadow War*.

I'd also like to give an honorable mention here to the late, great Angelo Codevilla of the Claremont Institute. While he was not directly involved in this book, shortly before his tragic death in 2021, he was gracious enough to spend an inordinate amount of time critiquing and giving me critical inputs for my first book, *Winning Space: How America Remains a Superpower*. As it relates to this work, Angelo's writings in the early 1990s in which he criticized President George H.W. Bush's handling of Desert Storm and challenged the very basis of the necessity of that war was a major inspiration for my interest both in writing this book as well as studying the Middle East and America's oftentimes haphazard involvement in that most dangerous region. We did not know each other personally very well, but I respected him and cherished the brief time I did get to know him in a professional manner. His mind and insights will be sorely missed in the years going ahead.

As I did in my first book, *Winning Space: How America Remains a Superpower*, I would like to credit the graduate program where I earned my Master of Arts (M.A.) in Statecraft and National Security Affairs from, the Institute of World Politics in Washington, D.C., as having been the basis of my education in geopolitics and national security. I had previously worked in government on national security policy yet I did not know how much I did not know until entering Marlatt Mansion and sitting in Dr. John Lenczowski's class for the first time. At IWP I learned that there were three ways of doing things in this world: the right way, the wrong way, and the Washington way.

For too long, especially in the Middle East, the United States had been doing things the "Washington way" and it showed. There is a right way to operate in the Middle East and *The Shadow War* was my attempt to light that path for policymakers who may be too blinkered by the Washington swamp. Whether anyone in power listens remains to be seen. But none of this would have been thinking had I not been set straight by the top-notch educators at IWP. This book is as much a result of the education I received at that special graduate school nestled in the heart of Washington, D.C. as it is anything else.

There were, of course, many more people involved in providing insights and ideas to me. Because of their day jobs, though, many could not go on record. For their input and time, I thank them and hope that one day I will be able to share their contribution to this important work. Iran is one of the most important geopolitical issues facing the United States and the world today. Yet, we continue ignoring Iran—and getting our Iran policy wrong—at our own peril. At some point, very soon, I fear we will reach the point of no return and Tehran will be able to fundamentally change the balance of power in the Middle East and likely trigger something worse. Many who contributed to my research and talked to me both on-and-off-the-record, concur with my assessment and wanted to get the word out. I am honored that they cooperated with my work so that I, too, could help them get the word out.

INDEX

China, People's Republic of, 7, 67, 274, 275,
287
  alliance with Iran, 22, 216
  global ambitions of, 219
  influence over Iran, 254–255
  pattern of deals with developing countries,
    23, 24
  trade war between the US and, 215
Christianity, 122, 154, 236
Churchill, Winston, 82–83, 120
CIA, 41, 83, 84, 138, 139, 141, 142,
162, 179, 202, 227, 229, 279, 280. *See also*
Mossadegh, Mohammad; Operation AJAX
  covert operations in Laos and Cambodia,
142
civil rights, 2
climate change, 219
Clinton, Bill, 245
Clinton, Hillary, 271, 279,
Cold War, 77, 81–86, 108, 125, 126, 128,
129, 211
Coll, Steve, 189
Colombia, 95. *See also* Revolutionary Armed
    Forces of Colombia (FARC)
communism, 77, 82, 126, 154, 185
  in Iran, 79
  Soviet, 114
  spread of, 130
Cooper, Scott, 103, 104
Copley, Gregory, 79, 80, 84, 109, 110,
132, 133, 135. *See also* International Strategic
Studies Association
Coppe, Danilo, 45
coronavirus, 20
COVID-19, 21, 289
Crusades, 236
Cuba,
  Iran and, 59, 61
  Soviet missiles in, 58
Cuban Missile Crisis, 59
cultural imperialism, 122
Cutler, Lloyd, 164. *See also* Carter, Jimmy

D
Damascus, 62, 67, 68
Darius the Great, 97, 123
Dark Ages, 235
Daugherty, William, J., 163, 164
DDoS attacks, 223
Death to America, 1, 2, 233–242

  and Ayatollah Khomeini, 113
  Iran daily cries of, 17, 298
  Plus, 6
Death to Israel, 113
death penalty, 107
Defense World, 39
Desert One, 177, 178, 179, 180, 184, 202
Desert Storm, 4, 193, 194
Die Welt, 38
dirty bomb, 41
Doha Agreement, 304–5
drone(s)
  Hamas' deployment of *Shahab*-type of, 54
  Iran's *Adabil*, 54
  long-range, 54

E
economic development, 237
Egypt, 258
  British influence over, 88, 237
  Muslim Brotherhood and, 88, 148, 237,
  238
  Obama administration's alliance with
  Islamists
    in, 118, 246
  rise of Islamism in, 91
  undemocratic regime in, 266, 273
Egyptian revolution of 2011, 148
eleventh imam, 89
Eisenhower administration, 120
Eisenhower, Dwight D., 82–83, 120, 140
  "Atoms for Peace" program, 202
Elkanian, Habib, 159, 160, 169, 171
Enlightenment, 235, 236
Environment, Conflict, and Cooperation
  (ECC)
    project, 197
ethnic Persians, 6
Europe,
  Germany's place in, 9

F
Fada'iyn-e Islam, 88
Fajr-5 missiles, 53
fake news, 42
Fakhrizadeh, Mohsen, 209
Fatah, 28
  alignment with Hezbollah, Hamas, and
  Iran, 48
  meeting with Hezbollah, 32

increasingly hostile stance toward the West, 59

industrialization of, 97

inflation in, 98, 104, 105, 107

influence of Muslim Brotherhood in, 236–237

inherently expansionistic and revolutionary nature of, 207

intelligence, surveillance, and reconnaissance capabilities, 228

internal political crisis in, 21

Iraq War, 193, 194, 195, 196–198, 199–200, 213

Islamic guidelines in, 226

Islamic reactionaries in, 108

Islamism in, 87–92, 235–236, 242

Islamist Revolution of 1979, 2, 3, 84, 89, 91, 92, 122, 138, 168, 184, 191, 192–193, 194, 238

Islamist regime of, 50

Islamists in, 5

Israel and, 5, 48, 59, 70

Jewish community in, 158–160

lack of balance of power between the US and, 59

Latin America and, 57–65

liberal reformers in, 83, 91

Majles, 73, 74, 75, 77, 78, 84, 85, 96

Marxism in, 107–108, 114, 240

Marxist guerillas in, 108, 133, 134, 149, 169

Marxist threat to, 135

massive executions in, 157–158

military, 55, 60, 61, 64, 80, 138, 139, 145, 148, 149, 150, 155, 156, 179, 198, 239, 252, 271, 309

minority rights in, 73

missile program, 53

model of decentralized regional resistance, 58

modernization in, 93–105, 106, 107

monarchists in, 78, 86, 91, 147, 149, 158, 166

Mujadedin-e Khalq (MEK), 108, 133, 134, 240

mullahs, 2, 6, 96

nationalism in, 76, 245

nationalists in, 74, 83, 91

Nazi Germany and, 75–76

new shipping route between Russia and, 25

nuclear agreement with US, 35, 205, 217, 218, 225, 246, 249, 253, 271

nuclear command, control, and communications capabilities, 228

nuclear energy in, 109, 202

nuclear program, 202, 208, 211, 244

nuclear weapons and, 3, 7, 8, 10, 244

Obama-era nuclear deal with, 66, 250

octogen production in, 39, 40, 43

oil war, 213–220, 225

OPEC and, 101–105

outbreak of COVID-19 in, 21

as outcast, 3

Parliament Day in, 75

physical connection to Israel through Iraq and Syria, 28

poverty in, 96

pre-Islamic history, 70, 97, 123

precision-guided munition, 44, 45, 49, 63, 209, 225, 229, 296

"Precision Project," 44

protests against regime in, 20

radicals rule of, 3

as a rational actor, 251, 310

religion and politics in, 71

religion and state, integration of, 122

religious beliefs, 6

religious fervor in, 86, 200

"resource curse," 123–25

rich history of, 3, 6

Russia and, 22, 24, 25, 26, 67, 72, 254–255

sanctions against, 4, 21, 25, 26, 250

satellite threat, 228–229

Saudi Arabia and, 46, 59

secularism in, 78

Shia Islam as official religion in, 72

Shiism in, 96

sociopolitical and economic dynamics of, 92

Soviet Union and, 126, 152

strategic ambitions of, 3

Sunni Arab states and, 5, 48

support for international terrorism, 70, 209, 216, 225

support of Hamas, 52–53, 55

support of Hezbollah, 27, 32, 33, 41, 55, 58, 229, 230

support of Houthi Rebels in Yemen, 214, 215

supremacist strategy of, 3

Z
Zahedi, General Fazlollah, 80, 84
Zarif, Javad, 70
Zebayar, Adel El, 63. *See also* Maduro, Nicolas;
    Revolutionary Armed Forces of Colombia
    (FARC)
Zimmerman, Warren, 154, 155. *See also*
    Ayatollah Ruhollah Khomeini; Carter,
    Jimmy; Yazdi, Ebrahim
al-Zobair, Haji Abdullah. *See* Williamson,
    William Richard
Zoroastrianism, 75, 86